Software Architecture Design Patterns in Java

Software Architecture Design Patterns in Java

Partha Kuchana

AUERBACH PUBLICATIONS

A CRC Press Company

Boca Raton   London   New York   Washington, D.C.

Library of Congress Cataloging-in-Publication Data

Kuchana, Partha.
    Software architecture design patterns in Java / Partha Kuchana.
        p. cm.
    Includes bibliographical references and index.
    ISBN 0-8493-2142-5 (alk. paper)
    1. Java (Computer program language) 2. Computer Software. 3. Computer architecture.
    4. Software patterns. I. Title.

QA76.73.J38K83 2004
005.13′3—dc22   2003070897

Visit the Auerbach Publications Web site at www.auerbach-publications.com

© 2004 by CRC Press LLC
Auerbach is an imprint of CRC Press LLC

No claim to original U.S. Government works
International Standard Book Number 0-8493-2142-5
Library of Congress Card Number 2003070897
Printed in the United States of America 1 2 3 4 5 6 7 8 9 0
Printed on acid-free paper

DEDICATION

To my family

CONTENTS

SECTION III: BASIC PATTERNS

SECTION IV: CREATIONAL PATTERNS

SECTION VII: BEHAVIORAL PATTERNS

FOREWORD

Partha Kuchana is an experienced enterprise systems architect. He understands that patterns are not about things that are just good ideas, but that patterns are about capturing knowledge bred from experience. This hard-won knowledge is what Partha is sharing with readers of his book. Here are some of the things I really like about what he has to say.

The book presents 42 design patterns, which include the 23 GoF patterns. These patterns are categorized as follows:

- 7 Basic patterns
- 5 Creational patterns
- 4 Collectional patterns
- 11 Structural patterns
- 11 Behavioral patterns
- 4 Concurrency patterns

The discussion of each pattern includes an example implemented in Java. Further, the source code for all examples is found on the following Web site for this book: http://www.crcpress.com/e_products/downloads/download.asp. The source code and the easily understood examples make this format work well.

Partha takes complex material and clearly explains the ideas so they are easy-to-understand, an important consideration for both the novice encountering the material for the first time and the experienced developer who quickly wants to extract the important bits for immediate use. Each pattern discussion also includes Practice Questions for exactly that — your own use to improve your skills or, if this book were to be chosen as a text, to help the time-pressured instructor.

Partha takes the time to compare and contrast the patterns. For example, in the discussion on the Mediator pattern, a table shows similarities and differences between Mediator and Façade. The reader will find that this analysis leads to a clearer understanding than simply trying to focus on each pattern in isolation. The text also includes consideration of relationships between patterns. For example, in the discussion on the Mediator pattern there is a reference to a previous design example for the Command pattern.

Finally, at the end of the book, the reader will be happy to find a case study that pulls some of the patterns together to illustrate how a more complicated problem would be tackled and how the patterns work together. As those who have studied the work of Christopher Alexander realize—patterns are not applied in isolation but collaborate within a specific domain to address large and small problems.

It has been ten years since the GoF book was published. A lot of patterns have been identified and captured in that time. A lot of patterns books have been written. This book is like the GoF book, a catalog; probably not one you will read cover-to-cover in a single setting, but which will find a place on your bookshelf. Keep it handy for all those "How do I do this in Java?" questions where you wish you had an expert in the office next door to provide answers. This book is the next best thing.

Linda Rising
Phoenix, AZ

ABOUT THE AUTHOR

Partha Kuchana is an experienced enterprise systems architect. He has eleven years of experience in all aspects of project delivery management (onsite/offshore models), enterprise architecture, design, development, mentoring and training. He is a Sun certified enterprise architect.

During the last several years, he has worked on numerous client–server, E-business, Web portal and enterprise application integration (EAI) projects at various client sites in the United Kingdom and the United States, involving iterative design methodologies such as Rational Unified Process (RUP) and extreme programming.

He has extensive experience applying design patterns in application architecture and design. He has successfully architected and designed business-to-business systems and complex heterogeneous systems integration using Web services, middleware and messaging products from various vendors. He has several published software-related publications.

Home page: http://members.ITJobsList.com/partha
E-mail: ParthaKuchana@ITJobsList.com

ACKNOWLEDGMENTS

First and foremost, I would like to thank my wife for her patience and support, for taking some of my workload especially in the areas of UML and Java programming and for her inspirational contributions at the time of frustrating moments. I would like to thank my parents, my sister, my brother and my dear friends whose support and encouragement throughout my life have made it possible for me to build the skill set necessary to succeed.

I would like to thank Venu Kuchana and D.R. Sudhakar for their contributions in terms of writing different Java programs. I would like to thank BalaLingam Kuchana for his contributions in the area of UML and for being in charge of creating the formatted version of my draft.

I would like to thank the entire team at Auerbach publications for their contributions in this project and for making this a remarkable experience. In particular, I have a deep sense of gratitude towards my acquisitions editor, John Wyzalek, for sharing my enthusiasm and providing me with great advice and help. I also would like to thank the managing editor, Claire Miller, for her invaluable advice and contribution in arranging the book in a presentable form.

My sincere thanks to Linda Rising for writing the Foreword.

I am truly appreciative and thankful to the following reviewers who have taken the time to read the draft and provide me with feedback.

- Pradyumn Sharma, CEO, Pragati Software Pvt. Ltd.
- Carsten Kuckuk, project lead, Design Patterns Study Group Stuttgart, RIB Software AG
- Tim Kemper, Boulder Design Patterns Group
- Geoffrey Sparks, CEO, Sparx Systems P/L
- Edward L. Howe, software architect, Employease, Inc.
- Christopher R. Gardner, software developer, McKesson Information Solutions
- David Deriso, senior software engineer, Employease, Inc.
- Mike Heinrich, software engineer, Canada
- Rodney Waldoff, director of systems architecture, Encyclopedia Brittanica Inc.
- Thomas SMETS, software engineer, Belgium
- Linda Rising, Ph.D., independent software consultant, Arizona State University
- Ray Tayek, coordinator LAJUG/OCJUG

In particular, thanks to Pradyumn Sharma, Carsten Kuckuk, and Tim Kemper for their insightful recommendations, their thoroughness, and their invaluable suggestions, including questions that an inquisitive reader might have about design patterns.

I would like to thank Mark Grand for his encouragement and advice on various aspects of writing a patterns book. I am sure I have forgotten someone important; please accept my sincere apologies.

I

AN INTRODUCTION TO DESIGN PATTERNS

1

DESIGN PATTERNS: ORIGIN AND HISTORY

During the late 1970s, an architect named Christopher Alexander carried out the first known work in the area of patterns. In an attempt to identify and describe the wholeness or aliveness of quality designs, Alexander and his colleagues studied different structures that were designed to solve the same problem. He identified similarities among designs that were of high quality. He used the term *pattern* in the following books to refer to these similarities.

- *A Pattern Language: Towns, Buildings, Construction* (Oxford University Press, 1977)
- *The Timeless Way of Building* (Oxford University Press, 1979)

The patterns identified and documented by Alexander are purely architectural and deal with structures like buildings, gardens and roadways.

ARCHITECTURAL TO SOFTWARE DESIGN PATTERNS

In 1987, influenced by the writings of Alexander, Kent Beck and Ward Cunningham applied the architectural pattern ideas for the software design and development. They used some of Alexander's ideas to develop a set of patterns for developing elegant user interfaces in Smalltalk. With the results of their work, they gave a presentation entitled *Using Pattern Languages for Object-Oriented Programming* at the Object-Oriented Programming Systems, Languages, and Applications (OOPSLA) '87 conference. Since then, many papers and presentations relating to patterns have been published by many eminent people in the Object Oriented (OO) world.

In 1994, the publication of the book entitled *Design Patterns: Elements of Reusable Object-Oriented Software* on design patterns by Erich Gamma, Richard Helm, Ralph Johnson and John Vlissides explained the usefulness of patterns and resulted in the widespread popularity for design patterns. These four authors together are referred to as the Gang of Four (GoF). In this book the authors documented the 23 patterns they found in their work of nearly four and a half years.

Since then, many other books have been published capturing design patterns and other best practices for software engineering.

WHAT IS A DESIGN PATTERN?

A design pattern is a documented best practice or core of a solution that has been applied successfully in multiple environments to solve a problem that recurs in a specific set of situations.

Architect Christopher Alexander describes a pattern as "a recurring solution to a common problem in a given context and system of forces." In his definition, the term *context* refers to the set of conditions/situations in which a given pattern is applicable and the term *system of forces* refers to the set of constraints that occur in the specific context.

MORE ABOUT DESIGN PATTERNS

- A design pattern is an effective means to convey/communicate what has been learned about high-quality designs. The result is:
  - A shared language for communicating the experience gained in dealing with these recurring problems and their solutions.
  - A common vocabulary of system design elements for problem solving discussions. A means of reusing and building upon the acquired insight resulting in an improvement in the software quality in terms of its maintainability and reusability.
- A design pattern is not an invention. A design pattern is rather a documented expression of the best way of solving a problem that is observed or discovered during the study or construction of numerous software systems.
- One of the common misconceptions about design patterns is that they are applied only in an object-oriented environment. Even though design patterns discussions typically refer to the object-oriented development, they are applicable in other areas as well. With only minor changes, a design pattern description can be adjusted to refer to software design patterns in general. From the preceding section, *Origin and History*, it can be seen that patterns have existed from the early days of architecture, long before the object-oriented design and programming era.
- Design patterns are not theoretical constructs. A design pattern can be seen as an encapsulation of a reusable solution that has been applied successfully to solve a common design problem.
- Though design patterns refer to the best known ways of solving problems, not all best practices in problem resolution are considered as patterns. A best practice must satisfy the Rule of Three to be treated as a design pattern. The Rule of Three states that a given solution must be verified to be a recurring phenomenon, preferably in at least three existing systems. Otherwise, the solution is not considered as a pattern. The goal is to ensure that some community of software professionals applied the solution described by the pattern to solve software design problems. Satisfying the

Rule of Three indicates that a design pattern provides a practical solution to deal with a real-world problem.

■ Design patterns do not provide solutions to every problem found in real-world software design and development. Design patterns are about providing elegant, reusable solutions to commonly encountered software development problems *in a particular context*. This means that a pattern that is meant to provide the best solution to a problem in a particular context may not produce an effective solution to the same problem *in a different context*. Sometimes, the solution proposed by the design pattern may not even be applicable in a different context.

Software frameworks can be confused with design patterns. They are closely related. Table 1.1 lists the similarities and differences between the two.

Table 1.1   Design Patterns versus Frameworks

Design Patterns	Frameworks
Design patterns are recurring solutions to problems that arise during the life of a software application in a particular context.	A framework is a group of components that cooperate with each other to provide a reusable architecture for applications with a given domain.
The primary goal is to: • Help improve the quality of the software in terms of the software being reusable, maintainable, extensible, etc. • Reduce the development time	The primary goal is to: • Help improve the quality of the software in terms of the software being reusable, maintainable, extensible, etc. • Reduce development time
Patterns are logical in nature.	Frameworks are more physical in nature, as they exist in the form of some software.
Pattern descriptions are usually independent of programming language or implementation details.	Because frameworks exist in the form of some software, they are implementation-specific.
Patterns are more generic in nature and can be used in almost any kind of application.	Frameworks provide domain-specific functionality.
A design pattern does not exist in the form of a software component on its own. It needs to be implemented explicitly each time it is used.	Frameworks are not complete applications on their own. Complete applications can be built by either inheriting the components const directly.
Patterns provide a way to do "good" design and are used to help design frameworks.	Design patterns may be used in the design and implementation of a framework. In other words, frameworks typically embody several design patterns.

ABOUT THIS BOOK

The objective of this book is to discuss design patterns in an easy to understand manner with simple examples. This book discusses 42 design patterns including the 23 patterns by GoF. These patterns are arranged in six categories:

- 7 Basic Patterns — Section III (Chapter 3 through Chapter 9)
- 5 Creational Patterns — Section IV (Chapter 10 through Chapter 14)
- 4 Collectional Patterns — Section V (Chapter 15 through Chapter 18)
- 11 Structural Patterns — Section VI (Chapter 19 through Chapter 29)
- 11 Behavioral Patterns — Section VII (Chapter 30 through Chapter 40)
- 4 Concurrency Patterns — Section VIII (Chapter 41 through Chapter 44)

Each pattern discussion starts with an explanation of the pattern followed by an example implemented in Java™ programming language. How a given pattern is applied in the example is discussed in detail along with code segments and UML diagrams (class, sequence). At the end of each pattern discussion, a few practice questions are provided for you to work on to improve your understanding of the pattern. Wherever applicable, patterns are compared with other similar looking patterns.

The examples in this book are kept simple for easy understanding. The objective is to enhance the explanation of each pattern with examples for a better understanding.

The UML section provides an overview of the Unified Modeling Language (UML) and discusses various elements of class and sequence diagrams.

The case study at the end of the book demonstrates the collective usage of different design patterns in a real-world application design scenario. This section discusses how various patterns can be used in designing a reusable application framework for a fictitious Web hosting company.

Source Code

The source code for all example applications is available on the following Web site for this book: http://www.crcpress.com/e_products/download.asp.

Source Code Disclaimer

Both the author and the publisher make no representations or warranties about the suitability of the software, either expressed or implied, including but not limited to the implied warranties of merchantability, fitness for a particular purpose or noninfringement. Both the author and the publisher shall not be liable for any damages suffered as a result of using, modifying or distributing the software or its derivatives.

Java is a trademark of Sun Microsystems, Inc. Windows is a registered trademark of Microsoft Corporation.

II

UNIFIED MODELING LANGUAGE (UML)

The Object Management Group (OMG) is a nonprofit consortium that produces and maintains computer industry standards and specifications for enterprise applications. UML is an application modeling specification from OMG. The primary objective of UML is to simplify the complex software engineering process. Using UML, one can specify, visualize and create artifacts of both software and nonsoftware systems. It is to be noted that UML is a modeling language only — that is, it defines the words and grammar, but not the process or procedure for creating models.

2

UML: A QUICK REFERENCE

UML offers 12 diagrams towards representing an application's requirements analysis and solution design. Each of these 12 diagrams can be classified into 3 categories as follows.

STRUCTURE DIAGRAMS

UML offers the following four structure diagrams, which can be used to represent the static structure of an application.

1. Class diagrams
2. Object diagrams
3. Component diagrams
4. Deployment diagrams

BEHAVIOR DIAGRAMS

UML offers the following five behavior diagrams, which can be used to represent the dynamic behavioral aspects of an application.

1. Use Case diagrams
2. Sequence diagrams
3. Activity diagrams
4. Collaboration diagrams
5. Statechart diagram

MODEL MANAGEMENT DIAGRAMS

UML offers the following three model management diagrams, which can be used to represent how different application modules are organized and managed.

1. Packages
2. Subsystems
3. Models

Class and sequence diagrams have been provided for examples in this book. This section provides a brief introduction to the class and sequence diagrams and explains the different class/sequence diagram elements used in this book.

CLASS DIAGRAMS

Class diagrams are part of the structure diagrams and are used to describe the static structure of a system. The structure and behavior of classes and their association with other classes are depicted inside of a class diagram.

Class

Figure 2.1 shows the generic representation of a class.

It consists of three compartments (rectangular sections). The class name is placed in the topmost compartment. The set of attributes (both instance variables and class variables) are listed in the second compartment beneath the class name compartment. The set of methods/operations is listed in the third compartment.

Though the generic representation consists of three compartments as described above, the compartments may vary in number and type. One can suppress compartments and also have additional compartments to accommodate such aspects as constraints and tagged values.

Figure 2.2 shows an example of a class.

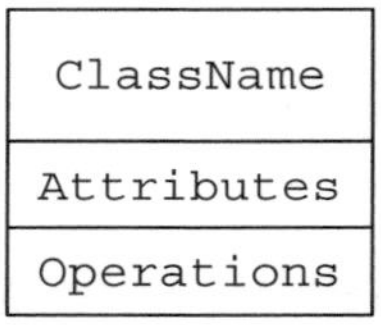

```
+------------+
| ClassName  |
+------------+
| Attributes |
+------------+
| Operations |
+------------+
```

Figure 2.1   Generic Class Representation

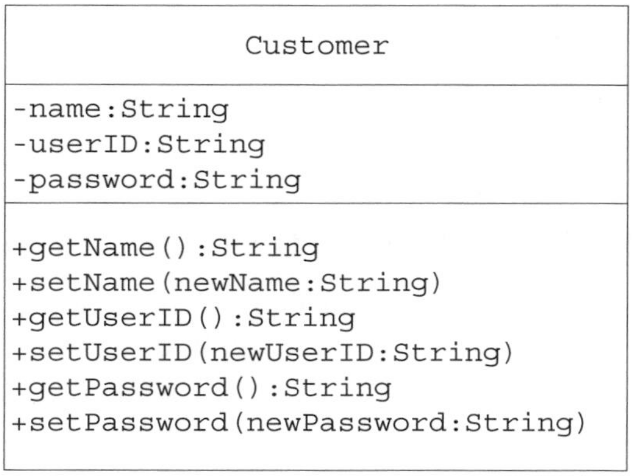

```
+----------------------------------------+
|                Customer                 |
+----------------------------------------+
| -name:String                           |
| -userID:String                         |
| -password:String                       |
+----------------------------------------+
| +getName():String                      |
| +setName(newName:String)               |
| +getUserID():String                    |
| +setUserID(newUserID:String)           |
| +getPassword():String                  |
| +setPassword(newPassword:String)       |
+----------------------------------------+
```

Figure 2.2   An Example Class Representation

Inner Class

An inner class is a class defined inside another class. The concept of an inner class exists in some of the object-oriented languages such as Java, C++ (through struct and enum) and C# (with true inner classes), but is not a standard object-oriented concept.

UML does not provide a definite way of representing an inner class. The notation shown in Figure 2.3 is used in this book to represent an inner class, where the inner class is placed in the operations section of class in which the inner class is defined.

Figure 2.4 shows an example of an inner class Memento defined inside the DataConverter class.

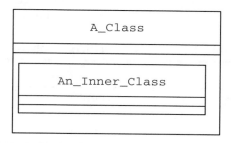

Figure 2.3   Inner Class Representation

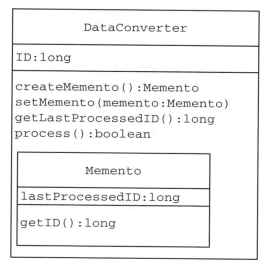

Figure 2.4   An Example Inner Class Representation

Access Specifiers

In Java, the visibility of different members of an object and their accessibility by different client objects is controlled using access specifiers. Access specifiers for attributes and operations can be specified using symbols from Table 2.1.

Table 2.2 lists Java access specifiers and their scope.

In Figure 2.2 (Customer class) name is a private attribute and getName is a public method.

Static

Underlining a variable or method of a class specifies it as static (with class level scope). In Figure 2.5, the method getInstance is a static method of the FileLogger class. Client objects can invoke the getInstance method on the FileLogger class without having to create its instances.

Table 2.1 Access Specifiers Symbols

Symbol	Scope
+	Public
#	Protected
−	Private

Table 2.2 Access Specifiers: Scope Details

Specifier	Classes in the Same Package	Classes in Other Packages	Subclasses in the Same Package	Subclasses in Other Packages
Public	Can Access	Can Access	Can Access	Can Access
Protected	Can Access	Cannot Access	Can Access	Can Access
Friendly (When no specifier is used) (Also referred to as Package scope)	Can Access	Cannot Access	Can Access	Cannot Access
Private	Cannot Access	Cannot Access	Cannot Access	Cannot Access

```
┌────────────────────────────────────┐
│            FileLogger              │
├────────────────────────────────────┤
│ +getInstance():FileLogger          │
└────────────────────────────────────┘
```

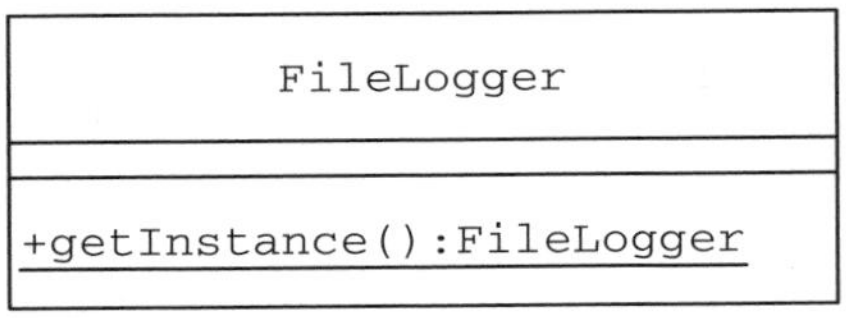

Figure 2.5 Static Method Representation

Abstract Class/Method

A method without body, in a class, is referred to as an abstract method. A class with at least one abstract method is treated as an abstract class. Client objects may not instantiate an abstract class. A subclass of an abstract class must implement all abstract methods of the abstract class or be declared as an abstract class itself.

Displaying a class/method name in italics specifies it as an abstract class/method. The Creator class in Figure 2.6 is an abstract class with an abstract method `factoryMethod`.

Exception

A dashed arrow with a stereotype label "throws" is used to indicate that a specific method throws an exception. The arrow points from the method to the exception class. Both the methods `isValid` and `save` in Figure 2.7 declare to (possibly) throw an exception of the `java.rmi.RemoteException` type.

Note

A note is attached to a UML diagram to provide additional information for a symbol such as comments, constraints or code. In general, notes can be attached to any diagram element in any UML diagram.

A note is denoted by a dog-eared rectangle and is attached to a diagram element by a dotted line. Figure 2.8 shows a note attached to the attribute of a class.

Generalization

Generalization is used to depict the object-oriented concept of inheritance when there is a base class with common behavior and each of its derived classes contains specific details/behavior.

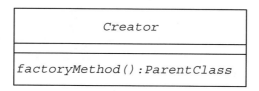

Figure 2.6 Abstract Class/Method Representation

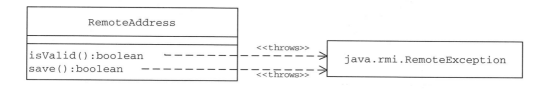

Figure 2.7 Representation of Methods Throwing Exceptions

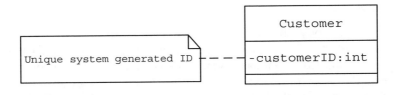

Figure 2.8 A Note to Provide Additional Information

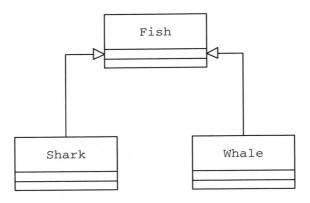

Figure 2.9 Inheritance Relationship

In Figure 2.9, the closed, hollow arrowhead pointing from the Shark/Whale subclass to the Fish superclass represents generalization.

Interface

An interface specifies the externally visible operations of a class, but not the actual implementation of those operations. An interface often specifies only a part of the behavior of an actual implementer class. An interface can be drawn using a class-like rectangular setup, with the text "interface" above the name of the interface. Figure 2.10 shows an interface named VisitorInterface.

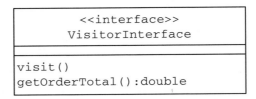

Figure 2.10 An Interface

Realization

A realization depicts the relationship between an interface and a class that provides the actual implementation. This can be drawn in two ways depending on how the interface is depicted.

1. Using a closed, hollow arrowhead pointing from the implementing class to the interface with a dashed line
2. With a line and a circle, where the circle represents the interface (with the name of the interface kept near the circle) and the line can be drawn pointing to the class that implements the interface represented by the circle.

In both Figure 2.11 and Figure 2.12, the OrderVisitor class implements the interface declared by the VisitorInterface (Java) interface.

Dependency

A dependency depicts the relationship between a source and a target component, when there is a dependency relationship between the two. It means, when there is a change in the target, the source element undergoes a necessary change but not vice versa.

The Order class in Figure 2.13 makes use of the execute method of the DBUtil class to execute SQL (structured query language) statements and hence is dependent on it.

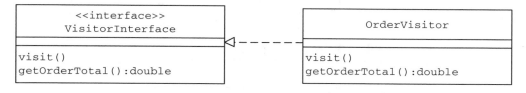

Figure 2.11   Interface-Implementer Representation I

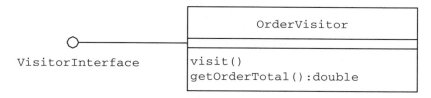

Figure 2.12   Interface-Implementer Representation II

Figure 2.13   One Class Dependent on the Other

The dashed arrow points from the dependent `Order` class to the target `DBUtil` class.

Class Association

Class association specifies the structural relationship between classes.

The concept of multiplicity discussed below is very closely tied to class associations.

Multiplicity

Multiplicity is used to indicate the number of instances of one class linked to one instance of the other class. Table 2.3 lists different values that can be used to indicate the multiplicity.

The following three different types of associations are used in example UML diagrams in this book.

Navigability

When Class A contains the information required to reach Class B, then the navigability is from Class A to Class B. In other words, Class A knows about Class B, but not vice versa.

In Figure 2.14, an instance of the `LogAbstraction` class internally maintains a `LoggerBridge` object and hence will be able to reach it directly. Hence a `LoggerBridge` object is navigable from a `LogAbstraction` instance.

Table 2.3   Multiplicity Values

Notation	Description
1	No More than One
0..1	Zero or One
*	Many
0..*	Zero or Many
1..*	One or Many

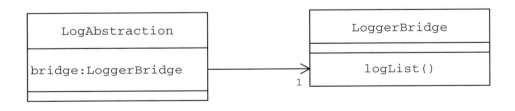

Figure 2.14   The Navigability from One Class to the Other

It is also possible for the navigability to be bidirectional. In that case, the solid line of association between the two classes either contains arrowheads on both the ends or none.

The following two associations are applicable when there is a *whole–part* relationship between two classes. In other words, one class contains the other.

Composition

Class A contains Class B.

This statement denotes a strong ownership between Class A, the *whole*, and Class B, its *part*. In other words, the part class *cannot meaningfully exist* on its own *without* the whole class.

In Figure 2.15:

- A line item is part of an order.
- A line item cannot exist without an order.

Aggregation

This is a lighter form of composition. The whole class plays a more important role than the part class, but unlike the case of composition, the part class *can meaningfully exist* on its own *without* the whole class.

In Figure 2.16:

- A `Player` is part of a `Team`.
- A `Player` can be part of more than one `Team` and hence, when a `Team` is dissolved, the `Player` still remains.

Figure 2.15   The Composite Relationship

Figure 2.16   The Aggregate Relationship

SEQUENCE DIAGRAMS

Sequence diagrams are used to depict interactions among collaborating objects in terms of messages exchanged over time for a specific result. In addition, a sequence diagram may also be used to model business flows. Let us take a quick look at some of the diagram elements used in creating sequence diagrams.

Object

An object is represented with the name of the class in a rectangle preceded by a colon. Figure 2.17 shows an object named `Controller`.

Message

A message is a communication between objects. The solid horizontal line indicating a message can be labeled with the name of the message/operation along with its argument values. Figure 2.18 is a message call named `save`.

In general, a message call in a sequence diagram will map to a class operation. The main exceptions are when you are not directly modeling a class interaction. For example, a sequence diagram may be used to model a user using an ATM machine where the interaction is more along the lines of the user sending a message to the system or the system sending a response to the user. In this case, the modeling is at a different conceptual level and the notion of direct mapping to class operations may not be appropriate. Sequence diagrams may also be used to model business flows, in which case the message may represent the passing of a note, a file, a letter, etc.

Figure 2.17   An Object in a Sequence Diagram

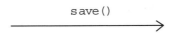

Figure 2.18   A Message Call from One Object to Another

Figure 2.19   A Message Call from an Object onto Itself

Self Call

This is a message call from an object onto itself. Figure 2.19 is a self call of a message named `createSQL`.

Let us create a sample sequence diagram (Figure 2.20) with the following functionality, using different sequence diagram symbols discussed above.

- An Internet user enters data in an online registration form and submits it.
- All user submissions are first received by a `Controller` object.
- The `Controller` object creates an `Account` object with the data submitted by the user.
- The `Account` object creates and uses a `DBManager` object to save the data to a database.

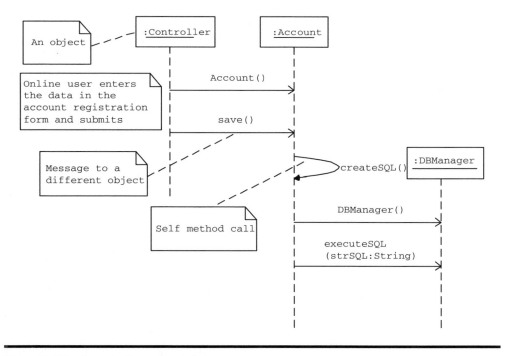

Figure 2.20   Sample Sequence Diagram

III

BASIC PATTERNS

The patterns discussed in this section are some of the most common, basic and important design patterns one can find in the areas of object-oriented design and programming. Some of these fundamental design patterns, such as the Interface, Abstract Parent, Private Methods, etc., are used extensively during the discussion of the other patterns in this book.

Chapter	Pattern Name	Description
3	Interface	Can be used to design a set of service provider classes that offer the same service so that a client object can use different classes of service provider objects in a seamless manner without having to alter the client implementation.
4	Abstract Parent Class	Useful for designing a framework for the consistent implementation of the functionality common to a set of related classes.
5	Private Methods	Provide a way of designing a class behavior so that external objects are not permitted to access the behavior that is meant only for the internal use.
6	Accessor Methods	Provide a way of accessing an object's state using specific methods. This approach discourages different client objects from directly accessing the attributes of an object, resulting in a more maintainable class structure.
7	Constant Data Manager	Useful for designing an easy to maintain, centralized repository for the constant data in an application.
8	Immutable Object	Used to ensure that the state of an object cannot be changed. May be used to ensure that the concurrent access to a data object by several client objects does not result in race conditions.
9	Monitor	A way of designing an application object so that it does not produce unpredictable results when more than one thread tries to access the object at the same time in a multithreaded environment.

The Java programming language has built-in support for some of the fundamental design patterns in the form of language features. The other fundamental patterns can very easily be implemented using the Java language constructs.

3

INTERFACE

This pattern was previously described in Grand98.

DESCRIPTION

In general, the functionality of an object-oriented system is encapsulated in the form of a set of objects. These objects provide different services either on their own or by interacting with other objects. In other words, a given object may rely upon the services offered by a different object to provide the service it is designed for. An object that requests a service from another object is referred as a client object. Some other objects in the system may seek the services offered by the client object.

From Figure 3.1, the client object assumes that the service provider objects corresponding to a specific service request are always of the same class type and interacts directly with the service provider object. This type of direct interaction ties the client with a specific class type for a given service request. This approach works fine when there is only one class of objects offering a given service, but may not be adequate when there is more than one class of objects that provide the same service required by the client (Figure 3.2). Because the client expects the service provider to be always of the same class type, it will not be able to make use of the different classes of service provider objects in a seamless manner. It requires changes to the design and implementation of the client and greatly reduces the reusability of the client by other objects.

In such cases, the Interface pattern can be used to better design different service provider classes that offer the same service to enable the client object to use different classes of service provider objects with little or no need for altering

Figure 3.1   Client–Service Provider Interaction

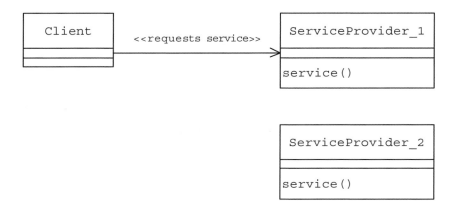

Figure 3.2   Different Classes of Service Providers Offering the Same Set of Services

the client code. Applying the Interface pattern, the common services offered by different service provider classes can be abstracted out and declared as a separate interface. Each of the service provider classes can be designed as implementers of this common interface.

With this arrangement, the client can safely assume the service provider object to be of the interface type. From the class hierarchy in Figure 3.3, objects of different service provider classes can be treated as objects of the interface type. This enables the client to use different types of service provider objects in a seamless manner without requiring any changes. The client does not need to be altered even when a new service provider is designed as part of the class hierarchy in Figure 3.3.

EXAMPLE

Let us build an application to calculate and display the salaries of different employees of an organization with the categorization of designations as listed in Table 3.1.

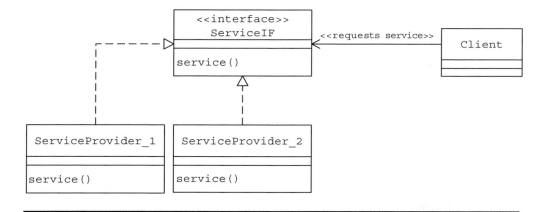

Figure 3.3   Common Interface with Different Service Providers as Implementers

Table 3.1   Different Categories of Designations

Designations	Category
Programmer, Designer and Consultant	Category-A
Sales Rep, Sales Manager, Account Rep	Category-B
...	...
C-Level Executives	Category-n
...	...

Let us assume that the application needs to consider only those employees whose designations are part of Category-A. The salary calculation functionality for all employees of Category-A can be designed in the form of the `CategoryA` class as follows:

```java
public class CategoryA {
    double baseSalary;
    double OT;
    public CategoryA(double base, double overTime) {
      baseSalary = base;
      OT = overTime;
    }
    public double getSalary() {
      return (baseSalary + OT);
    }
}
```

The class representation of an employee, in its simplest form, can be designed as in the following listing with two attributes: the employee name and the category of designation.

```java
public class Employee {
  CategoryA salaryCalculator;
  String name;
  public Employee(String s, CategoryA c) {
    name = s;
    salaryCalculator = c;
  }
  public void display() {
    System.out.println("Name=" + name);
    System.out.println("salary= " +
                    salaryCalculator.getSalary());
  }
}
```

A client object can configure an `Employee` object with values for the name and the category type attributes at the time of invoking its constructor. Subsequently the client object can invoke the `display` method to display the details of the employee name and salary. Because we are dealing only with employees who belong to Category-A, instances of the `Employee` class always expect the category type and hence the salary calculator to be always of the `CategoryA` type. As part of its implementation of the `display` method, the `Employee` class uses the salary calculation service provided by the `CategoryA` class.

The main application object `MainApp` that needs to display the salary details of employees performs the following tasks:

- Creates an instance of the `CategoryA` class by passing appropriate details required for the salary calculation.
- Creates an `Employee` object and configures it with the `CategoryA` object created above.
- Invokes the `display` method on the `Employee` object.
- The `Employee` object makes use of the services of the `CategoryA` object in calculating the salary of the employee it represents. In this aspect, the `Employee` object acts as a client to the `CategoryA` object.

```java
public class MainApp {
  public static void main(String [] args) {
    CategoryA c = new CategoryA(10000, 200);
    Employee e = new Employee ("Jennifer,"c);
    e.display();
  }
}
```

This design works fine as long as the need is to calculate the salary for Category-A employees only and there is only one class of objects that provides this service. But the fact that the `Employee` object expects the salary calculation service provider object to be always of the `CategoryA` class type affects the maintainability and results in an application design that is restrictive in terms of its adaptability.

Let us assume that the application also needs to calculate the salary of employees who are part of Category-B, such as sales representatives and account representatives, and the corresponding salary calculation service is provided by objects of a different class `CategoryB`.

```java
public class CategoryB {
  double salesAmt;
  double baseSalary;
  final static double commission = 0.02;
  public CategoryB(double sa, double base) {
    baseSalary = base;
```

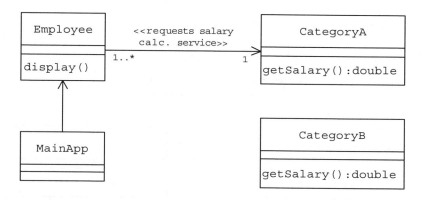

Figure 3.4   Employee/Consultant/Salesrep Class Association

```
      salesAmt = sa;
   }
   public double getSalary() {
     return (baseSalary + (commission * salesAmt));
   }
}
```

The main application object `MainApp` will be able to create an instance of the `CategoryB` class but will not be able to configure the `Employee` object with this instance. This is because the `Employee` object expects the salary calculator to be always of the `CategoryA` type. As a result, the main application will not be able to reuse the existing `Employee` class to represent different types of employees (Figure 3.4). The existing `Employee` class implementation needs to undergo necessary modifications to accept additional salary calculator service provider types. These limitations can be addressed by using the Interface pattern resulting in a much more flexible application design.

Applying the Interface pattern, the following three changes can be made to the application design.

1. The common salary calculating service provided by different objects can be abstracted out to a separate `SalaryCalculator` interface.

```
public interface SalaryCalculator {
   public double getSalary();
}
```

2. Each of the `CategoryA` and the `CategoryB` classes can be designed as implementers of the `SalaryCalculator` interface (Figure 3.5).

```
public class CategoryA implements SalaryCalculator {
   double baseSalary;
   double OT;
```

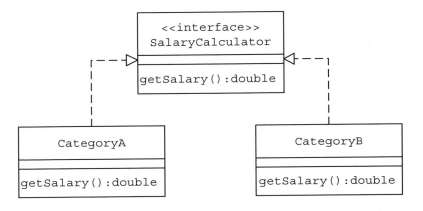

Figure 3.5 Salary Calculation Service Provider Class Hierarchy

```
public CategoryA(double base, double overTime) {
  baseSalary = base;
  OT = overTime;
}
public double getSalary() {
  return (baseSalary + OT);
}
}
public class CategoryB implements SalaryCalculator {
  double salesAmt;
  double baseSalary;
  final static double commission = 0.02;
  public CategoryB(double sa, double base) {
    baseSalary = base;
    salesAmt = sa;
  }
  public double getSalary() {
    return (baseSalary + (commission * salesAmt));
  }
}
```

3. The Employee class implementation needs to be changed to accept a salary calculator service provider of type SalaryCalculator.

```
public class Employee {
  SalaryCalculator empType;
  String name;
```

```
public Employee(String s, SalaryCalculator c) {
   name = s;
   empType = c;
}
public void display() {
   System.out.println("Name=" + name);
   System.out.println("salary= " + empType.getSalary());
}
}
```

With these changes in place, the main application object `MainApp` can now create objects of different types of salary calculator classes and use them to configure different `Employee` objects. Because the `Employee` class, in the revised design, accepts objects of the `SalaryCalculator` type, it can be configured with an instance of any `SalaryCalculator` implementer class (or its subclass). Figure 3.6 shows the application object association.

```
public class MainApp {
   public static void main(String [] args) {
      SalaryCalculator c = new CategoryA(10000, 200);
      Employee e = new Employee ("Jennifer",c);
      e.display();
      c = new CategoryB(20000, 800);
      e = new Employee ("Shania",c);
      e.display();
   }
}
```

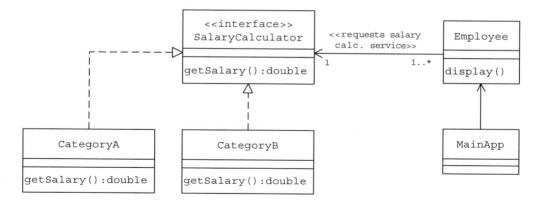

Figure 3.6   Example Application/Class Association

PRACTICE QUESTIONS

1. Design a `Search` interface that declares methods for searching an item in a list. Design and implement two implementers — `BinarySearch` and `LinearSearch` — to conduct a binary and linear search of the list, respectively.

2. Design an `AddressValidator` interface that declares methods for validating different parts of a given address. Design and implement two implementer classes — `USAddress` and `CAAddress` — to validate a given U.S. and Canadian address, respectively.

4

ABSTRACT PARENT CLASS

This pattern was previously described in Grand98.

DESCRIPTION

The Abstract Parent Class pattern is useful for designing a framework for the consistent implementation of functionality common to a set of related classes.

An abstract method is a method that is declared, but contains no implementation. An abstract class is a class with one or more abstract methods. Abstract methods, with more than one possible implementation, represent variable parts of the behavior of an abstract class. An abstract class may contain implementations for other methods, which represent the invariable parts of the class functionality.

Different subclasses may be designed when the functionality outlined by abstract methods in an abstract class needs to be implemented differently. An abstract class, as is, may not be directly instantiated. When a class is designed as a subclass of an abstract class, it *must* implement all of the abstract methods declared in the parent abstract class. Otherwise the subclass itself becomes an abstract class. Only nonabstract subclasses of an abstract class can be instantiated. The requirement that every concrete subclass of an abstract class must implement all of its abstract methods ensures that the variable part of the functionality will be implemented in a consistent manner in terms of the method signatures. The set of methods implemented by the abstract parent class is automatically inherited by all subclasses. This eliminates the need for redundant implementations of these methods by each subclass. Figure 4.1 shows an abstract class with two concrete subclasses.

In the Java programming language there is no support for multiple inheritance. That means a class can inherit only from one single class. Hence inheritance should be used only when it is absolutely necessary. Whenever possible, methods denoting the common behavior should be declared in the form of a Java interface to be implemented by different implementer classes. But interfaces suffer from the limitation that they cannot provide method implementations. This means that every implementer of an interface must explicitly implement all methods declared in an interface, even when some of these methods represent the invariable part of the functionality and have exactly the same implementation in all of the

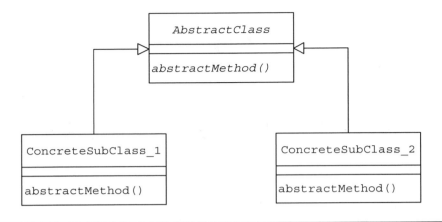

Figure 4.1 An Abstract Class with Two Concrete Subclasses

implementer classes. This leads to redundant code. The following example demonstrates how the Abstract Parent Class pattern can be used in such cases without requiring redundant method implementations.

EXAMPLE

In a typical organization, it is very common to have employees with different designations. This can be represented in form of a class hierarchy with a base **Employee** class and a set of subclasses each corresponding to employees with a specific designation.

Let us consider the following operations as part of designing the representation of an employee.

1. Save employee data
2. Display employee data
3. Access employee attributes such as name and ID
4. Calculate compensation

While Operation 1 through Operation 3 remain the same for all employees, the compensation calculation will be different for employees with different designations. Such an operation, which can be performed in different ways, is a good candidate to be declared as an abstract method. This forces different concrete subclasses of the **Employee** class to provide a custom implementation for the salary calculation operation.

From the base **Employee** class implementation in Listing 4.1, it can be seen that the base **Employee** class provides implementation for the **save, getID, getName** and **toString** methods while it declares the **computeCompensation** method as an abstract method.

Let us define two concrete subclasses — **Consultant** and **SalesRep** — of the **Employee** class (Listing 4.2) representing employees who are consultants and sales representatives, respectively. Each of these subclasses must implement the **computeCompensation** method. Otherwise these subclasses need to be

Listing 4.1   Abstract Employee Class

```java
public abstract class Employee {
   String name;
   String ID;
   //invariable parts
   public Employee(String empName, String empID) {
      name = empName;
      ID = empID;
   }
   public String getName() {
      return name;
   }
   public String getID() {
      return ID;
   }
   public String toString() {
      String str = " Emp Name:: " + getName() + " EmpID:: " +
                 getID();
      return str;
   }
   public void save() {
      FileUtil futil = new FileUtil();
      futil.writeToFile("emp.txt",this.toString(), true, true);
   }
   //variable part of the behavior
   public abstract String computeCompensation();
}
```

declared as abstract and it becomes impossible to instantiate them. Figure 4.2 shows the class hierarchy with **Consultant** and **SalesRep** concrete subclasses of the **Employee** class.

Abstract Parent Class versus Interface

As an alternate design strategy, we could design the employee representation as a Java interface, instead of designing it as an abstract class, with both the **Consultant** and the **SalesRep** classes as its implementers. Figure 4.3 shows the resulting class hierarchy.

But doing so would require *both* the implementers to implement the **save**, **getID**, **getName**, **toString** and the **computeCompensation** methods. Because the implementation of the **save**, **getID**, **getName** and **toString**

Listing 4.2   Concrete Employee Subclasses

```
public class Consultant extends Employee {
  public String computeCompensation() {
    return ("consultant salary is base + " +
            " allowance + OT - tax deductions");
  }
  public Consultant(String empName, String empID) {
    super(empName, empID);
  }
}
public class SalesRep extends Employee {
  //variable part behavior
  public String computeCompensation() {
    return ("sales Rep Salary is Base + commission + " +
            " allowance — tax deductions");
  }
  public SalesRep(String empName, String empID) {
    super(empName, empID);
  }
}
```

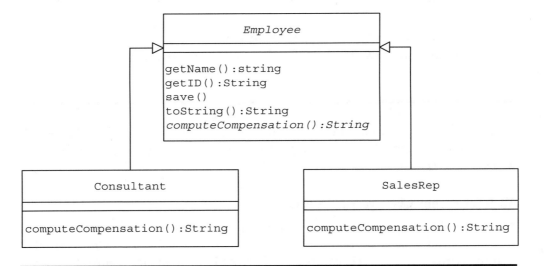

Figure 4.2   Employee Class Hierarchy

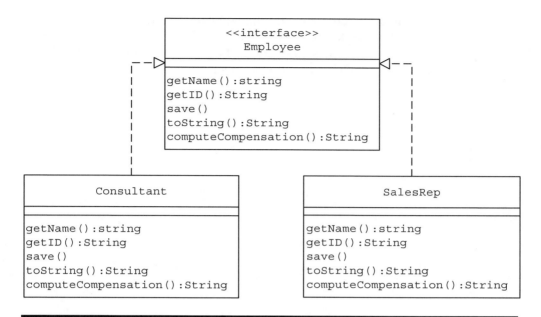

Figure 4.3   Employee as an Interface with Two Implementers

methods remains *the same* for *all* implementers, this leads to redundant code in the application. The implementation of these invariable methods cannot be made part of the **Employee** interface. This is because a Java interface cannot provide implementation for a method. An interface is used for the declaration purpose only. By designing the Employee class as an abstract class, the need for a redundant implementation can be eliminated.

PRACTICE QUESTIONS

1. Consider the details of different bank account types as follows:
   a. All bank accounts allow
      i. Deposits
      ii. Balance enquiries
   b. Savings accounts
      i. Allow no checking
      ii. Do not charge service fee
      iii. Give interest
   c. Checking accounts
      i. Allow checking
      ii. Charge service fee
      iii. Do not give interest

Design a class hierarchy with **Account** as an abstract class with the class representations for both the savings account and the checking account as two concrete subclasses of it.

2. Both the right-angled triangle and the equilateral triangle are triangles with specific differences. Design a class hierarchy with **Triangle** as an abstract class with the class representations for both the right-angled triangle and the equilateral triangle as two concrete subclasses of it.

5

PRIVATE METHODS

DESCRIPTION

Typically a class is designed to offer a well-defined and related set of services to its clients. These services are offered in the form of its methods, which constitute the overall behavior of that object. In case of a well-designed class, each method is designed to perform a single, defined task. Some of these methods may use the functionality offered by other methods or even other objects to perform the task they are designed for. Not all methods of a class are always meant to be used by external client objects. Those methods that offer defined services to different client objects make up an object's public protocol and are to be declared as public methods. Some of the other methods may exist to be used internally by other methods or inner classes of the same object. The Private Methods pattern recommends designing such methods as *private methods*.

In Java, a method signature starts with an access specifier (private/protected/public). Access specifiers indicate the scope and visibility of a method/variable.

A method is declared as private by using the "private" keyword as part of its signature. e.g.,

```
private int hasValidChars(){
    //...
}
```

External client objects cannot directly access private methods. This in turn hides the behavior contained in these methods from client objects.

EXAMPLE

Let us design an `OrderManager` class as in Figure 5.1 that can be used by different client objects to create orders.

```
public class OrderManager {
  private int orderID = 0;
  //Meant to be used internally
```

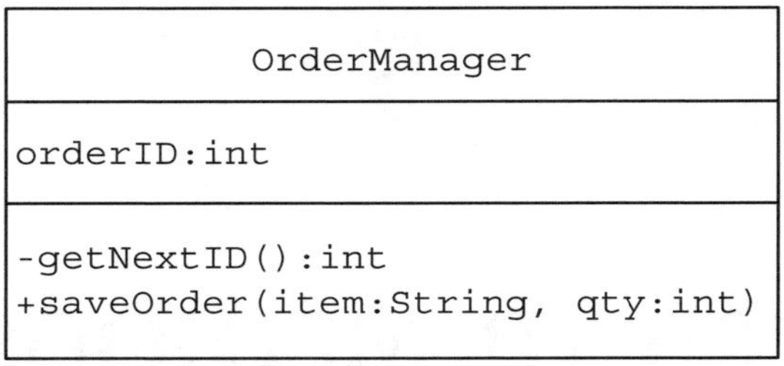

```
                        OrderManager
  ┌──────────────────────────────────────────┐
  │ orderID:int                              │
  ├──────────────────────────────────────────┤
  │ -getNextID():int                         │
  │ +saveOrder(item:String, qty:int)         │
  └──────────────────────────────────────────┘
```

Figure 5.1   OrderManager

```
    private int getNextID() {
      ++orderID;
      return orderID;
    }
    //public method to be used by client objects
    public void saveOrder(String item, int qty) {
      int ID = getNextID();
      System.out.println("Order ID=" + ID + "; Item=" + item +
                     "; Qty=" + qty + " is saved. ");
    }
  }
```

From the `OrderManager` implementation it can be observed that the `saveOrder` method is declared as public as it is meant to be used by client objects, whereas the `getNextID` method is used internally by the `saveOrder` method and is not meant to be used by client objects directly. Hence the `getNextID` method is designed as a private method. This automatically prevents client objects from accessing the `getNextID` method directly.

PRACTICE QUESTIONS

1. Design a `CreditCard` class, which offers the functionality to validate credit card numbers. Design the card validation method to internally use a private method to check if the card number has valid characters.
2. The `OrderManager` class built during the example discussion does not define a constructor. Add a private constructor to the `OrderManager` class. What changes must be made to the `OrderManager` class so that client objects can create `OrderManager` instances?

6

ACCESSOR METHODS

DESCRIPTION

The Accessor Methods pattern is one of the most commonly used patterns in the area of object-oriented programming. In fact, this pattern has been used in most of the examples discussed in this book for different patterns. In general, the values of different instance variables of an object, at a given point of time, constitute its state. The state of an object can be grouped into two categories — public and private. The public state of an object is available to different client objects to access, whereas the private state of an object is meant to be used internally by the object itself and not to be accessed by other objects.

Consider the class representation of a customer in Figure 6.1.

The instance variable ID is maintained separately and used internally by each Customer class instance and is not to be known by other objects. This makes the variable ID the private state of a Customer object to be used internally by the Customer object. On the other hand, variables such as name, SSN (Social Security Number) and the address make up the public state of the Customer object and are supposed to be used by client objects. In case of such an object, the Accessor Method pattern recommends:

- All instance variables being declared as private and provide public methods known as *accessor methods* to access the public state of an object. This prevents external client objects from accessing object instance variables directly. In addition, accessor methods hide from the client whether a property is stored as a direct attribute or as a derived one.

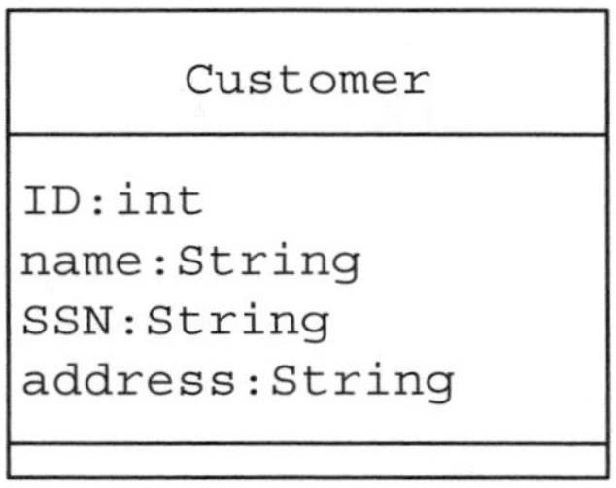

```
          Customer

ID:int
name:String
SSN:String
address:String
```

Figure 6.1   Customer Class

- Client objects can make use of accessor methods to move a Customer object from one state (source) to another state (target). In general, if the object cannot reach the target state, it should notify the caller object that the transition could not be completed. This can be accomplished by having the accessor method throw an exception.
- An object can access its private variables directly. But doing so could greatly affect the maintainability of an application, which the object is part of. When there is a change in the way a particular instance variable is to be defined, it requires changes to be made in every place of the application code where the instance variable is referenced directly. Similar to its client objects, if an object is designed to access its instance variables through accessor methods, any change to the definition of an instance variable requires a change only to its accessor methods.

ACCESSOR METHOD NOMENCLATURE

There is no specific requirement for an accessor method to be named following a certain naming convention. But most commonly the following naming rules are followed:

- To access a non-Boolean instance variable:
  - Define a `getXXXX` method to read the values of an instance variable XXXX. E.g., define a `getFirstName()` method to read the value of an instance variable named `firstName`.
  - Define a `setXXXX(new value)` method to alter the value of an instance variable XXXX. E.g., define a `setFirstName(String)` method to alter the value of an instance variable named `firstName`.
- To access a Boolean instance variable:
  - Define an `isXXXX()` method to check if the value of an instance variable XXXX is true or false. E.g., define an `isActive()` method on a Customer object to check if the customer represented by the Customer object is active.
  - Define a `setXXXX(new value)` method to alter the value of a Boolean instance variable XXXX. E.g., define a `setActive(boolean)` method on a Customer object to mark the customer as active.

The following `Customer` class example explains the usage of accessor methods.

EXAMPLE

Suppose that you are designing a Customer class as part of a large application. A generic representation of a customer in its simplest form can be designed as in Figure 6.2.

Applying the Accessor Method pattern, the set of accessor methods listed in Table 6.1 can be defined corresponding to each of the instance variables (Listing 6.1).

Figure 6.3 shows the resulting class structure.

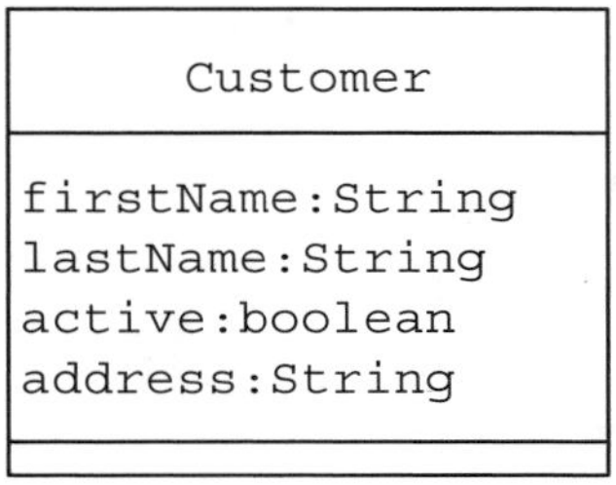

```
          Customer

firstName:String
lastName:String
active:boolean
address:String
```

Figure 6.2   Customer Representation

Table 6.1   List of Accessor Methods

Variable	Method	Purpose
firstName	getFirstName	To read the value of the firstName instance variable
	setFirstName	To alter the value of the firstName instance variable
lastName	getLastName	To read the value of the lastName instance variable
	setLastName	To alter the value of the lastName instance variable
address	getAddress	To read the value of the address instance variable
	setAddress	To alter the value of the address instance variable
active	isActive	To read the value of the active Boolean instance variable
	setActive	To alter the value of the active Boolean instance variable

Different client objects can access the object state variables using the accessor methods listed in Table 6.1. The Customer object itself can access its state variables directly, but using the accessor methods will greatly improve the maintainability of the Customer class code. This in turn contributes to the overall application maintainability.

DIRECT REFERENCE VERSUS ACCESSOR METHODS

Let us suppose that we need to add the following two new methods to the Customer class.

1. isValidCustomer — To check if the customer data is valid.
2. save — To save the customer data to a data file.

As can be seen from the Customer class implementation in Listing 6.2, the newly added methods access different instance variables directly. Different client

Listing 6.1   Customer Class with Accessor Methods

```java
public class Customer {
  private String firstName;
  private String lastName;
  private String address;
  private boolean active;
  public String getFirstName() {
    return firstName;
  }
  public String getLastName() {
    return lastName;
  }
  public String getAddress() {
    return address;
  }
  public boolean isActive() {
    return active;
  }
  public void setFirstName(String newValue) {
    firstName = newValue;
  }
  public void setLastName(String newValue) {
    lastName = newValue;
  }
  public void setAddress(String newValue) {
    address = newValue;
  }
  public void isActive(boolean newValue) {
    active = newValue;
  }
}
```

objects can use the Customer class in this form without any difficulty. But when there is a change in the definition of any of the instance variables, it requires a change to the implementation of all the methods that access these instance variables directly. For example, if the address variable need to be changed from its current definition as a string to a StringBuffer or something different, then all methods that refer to the address variable directly needs to be altered.

As an alternative approach, Customer object methods can be redesigned to access the object state through its accessor methods (Listing 6.3).

```
┌─────────────────────────────────────────┐
│                Customer                   │
├─────────────────────────────────────────┤
│ firstName:String                          │
│ lastName:String                           │
│ active:boolean                            │
│ address:String                            │
├─────────────────────────────────────────┤
│ getFirstName():String                     │
│ getLastName():String                      │
│ getAddress():String                       │
│ isActive():boolean                        │
│ setFirstName(newValue:String)             │
│ setLastName(newValue:String)              │
│ setAddress(newValue:String)              │
│ setActive(newValue:boolean)               │
│                                           │
└─────────────────────────────────────────┘
```

Figure 6.3 Customer Class with Accessor Methods

In this approach, any change to the definition of any of the instance variables requires a change *only* to the implementation of the corresponding accessor methods. No changes are required for any other part of the class implementation and the class becomes more maintainable.

PRACTICE QUESTIONS

1. Design an Order class with accessor methods for its instance variables.
2. Identify the effect of using accessor methods when a class is subclassed.

Listing 6.2   Customer Class Directly Accessing Its Instance Variables

```java
public class Customer {
        …

        …

  public String getFirstName() {
    return firstName;
  }
        …

        …

  public boolean isValidCustomer() {
    if ((firstName.length() > 0) && (lastName.length() > 0) &&
        (address.length() > 0))
      return true;
    return false;
  }
 public void save() {
    String data =
      firstName + "," + lastName + "," + address +
      "," + active;
    FileUtil futil = new FileUtil();
    futil.writeToFile("customer.txt",data, true, true);
  }
}
```

Listing 6.3   Customer Class Using Accessor Methods to Access Its Instance Variables

```
public class Customer {

        ...

        ...

  public String getFirstName() {
    return firstName;
  }

        ...

        ...

  public boolean isValidCustomer() {
    if ((getFirstName().length() > 0) &&
        (getLastName().length() > 0) &&
        (getAddress().length() > 0))
      return true;
    return false;
  }
  public void save() {
    String data =
      getFirstName() + "," + getLastName() + "," +
      getAddress() + "," + isActive();
    FileUtil futil = new FileUtil();
    futil.writeToFile("customer.txt",data, true, true);
  }
}
```

7

CONSTANT DATA MANAGER

DESCRIPTION

Objects in an application usually make use of different types of data in offering the functionality they are designed for. Such data can either be variable data or constant data. The Constant Data Manager pattern is useful for designing an efficient storage mechanism for the constant data used by different objects in an application. In general, application objects access different types of constant data items such as data file names, button labels, maximum and minimum range values, error codes and error messages, etc.

Instead of allowing the constant data to be present in different objects, the Constant Data Manager pattern recommends all such data, which is considered as constant in an application, be kept in a separate object and accessed by other objects in the application. This type of separation provides an easy to maintain, centralized repository for the constant data in an application.

EXAMPLE

Let us consider a Customer Data Management application that makes use of three types of objects — Account, Address and CreditCard — to represent different parts of the customer data (Figure 7.1). Each of these objects makes use of different items of constant data as part of offering the services it is designed for (Listing 7.1).

Instead of allowing the distribution of the constant data across different classes, it can be encapsulated in a separate ConstantDataManager (Listing 7.2) object and is accessed by each of the Account, Address and CreditCard objects.

The interaction among these classes can be depicted as in Figure 7.2.

Whenever any of the constant data items needs to be modified, only the ConstantDataManager needs to be altered without affecting other application objects. On the other side, it is easy to lose track of constants that do not get used anymore when code gets thrown out over the years but constants remain in the class.

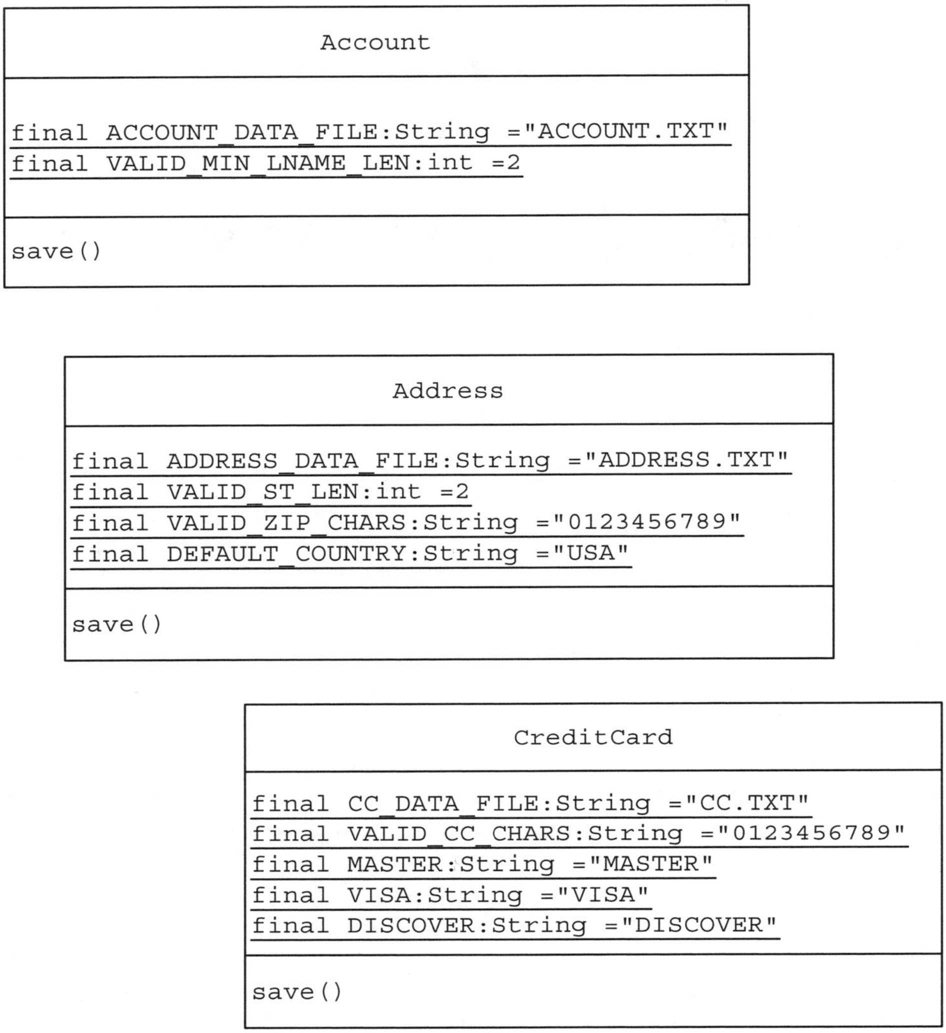

```
+-------------------------------------------------------+
|                       Account                         |
+-------------------------------------------------------+
| final ACCOUNT_DATA_FILE:String ="ACCOUNT.TXT"         |
| final VALID_MIN_LNAME_LEN:int =2                      |
+-------------------------------------------------------+
| save()                                                |
+-------------------------------------------------------+


    +-------------------------------------------------------+
    |                       Address                         |
    +-------------------------------------------------------+
    | final ADDRESS_DATA_FILE:String ="ADDRESS.TXT"         |
    | final VALID_ST_LEN:int =2                             |
    | final VALID_ZIP_CHARS:String ="0123456789"            |
    | final DEFAULT_COUNTRY:String ="USA"                   |
    +-------------------------------------------------------+
    | save()                                                |
    +-------------------------------------------------------+


        +-------------------------------------------------------+
        |                     CreditCard                        |
        +-------------------------------------------------------+
        | final CC_DATA_FILE:String ="CC.TXT"                   |
        | final VALID_CC_CHARS:String ="0123456789"             |
        | final MASTER:String ="MASTER"                         |
        | final VISA:String ="VISA"                             |
        | final DISCOVER:String ="DISCOVER"                     |
        +-------------------------------------------------------+
        | save()                                                |
        +-------------------------------------------------------+
```

Figure 7.1   Different Application Objects

PRACTICE QUESTIONS

1. Constant data can also be declared in a Java interface. Any class that implements such an interface can use the constants declared in it without any qualifications. Redesign the example application with the `Constant-DataManager` as an interface.
2. Identify how the Constant Data Manager pattern can be used to store different application-specific error messages.

Listing 7.1   Application Classes: Account, Address and CreditCard

```
public class Account {
  public static final String ACCOUNT_DATA_FILE = "ACCOUNT.TXT";
  public static final int VALID_MIN_LNAME_LEN = 2;
  public void save() {
  }
}
public class Address {
  public static final String ADDRESS_DATA_FILE = "ADDRESS.TXT";
  public static final int VALID_ST_LEN = 2;
  public static final String VALID_ZIP_CHARS = "0123456789";
  public static final String DEFAULT_COUNTRY = "USA";
  public void save() {
  }
}
public class CreditCard {
  public static final String CC_DATA_FILE = "CC.TXT";
  public static final String VALID_CC_CHARS = "0123456789";
  public static final String MASTER = "MASTER";
  public static final String VISA = "VISA";
  public static final String DISCOVER = "DISCOVER";
  public void save() {
  }
}
```

3. The ConstantDataManager in Listing 7.2 contains hard-coded values for different constant items. Enhance the ConstantDataManager class to read values from a file and initialize different constant data items when it is first constructed.

Listing 7.2 `ConstantDataManager` Class

```java
public class ConstantDataManager {
  public static final String ACCOUNT_DATA_FILE = "ACCOUNT.TXT";
  public static final int VALID_MIN_LNAME_LEN = 2;
  public static final String ADDRESS_DATA_FILE = "ADDRESS.TXT";
  public static final int VALID_ST_LEN = 2;
  public static final String VALID_ZIP_CHARS = "0123456789";
  public static final String DEFAULT_COUNTRY = "USA";
  public static final String CC_DATA_FILE = "CC.TXT";
  public static final String VALID_CC_CHARS = "0123456789";
  public static final String MASTER = "MASTER";
  public static final String VISA = "VISA";
  public static final String DISCOVER = "DISCOVER";
}
```

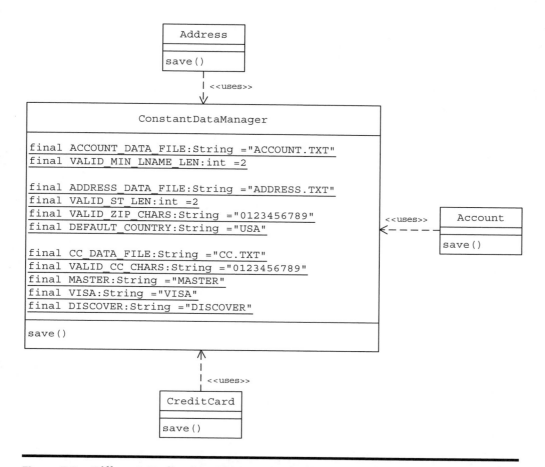

Figure 7.2   Different Application Objects Access the `ConstantDataManager` for the Constant Data

8

IMMUTABLE OBJECT

This pattern was previously described in Grand98.

DESCRIPTION

In general, classes in an application are designed to carry data and have behavior. Sometimes a class may be designed in such a way that its instances can be used just as carriers of related data without any specific behavior. Such classes can be called data model classes and instances of such classes are referred to as data objects. For example, consider the Employee class in Figure 8.1 and Listing 8.1.

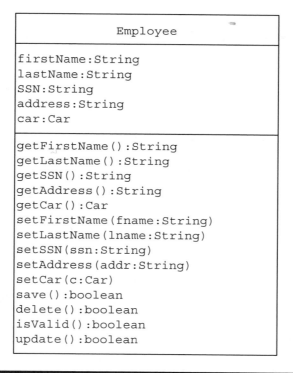

Figure 8.1 Employee Representation

Listing 8.1   Employee Class

```java
public class Employee {
  //State
  private String firstName;
  private String lastName;
  private String SSN;
  private String address;
  private Car car;
  //Constructor
  public Employee(String fn, String ln, String ssn,
                  String addr, Car c) {
    firstName = fn;
    lastName = ln;
    SSN = ssn;
    address = addr;
    car = c;
  }
  //Behavior
  public boolean save() {
    //…
    return true;
  }
  public boolean isValid() {
    //…
    return true;
  }
  public boolean update() {
    //…
    return true;
  }
```

(continued)

Listing 8.1   Employee Class (Continued)

```
    //Setters
    public void setFirstName(String fname) {
      firstName = fname;
    }
    public void setLastName(String lname) {
      lastName = lname;
    }
    public void setSSN(String ssn) {
      SSN = ssn;
    }
    public void setCar(Car c) {
      car = c;
    }
    public void setAddress(String addr) {
      address = addr;
    }
    //Getters
    public String getFirstName() {
      return firstName;
    }
    public String getLastName() {
      return lastName;
    }
    public String getSSN() {
      return SSN;
    }
    public Car getCar() {
      return car;
    }
    public String getAddress() {
      return address;
    }
  }
```

Instances of the Employee class above have both the data and the behavior. The corresponding data model class can be designed as in Figure 8.2 and Listing 8.2 without any behavior.

In a typical application scenario, several client objects may simultaneously access instances of such data model classes. This could lead to problems if changes

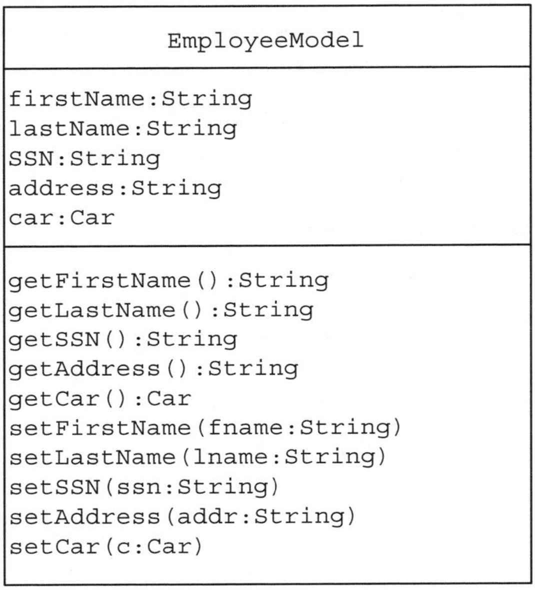

```
                    EmployeeModel

          firstName:String
          lastName:String
          SSN:String
          address:String
          car:Car

          getFirstName():String
          getLastName():String
          getSSN():String
          getAddress():String
          getCar():Car
          setFirstName(fname:String)
          setLastName(lname:String)
          setSSN(ssn:String)
          setAddress(addr:String)
          setCar(c:Car)
```

Figure 8.2 `EmployeeModel` **Class**

Listing 8.2 `EmployeeModel` **Class**

```java
public class EmployeeModel {
  //State
  private String firstName;
  private String lastName;
  private String SSN;
  private String address;
  private Car car;
  //Constructor
  public EmployeeModel(String fn, String ln, String ssn,
      String addr, Car c) {
    firstName = fn;
    lastName = ln;
    SSN = ssn;
    address = addr;
    car = c;
  }
```

(continued)

Listing 8.2 EmployeeModel Class (Continued)

```
  //Setters
  public void setFirstName(String fname) {
    firstName = fname;
  }
  public void setLastName(String lname) {
    lastName = lname;
  }
  public void setSSN(String ssn) {
    SSN = ssn;
  }
  public void setCar(Car c) {
    car = c;
  }
  public void setAddress(String addr) {
    address = addr;
  }
  //Getters
  public String getFirstName() {
    return firstName;
  }
  public String getLastName() {
    return lastName;
  }
  public String getSSN() {
    return SSN;
  }
  public Car getCar() {
    return car;
  }
  public String getAddress() {
    return address;
  }
}
```

to the state of a data object are not coordinated properly. The Immutable Object pattern can be used to ensure that the concurrent access to a data object by several client objects does not result in any problem. The Immutable Object pattern accomplishes this without involving the overhead of synchronizing the methods to access the object data.

Applying the Immutable Object pattern, the data model class can be designed in such a way that the data carried by an instance of the data model class remains unchanged over its entire lifetime. That means the instances of the data model class become *immutable*.

In general, concurrent access to an object creates problems when one thread can change data while a different thread is reading the same data. The fact that the data of an immutable object cannot be modified makes it automatically thread-safe and eliminates any concurrent access related problems.

Though using the Immutable Object pattern opens up an application for all kinds of performance tuning tricks, it must be noted that designing an object as immutable is an important decision. Every now and then it turns out that objects that were once thought of as immutables are in fact mutable, which could result in difficult implementation changes.

EXAMPLE

As an example, let us redesign the `EmployeeModel` class to make it immutable by applying the following changes.

1. All instance variables (state) must be set in the constructor alone. No other method should be provided to modify the state of the object. The constructor is automatically thread-safe and hence does not lead to problems.
2. It may be possible to override class methods to modify the state. In order to prevent this, declare the class as *final*. Declaring a class as final does not allow the class to be extended further.
3. All instance variables should be declared *final* so that they can be set only once, inside the constructor.
4. If any of the instance variables contain a reference to an object, the corresponding *getter* method should return a copy of the object it refers to, but *not* the actual object itself.

Figure 8.3 and Listing 8.3 show the resulting immutable version of the `EmployeeModel` class.

The immutable version of the `EmployeeModel` objects can safely be used in a multithreaded environment.

PRACTICE QUESTIONS

1. Design an immutable class that contains the line styles and colors used in a given image.
2. Design an immutable class to carry the data related to a company such as the company address, phone, fax, company name and other details.

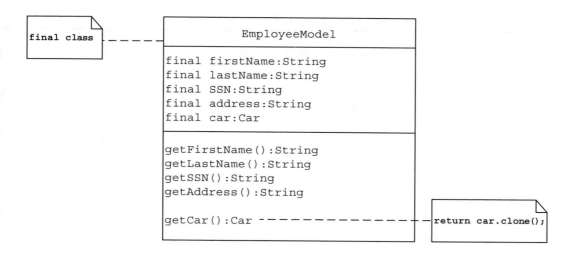

Figure 8.3 **EmployeeModel Class: Immutable Version**

Listing 8.3 EmployeeModel Class: Immutable Version

```java
public final class EmployeeModel {
  //State
  private final String firstName;
  private final String lastName;
  private final String SSN;
  private final String address;
  private final Car car;
  //Constructor
  public EmployeeModel(String fn, String ln, String ssn,
      String addr, Car c) {
    firstName = fn;
    lastName = ln;
    SSN = ssn;
    address = addr;
    car = c;
  }
  //Getters
  public String getFirstName() {
    return firstName;
  }
  public String getLastName() {
    return lastName;
  }
  public String getSSN() {
    return SSN;
  }
  public Car getCar() {
    //return a copy of the car object
    return (Car) car.clone();
  }
  public String getAddress() {
    return address;
  }
}
```

9

MONITOR

DESCRIPTION

In general, an object may need to access shared resources such as files as part of its implementation to provide the services it is designed for. In a multithreaded environment, when methods of such an object are accessed simultaneously by more than one thread, it could result in unpredictable behavior. Instances of such incorrect and irregular behavior resulting from the concurrent access to an object's methods by multiple threads are referred to as *race conditions*.

The monitor is a mechanism to obtain a lock on such an object to ensure that only one thread is allowed to execute any method on that object at any given time. Instead of keeping the responsibility on its client objects, the actual service provider object itself can be designed to be responsible to ensure that no two threads can execute its methods simultaneously. This can be accomplished using the monitor concept. In Java this can be accomplished by declaring the methods of an object using the synchronized keyword.

The following example demonstrates the use of synchronizing an object's methods to prevent race conditions.

EXAMPLE

Let us build a utility class whose instances can be used to log messages in a multithreaded environment.

A simple message logging utility class can be designed as in Listing 9.1.

Other application objects can log messages to the log file by invoking the log method on a FileLogger instance. Inside the log method, the FileLogger performs the necessary file operations required to log an input message. It is to be noted that the log method is declared with the synchronized keyword. Without synchronization, when multiple threads simultaneously try to log messages by invoking the log method on the same FileLogger object, it could result in unpredictable behavior. This is because multiple threads try to perform the same set of open, write and close operations on the same log file at the same time.

The synchronized keyword ensures that only one thread is allowed to execute the log method *on a given* FileLogger object at any given point in time. This guarantee comes at a price. Declaring an object's methods as synchronized can have negative impact on the performance of an application that makes use of

Listing 9.1 A Simple Message Logger

```
public class FileLogger {
  public synchronized void log(String msg) {
    DataOutputStream dos = null;
    try {
      dos = new DataOutputStream(
            new FileOutputStream("log.txt",true));
      dos.writeBytes(msg);
      dos.close();
    } catch (FileNotFoundException ex) {
    //
    }
    catch (IOException ex) {
    //
    }
  }
}
```

those methods. In general, synchronized methods run many times slower than their nonsynchronized counterparts. Hence an object's methods should be designed as synchronized methods only after careful consideration.

An object can have any number of synchronized methods. For a thread to execute a synchronized method on an object, it needs to get a lock on that object. The thread holds the lock on the object as long as the method execution continues. While a thread holds a lock on an object, no other thread is given a lock on the same object and hence other threads cannot execute any of the synchronized methods on the same object.

PRACTICE QUESTIONS

1. Design a thread-safe LogReader class to read messages from the log file log.txt.
2. As can be seen from the example, the monitor concept ensures the prevention of race conditions by providing a lock on an object to a thread. Identify how to provide a lock on an entire class of objects when a thread is executing some code on an instance of that class. In other words, when a thread is executing a method on an object, no other thread should be allowed to execute the same method even on a different instance of the same class.

IV

CREATIONAL PATTERNS

Creational Patterns:

- Deal with one of the most commonly performed tasks in an OO application, the creation of objects.
- Support a uniform, simple, and controlled mechanism to create objects.
- Allow the encapsulation of the details about what classes are instantiated and how these instances are created.
- Encourage the use of interfaces, which reduces coupling.

Chapter	Pattern Name	Description
10	Factory Method	When a client object does not know which class to instantiate, it can make use of the factory method to create an instance of an appropriate class from a class hierarchy or a family of related classes. The factory method may be designed as part of the client itself or in a separate class. The class that contains the factory method or any of its subclasses decides on which class to select and how to instantiate it.
11	Singleton	Provides a controlled object creation mechanism to ensure that only one instance of a given class exists.
12	Abstract Factory	Allows the creation of an instance of a class from a suite of related classes without having a client object to specify the actual concrete class to be instantiated.
13	Prototype	Provides a simpler way of creating an object by cloning it from an existing (prototype) object.
14	Builder	Allows the creation of a complex object by providing the information on only its type and content, keeping the details of the object creation transparent to the client. This allows the same construction process to produce different representations of the object.

10

FACTORY METHOD

This pattern was previously described in GoF95.

DESCRIPTION

In general, all subclasses in a class hierarchy inherit the methods implemented by the parent class. A subclass may override the parent class implementation to offer a different type of functionality for the same method. When an application object is aware of the exact functionality it needs, it can directly instantiate the class from the class hierarchy that offers the required functionality.

At times, an application object may only know that it needs to access a class from within the class hierarchy, but does not know exactly which class from among the set of subclasses of the parent class is to be selected. The choice of an appropriate class may depend on factors such as:

- The state of the running application
- Application configuration settings
- Expansion of requirements or enhancements

In such cases, an application object needs to implement the class selection criteria to instantiate an appropriate class from the hierarchy to access its services (Figure 10.1).

This type of design has the following disadvantages:

- Because every application object that intends to use the services offered by the class hierarchy needs to implement the class selection criteria, it results in a high degree of coupling between an application object and the service provider class hierarchy.
- Whenever the class selection criteria change, every application object that uses the class hierarchy must undergo a corresponding change.
- Because class selection criteria needs to take all the factors that could affect the selection process into account, the implementation of an application object could contain inelegant conditional statements.

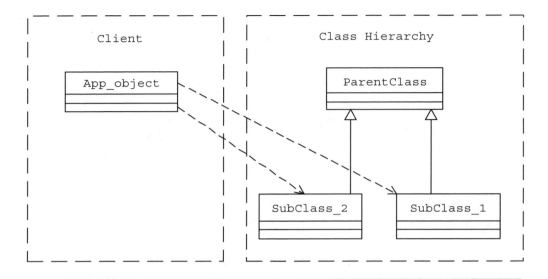

Figure 10.1   Client Object Directly Accessing a Service Provider Class Hierarchy

- If different classes in the class hierarchy need to be instantiated in diverse manners, the implementation of an application object can become more complex.
- It requires an application object to be fully aware of the existence and the functionality offered by each class in the service provider class hierarchy.

In such cases, the Factory Method pattern recommends encapsulating the functionality required, to select and instantiate an appropriate class, inside a designated method referred to as a *factory method*. Thus, a factory method can be defined as a method in a class that:

- Selects an appropriate class from a class hierarchy based on the application context and other influencing factors
- Instantiates the selected class and returns it as an instance of the parent class type

Encapsulation of the required implementation to select and instantiate an appropriate class in a separate method has the following advantages:

- Application objects can make use of the factory method to get access to the appropriate class instance. This eliminates the need for an application object to deal with the varying class selection criteria.
- Besides the class selection criteria, the factory method also implements any special mechanisms required to instantiate the selected class. This is applicable if different classes in the hierarchy need to be instantiated in different ways. The factory method hides these details from application objects and eliminates the need for them to deal with these intricacies.

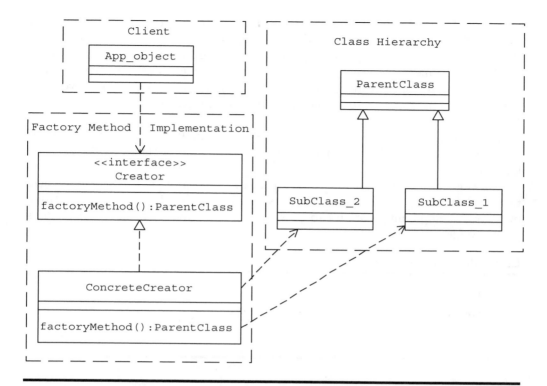

Figure 10.2   A Client Object Accessing a Service Provider Class Hierarchy Using a Factory Method

■ Because the factory method returns the selected class instance as an object of the parent class type, an application object does not have to be aware of the existence of the classes in the hierarchy.

One of the simplest ways of designing a factory method is to create an abstract class or an interface that *just declares* the factory method. Different subclasses (or implementer classes in the case of an interface) can be designed to implement the factory method in its entirety as depicted in Figure 10.2. Another strategy is to create a concrete creator class with default implementation for the factory method in it. Different subclasses of this concrete class can override the factory method to implement specialized class selection criteria.

EXAMPLE

Let us design the functionality to log messages in an application. In general, logging messages is one of the most commonly performed tasks in software applications. Logging appropriate messages at appropriate stages can be extremely useful for debugging and monitoring applications.

Because the message logging functionality could be needed by many different clients, it would be a good idea to keep the actual message logging functionality inside a common utility class so that client objects do not have to repeat these details.

Let us define a Java interface Logger (Listing 10.1) that declares the interface to be used by the client objects to log messages.

In general, an incoming message could be logged to different output media, in different formats. Different concrete implementer classes of the Logger interface can handle these differences in implementation. Let us define two such implementers as in Table 10.1. The resulting class hierarchy is depicted in Figure 10.3.

Each of the Logger implementer classes (Listing 10.2) offers the respective functionality stated in Table 10.1 inside the log method declared by the Logger interface.

Consider an application object LoggerTest that intends to use the services provided by the Logger implementers. Suppose that the overall application message logging configuration can be specified using the logger.properties property file.

Listing 10.1 Logger Interface

```
public interface Logger {
  public void log(String msg);
}
```

Table 10.1 Logger Implementers

Implementer	Functionality
FileLogger	Stores incoming messages to a log file
ConsoleLogger	Displays incoming messages on the screen

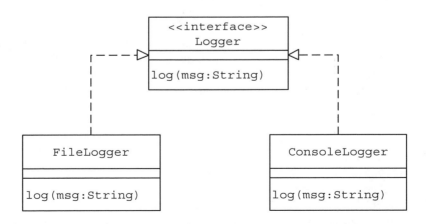

Figure 10.3 Message Logging Utility Class Hierarchy

Listing 10.2   Logger Implementer Classes

```
public class FileLogger implements Logger {
  public void log(String msg) {
    FileUtil futil = new FileUtil();
    futil.writeToFile("log.txt", msg, true, true);
  }
}
public class ConsoleLogger implements Logger {
  public void log(String msg) {
    System.out.println(msg);
  }
}
```

Sample `logger.properties` file contents
```
FileLogging=OFF
```

Depending on the value of the `FileLogging` property, an appropriate Logger implementer needs to be used to log messages. For example, if the `FileLogging` property is set to `ON`, messages are to be logged to a file and hence a `FileLogger` object can be used to log messages. Similarly, if the `FileLogging` property is set to `OFF`, messages are to be displayed on the console and hence a `ConsoleLogger` object can be used.

To log messages, an application object such as the `LoggerTest` needs to:

- Identify an appropriate Logger implementer by reading the `FileLogging` property value from the `logger.properties` file
- Instantiate the Logger implementer and invoke the `log` method by passing the message text to be logged as an argument

This requires every application object to:

- Be aware of the existence and the functionality of all implementers of the Logger interface and their subclasses
- Provide the implementation required to select and instantiate an appropriate Logger implementer

Figure 10.4 depicts this design strategy.

Applying the Factory Method pattern, the necessary implementation for selecting and instantiating an appropriate Logger implementer can be encapsulated inside a separate `getLogger` method in a separate class `LoggerFactory`

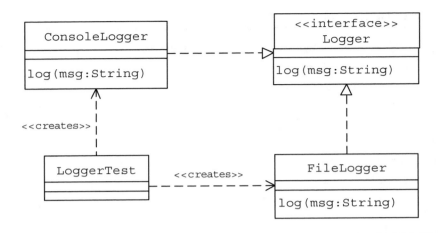

Figure 10.4 Client LoggerTest Accessing Logger Implementers Directly

(Listing 10.3). The LoggerFactory, with the getLogger factory method, plays the role of the ConcreteCreator shown in Figure 10.2.

As part of its implementation, the factory method getLogger checks the logger.properties property file to see if file logging is enabled and decides which Logger implementation is to be instantiated. The selected Logger implementer instance is returned as an object of type Logger.

With the factory method in place, client objects do not need to deal with the intricacies involved in selecting and instantiating an appropriate Logger implementer. Client objects do not need to know the existence of different implementers of the Logger interface and their associated functionality (Figure 10.5).

Whenever a client object such as the LoggerTest (Listing 10.4) needs to log a message, it can:

■ Invoke the factory method getLogger. When the factory method returns, the client object does not have to know the exact Logger subtype that is instantiated as long as the returned object is of the Logger type.
■ Invoke the log method exposed by the Logger interface on the returned object.

Figure 10.6 shows the message flow when the client object LoggerTest uses the LoggerFactory factory method to create an appropriate Logger implementer to log a message.

In this example application design, the creator class LoggerFactory is designed as a concrete class with default implementation for the factory method getLogger. There can be variations in the way in which the class selection criterion is implemented. Such variations can be implemented by overriding the getLogger method in LoggerFactory subclasses.

Listing 10.3 LoggerFactory Class

```java
public class LoggerFactory {
  public boolean isFileLoggingEnabled() {
    Properties p = new Properties();
    try {
      p.load(ClassLoader.getSystemResourceAsStream(
        "Logger.properties"));
      String fileLoggingValue =
        p.getProperty("FileLogging");
      if (fileLoggingValue.equalsIgnoreCase("ON") == true)
        return true;
      else
        return false;
    } catch (IOException e) {
      return false;
    }
  }
  //Factory Method
  public Logger getLogger() {
    if (isFileLoggingEnabled()) {
      return new FileLogger();
    } else {
      return new ConsoleLogger();
    }
  }
}
```

PRACTICE QUESTIONS

1. Add a new logger DBLogger that logs messages to a database.
2. Create a subclass of the LoggerFactory class and override the getLogger implementation to implement a different class selection criterion.

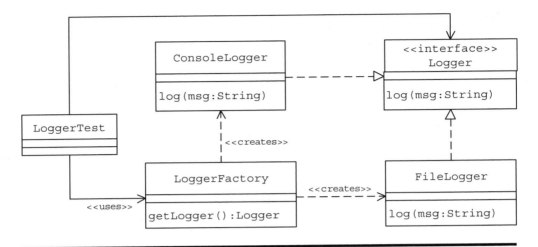

Figure 10.5 The Client LoggerTest Accessing the Logger Class Hierarchy after the Factory Method Pattern Is Applied

Listing 10.4 Client LoggerTest Class

```
public class LoggerTest {
  public static void main(String[] args) {
    LoggerFactory factory = new LoggerFactory();
    Logger logger = factory.getLogger();
    logger.log("A Message to Log");
  }
}
```

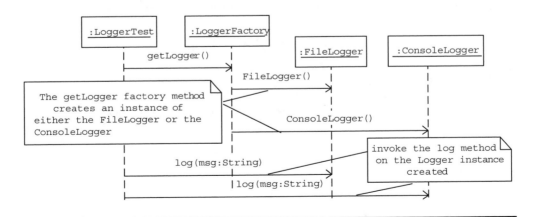

Figure 10.6 Message Flow When a Client Uses the LoggerFactory to Create an Appropriate Logger to Log a Message

11

SINGLETON

This pattern was previously described in GoF95.

DESCRIPTION

The Singleton pattern is an easy to understand design pattern. Sometimes, there may be a need to have one and only one instance of a given class during the lifetime of an application. This may be due to necessity or, more often, due to the fact that only a single instance of the class is sufficient. For example, we may need a single database connection object in an application. The Singleton pattern is useful in such cases because it ensures that there exists one and only one instance of a particular object ever. Further, it suggests that client objects should be able to access the single instance in a consistent manner.

WHO SHOULD BE RESPONSIBLE?

Having an instance of the class in a global variable seems like an easy way to maintain the single instance. All client objects can access this instance in a consistent manner through this global variable. But this does not prevent clients from creating other instances of the class. For this approach to be successful, all of the client objects have to be responsible for controlling the number of instances of the class. This widely distributed responsibility is not desirable because a client should be free from any class creation process details. The responsibility for making sure that there is only one instance of the class should belong to the class itself, leaving client objects free from having to handle these details.

A class that maintains its single instance nature by itself is referred to as a *Singleton* class.

EXAMPLE

Let us continue to work on the message logging utility example we have designed during the Factory Method pattern discussion in the previous chapter. One of the implementers of the **Logger** interface, the **FileLogger** class, logs incoming messages to the file **log.txt**. Having a singleton is helpful when there is only one physical instance of what the object represents. This is true in case of the

`FileLogger` because there is only one physical log file. In an application, when different client objects try to log messages to the file, there could potentially be multiple instances of the `FileLogger` class in use by each of the client objects. This could lead to different issues due to the concurrent access to the same file by different objects.

One of the solutions is to maintain an instance of the `FileLogger` class in a global variable within the application. This instance can be accessed in a consistent manner by all clients providing them with a single, global point of access to it. However this does not solve the problem fully.

■ It does not prevent clients from creating new instances of the `FileLogger` class.
■ It does not prevent multiple threads within the same client from executing the `log` method.

Another solution is to apply the monitor concept and declare the `log(String)` method as synchronized.

The monitor concept, discussed under Basic Patterns, ensures that no two threads are allowed to access the same object at the same time.

This does prevent multiple threads from entering the same method for execution, but does not prevent the client objects from creating multiple instances of the `FileLogger` class.

In addition to declaring the `log` method as synchronized, what is needed is a way to ensure that there exists one and only one instance of the `FileLogger` class during the lifetime of an application. This needs to be done in such a way that the client objects do not have to monitor the creation process or keep track of the number of `FileLogger` instances that exist.

To accomplish this using the Singleton pattern, the following changes can be made to the `FileLogger` class to make it a singleton class (Figure 11.1 and Listing 11.1).

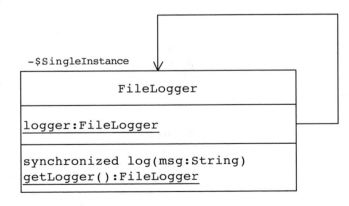

Figure 11.1 `FileLogger` Class as a Singleton

Listing 11.1 Singleton `FileLogger` Class

```
public class FileLogger implements Logger {
  private static FileLogger logger;
  //Prevent clients from using the constructor
  private FileLogger() {
  }
  public static FileLogger getFileLogger() {
    if (logger == null) {
      logger = new FileLogger();
    }
    return logger;
  }
  public synchronized void log(String msg) {
    FileUtil futil = new FileUtil();
    futil.writeToFile("log.txt",msg, true, true);
  }
}
```

Make the Constructor Private

Making the constructor private prevents client objects from creating `FileLogger` objects by invoking its constructor. At the same time, other methods inside `FileLogger` will have access to the private constructor.

Static Public Interface to Access an Instance

Provide a public interface, in the form of a static method `getInstance`, for clients to be able to get access to an instance of the `FileLogger` class. This public method must be static for a client to be able to access this method without having to instantiate the class.

Inside the `getInstance` method, create and return an instance of the `FileLogger` class by accessing its private constructor. This is done *only during the first invocation* of the `getInstance` method. Every subsequent call to the `getInstance` method returns the *same* `FileLogger` instance that is created during the first invocation. A new instance of the class is *not* created again.

A design like this ensures that there exists only one instance of the `FileLogger` class and that no two threads are allowed to execute the `log` method at the same time. This solves the problems the earlier design approach has posed.

In the case of clients expecting to use the singleton `FileLogger` object (the `LoggerTest` in this case), nothing really changes in the way they interact with the singleton `FileLogger` object.

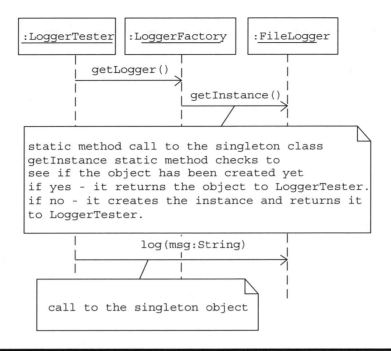

Figure 11.2   Message Flow When a Client Accesses the Singleton `FileLogger` and Invokes Its Method to Log a Message

```
//client code
public class LoggerTest{
  public static void main(String[] args){
    LoggerFactory factory=new LoggerFactory();
    //factory method call
    Logger logger=factory.getLogger();
    logger.log("A Message to Log");
  }
}
```

Figure 11.2 shows the message flow when the client **LoggerTest** accesses the singleton **FileLogger**.

The only change is for those client objects that attempt to create an instance of the **FileLogger** class (the **LoggerFactory** in this case). Instead of invoking the constructor method, they will have to use the public method **getInstance** to get an instance of the **FileLogger** class as in Listing 11.2.

Listing 11.2 LoggerFactory Class: Revised

```
public class LoggerFactory {
  public boolean isFileLoggingEnabled() {
    Properties p = new Properties();
    try {
      p.load(ClassLoader.getSystemResourceAsStream(
        "Logger.properties"));
      String fileLoggingValue =
        p.getProperty("FileLogging");
      if (fileLoggingValue.equalsIgnoreCase("ON") == true)
        return true;
      else
        return false;
    } catch (IOException e) {
      return false;
    }
  }
  public Logger getLogger() {
    if (isFileLoggingEnabled()) {
      return FileLogger.getFileLogger();
    } else {
      return new ConsoleLogger();
    }
  }
}
```

PRACTICE QUESTIONS

1. Besides the approach adopted in the example above, there can be different ways to ensure the singleton nature of an object. Think of other ways of accomplishing it.
2. Design and implement a database connection class as singleton.

12

ABSTRACT FACTORY

This pattern was previously described in GoF95.

DESCRIPTION

During the discussion of the Factory Method pattern we saw that:

- In the context of a factory method, there exists a class hierarchy composed of a set of subclasses with a common parent class.
- A factory method is used when a client object knows when to create an instance of the parent class type, but does not know (or should not know) exactly which class from among the set of subclasses (and possibly the parent class) should be instantiated. Besides the class selection criteria, a factory method also hides any special mechanism required to instantiate the selected class.

The Abstract Factory pattern takes the same concept to the next level. In simple terms, an *abstract factory* is a class that provides an interface to produce a family of objects. In the Java programming language, it can be implemented either as an interface or as an abstract class.

In the context of an abstract factory there exist:

- Suites or families of related, dependent classes.
- A group of concrete factory classes that implements the interface provided by the abstract factory class. Each of these factories controls or provides access to a particular suite of related, dependent objects and implements the abstract factory interface in a manner that is specific to the family of classes it controls.

The Abstract Factory pattern is useful when a client object wants to create an instance of one of a suite of related, dependent classes without having to know which specific concrete class is to be instantiated. In the absence of an abstract factory, the required implementation to select an appropriate class (in other words, the class selection criterion) needs to be present everywhere such an instance is created. An abstract factory helps avoid this duplication by providing the necessary

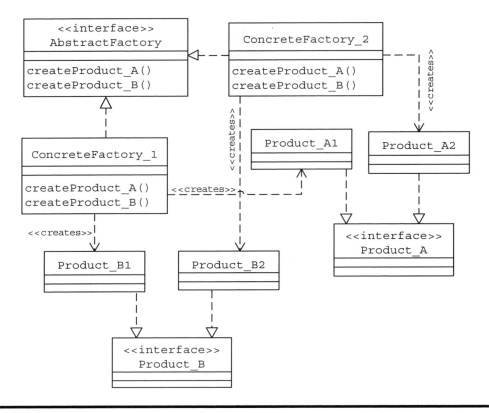

Figure 12.1 Generic Class Associations While Applying the Abstract Factory Pattern

interface for creating such instances. Different concrete factories implement this interface. Client objects make use of these concrete factories to create objects and, therefore, do not need to know which concrete class is actually instantiated. Figure 12.1 shows the generic class association when the Abstract Factory pattern is applied.

The abstract factory shown in the Figure 12.1 class diagram is designed as a Java interface with its implementers as concrete factories. In Java, an abstract factory can also be designed as an abstract class with its concrete subclasses as factories, where each factory is responsible for creating and providing access to the objects of a particular suite of classes.

ABSTRACT FACTORY VERSUS FACTORY METHOD

Abstract Factory is used to create groups of related objects while hiding the actual concrete classes. This is useful for plugging in a different group of objects to alter the behavior of the system. For each group or family, a concrete factory is implemented that manages the creation of the objects and the interdependencies and consistency requirements between them. Each concrete factory implements the interface of the abstract factory.

This situation often arises when designing a framework or a library, which needs to be kept extensible. One example is the JDBC (Java Database Connectivity) driver system, where each driver contains classes that implement the `Connection`, the `Statement` and the `ResultSet` interfaces. The set of classes that the Oracle JDBC driver contains are different from the set of classes that the DB2 JDBC driver contains and they must not be mixed up. This is where the role of the factory comes in: It knows which classes belong together and how to create objects in a consistent way.

Factory Method is specifying a method for the creation of an object, thus allowing subclasses or implementing classes to define the concrete object. Abstract Factories are usually implemented using the Factory Method pattern. Another approach would be to use the Prototype pattern.

EXAMPLE I

Let us design an application to query the features of different types of vehicles. For simplicity, let us consider two types of vehicles: cars and SUVs. Further, a vehicle can be of either luxury or nonluxury category.

Let us define a common `Car` interface (Figure 12.2, Listing 12.1) that declares the interface to be implemented by different classes that represent different types of cars.

Let us design two classes (Listing 12.2) that implement the `Car` interface — `LuxuryCar` and `NonLuxuryCar` — representing luxury cars and nonluxury cars, respectively. Figure 12.2 shows the resulting class hierarchy.

A similar class hierarchy can be designed to represent SUVs (Figure 12.3, Listing 12.3). In Figure 12.3, the `SUV` interface declares the common interface to be offered by different classes that represent SUVs and its implementers — `LuxurySUV` and `NonLuxurySUV` — (Listing 12.4) represent luxury and nonluxury SUVs, respectively.

For simplicity, both the `Car` and the `SUV` class hierarchies are designed to offer only two basic operations to retrieve the details of a car or SUV. Together these class hierarchies contain two families of classes as listed in Table 12.1.

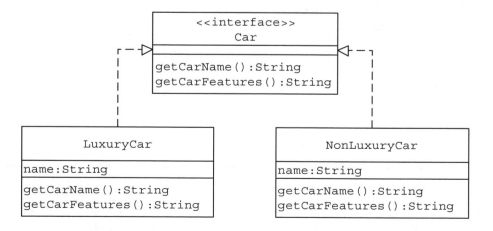

Figure 12.2 The Car Class Hierarchy

Listing 12.1 The Common Car Interface

```java
public interface Car {
  public String getCarName();
  public String getCarFeatures();
}//End of class
```

Listing 12.2 Classes Representing Luxury and NonLuxury Cars

```java
public class LuxuryCar implements Car {
  private String name;
  public LuxuryCar(String cName) {
    name = cName;
  }
  public String getCarName() {
    return name;
  }
  public String getCarFeatures() {
    return "Luxury Car Features ";
  };
}//End of class
public class NonLuxuryCar implements Car {
  private String name;
  public NonLuxuryCar(String cName) {
    name = cName;
  }
  public String getCarName() {
    return name;
  }
  public String getCarFeatures() {
    return "Non-Luxury Car Features ";
  };
}//End of class
```

An application object can make use of the services of different Car/SUV implementers (Table 12.1) to query the features of a car or SUV. If such an application object is to directly deal with different concrete Car/SUV classes, it needs to be aware of the existence of different concrete Car/SUV implementers. In addition, this approach results in the required implementation to select and instantiate an appropriate Car/SUV class to be present everywhere an application

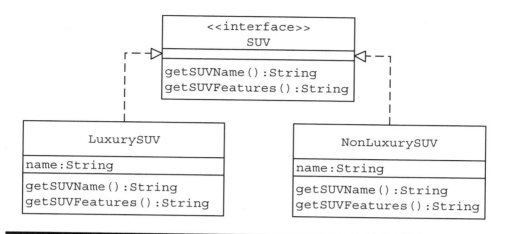

Figure 12.3   The SUV Class Hierarchy

Listing 12.3   The Common SUV Interface

```
public interface SUV {
  public String getSUVName();
  public String getSUVFeatures();
}//End of class
```

object needs to query the features of a car or SUV. Using the Abstract Factory pattern in such cases, the responsibility of selecting and instantiating an appropriate Car/SUV implementer can be moved out of application objects to a separate designated abstract factory class. The abstract factory class may simply declare the required interface, leaving the actual implementation details of class selection and instantiation to its implementers. This type of design eliminates the need for an application object to be aware of the existence of different concrete Car/SUV classes.

Applying the Abstract Factory pattern in this case, let us define an interface in the form of an abstract class VehicleFactory (Figure 12.4, Listing 12.5).

The VehicleFactory class acts as an abstract factory. A client object can use an instance of a concrete factory that implements the VehicleFactory interface to create objects representing vehicles of different types and categories without having to know the actual concrete class that needs to be instantiated. As we proceed with the design, we will create a utility method that can be used by different client objects to obtain an appropriate concrete factory (which implements the abstract factory interface).

As part of applying the Abstract Factory pattern, let us define two concrete factory classes — LuxuryVehicleFactory and NonLuxuryVehicleFactory — as concrete subclasses (Listing 12.6) of the VehicleFactory with responsibilities as detailed in Table 12.2. The class diagram in Figure 12.5 shows the resulting class hierarchy.

Listing 12.4   Classes Representing Luxury and NonLuxury SUVs

```java
public class LuxurySUV implements SUV {
  private String name;
  public LuxurySUV(String sName) {
    name = sName;
  }
  public String getSUVName() {
    return name;
  }
  public String getSUVFeatures() {
    return "Luxury SUV Features ";
  };
}//End of class
public class NonLuxurySUV implements SUV {
  private String name;
  public NonLuxurySUV(String sName) {
    name = sName;
  }
  public String getSUVName() {
    return name;
  }
  public String getSUVFeatures() {
    return "Non-Luxury SUV Features ";
  };
}//End of class
```

Table 12.1   Families of Vehicle Classes

Family	Member Classes
Luxury	LuxuryCar, LuxurySUV
Nonluxury	NonLuxuryCar, NonLuxurySUV

Now, it also needs to be ensured that client objects do not have to know about the existence of these concrete factory classes. A client object should be provided with an appropriate factory object as needed.

To facilitate this, let us add a static method getVehicleFactory(String type) to the VehicleFactory abstract class (Figure 12.6). This new method can be implemented to return an appropriate concrete vehicle factory object

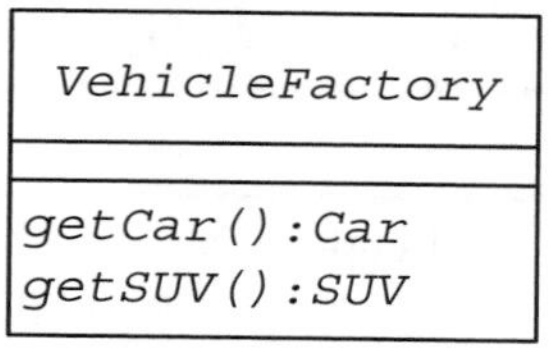

```
┌─────────────────────────┐
│   VehicleFactory        │
├─────────────────────────┤
│                         │
├─────────────────────────┤
│ getCar():Car            │
│ getSUV():SUV            │
└─────────────────────────┘
```

Figure 12.4   The Abstract Factory Class

Listing 12.5   Abstract VehicleFactory Class

```java
public abstract class VehicleFactory {
  public static final String LUXURY_VEHICLE = "Luxury";
  public static final String NON_LUXURY_VEHICLE = "Non-Luxury";
  public abstract Car getCar();
  public abstract SUV getSUV();
        ...
        ...
}//End of class
```

Listing 12.6   Concrete Factory Subclasses of the Abstract VehicleFactory Class

```java
public class LuxuryVehicleFactory extends VehicleFactory {
  public Car getCar() {
    return new LuxuryCar("L-C");
  }
  public SUV getSUV() {
    return new LuxurySUV("L-S");
  }
}//End of class
public class NonLuxuryVehicleFactory extends VehicleFactory {
  public Car getCar() {
    return new NonLuxuryCar("NL-C");
  }
  public SUV getSUV() {
    return new NonLuxurySUV("NL-S");
  }
}//End of class
```

Table 12.2   Different Concrete Vehicle Factories

Concrete Factory	Responsibility
LuxuryVehicleFactory	Responsible for creating instances of classes representing luxury vehicles
NonLuxuryVehicleFactory	Responsible for creating instances of classes representing nonluxury vehicles

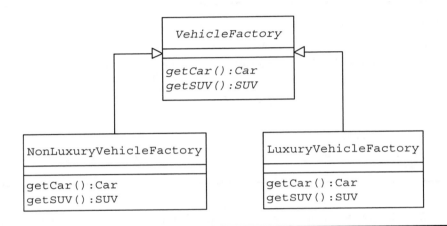

Figure 12.5   Abstract VehicleFactory Class Hierarchy

```
                    VehicleFactory
                    
                    getCar():Car
                    getSUV():SUV
```

```
     VehicleFactory

     getCar():Car
     getSUV():SUV
     getVehicleFactory(type:String):VehicleFactory
```

Figure 12.6   Revised Abstract Factory Class

(LuxuryVehicleFactory or NonLuxuryVehicleFactory in this case) to a calling client object (Listing 12.7).

The getVehicleFactory(String type) method does not need to be within the abstract factory as we designed in this example application. It can be in a different class altogether. In such a case, the abstract factory can be implemented as a Java interface instead of its current design as an abstract class.

Listing 12.7   Abstract `VehicleFactory` Class: Revised

```
public abstract class VehicleFactory {

    ...

    ...

  public static VehicleFactory getVehicleFactory(String type) {
    if (type.equals(VehicleFactory.LUXURY_VEHICLE))
      return new LuxuryVehicleFactory();
    if (type.equals(VehicleFactory.NON_LUXURY_VEHICLE))
      return new NonLuxuryVehicleFactory();
    return new LuxuryVehicleFactory();
  }
}//End of class
```

Let us see how a typical client object can make use of the class structure we have put together so far in this example.

The example client object `AutoSearchUI` (Listing 12.8) displays the necessary user interface as in Figure 12.7 for querying different vehicle features.

When the `Search` button is clicked after a vehicle category and type combination is selected:

1. The client `AutoSearchUI` invokes the static `getVehicleFactory(String type)` method on the abstract `VehicleFactory` class.
2. The `getVehicleFactory` method creates an appropriate factory object and returns it as an object of `VehicleFactory` type.
3. The client `AutoSearchUI` does not need to know the existence of any concrete vehicle factory class. It simply invokes the required abstract vehicle factory method such as `getCar` or `getSUV` on the returned factory instance.
4. The factory object internally creates an instance of an appropriate class from among the family of classes it controls (LuxuryCar/LuxurySUV or NonLuxuryCar/NonLuxurySUV) and returns it as an object of `Car/SUV` type.
5. The client `AutoSearchUI` does not need to be aware of the existence of different concrete `Car/SUV` classes. It simply invokes methods declared by the `Car/SUV` interface such as `getName` or `getFeatures` on the object returned in Step 4 above.

The sequence diagram in Figure 12.8 depicts the message exchange between objects when the client `AutoSearchUI` uses `VehicleFactory` (i.e., the abstract factory) to retrieve luxury car details.

Listing 12.8   Client `AutoSearchUI` Class

```java
public class AutoSearchUI extends JFrame {
        ...

        ...

  public void actionPerformed(ActionEvent e) {
    String searchResult = null;
     if (e.getActionCommand().equals(AutoSearchUI.EXIT)) {
       System.exit(1);
    }
    if (e.getActionCommand().equals(AutoSearchUI.SEARCH)) {
      //get input values
      String vhCategory =
        objAutoSearchUI.getSelectedCategory();
      String vhType = objAutoSearchUI.getSelectedType();
      //get one of Luxury or NonLuxury vehicle factories
      VehicleFactory vf =
        VehicleFactory.getVehicleFactory(vhCategory);
      if (vhType.equals(AutoSearchUI.CAR)) {
        Car c = vf.getCar();
        searchResult =
          "Name: " + c.getCarName() + " Features: " +
          c.getCarFeatures();
      }
      if (vhType.equals(AutoSearchUI.SUV)) {
        SUV s = vf.getSUV();
        searchResult =
          "Name: " + s.getSUVName() + " Features: " +
          s.getSUVFeatures();
      }
      objAutoSearchUI.setResult(searchResult);
    }
  }
        ...
        ...
}
```

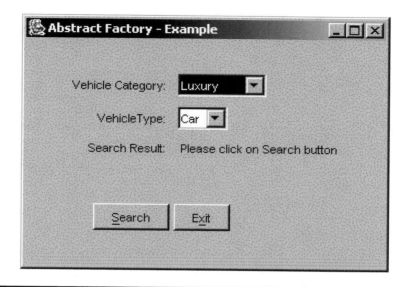

Figure 12.7   Vehicle Query User Interface

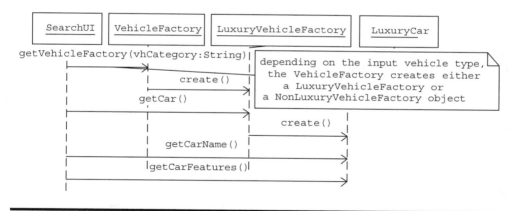

Figure 12.8   Luxury Car Details Query: Message Flow

EXAMPLE II

Let us design a simple customer data management application with the following features:

- The basic functionality is to validate and save the input customer data consisting of account, address and credit card data.
- The application should be functional in both local and remote modes.
- In the remote mode, the application should make use of remote objects using Java Remote Method Invocation (RMI) and save the data to a central server.

Account
firstName:String lastName:String
isValid():boolean save():boolean getFirstName():String getLastName():String

Address
address:String city:String state:String
isValid():boolean save():boolean getAddress():String getState():String

CreditCard
cardType:String cardNumber:String cardExpDate:String
isValid():String save():String getCardType():String getCardNumber():String getCardExpDate():String

Figure 12.9   Classes Representing the Customer Data

- When the remote server is not available, users should be able to operate the application locally without interruption.
- The process of synchronizing both the local and the central databases is not considered as part of this example application.

Let us design three classes — Account, Address and CreditCard — as in Figure 12.9 representing the three different parts of the customer data.

Each of the customer data classes in Figure 12.9 offers methods to accept, validate and save appropriate parts of the customer data. Instances of these classes can be used by the application while operating in the local mode. As stated earlier, the application must function in remote mode as well and should make use of remote objects using RMI. The set of customer data classes in Figure 12.9 cannot be readily used as remote objects. This is because for a class instance to be accessible via RMI as a remote object, the class must:

- Extend the built-in java.rmi.server.UnicastRemoteObject class
- Implement the built-in java.rmi.Remote interface or any interface that is derived from the java.rmi.Remote interface
- Declare all of its methods to throw the built-in java.rmi.RemoteException exception

Hence, for the application to be functional in the remote mode, a second set of customer data classes is needed, whose instances can be accessed using RMI. In

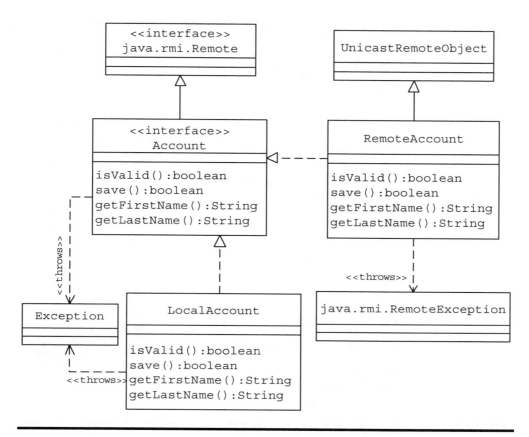

Figure 12.10 Account Class Hierarchy

addition, both the local and the remote objects must offer the same interface to enable the application to use both local and remote objects in a seamless manner.

The common interface for both the local and the remote class representations of the account data can be designed in the form of a Java interface Account (Figure 12.10) with the following features:

- Derived from the built-in java.rmi.Remote interface to enable its implementers to be used as remote objects accessible via RMI.
- Declares all of its methods to throw the java.lang.Exception exception. This allows an implementer class to throw any subclass of the java.lang.Exception class as part of implementing the interface methods.

As seen earlier, a remote class must declare all of its methods to throw the java.rmi.RemoteException. Because the java.rmi.RemoteException is a subclass of the java.lang.Exception class, the remote class representation of the account data can safely declare its methods to throw the java.rmi.Remote-Exception at the time of implementing the common Account interface methods. Because there are no special requirements for the local class representation of the customer account data, the local class can be designed to implement the same

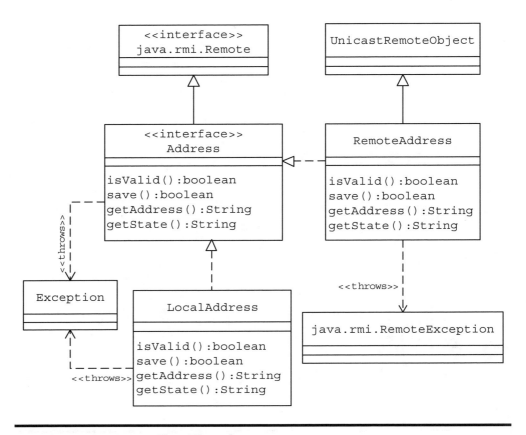

Figure 12.11 Address Class Hierarchy

Account interface as the remote class. As a result, both LocalAccount and RemoteAccount classes, which are the local and remote class representations of the account data, share the same common Account interface. Figure 12.10 shows the Account class hierarchy and its relationship with exception and RMI-specific classes.

In a similar manner, the class representations for both the address and the credit card parts of the customer data can be designed as in Figures 12.11 and 12.12, respectively.

Let us design an interface in the form of the CustomerFactory Java interface, which declares the methods to create instances of local or remote family of customer data classes (Account, Address and CreditCard). Let us further design two concrete implementers of the CustomerFactory interface as detailed in Table 12.3.

In this design, the CustomerFactory interface acts as an abstract factory and each of its concrete implementers act as factories. Figure 12.13 depicts the resulting factory class hierarchy.

To eliminate the need for a client object to deal with the factory objects directly, let us design a utility class CustomerUtil with a static method getCustFactory(String mode) that takes the current mode of operation as input and returns an appropriate CustomerFactory implementer object to the calling client object.

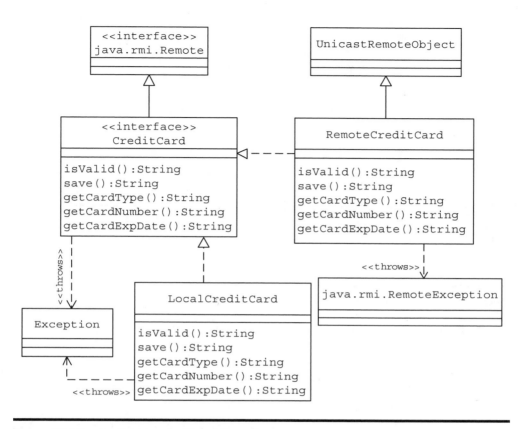

Figure 12.12 `CreditCard` **Class Hierarchy**

Table 12.3 Concrete Customer Factory Classes

Implementer Class	Responsibility
`LocalCustomerFactory`	Responsible for creating instances of classes representing the customer data in the local mode: `LocalAccount`, `LocalAddress` and `LocalCreditCard`
`RemoteCustomerFactory`	Responsible for creating instances of classes representing the customer data in the remote mode: `RemoteAccount`, `RemoteAddress` and `RemoteCreditCard`

Logical Flow When the Application Is Run

■ The client object that needs to access the services of the customer data objects to validate and save the customer data is assumed to be aware of the current mode of operation (i.e., local or remote).

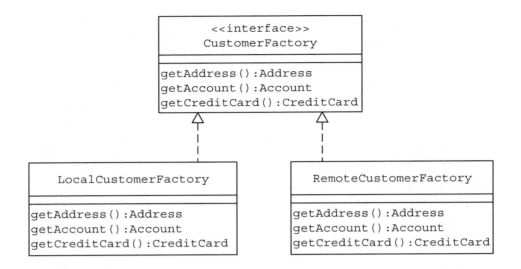

Figure 12.13 `CustomerFactory` **Class Hierarchy**

- By passing the application mode as the parameter, the client object can invoke the `getCustFactory(String)` static method of the `CustomerUtil` class.
- Inside the `getCustFactory(String)` method, the `CustomerUtil` creates an appropriate customer factory object and returns it to the client as an object of the `CustomerFactory` type.
- The client object can create the required customer data class (`Account`, `Address` or `CreditCard`) by invoking the `CustomerFactory` methods on the returned factory instance.
- Once an appropriate customer data object is created, the class object can use it to validate and save data.

PRACTICE QUESTIONS

1. Implement the example-II customer data management application.
2. Draw sequence diagrams to depict the message flow when the application is run.
3. Consider a Web hosting company that offers hosting services on both Windows and UNIX platforms. Suppose that the Web hosting company offers three different types of hosting packages — Basic, Premium and Premium Plus — on both platforms. Design an application using the Abstract Factory pattern to query the features of different types of hosting packages offered by the Web hosting company.

13

PROTOTYPE

This pattern was previously described in GoF95.

DESCRIPTION

As discussed in earlier chapters, both the Factory Method and the Abstract Factory patterns allow a system to be independent of the object creation process. In other words, these patterns enable a client object to create an instance of an appropriate class by invoking a designated method without having to specify the exact concrete class to be instantiated. While addressing the same problem as the Factory Method and Abstract Factory patterns, the Prototype pattern offers a different, more flexible way of achieveing the same result.

Other uses of the Prototype pattern include:

- When a client needs to create a set of objects that are alike or differ from each other only in terms of their state and it is expensive to create such objects in terms of the time and the processing involved.
- As an alternative to building numerous factories that mirror the classes to be instantiated (as in the Factory Method).

In such cases, the Prototype pattern suggests to:

- Create one object upfront and designate it as a prototype object.
- Create other objects by simply making a copy of the prototype object and making required modifications.

In the real world, we use the Prototype pattern on many occasions to reduce the time and effort spent on different tasks. The following are two such examples:

1. *New Software Program Creation* — Typically programmers tend to make a copy of an existing program with similar structure and modify it to create new programs.
2. *Cover Letters* — When applying for positions at different organizations, an applicant may not create cover letters for each organization individually from scratch. Instead, the applicant would create one cover letter in the

most appealing format, make a copy of it and personalize it for every organization.

As can be seen from the examples above, some of the objects are created from scratch, whereas other objects are created as copies of existing objects and then modified. But the system or the process that uses these objects does not differentiate between them on the basis of how they are actually created. In a similar manner, when using the Prototype pattern, a system should be independent of the creation, composition and representation details of the objects it uses.

One of the requirements of the prototype object is that it should provide a way for clients to create a copy of it. By default, all Java objects inherit the built-in `clone()` method from the topmost `java.lang.Object` class. The built-in `clone()` method creates a clone of the original object as a shallow copy.

SHALLOW COPY VERSUS DEEP COPY

When an object is cloned as a shallow copy:

- The original top-level object and all of its primitive members are duplicated.
- Any lower-level objects that the top-level object contains are not duplicated. Only references to these objects are copied. This results in both the orginal and the cloned object referring to the same copy of the lower-level object. Figure 13.1 shows this behavior.

In contrast, when an object is cloned as a deep copy:

- The original top-level object and all of its primitive members are duplicated.
- Any lower-level objects that the top-level object contains are also duplicated. In this case, both the orginal and the cloned object refer to two different lower-level objects. Figure 13.2 shows this behavior.

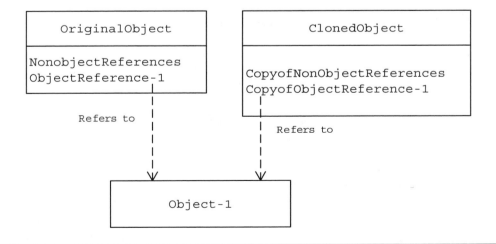

Figure 13.1   Shallow Copy

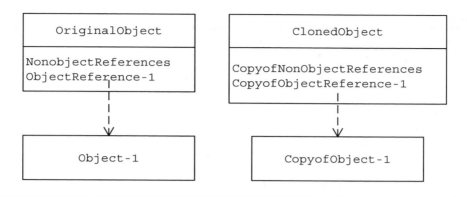

Figure 13.2   Deep Copy

Shallow Copy Example

The following is an example of creating a shallow copy using the built-in `java.lang.Object clone()` method. Let us design a `Person` class (Listing 13.1) as an implementer of the built-in Java `java.lang.Cloneable` interface with two attributes, a string variable name and a `Car` object `car`.

In general, a class must implement the `Cloneable` interface to indicate that a field-for-field copy of instances of that class is allowed by the `Object.clone()` method. When a class implements the `Cloneable` interface, it should override the `Object.clone` method with a public method. Note that when the `clone` method is invoked on an object that does not implement the `Cloneable` interface, the exception `CloneNotSupportedException` is thrown.

As part of its implementation of the public `clone` method, the `Person` class simply invokes the built-in `clone` method. The built-in `clone` method creates a clone of the current object as a shallow copy, which is returned to the calling client object.

Let us design a client `ShallowCopyTest` (Listing 13.2) to demonstrate the behavior of a shallow copy object. To demonstrate the fact that the shallow copy process duplicates nonobject references only but not object references, the client:

- Creates an instance of the `Person` class
- Creates a clone of the `Person` object created above and alters the values of its attributes
- Displays the values of its attributes at different stages

When the `Car` object associated with the cloned object is modified, it can be seen that the `Car` object associated with the original object gets affected. This is because the lower-level `Car` object is not duplicated and is shared by both the original and the cloned `Person` objects, whereas the name attribute value of the orginal object does not get affected when the cloned object's name attribute value is altered. This is because the shallow copy process duplicates attributes that are of primitive types.

Listing 13.1 Person Class

```java
class Person implements Cloneable {
  //Lower-level object
  private Car car;

  private String name;
  public Car getCar() {
    return car;
  }
  public String getName() {
    return name;
  }
  public void setName(String s) {
    name = s;
  }
  public Person(String s, String t) {
    name = s;
    car = new Car(t);
  }
  public Object clone() {
    //shallow copy
    try {
      return super.clone();
    } catch (CloneNotSupportedException e) {
      return null;
    }
  }
}
class Car {

  private String name;

  public String getName() {
    return name;
  }
  public void setName(String s) {
    name = s;
  }
  public Car(String s) {
    name = s;
  }
```

Listing 13.2   Client `ShallowCopyTest` Class

```
public class ShallowCopyTest {
  public static void main(String[] args) {
    //Original Object
    Person p = new Person("Person-A,""Civic");
    System.out.println("Original (orginal values): " +
                    p.getName() + " - " +
                    p.getCar().getName());
    //Clone as a shallow copy
    Person q = (Person) p.clone();
    System.out.println("Clone (before change): " +
                    q.getName() + " - " +
                    q.getCar().getName());
    //change the primitive member
    q.setName("Person-B");
    //change the lower-level object
    q.getCar().setName("Accord");
    System.out.println("Clone (after change): " +
                    q.getName() + " - " +
                    q.getCar().getName());
    System.out.println(
      "Original (after clone is modified): " +
      p.getName() + " - " + p.getCar().getName());
  }
}
```

When this program is run, the following output is displayed:

```
Original (orginal values): Person-A - Civic
Clone (before change): Person-A - Civic
Clone (after change): Person-B - Accord
Original (after clone is modified): Person-A - Accord
```

Deep Copy Example

The same example above can be redesigned by overriding the built-in `clone()` method to create a deep copy of the `Person` object (Listing 13.3). As part of its implementation of the `clone` method, to create a deep copy, the `Person` class creates a new `Person` object with its attribute values the same as the original object and returns it to the client object.

Listing 13.3 `Person` Class Revised

```java
class Person implements Cloneable {
  //Lower-level object
  private Car car;
  private String name;
  public Car getCar() {
    return car;
  }
  public String getName() {
    return name;
  }
  public void setName(String s) {
    name = s;
  }
  public Person(String s, String t) {
    name = s;
    car = new Car(t);
  }
  public Object clone() {
    //Deep copy
    Person p = new Person(name, car.getName());
    return p;
  }
}
class Car {
  private String name;
  public String getName() {
    return name;
  }
  public void setName(String s) {
    name = s;
  }
  public Car(String s) {
    name = s;
  }
}
```

Listing 13.4 Client `DeepCopyTest` Class

```java
public class DeepCopyTest {
  public static void main(String[] args) {
    //Original Object
    Person p = new Person("Person-A","Civic");
    System.out.println("Original (orginal values): " +
                      p.getName() + " - " +
                      p.getCar().getName());
    //Clone as a shallow copy
    Person q = (Person) p.clone();
    System.out.println("Clone (before change): " +
                      q.getName() + " - " +
                      q.getCar().getName());
    //change the primitive member
    q.setName("Person-B");
    //change the lower-level object
    q.getCar().setName("Accord");
    System.out.println("Clone (after change): " +
                      q.getName() + " - " +
                      q.getCar().getName());
    System.out.println(
      "Original (after clone is modified): " +
      p.getName() + " - " + p.getCar().getName());
  }
}
```

Similar to the client `ShallowCopyTest`, a new client `DeepCopyTest` (Listing 13.4) can be designed to:

- Create an instance of the `Person` class
- Create a clone of the `Person` object created above and alter the values of its attributes
- Display the values of its attributes at different stages

When the `Car` object associated with the cloned object is modified, it can be seen that the `Car` object associated with the original object *does not* get affected. This is because the lower-level `Car` object is duplicated and is not shared by both the original and the cloned `Person` objects.

Similar to a shallow copy, the name attribute value of the orginal object does not get affected when the cloned object's name attribute value is altered. This is because in addition to attributes that are object references, the deep copy process duplicates those attributes that are of primitive types.

When the client DeepCopyTest is run, it displays the following output. From the output it can be seen that the lower-level Car object of the original Person object is unaffected when its clone is modified.

```
Original (orginal values): Person-A - Civic
Clone (before change): Person-A - Civic
Clone (after change): Person-B - Accord
Original (after clone is modified): Person-A - Civic
```

EXAMPLE I

Let us consider Practice Question 3 from Chapter 12 — Abstract Factory. The representation of different hosting packages would have resulted in a class hierarchy as shown in Figure 13.3.

Applying the Abstract Factory pattern, the application design would have resulted in a factory class hierarchy as shown in Figure 13.4.

In Figure 13.4, the HostingPlanFactory plays the role of an abstract factory whereas WinPlanFactory and UnixPlanFactory act as concrete factories. Each of these concrete factories would be responsible for the creation of a family of related classes that represent hosting packages on a specific platform as follows:

■ WinPlanFactory would be responsible for the creation of WinBasic, WinPremium and WinPremiumPlus objects.

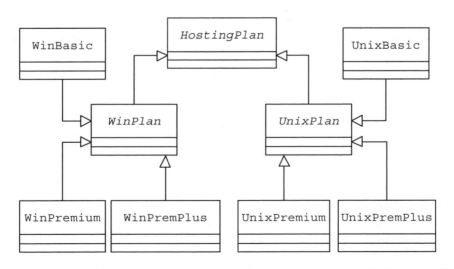

Figure 13.3   Hosting Packages Class Hierarchy

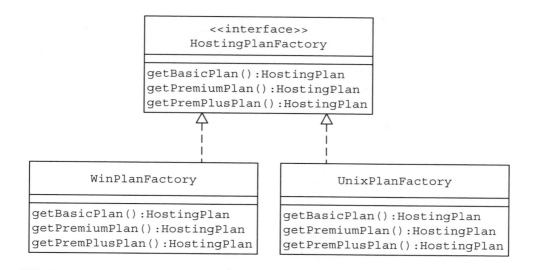

Figure 13.4   Hosting Packages Factory Class Hierarchy

- UnixPlanFactory would be responsible for the creation of UnixBasic, UnixPremium and UnixPremiumPlus objects.

Client objects can make use of an appropriate concrete factory class instance to create required HostingPlan objects.

Let us design the same application using the Prototype pattern. Applying the Prototype pattern, the HostingPlanFactory class hierarchy in Figure 13.4 can be replaced with a single concrete class HostingPlanKit (Figure 13.5 and Listing 13.5).

Design Highlights of the HostingPlanKit Class

- Maintains different prototypical objects that represent different types of hosting packages in its instance variables.

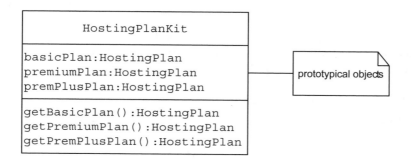

Figure 13.5   Single Class Equivalent of the Abstract Factory Class Hierarchy

Listing 13.5 `HostingPlanKit` Class

```java
public class HostingPlanKit {
  private HostingPlan basicPlan;
  private HostingPlan premiumPlan;
  private HostingPlan premPlusPlan;
  public HostingPlanKit(HostingPlan basic, HostingPlan premium,
      HostingPlan premPlus) {
    basicPlan = basic;
    premiumPlan = premium;
    premPlusPlan = premPlus;
  }
  public HostingPlan getBasicPlan() {
    return (HostingPlan) basicPlan.clone();
  }
  public HostingPlan getPremiumPlan() {
    return (HostingPlan) premiumPlan.clone();
  }
  public HostingPlan getPremPlusPlan() {
    return (HostingPlan) premPlusPlan.clone();
  }
}
```

■ Offers a set of methods that can be used by different client objects to get access to objects representing different hosting plans. As part of its implementation of these methods, it returns copies of the prototypical objects it contains.

For a client object to be able to make use of a `HostingPlanKit` instance, the `HostingPlanKit` instance must be configured with appropriate prototypical objects.

Let us design a separate class `HostingPlanManager` (Figure 13.6) with the responsibility of configuring a `HostingPlanKit` object with appropriate prototypical objects and return it to client objects.

```java
public class HostingPlanManager {
  public static HostingPlanKit getHostingPlanKit(
    String platform) {
    HostingPlan basicPlan = null;
    HostingPlan premiumPlan = null;
    HostingPlan premPlusPlan = null;
    if (platform.equalsIgnoreCase("Win")) {
```

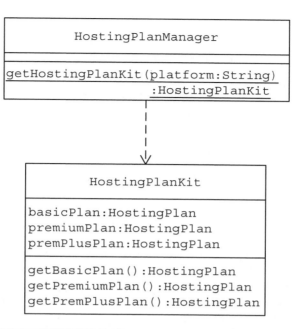

Figure 13.6 `HostingPlanManager` Class Representation

```
      basicPlan = new WinBasic();
      premiumPlan = new WinPremium();
      premPlusPlan = new WinPremPlus();
    }
    if (platform.equalsIgnoreCase("Unix")) {
      basicPlan = new UnixBasic();
      premiumPlan = new UnixPremium();
      premPlusPlan = new UnixPremPlus();
    }
    return new HostingPlanKit(basicPlan, premiumPlan,
         premPlusPlan);
  }
}
```

The `HostingPlanManager` offers a static method `getHostingPlanKit` that can be used by client objects to get access to a `HostingPlanKit` object configured with prototypical `HostingPlan` objects that represent hosting plans on the specified platform. As an alternative design strategy, the static method `getHostingPlanKit` can be designed as part of the `HostingPlanKit` class itself.

Once the `HostingPlanKit` object is received, a client can make use of `getBasicPlan/getPremiumPlan/getPremPlusPlan` methods to get access to `HostingPlan` objects.

```
public class TestClient {
  public static void main(String[] args) {
    HostingPlanManager manager = new HostingPlanManager();
    HostingPlanKit kit = manager.getHostingPlanKit("Win");
    HostingPlan plan = kit.getBasicPlan();
    System.out.println(plan.getFeatures());
    plan = kit.getPremiumPlan();
    System.out.println(plan.getFeatures());
  }
}
```

EXAMPLE II

A computer user in a typical organization is associated with a user account. A user account can be part of one or more groups. Permissions on different resources (such as servers, printers, etc.) are defined at the group level. A user gets all the permissions defined for all groups that his or her account is part of. Let us build an application to facilitate the creation of user accounts. For simplicity, let us consider only two groups — Supervisor and AccountRep — representing users who are supervisors and account representatives, respectively.

Let us define a `UserAccount` class (Figure 13.7 and Listing 13.6) that represents a typical user account.

A typical `UserAccount` object maintains user-specific data such as firstname and lastname as strings and maintains the set of user permissions in the form of a vector.

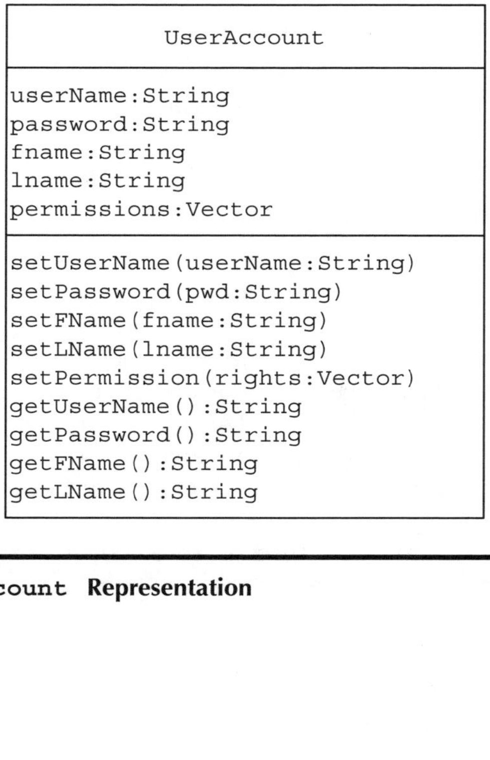

```
UserAccount
─────────────────────────
userName:String
password:String
fname:String
lname:String
permissions:Vector
─────────────────────────
setUserName(userName:String)
setPassword(pwd:String)
setFName(fname:String)
setLName(lname:String)
setPermission(rights:Vector)
getUserName():String
getPassword():String
getFName():String
getLName():String
```

Figure 13.7 `UserAccount` Representation

Listing 13.6 UserAccount Class

```
public class UserAccount {
  private String userName;
  private String password;
  private String fname;
  private String lname;
  private Vector permissions = new Vector();
  public void setUserName(String uName) {
    userName = uName;
  }
  public String getUserName() {
    return userName;
  }
  public void setPassword(String pwd) {
    password = pwd;
  }
  public String getPassword() {
    return password;
  }
  public void setFName(String name) {
    fname = name;
  }
  public String getFName() {
    return fname;
  }
  public void setLName(String name) {
    lname = name;
  }
  public String getLName() {
    return lname;
  }
  public void setPermissions(Vector rights) {
    permissions = rights;
  }
  public Vector getPermissions() {
    return permissions;
  }
}
```

For simplicity, let us define the set of permissions for each of the Supervisor and the AccountRep groups in the form of two text files — `supervisor.txt` and `accountrep.txt`, respectively. With this arrangement, one of the simplest ways to create a user account is to:

■ Instantiate the `UserAccount` class
■ Read permissions from an appropriate data file
■ Set these permissions in the `UserAccount` object

Though this approach looks straightforward, it is not efficient as it involves expensive file I/O (input/output) each time an account is created. This process can be designed more efficiently using the Prototype pattern. Applying the Prototype pattern, let us make the following changes to the design.

Redesign the `UserAccount` Class

The `UserAccount` class needs to be redesigned to provide a way for clients to create a clone of it (Listing 13.7). This can be accomplished by:

■ Designing the `UserAccount` class to implement the `Cloneable` interface
■ Returning a shallow copy of itself as part of its implementation of the clone method

Listing 13.7 `UserAccount` Class Revised

```java
public class UserAccount implements Cloneable {
  private String userName;
  private String password;
  private String fname;
  private String lname;
  private Vector permissions = new Vector();
        ...

        ...

  public Object clone() {
    //Shallow Copy
    try {
      return super.clone();
    } catch (CloneNotSupportedException e) {
      return null;
    }
        ...

        ...

  }
}
```

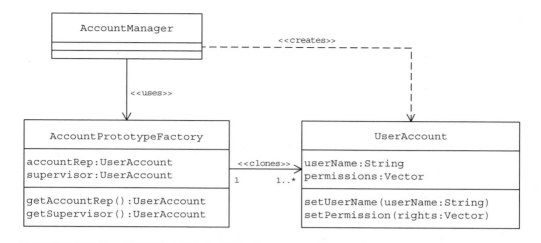

Figure 13.8 `UserAccount` **Creation Utility: Class Association**

Create a Prototype Factory Class

A new class, `AccountPrototypeFactory`, can be defined to hold prototypical `UserAccount` objects representing Supervisor and AccountRep type accounts. When requested by a client, the `AccountPrototypeFactory` returns a copy of an appropriate `UserAccount` object. Figure 13.8 shows the resulting class association.

```
public class AccountPrototypeFactory {
  private UserAccount accountRep;
  private UserAccount supervisor;
  public AccountPrototypeFactory(UserAccount supervisorAccount,
      UserAccount arep) {
    accountRep = arep;
    supervisor = supervisorAccount;
  }
  public UserAccount getAccountRep() {
    return (UserAccount) accountRep.clone();
  }
  public UserAccount getSupervisor() {
    return (UserAccount) supervisor.clone();
  }
}
```

With these modifications in place, in order to create user accounts, a typical client (Listing 13.8):

Listing 13.8   Client `AccountManager` Class

```
public class AccountManager {
  public static void main(String[] args) {
    /*
        Create Prototypical Objects
    */
    Vector supervisorPermissions =
      getPermissionsFromFile("supervisor.txt");
    UserAccount supervisor = new UserAccount();
    supervisor.setPermissions(supervisorPermissions);
    Vector accountRepPermissions =
      getPermissionsFromFile("accountrep.txt");
    UserAccount accountRep = new UserAccount();
    accountRep.setPermissions(accountRepPermissions);
    AccountPrototypeFactory factory =
      new AccountPrototypeFactory(supervisor,
          accountRep);
    /* Using protype objects to create other user accounts */
    UserAccount newSupervisor = factory.getSupervisor();
    newSupervisor.setUserName("PKuchana");
    newSupervisor.setPassword("Everest");
    System.out.println(newSupervisor);
    UserAccount anotherSupervisor = factory.getSupervisor();
    anotherSupervisor.setUserName("SKuchana");
    anotherSupervisor.setPassword("Everest");
    System.out.println(anotherSupervisor);
    UserAccount newAccountRep = factory.getAccountRep();
    newAccountRep.setUserName("VKuchana");
    newAccountRep.setPassword("Vishal");
    System.out.println(newAccountRep);
  }
          ...
          ...
}
```

■ First creates two `UserAccount` objects representing Supervisor and AccountRep type accounts. These instances are then stored inside the `AccountPrototypeFactory` as prototype objects. This is the only time permissions are read from data files.

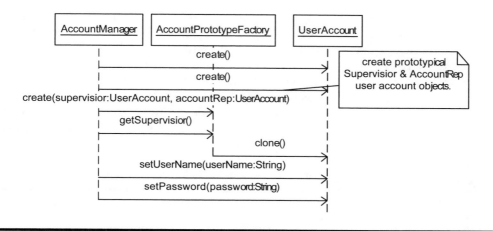

Figure 13.9 UserAccount Creation: Message Flow

■ Each time a new Supervisor or AccountRep type account needs to be created, the client invokes one of the getSupervisor or the getAccountRep methods of the AccountPrototypeFactory. In response, the AccountPrototypeFactory clones an appropriate prototype UserAccount object and returns it to the client. Once the UserAccount clone is received, the client can make necessary changes such as setting the new username and password.

Unlike the earlier design, this approach does not involve creating each UserAccount object from scratch by reading from the data file. Instead, it makes use of object cloning to create new objects. The sequence diagram in Figure 13.9 depicts the message flow when a new supervisor account is created.

PRACTICE QUESTIONS

1. In the example application above, every new Supervisor type account is given exactly the same set of permissions as the prototypical Supervisor UserAccount object. Let us consider a new user account group to represent marketing coordinators. In addition to all the permissions of a regular supervisor, a marketing coordinator is to be given access to the color printer. Hence, whenever a marketing coordinator is to be created, the existing Supervisor prototype account object can be cloned and the required new color printer access privilege can be added. In terms of implementation, this means adding a new permission object to the permissions vector after the clone is received through the getSupervisor method call. In this case, is the existing shallow copy implementation, of the clone method sufficient, or does it need to be changed and why?

2. During the discussion of the Abstract Factory pattern, we designed an application that deals with different types of vehicles. Besides the families of vehicle classes, the application design is comprised of an abstract `VehicleFactory` with two concrete factory subclasses as listed in Table 13.1. Applying the Prototype pattern, redesign this application so that only one concrete factory class is needed. The concrete factory can be configured with the prototypical instance of each vehicle type in the vehicle family. The concrete factory then uses these prototypes to create new objects. Make any necessary assumptions about the application functionality.

Table 13.1 Concrete Factory Classes

Concrete Factory	Responsibility
LuxuryVehicleFactory	Responsible for creating instances of classes representing luxury vehicles
NonLuxuryVehicleFactory	Responsible for creating instances of classes representing nonluxury vehicles

14

BUILDER

This pattern was previously described in GoF95.

DESCRIPTION

In general, object construction details such as instantiating and initializing the components that make up the object are kept within the object, often as part of its constructor. This type of design closely ties the object construction process with the components that make up the object. This approach is suitable as long as the object under construction is simple and the object construction process is definite and always produces the same representation of the object.

This design may not be effective when the object being created is complex and the series of steps constituting the object creation process can be implemented in different ways producing different representations of the object. Because different implementations of the construction process are all kept within the object, the object can become bulky (construction bloat) and less modular. Subsequently, adding a new implementation or making changes to an existing implementation requires changes to the existing code.

Using the Builder pattern, the process of constructing such an object can be designed more effectively. The Builder pattern suggests moving the construction logic out of the object class to a separate class referred to as *a builder* class. There can be more than one such builder class each with different implementation for the series of steps to construct the object. Each such builder implementation results in a different representation of the object. This type of separation reduces the object size. In addition:

- The design turns out to be more modular with each implementation contained in a different builder object.
- Adding a new implementation (i.e., adding a new builder) becomes easier.
- The object construction process becomes independent of the components that make up the object. This provides more control over the object construction process.

In terms of implementation, each of the different steps in the construction process can be declared as methods of a common interface to be implemented by different concrete builders. Figure 14.1 shows the resulting builder class hierarchy.

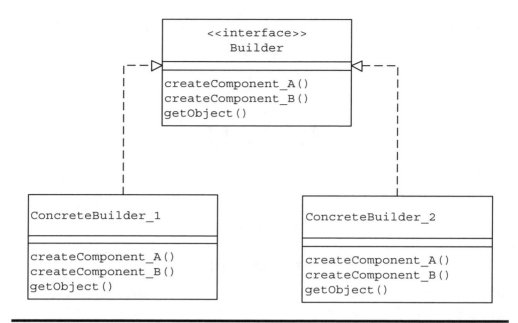

Figure 14.1 Generic `Builder` Class Hierarchy

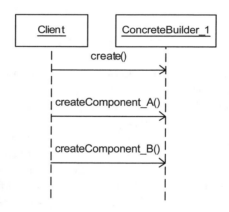

Figure 14.2 `Client/Builder` Direct Interaction

A client object can create an instance of a concrete builder and invoke the set of methods required to construct different parts of the final object. Figure 14.2 shows the corresponding message flow.

This approach requires every client object to be aware of the construction logic. Whenever the construction logic undergoes a change, all client objects need to be modified accordingly. The Builder pattern introduces another level of separation that addresses this problem. Instead of having client objects invoke different builder methods directly, the Builder pattern suggests using a dedicated object referred to as a *Director*, which is responsible for invoking different builder methods required for the construction of the final object. Different client objects can make use of the Director object to create the required object. Once the object is constructed, the client object can directly request from the builder the fully constructed object. To facilitate this process, a new method getObject can be declared in the common Builder interface to be implemented by different concrete builders.

The new design eliminates the need for a client object to deal with the methods constituting the object construction process and encapsulates the details of how the object is constructed from the client. Figure 14.3 shows the association between different classes.

The interaction between the client object, the Director and the Builder objects can be summarized as follows:

- The client object creates instances of an appropriate concrete Builder implementer and the Director. The client may use a factory for creating an appropriate Builder object.
- The client associates the Builder object with the Director object.
- The client invokes the build method on the Director instance to begin the object creation process. Internally, the Director invokes different Builder methods required to construct the final object.
- Once the object creation is completed, the client invokes the getObject method on the concrete Builder instance to get the newly created object. Figure 14.4 shows the overall message flow.

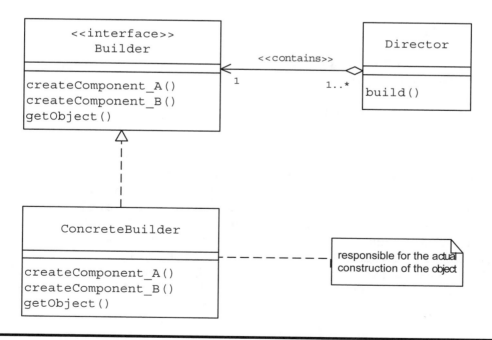

Figure 14.3   Class Association

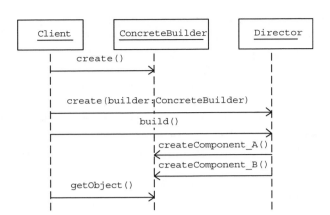

Figure 14.4 Object Creation When the Builder Pattern Is Applied

EXAMPLE I

A typical online job site maintains employer-, candidate- and jobs-related data. Let us build an application using the Builder pattern that displays the necessary user interface to allow a user to search for different employers and candidates in the database. For simplicity, let us consider only three fields for each search, which users can use to specify the search criteria.

- Employer Search
  - Name
  - City
  - Membership Renewal Date
- Candidate Search
  - Name
  - Experience (minimum number of years)
  - Skill Set

The required user interface (UI) for each of these searches requires a different combination of UI controls. In terms of implementation, the required set of UI controls can be placed in a `JPanel` container. The Builder pattern can be used in this case with different builder objects constructing the `JPanel` object with the necessary UI controls and initializing them appropriately.

Applying the Builder pattern, let us define the common builder interface in the form of an abstract `UIBuilder` class as in Listing 14.1.

Let us define two concrete subclasses (Figure 14.5 and Listing 14.2) of the `UIBuilder` class with responsibilities as listed in Table 14.1. These subclasses act as concrete builder classes.

A Side Note ...

For simplicity, the `getSQL` method in both the `EmpSrchBuilder` the `Cand-SrchBuilder` is implemented to create the SQL statement as a string by simply

Listing 14.1 Abstract UIBuilder Class

```
public abstract class UIBuilder {
  protected JPanel searchUI;
  //add necessary UI controls and initialize them
  public abstract void addUIControls();
  public abstract void initialize();
  //return the SELECT sql command for the specified criteria
  public abstract String getSQL();
  //common to all concrete builders.
  //returns the fully constructed search UI
  public JPanel getSearchUI() {
    return searchUI;
  }
}
```

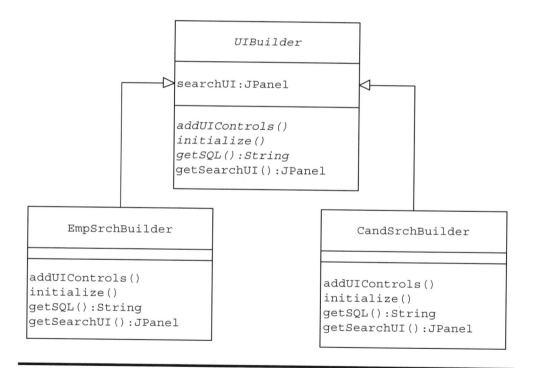

Figure 14.5 UIBuilder: Class Hierarchy

including the user input values, without any validations, in the SQL string. This type of implementation is likely to introduce an SQL injection problem. SQL injection is a technique that enables a malicious user to execute unauthorized

Listing 14.2 `UIBuilder` Concrete Subclasses

```
class EmpSrchBuilder extends UIBuilder {
        ...

        ...

  public void addUIControls() {
    searchUI = new JPanel();
    JLabel lblUserName = new JLabel("Name :");
    JLabel lblCity = new JLabel("City:");
    JLabel lblRenewal = new JLabel("Membership Renewal :");
    GridBagLayout gridbag = new GridBagLayout();
    searchUI.setLayout(gridbag);
    GridBagConstraints gbc = new GridBagConstraints();
    searchUI.add(lblUserName);
    searchUI.add(txtUserName);
    searchUI.add(lblCity);
    searchUI.add(txtCity);
    searchUI.add(lblRenewal);
    searchUI.add(txtRenewal);
            ...

            ...

    gbc.gridx = 0;
    gbc.gridy = 0;
    gridbag.setConstraints(lblUserName, gbc);
    gbc.gridx = 0;
    gbc.gridy = 1;
    gridbag.setConstraints(lblCity, gbc);
    gbc.gridx = 0;
    gbc.gridy = 2;
    gridbag.setConstraints(lblRenewal, gbc);
            ...

            ...

  }
  public void initialize() {
    Calendar cal = Calendar.getInstance();
    cal.setTime(new java.util.Date());
    txtUserName.setText("Enter UserName Here");
    txtRenewal.setText((cal.get(Calendar.MONTH) + 1) + "/" +
                   cal.get(Calendar.DATE) + "/" +
                   cal.get(Calendar.YEAR));
  }
```

(continued)

Listing 14.2 `UIBuilder` **Concrete Subclasses (Continued)**

```
    public String getSQL() {
      return ("Select * from Employer where Username='" +
              txtUserName.getText() + "'" + " and City='" +
              txtCity.getText() + "' and DateRenewal='" +
              txtRenewal.getText() + "'");
    }
  }
  class CandSrchBuilder extends UIBuilder {
          ...

          ...

    public void addUIControls() {
      searchUI = new JPanel();
      JLabel lblUserName = new JLabel("Name :");
      JLabel lblExperienceRange =
        new JLabel("Experience(min Yrs.):");
      JLabel lblSkill = new JLabel("Skill :");
      cmbExperience.addItem("<5");
      cmbExperience.addItem(">5");
      GridBagLayout gridbag = new GridBagLayout();
      searchUI.setLayout(gridbag);
      GridBagConstraints gbc = new GridBagConstraints();
      gbc.anchor = GridBagConstraints.WEST;
      searchUI.add(lblUserName);
      searchUI.add(txtUserName);
      searchUI.add(lblExperienceRange);
      searchUI.add(cmbExperience);
      searchUI.add(lblSkill);
      searchUI.add(txtSkill);
              ...

              ...
```

(continued)

Listing 14.2 `UIBuilder` Concrete Subclasses (Continued)

```
            gbc.gridx = 0;
            gbc.gridy = 0;
            gridbag.setConstraints(lblUserName, gbc);
            gbc.gridx = 0;
            gbc.gridy = 1;
            gridbag.setConstraints(lblExperienceRange, gbc);
            gbc.gridx = 0;
            gbc.gridy = 2;
            gridbag.setConstraints(lblSkill, gbc);

                ...

                ...

    }
    public void initialize() {
        txtUserName.setText("Enter UserName Here");
        txtSkill.setText("Internet Tech");
    }
    public String getSQL() {
        String experience =
            (String) cmbExperience.getSelectedItem();
        return ("Select * from Candidate where Username='" +
                txtUserName.getText() + "' and Experience " +
                experience + " and Skill='" +
                txtSkill.getText() + "'");

    }
}
```

SQL commands by taking advantage of poor or no input validation when an SQL statement is built as a string, using user input values.

A malicious user could enter something like `joe';delete * from Employer` into the `Username` field, which results in an SQL statement as follows:

```
Select * from Employer where Username='joe';'delete *
from employer...
```

Most commercial database servers treat this as a batch of SQL statements. The first occurrence of `;` terminates the first SQL command and the server attempts to execute the next SQL statement in the batch, which is `delete * from employer`.

In this manner, attackers can trick the program into executing whatever SQL statement they want. In a real-world application, prepared statements (with

Table 14.1   Responsibilities of `EmpSrchBuilder` and `CandSrchBuilder` Concrete Builder Classes

Builder	Responsibility
`EmpSrchBuilder`	• Builds a `JPanel` object with the necessary UI controls for the employer search • Initializes UI controls • Returns the fully constructed `JPanel` object as part of the `getSearchUI` method • Builds the required SQL select command and returns it as part of the `getSQL` method
`CandSrchBuilder`	• Builds a `JPanel` object with the necessary UI controls for the candidate search • Initializes UI controls • Returns the fully constructed `JPanel` object as part of the `getSearchUI` method • Builds the required SQL select command and returns it as part of the `getSQL` method

placeholders instead of textual parameter insertion) should be used and parameters should be examined for dangerous characters before being passed on to the database.

Back to the Example Application ...

Let us define a Director class `UIDirector` as in Listing 14.3.

The `UIDirector` maintains an object reference of type `UIBuilder`. This `UIBuilder` object can be passed to the `UIDirector` as part of a call to its constructor. As part of the `build` method, the `UIDirector` invokes different `UIBuilder` methods on this object for constructing the `JPanel` `searchUI` object.

Listing 14.3   `UIDirector` Class

```
public class UIDirector {
  private UIBuilder builder;
  public UIDirector(UIBuilder bldr) {
    builder = bldr;
  }
  public void build() {
    builder.addUIControls();
    builder.initialize();
  }
}
```

The client `SearchManager` can be designed (Listing 14.5) such that:

- It displays the necessary UI to allow a user to select the type of the search. The initial display contains an empty panel for the display of the search criteria UI (Figure 14.6).
- When the user selects a search type, the client object creates an instance of an appropriate `UIBuilder` using a `BuilderFactory` factory object. The `BuilderFactory` `getUIBuilder` method (Listing 14.4):
  - Accepts the type of the search selected by the user as input.
  - Creates an appropriate `UIBuilder` object based on this input and returns the `UIBuilder` object to the client.
- The client creates a `UIDirector` object and configures it with the `UIBuilder` object created above.
- The client invokes the `build` method of the `UIDirector` to begin the UI panel construction process. The `UIDirector` invokes the set of `UIBuilder` methods required to construct the `JPanel` object with the necessary UI controls.
- The client invokes the `getSearchUI` method on the `UIBuilder` object to access the fully constructed `JPanel` object, which contains the necessary user interface controls to allow a user to specify the search criteria. The `JPanel` search criteria UI is then displayed in the main UI window. Figures 14.7 and 14.8 show the UI displays for the employer search and candidate search, respectively.
- Once the user enters the search criteria and clicks on the `GetSQL` button, the client invokes the `getSQL` method on the `UIBuilder` object. Different concrete `UIBuilder` subclasses display different UI controls and the SQL statement depends on the fields represented by these controls but the client does not have to deal with these differences. Each of the concrete `UIBuilder` objects hides these details from the client and provides the implementation for the `getSQL` method, taking into account the representation of the object it builds.

Listing 14.4 `BuilderFactory` Class

```
class BuilderFactory {
  public UIBuilder getUIBuilder(String str) {
    UIBuilder builder = null;
    if (str.equals(SearchManager.CANDIDATE_SRCH)) {
      builder = new CandSrchBuilder();
    } else if (str.equals(SearchManager.EMPLOYER_SRCH)) {
      builder = new EmpSrchBuilder();
    }
    return builder;
  }
}
```

Listing 14.5 The Client `SearchManager` Class

```
public class SearchManager extends JFrame {
        ...

        ...

  public void actionPerformed(ActionEvent e) {
        ...

        ...

    if (e.getActionCommand().equals(SearchManager.GET_SQL)) {
      manager.setSQL(builder.getSQL());
    }
    if (e.getSource() == manager.getSearchTypeCtrl()) {
      String selection = manager.getSearchType();
      if (selection.equals("") == false) {
        BuilderFactory factory = new BuilderFactory();
        //create an appropriate builder instance
        builder = factory.getUIBuilder(selection);
        //configure the director with the builder
        UIDirector director = new UIDirector(builder);
        //director invokes different builder
        //methods
        director.build();
        //get the final build object
        JPanel UIObj = builder.getSearchUI();
        manager.displayNewUI(UIObj);
      }
    }
  }
        ...

        ...

  public buttonHandler(SearchManager inManager) {
    manager = inManager;
  }
}
```

The database interaction is not included in this example to keep it simple. The final SQL statement is simply displayed in the UI (Figure 14.9).

The class association can be depicted as in Figure 14.10.

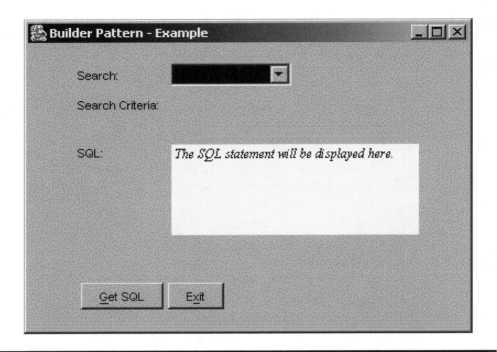

Figure 14.6 `SearchManager`: **Initial UI Display**

The `BuilderFactory` factory is not shown in the Figure 14.10 class diagram because it is not part of the Builder pattern implementation. The client `Search-Manager` uses it only as a helper class.

The sequence diagram in Figure 14.11 shows the message flow when the user conducts an employer search.

EXAMPLE II

Let us design the following functionality for an online shopping site.

- A server side component receives the order information submitted by a user in the form of an XML string.
- The order XML is then parsed and validated to create an `Order` object.
- The `Order` object is finally saved to the disk.

A typical order XML record is shown follows:

```
<Order>
  <LineItems>
    <Item>
      <ID>100</ID>
      <Qty>1</Qty>
    </Item>
```

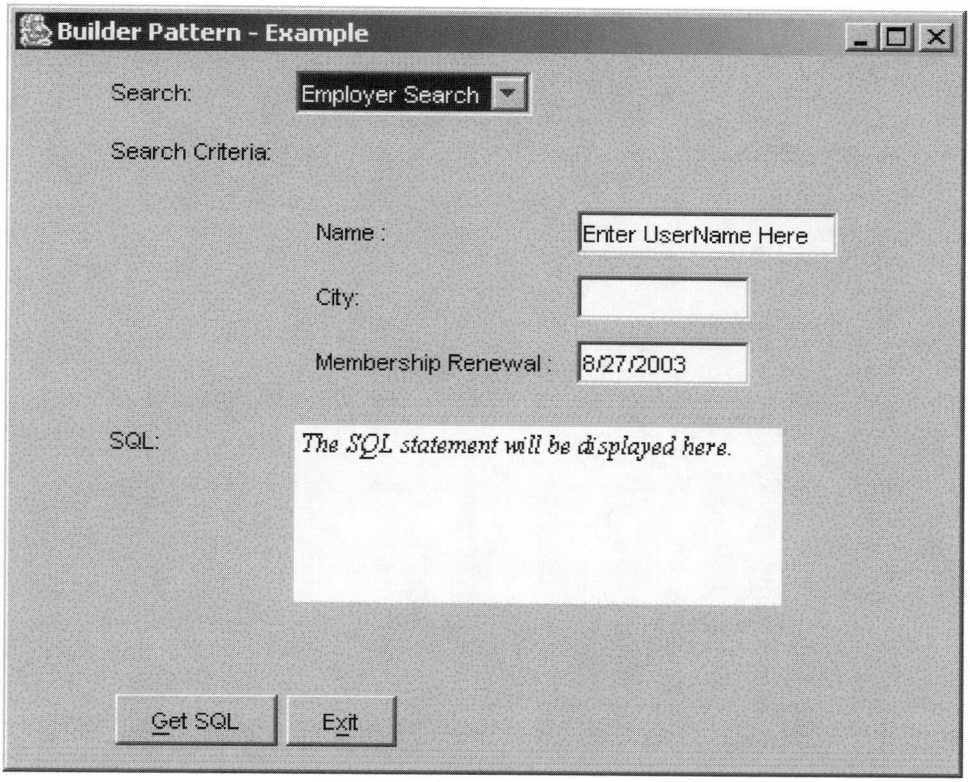

Figure 14.7 UI Display for the Employer Search

```
    <Item>
      <ID>200</ID>
      <Qty>2</Qty>
    </Item>
  </LineItems>
  <ShippingAddress>
    <Address1>101 Arrowhead Trail </Address1>
    <Address2> Suite 100</Address2>
    <City>Anytown</City>
    <State>OH</State>
    <Zip>12345</Zip>
  </ShippingAddress>
  <BillingAddress>
    <Address1>2669 Knox St </Address1>
    <Address2> Unit 444</Address2>
    <City>Anytown</City>
    <State>CA</State>
```

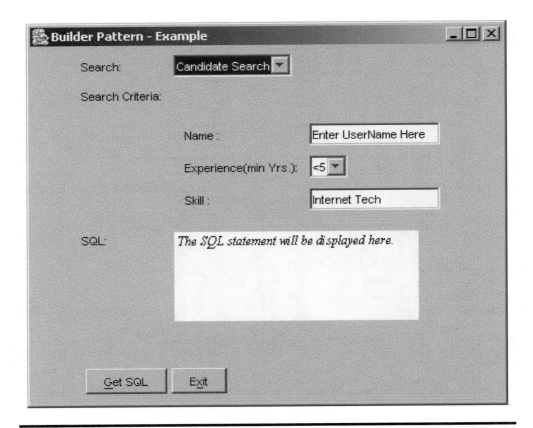

Figure 14.8 UI Display for the Candidate Search

```
    <Zip>56789</Zip>
  </BillingAddress>
</Order>
```

Payment details are not included in XML in order to keep the example simple. Let us consider three types of orders as in Table 14.2.

The class representation of a generic order can be designed as in Figure 14.12 with the required attributes and methods.

The save method can be used by different client objects to save the Order object to disk.

The series of steps required for the creation of an Order object can be summarized as follows:

- Parse the input XML string
- Validate the data
- Calculate the tax
- Calculate the shipping
- Create the actual object with:
    - Line items from the input XML string
    - Tax and shipping details calculated as per the details listed in Table 14.2

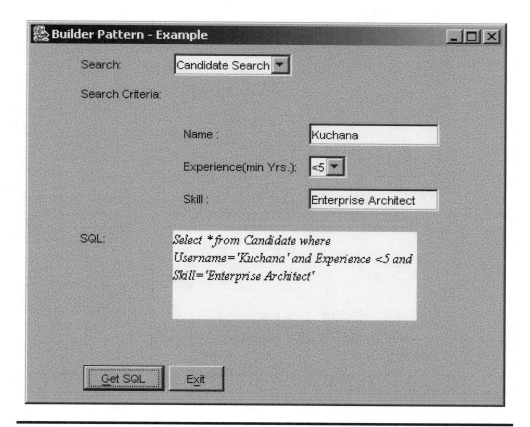

Figure 14.9   UI Display with SQL Statement Output

Let us design an interface `OrderBuilder` as in Figure 14.13 that declares the methods representing different steps in the `Order` object creation.

Because an order can exist in three different forms (California, Non-California or Overseas), let us define three concrete `OrderBuilder` implementers (Figure 14.14), where each implementer is responsible for the construction of a specific order type representation.

Each concrete `OrderBuilder` implementer can be designed to carry out the validations and tax and shipping calculation rules listed in Table 14.2 for the type of the `Order` object it constructs.

As a next step, let us define an `OrderDirector` as in Figure 14.15.

The `OrderDirector` contains an object reference of type `OrderBuilder`. The parse method is used internally by the `OrderDirector` to parse the input XML record. Figure 14.16 shows the overall association between different classes.

The server-side object that first receives the order XML acts as the client object in this case. The client makes use of the `OrderDirector` and concrete `Order-Builder` implementer objects to create different representations of the `Order` object using the same construction process described as follows:

■ The client first receives the order in the form of an XML record.

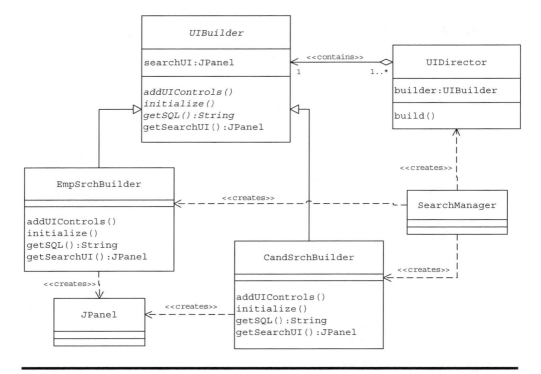

Figure 14.10 Class Association

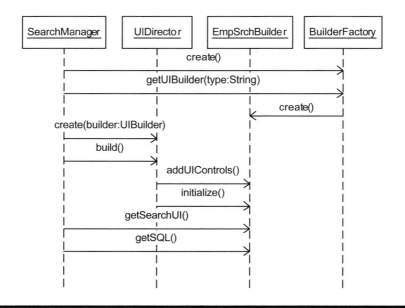

Figure 14.11 Message Flow

Table 14.2   Different Order Types

S. No	Order Type	Details
1	Overseas orders	• Orders from countries other than the United States. Additional shipping and handling is charged for these orders. • Overseas orders are accepted only if the order amount is greater than $100.
2	California orders	• U.S. orders with shipping address in California and are charged additional sales tax. • Orders with $100 or more order amount receive free regular shipping.
3	Non-California orders	• U.S. orders with shipping address not in California. Additional sales tax is not applicable. • Orders with $100 or more order amount receive free regular shipping.

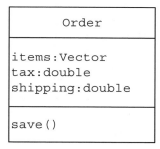

Figure 14.12   Generic Order Representation

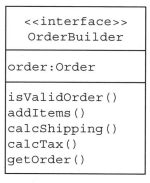

Figure 14.13   Builder Interface for Order Objects

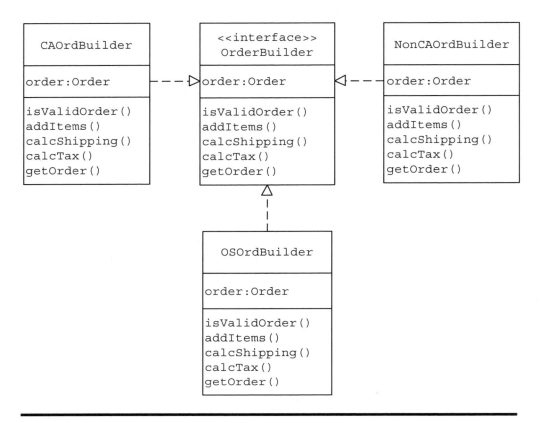

Figure 14.14 OrderBuilder Hierarchy

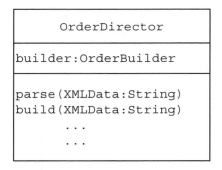

Figure 14.15 Director for the Creation of Order Objects

- The client creates an appropriate OrderBuilder object. It then instantiates the OrderDirector, passing the OrderBuilder object as a parameter.
- The client invokes the build method on the OrderDirector, passing the input XML data to initiate the Order object construction process.
    - If a problem is encountered during the construction process, a BuilderException is thrown. In general, error handling should be

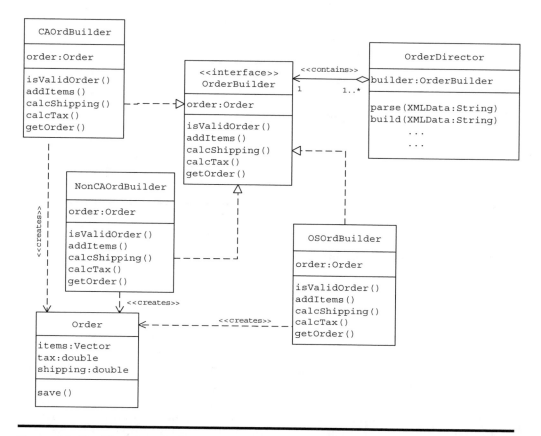

Figure 14.16 Class Association

done in a proper way with `Builders` to avoid the risk of having half-created objects lying around.

■ The `OrderDirector` invokes different `OrderBuilder` methods to complete the construction of the `Order` object.
■ The client calls the `getOrder` method of the `OrderBuilder` to get the final constructed `Order` object.
■ The client can invoke the `save` method on the returned `Order` object to save the order to the disk.

EXAMPLE III

Let us design the order handling functionality for a different type of an online shopping site that transmits orders to different order fulfilling companies based on the type of the goods ordered. Suppose that the group of order processing companies can be classified into three categories based on the format of the order information they expect to receive. These formats include comma-separated value (CSV), XML and a custom object. When the order information is transformed into one of these formats, appropriate header and footer information that is specific to a format needs to be added to the order data.

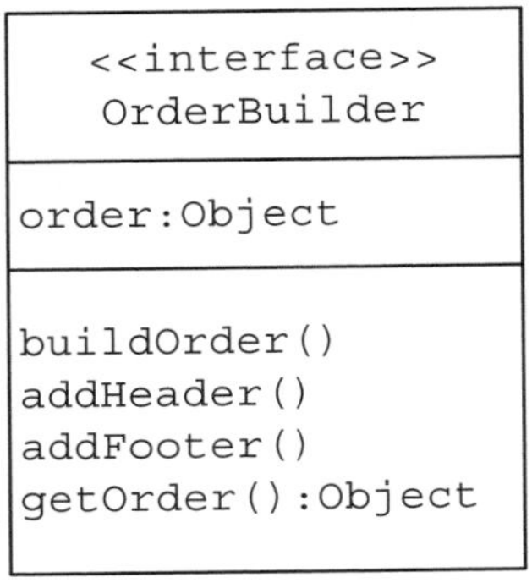

```
        <<interface>>
        OrderBuilder

  order:Object

  buildOrder()
  addHeader()
  addFooter()
  getOrder():Object
```

Figure 14.17   Builder Interface for Order Objects

The series of steps required for the creation of an Order object can be summarized as follows:

- Create the header specific to the format
- Add the order data
- Create the footer specific to the format

Let us design an interface OrderBuilder as in Figure 14.17 that declares the methods representing different steps in the Order object creation.

Because an order can exist in three different forms (CSV, XML and custom object), let us define three concrete OrderBuilder implementers as in Figure 14.18, where each implementer is responsible for the construction of a specific order representation.

Each concrete OrderBuilder implementer can be designed to implement the details of:

- Transforming input order information into a specific format
- Creating header or footer specific to the representation of the order being created

As a next step, let us define an OrderDirector as in Figure 14.19.

The OrderDirector contains an object reference of type OrderBuilder. Figure 14.20 shows the overall association between different classes.

Client objects can make use of the OrderDirector and concrete Order-Builder implementer objects to create different representations of the Order object using the same construction process described as follows:

- The client creates an appropriate OrderBuilder object. It then instantiates the OrderDirector, passing the OrderBuilder object as a parameter.
- The client invokes the build method on the OrderDirector, passing the input order data to initiate the Order object construction process.

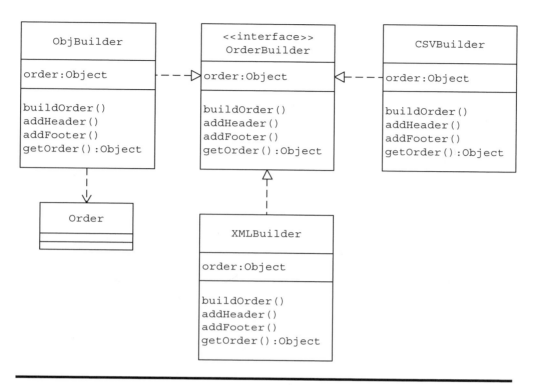

Figure 14.18 `OrderBuilder` **Hierarchy**

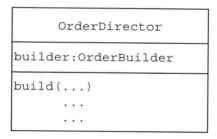

Figure 14.19 **Director for the Creation of Order Objects**

- If a problem is encountered during the construction process, an exception `BuilderException` is thrown.
■ The `OrderDirector` invokes the `buildOrder`, `addHeader` and `add-Footer OrderBuilder` methods to complete the construction of the `Order` object.
■ The client calls the `getOrder` method of the `OrderBuilder` to get the final constructed `Order` object.
■ The client can transmit the order to an appropriate order handling company.

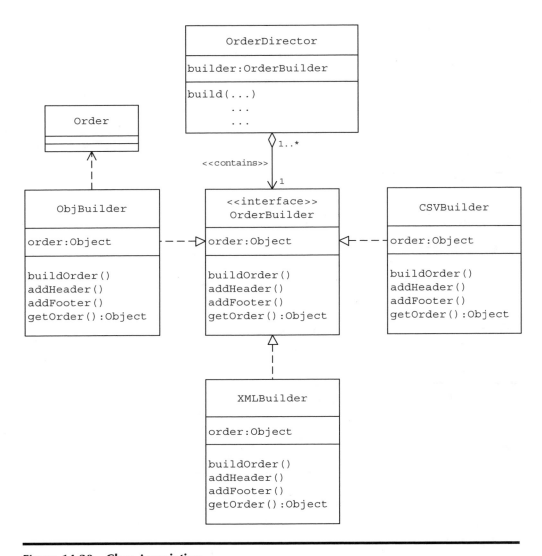

Figure 14.20 Class Association

PRACTICE QUESTIONS

1. Enhance the Example I application above to allow users to query on jobs as well. Create a new concrete builder to construct the necessary user interface.
2. Implement Examples II and III discussed above. Draw sequence diagrams to depict the message flow when the application is run.

V

COLLECTIONAL PATTERNS

Collectional patterns primarily:

- Deal with groups or collections of objects
- Deal with the details of how to compose classes and objects to form larger structures
- Concentrate on the most efficient way of designing a class so that its instances do not carry any duplicate data
- Allow the definition of operations on collections of objects

Chapter	Pattern Name	Description
15	Composite	Allows both individual objects and composite objects to be treated uniformly.
16	Iterator	Allows a client to access the contents of an aggregate object (collection of objects) in some sequential manner, without having any knowledge about the internal representation of its contents.
17	Flyweight	The intrinsic, invariant common information and the variable parts of a class are separated into two classes, leading to savings in terms of the memory usage and the amount of time required for the creation of a large number of its instances.
18	Visitor	Allows an operation to be defined across a collection of different objects without changing the classes of objects on which it operates.

15

COMPOSITE

This pattern was previously described in GoF95.

DESCRIPTION

Every component or object can be classified into one of the two categories — Individual Components or Composite Components — which are composed of individual components or other composite components. The Composite pattern is useful in designing a common interface for both individual and composite components so that client programs can view both the individual components and groups of components uniformly. In other words, the Composite design pattern allows a client object to treat both single components and collections of components in an identical manner.

This can also be explained in terms of a tree structure. The Composite pattern allows uniform reference to both Nonterminal nodes (which represent collections of components or composites) and terminal nodes (which represent individual components).

EXAMPLE

Let us create an application to simulate the Windows/UNIX file system. The file system consists mainly of two types of components — directories and files. Directories can be made up of other directories or files, whereas files cannot contain any other file system component. In this aspect, directories act as nonterminal nodes and files act as terminal nodes of a tree structure.

DESIGN APPROACH I

Let us define a common interface for both directories and files in the form of a Java interface `FileSystemComponent` (Figure 15.1). The `FileSystemComponent` interface declares methods that are common for both file components and directory components.

Let us further define two classes — `FileComponent` and `DirComponent` — as implementers of the common `FileSystemComponent` interface. Figure 15.2 shows the resulting class hierarchy.

```
            <<interface>>
         FileSystemComponent

      getComponentSize():long
```

Figure 15.1 The Common `FileSystemComponent` Interface

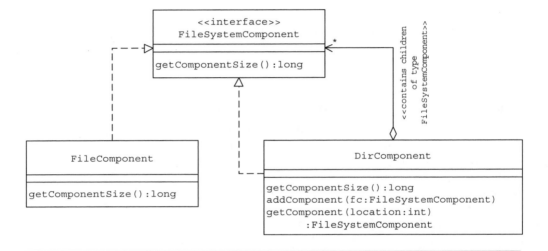

Figure 15.2 The `FileSystemComponent` Class Hierarchy

FileComponent

The `FileComponent` class represents a file in the file system and offers implementation for the following methods.

getComponentSize()

This method returns the size (in kilobytes) of the file represented by the `File-Component` object.

DirComponent

This class represents a directory in the file system. Since directories are composite entities, the `DirComponent` provides methods to deal with the components it contains. These methods are in addition to the common `getComponentSize` method declared in the `FileSystemComponent` interface.

addComponent(FileSystemComponent)

This method is used by client applications to add different `DirComponent` and `FileComponent` objects to a `DirComponent` object.

getComponent(int)

The `DirComponent` stores the other `FileSystemComponent` objects inside a vector. This method is used to retrieve one such object stored at the specified location.

getComponentSize()

This method returns the size (in kilobytes) of the directory represented by the `DirComponent` object. As part of the implementation, the `DirComponent` object iterates over the collection of `FileSystemComponent` objects it contains, in a recursive manner, and sums up the sizes of all individual `FileComponents`. The final sum is returned as the size of the directory it represents.

A typical client would first create a set of `FileSystemComponent` objects (both `DirComponent` and `FileComponent` instances). It can use the `addComponent` method of the `DirComponent` to add different `FileSystemComponents` to a `DirComponent`, creating a hierarchy of file system (`FileSystemComponent`) objects.

When the client wants to query any of these objects for its size, it can simply invoke the `getComponentSize` method. The client does not have to be aware of the calculations involved or the manner in which the calculations are carried out in determining the component size. In this aspect, the client treats both the `FileComponent` and the `DirComponent` object in the same manner. No separate code is required to query `FileComponent` objects and `DirComponent` objects for their size.

Though the client treats both the `FileComponent` and `DirComponent` objects in a uniform manner in the case of the common `getComponentSize` method, it does need to distinguish when calling composite specific methods such as `addComponent` and `getComponent` defined exclusively in the `DirComponent`. Because these methods are not available with `FileComponent` objects, the client needs to check to make sure that the `FileSystemComponent` object it is working with is in fact a `DirComponent` object.

The following Design Approach II eliminates this requirement from the client.

DESIGN APPROACH II

The objective of this approach is to:

- Provide the same advantage of allowing the client application to treat both the composite `DirComponent` and the individual `FileComponent` objects in a uniform manner while invoking the `getComponentSize` method

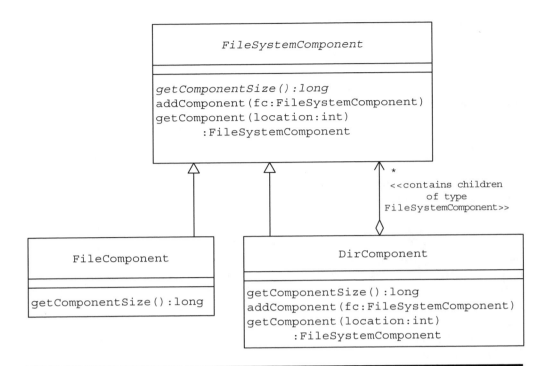

Figure 15.3   Class Association

■ Free the client application from having to check to make sure that the FileSystemComponent it is dealing with is an instance of the DirComponent class while invoking any of the composite-specific methods such as addComponent or getComponent

In the new design (Figure 15.3), the composite-specific addComponent and getComponent methods are moved to the common interface FileSystem-Component. The FileSystemComponent provides the default implementation for these methods and is designed as an abstract class (Listing 15.1).

The default implementation of these methods consists of what is applicable to FileComponent objects. FileComponent objects are individual objects and do not contain other FileSystemComponent objects within. Hence, the default implementation does nothing and simply throws a custom CompositeException exception. The derived composite DirComponent class overrides these methods to provide custom implementation (Listing 15.2).

Because there is no change in the way the common getComponentSize method is designed, the client will still be able to treat both the composite DirComponent and FileComponent objects identically.

Because the common parent FileSystemComponent class now contains default implementations for the addComponent and the getComponent methods, the client application does not need to make any check before making a call to these composite-specific methods.

Listing 15.1 `FileSystemComponent` **Abstract Class**

```
public abstract class FileSystemComponent {
  String name;
  public FileSystemComponent(String cName) {
    name = cName;
  }
  public void addComponent(FileSystemComponent component)
    throws CompositeException {
    throw new CompositeException(
      "Invalid Operation. Not Supported");
  }
  public FileSystemComponent getComponent(int componentNum)
    throws CompositeException {
    throw new CompositeException(
      "Invalid Operation. Not Supported");
  }
  public abstract long getComponentSize();
}//End of class FileSystemComponent
```

Whenever a new composite-specific method such as `removeComponent` is to be added to the composite `DirComponent`, it also needs to be added to the parent `FileSystemComponent` class. The `FileSystemComponent` class must provide a `FileComponent`-specific default implementation for the new method.

The test client application `CompositeDemo` (Listing 15.3) creates a set of `DirComponent`, `FileComponent` objects. Using the composite method `addComponent`, it builds a file system component hierarchy as in Figure 15.4.

When the client needs to find the size of a file system component, it simply invokes the `getComponentSize` method on the `DirComponent` or `FileComponent` object that represents the file system component. The client does not need to treat the component differently depending on if the component is an individual component (`FileComponent`) or a composite component (`DirComponent`). When the client `CompositeDemo` is run, the following output is displayed:

```
Main Folder Size= 10000kb
Sub Folder1 Size= 3000kb
File1 in Folder1 Size= 1000kb
```

Listing 15.2 `FileSystemComponent` Concrete Subclasses: `FileComponent` and `DirComponent`

```
public class FileComponent extends FileSystemComponent {
  private long size;
  public FileComponent(String cName, long sz) {
    super(cName);
    size = sz;
  }
  public long getComponentSize() {
    return size;
  }
}//End of class
public class DirComponent extends FileSystemComponent {
  Vector dirContents = new Vector();
  //individual files/sub folders collection
  public DirComponent(String cName) {
    super(cName);
  }
  public void addComponent(FileSystemComponent fc)
    throws CompositeException {
    dirContents.add(fc);
  }
  public FileSystemComponent getComponent(int location)
  throws CompositeException {
    return (FileSystemComponent) dirContents.elementAt(
            location);
  }
  public long getComponentSize() {
    long sizeOfAllFiles = 0;
    Enumeration e = dirContents.elements();
    while (e.hasMoreElements()) {
      FileSystemComponent component =
        (FileSystemComponent) e.nextElement();
      sizeOfAllFiles = sizeOfAllFiles +
                      (component.getComponentSize());
    }
    return sizeOfAllFiles;
  }
}//End of class
```

Listing 15.3   Client CompositeDemo Class

```java
public class CompositeDemo {
  public static final String SEPARATOR = ", ";
  public static void main(String[] args) {
    FileSystemComponent mainFolder =
      new DirComponent("Year2000");
    FileSystemComponent subFolder1 = new DirComponent("Jan");
    FileSystemComponent subFolder2 = new DirComponent("Feb");
    FileSystemComponent folder1File1 =
      new FileComponent("Jan1DataFile.txt,"1000);
    FileSystemComponent folder1File2 =
      new FileComponent("Jan2DataFile.txt",2000);
    FileSystemComponent folder2File1 =
      new FileComponent("Feb1DataFile.txt",3000);
    FileSystemComponent folder2File2 =
      new FileComponent("Feb2DataFile.txt",4000);
    try {
      mainFolder.addComponent(subFolder1);
      mainFolder.addComponent(subFolder2);
      subFolder1.addComponent(folder1File1);
      subFolder1.addComponent(folder1File2);
      subFolder2.addComponent(folder2File1);
      subFolder2.addComponent(folder2File2);
    } catch (CompositeException ex) {
      //
    }
    //Client refers to both composite &
    //individual components in a uniform manner
    System.out.println(" Main Folder Size= " +
                    mainFolder.getComponentSize() + "kb");
    System.out.println(" Sub Folder1 Size= " +
                    subFolder1.getComponentSize() + "kb");
    System.out.println(" File1 in Folder1 size= " +
                    folder1File1.getComponentSize() + "kb");
  }
}
```

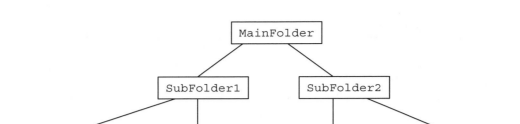

Figure 15.4   Example Application: `FileSystemComponent` Hierarchy

PRACTICE QUESTIONS

1. The following is an example of the FQDN (fully qualified domain name) on the Internet:

   ```
   nwest.sales.DomainName.com
   ```

   It consists of different subdomains. Each such subdomain can be mapped onto a specific directory on the file system of the computer where the `DomainName.com` is hosted. Each such subdomain can have different HTML files, which can be accessed through a URL. Thus a subdomain and the set of HTML files can be viewed as two main components of a Web site.

   a. Define a subdomain hierarchy for an example domain.
   b. Create an application that uses the Composite pattern to:
      i. Display the directory a given subdomain is mapped onto
      ii. Display the URLs of Web site components (either subdomains or single HTML files) in a uniform manner

2. Let us consider the HTML `<frameset>` tag. The `<frameset>` tag is used to divide a Web page into different sections for the purpose of displaying multiple Web pages. Each such section can display a separate Web page. The actual Web page to be displayed inside a section can be specified using the `<frame>` tag. Further, a `<frameset>` tag can be nested, allowing further division of these sections.

```
E.g.,
<html>
<head></head>
<frameset rows="20%,80%">
    <frameset rows="100,200">
        <frame src="frame1.html">
          <frame src="frame2.html">
    </frameset>
    <frame src="frame3.html">
```

```
</frameset>
</html>
```

From the description of the `<frameset>` and `<frame>` tags above, it can be seen that these can be arranged in a tree-like structure with each `<frameset>` tag as a nonterminal node and each `<frame>` tag as a terminal node.

a. Design two classes — `FrameSet` and `Frame` — to represent the `<frameset>` and the `<frame>` tags, respectively.

b. Define an operation `getSourceFiles()` on these classes that returns the HTML file(s) specified to be displayed by a specific `FrameSet` or `Frame` object.

c. Design and implement this operation applying the Composite pattern so that a client can refer to these classes in an identical manner.

3. A typical product database consists of two types of product components — product categories and product items. A product category is generally composite in nature. It can contain product items and also other product categories as its subcategories.

Example Product Categories:

a. Computers
b. Desktops
c. Laptops
d. Peripherals
e. Printers
f. Cables

The Computers product category contains both the Desktops and the Laptops product categories as its subcategories. The Desktop category can contain a product item such as Compaq Presario 5050.

Product items are usually individual, in the sense that they do not contain any product component within.

Design and implement an application to list the dollar value of a product component. Use the Composite pattern to allow the client application to refer to both the product categories and the product items in a uniform manner.

16

ITERATOR

This pattern was previously described in GoF95.

DESCRIPTION

The Iterator pattern allows a client object to access the contents of a container in a sequential manner, without having any knowledge about the internal representation of its contents.

The term *container*, used above, can simply be defined as *a collection of data or objects*. The objects within the container could in turn be collections, making it a collection of collections. The Iterator pattern enables a client object to traverse through this collection of objects (or the container) without having the container to reveal how the data is stored internally.

To accomplish this, the Iterator pattern suggests that a `Container` object should be designed to provide a public interface in the form of an *Iterator* object for different client objects to access its contents. An `Iterator` object contains public methods to allow a client object to navigate through the list of objects within the container.

ITERATORS IN JAVA

One of the simplest iterators available in Java is the `java.sql.ResultSet` class, which is used to hold database records. This class offers a method `next()` for navigating along rows and a set of `getter` methods for column positioning.

Java also offers an interface `Enumeration` as part of the `java.util` package, which declares the methods listed in Table 16.1.

Table 16.1 Enumeration Methods

Method	Return	Description
hasMoreElements()	boolean	Checks if there are more elements in the collection
nextElement()	Object	Returns the next element in the collection

Table 16.2   Iterator Interface Methods

Method	Return	Description
hasNext()	boolean	Checks if there are more elements in the collection.
next()	Object	Returns the next element in the collection.
remove()	void	Removes from the collection, the last element returned by the iterator.

Concrete iterators can be built as implementers of the Enumeration interface by providing implementation for its methods.

In addition, the java.util.Vector class offers a method:

```
public final synchronized Enumeration elements()
```

that returns an enumeration of elements or objects. The returned Enumeration object works as an iterator for the Vector object. The Java Enumeration interface methods listed in Table 16.1 can be used on the returned Enumeration object to sequentially fetch elements stored in the Vector object.

Besides the Enumeration interface, Java also offers the java.util.Iterator interface. The Iterator interface declares three methods as in Table 16.2.

Similar to the Enumeration interface, concrete iterators can be built as implementers of the java.util.Iterator interface.

Though it is considered useful to employ existing Java iterator interfaces such as Iterator or Enumeration, it is not necessary to utilize one of these built-in Java interfaces to implement an iterator. One can design a custom iterator interface that is more suitable for an application need.

FILTERED ITERATORS

In the case of the java.util.Vector class, its iterator simply returns the next element in the collection. In addition to this basic behavior, an iterator may be implemented to do more than simply returning the next object in line. For instance, an iterator object can return a selected set of objects (instead of all objects) in a sequential order. This filtering can be based on some form of input from the client. These types of iterators are referred to as *filtered iterators*.

INTERNAL VERSUS EXTERNAL ITERATORS

An iterator can be designed either as an internal iterator or as an external iterator.

- ■ **Internal iterators**
  - The collection itself offers methods to allow a client to visit different objects within the collection. For example, the java.util.ResultSet class contains the data and also offers methods such as next() to navigate through the item list.
  - There can be only one iterator on a collection at any given time.
  - The collection has to maintain or save the state of iteration.

■ **External iterators**
  – The iteration functionality is separated from the collection and kept inside a different object referred to as an *iterator*. Usually, the collection itself returns an appropriate iterator object to the client depending on the client input. For example, the java.util.Vector class has its iterator defined in the form of a separate object of type Enumeration. This object is returned to a client object in response to the elements() method call.
  – There can be multiple iterators on a given collection at any given time.
  – The overhead involved in storing the state of iteration is not associated with the collection. It lies with the exclusive Iterator object.

EXAMPLE: INTERNAL ITERATOR

Let us build an application to display data from a file Candidates.txt containing details of different IT professionals who have offered their candidature for a job opening. For simplicity, let us consider only three attributes — name, current working location and certification type. As discussed in the preceding section "Internal versus External Iterators", in case of an internal iterator, the container (or the collection) is responsible for providing the interface for a client object to navigate through the container's contents.

Let us define a container class AllCandidates (Listing 16.1) that:

■ Reads data from the data file as part of its constructor and stores the data in the form of a group of Candidate objects inside of an instance variable of Vector type.
■ Implements the built-in java.util.Iterator interface and provides implementation for its methods as follows:
  – hasNext() – Checks to see if there are any more candidates in the collection.
  – next() – Returns the next candidate object, if any, from the collection. If there is none, it throws a NoSuchElementException exception.
  – remove() – Because the application does not deal with the candidate data deletion, this method implementation does nothing.

Figure 16.1 shows the class association of the example application using an internal iterator.

A client SearchManager can be designed to make use of the AllCandidates container to display different candidates data.

CLIENT/CONTAINER INTERACTION

The client SearchManager creates the necessary user interface for the display of the data (Figure 16.2). When a user clicks on the Show All button, it creates an instance of the container AllCandidates. As part of its constructor, the AllCandidates object reads the data file and stores it inside a Vector in the form of a group of Candidate objects. The client does not have to be aware of how the data is stored, in which form and other details. In other words, the client SearchManager only needs to know that the container AllCandidates

Listing 16.1 AllCandidates Class

```java
public class AllCandidates implements Iterator {
  private Vector data;
  Enumeration ec;
  Candidate nextCandidate;
  public AllCandidates() {
    initialize();
    ec = data.elements();
  }
  private void initialize() {
    /*
      Get data from db.
    */
    data = new Vector();
    FileUtil util = new FileUtil();
    Vector dataLines = util.fileToVector("Candidates.txt");
    for (int i = 0; i < dataLines.size(); i++) {
      String str = (String) dataLines.elementAt(i);
      StringTokenizer st = new StringTokenizer(str, ",");
      data.add(
        new Candidate(st.nextToken(), st.nextToken(),
                  st.nextToken()));
    }
  }
  public boolean hasNext() {
    boolean matchFound = false;
    nextCandidate = null;
    while (ec.hasMoreElements()) {
      Candidate tempObj = (Candidate) ec.nextElement();
      nextCandidate = tempObj;
      break;
    }
    return (nextCandidate != null);
  }
```

(continued)

Listing 16.1 AllCandidates Class (Continued)

```java
public Object next() {
  if (nextCandidate == null) {
    throw new NoSuchElementException();
  } else {
    return nextCandidate;
  }
}
  public void remove() {};
}
```

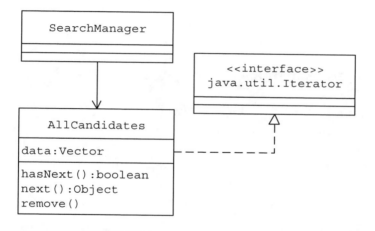

Figure 16.1 Internal Iterator: Class Association

functions as a data store for the candidate data in the form of a group of
Candidate objects. It does not need to know how these objects are stored (in
a Vector or Hashmap, etc.) inside the container.

For the client, the AllCandidates object functions both as a container and
an iterator. It makes use of the hasNext() and the next() methods to retrieve
different Candidate objects and displays them in the user interface (Figure 16.2).

```java
      ...

      ...

public void actionPerformed(ActionEvent e) {
  if (e.getActionCommand().equals(SearchManager.EXIT)) {
    System.exit(1);
  }
  if (e.getActionCommand().equals(SearchManager.SHOW_ALL)) {
```

```
AllCandidates ac = new AllCandidates();
String selectedCandidates =
  "Name — - Cert Type — - Location" + "\n" +
   " — _ _ _ _ _ _ _ _ _ _ _ _ _ _ _ _ ";
while (ac.hasNext()) {
  Candidate c = (Candidate) ac.next();
  selectedCandidates = selectedCandidates + "\n" +
    c.getName() + " - " +
    c.getCertificationType() + " - " +
    c.getLocation();
}
manager.setSelectedCandidates(selectedCandidates);
}
}
        ...
        ...
```

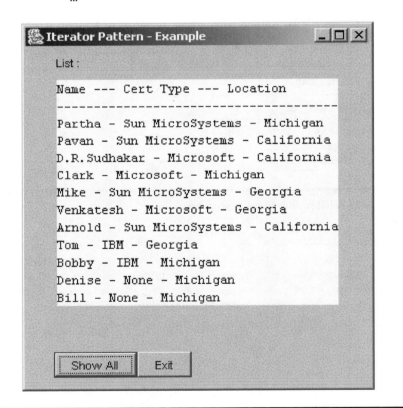

Figure 16.2 Client User Interface: Results Display

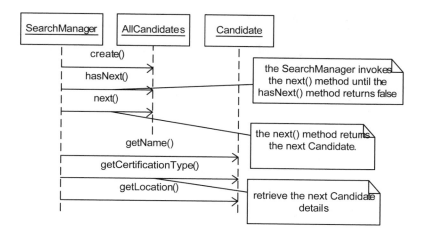

Figure 16.3   Internal Iterator: Message Flow

Figure 16.3 shows the application message flow when the user clicks on the Show All button.

EXAMPLE: EXTERNAL FILTERED ITERATOR

Let us enhance the example application to allow a user to filter candidates by the type of certification they have. This enhancement can be designed using an external filtered iterator.

In the case of an external iterator, the implementation is decoupled from the container and is kept inside a separate iterator class.

Let us design an external iterator class CertifiedCandidates (Listing 16.2) as an implementer of the built-in java.util.Iterator interface. As part of its constructor, the CertifiedCandidates iterator accepts a certification type and an instance of AllCandidates as input. It works as a filtered iterator for the candidate data contained in the AllCandidates container and returns the group of candidates with the specified certification type in a sequential manner. It implements the java.util.Iterator methods as follows:

- hasNext() – Checks to see if there are any more candidates with the specified certification type.
- next() – Returns the next candidate, if any, with the specified certification type. If there is none, it throws a NoSuchElementException exception. Ideally, a client would invoke the next() method only if a prior call to the hasNext() method returns true.
- remove() – Because the scope of the example application does not deal with deleting the profile of a candidate, this method implementation does nothing.

Besides the external iterator definition, as part of the new design, the container AllCandidates class needs to be modified (Listing 16.3) so that:

Listing 16.2 `CertifiedCandidates` **Class**

```java
public class CertifiedCandidates implements Iterator {
  private Vector v;
  AllCandidates ac;
  String certificationType;
  Candidate nextCandidate;
  Enumeration ec;
  public CertifiedCandidates(AllCandidates inp_ac,
      String certType) {
    ac = inp_ac;
    certificationType = certType;
    ec = inp_ac.getAllCandidates();
  }
  public boolean hasNext() {
    boolean matchFound = false;
    while (ec.hasMoreElements()) {
      Candidate tempObj = (Candidate) ec.nextElement();
      if (tempObj.getCertificationType().equals(
            certificationType)) {
        matchFound = true;
        nextCandidate = tempObj;
        break;
      }
    }
    if (matchFound == true) {
    } else {
      nextCandidate = null;
    }
    return matchFound;
  }
  public Object next() {
    if (nextCandidate == null) {
      throw new NoSuchElementException();
    } else {
      return nextCandidate;
    }
  }
  public void remove() {};
}
```

Listing 16.3 AllCandidates Class: Modified

```
public class AllCandidates {
  private Vector data;
  public AllCandidates() {
    initialize();
  }
  private void initialize() {
    /*
      Get data from db.
    */
    data = new Vector();
    FileUtil util = new FileUtil();
    Vector dataLines = util.fileToVector("Candidates.txt");
    for (int i = 0; i < dataLines.size(); i++) {
      String str = (String) dataLines.elementAt(i);
      StringTokenizer st = new StringTokenizer(str, ",");
      data.add(
        new Candidate(st.nextToken(), st.nextToken(),
                  st.nextToken()));
    }
  }
  public Enumeration getAllCandidates() {
    return data.elements();
  }
  public Iterator getCertifiedCandidates(String type) {
    return new CertifiedCandidates(this, type);
  }
}
```

- It is still responsible for reading the data file and carrying the data inside it, in the form of Candidate objects.
- It offers a public method getCertifiedCandidates(String type). This method creates and returns an iterator as an object of type java.util.Iterator. The client SearchManager can use this method when it wants to filter the candidate data by a specific certification type.

While creating an instance of the iterator CertifiedCandidates, the container AllCandidates sends itself as an argument to the iterator. The iterator uses this instance to access the data stored inside the AllCandidates container.

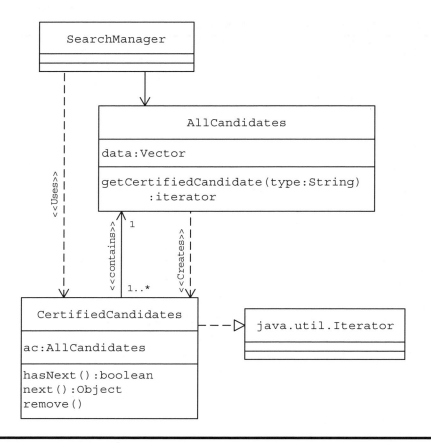

Figure 16.4   External Iterator: Class Association

The class diagram in Figure 16.4 shows the class association in the example application using an external filtered iterator.

The client `SearchManager` creates the necessary user interface to allow a user to select a certification type and to display the data (Figure 16.5). When a user selects a certification type and clicks on the `Retrieve` button, the `Search-Manager`:

- Creates an instance of the container `AllCandidates`. As part of its constructor, the `AllCandidates` object reads the data file and stores the data inside an instance variable data of type `Vector`. The client does not have to be aware of the data format or how the data is stored.
- Invokes the `getCertifiedCandidates(String type)` method on the `AllCandidates` container object by passing the selected certification type as an argument. The `getCertifiedCandidates` method creates an instance of the `CertifiedCandidates` class and returns it as an object of type `java.util.Iterator`.

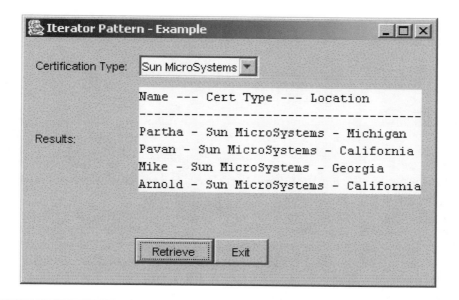

Figure 16.5 Client User Interface: Results Display

Once the Iterator object is received, the client SearchManager makes use of the hasNext() and the next() methods to retrieve the matching Candidate objects and displays them in the user interface (Figure 16.5).

```
          ...

          ...
public void actionPerformed(ActionEvent e) {
  if (e.getActionCommand().equals(SearchManager.EXIT)) {
    System.exit(1);
  }
  if (e.getActionCommand().equals(
        SearchManager.GET_CANDIDATES)) {
    String selection = manager.getCertificationType();
    AllCandidates ac = new AllCandidates();
    Iterator certCandidates =
      ac.getCertifiedCandidates(selection);
    String selectedCandidates =
      "Name — - Cert Type — - Location" + "\n" +
      " — — — — — — — — — — — — — — — — — ";
    while (certCandidates.hasNext()) {
      Candidate c = (Candidate) certCandidates.next();
      selectedCandidates = selectedCandidates + "\n" +
```

```
                  c.getName() + " - " + c.getCertificationType() +
                    " - " + c.getLocation();
              }
            manager.setSelectedCandidates(selectedCandidates);
          }
        }
                ...
                ...
```

The sequence diagram in Figure 16.6 shows the message flow when the user clicks on the `Retrieve` button.

In the case of both iterators, the client `SearchManager` does not contain any implementation that is tied to the way data is stored inside the container. All such implementation is completely moved out of the client to either the container (internal iterator) or to the iterator object (external iterator). The resulting design protects the client `SearchManager` from any changes to the way the data is maintained inside the container. For instance, if the internal representation of the data is changed so that the data is stored in an `array` or in some other form instead of a `Vector`, no changes are required to the client `SearchManager` implementation.

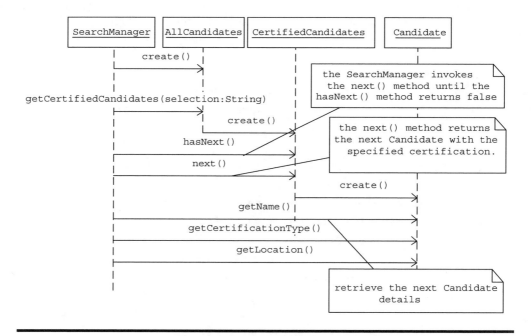

Figure 16.6   Message Flow When the External Iterator Is in Use

PRACTICE QUESTIONS

1. Design and implement a new filtered external iterator to filter the list of candidates by location and integrate it into the example application.
2. Consider the following author details XML data file contents.

```
<Authors>
  <Author>
    <Name>Auth_1</Name>
    <Books>
      <Book>
        <Title>B1</Title>
      </Book>
      <Book>
        <Title>B2</Title>
      </Book>
    <Books>
  </Author>
  <Author>
    <Name>Auth_2</Name>
      <Books>
        <Book>
          <Title>B3</Title>
        </Book>
        <Book>
          <Title>B4</Title>
        </Book>
    <Books>
  </Author>
</Authors>
```

Design an application to go through this list of authors and their books using the components listed in Table 16.3.
Design a client to use these two iterators together to access each author, the author's books and display them in a desired format.

Table 16.3 Application Components

Name	Role	Responsibility
AuthorCollection	Container	This class is responsible for reading from the physical XML file and holding the data. Offers methods to create two external iterators — AuthorIterator and BookIterator — on its data.
AuthorIterator	Iterator	An external iterator that returns all authors one by one in response to its next() method call.
BookIterator	Iterator	An external filtered iterator that returns all books written by a specified author one by one in response to its next() method call.

17

FLYWEIGHT

This pattern was previously described in GoF95.

DESCRIPTION

Every object can be viewed as consisting of one or both of the following two sets of information:

1. *Intrinsic Information* — The intrinsic information of an object is independent of the object context. That means the intrinsic information is the common information that remains constant among different instances of a given class. For example, the company information on a visiting card is the same for all employees.
2. *Extrinsic Information* — The extrinsic information of an object is dependent upon and varies with the object context. That means the extrinsic information is unique for every instance of a given class. For example, the employee name and title are extrinsic on a visiting card as this information is unique for every employee.

Consider an application scenario that involves creating a large number of objects that are unique only in terms of a few parameters. In other words, these objects contain some intrinsic, invariant data that is common among all objects. This intrinsic data needs to be created and maintained as part of every object that is being created. The overall creation and maintenance of a large group of such objects can be very expensive in terms of memory-usage and performance.

The Flyweight pattern can be used in such scenarios to design a more efficient way of creating objects.

The Flyweight pattern suggests separating all the intrinsic common data into a separate object referred to as a *Flyweight* object. The group of objects being created can share the **Flyweight** object as it represents their intrinsic state. This eliminates the need for storing the same invariant, intrinsic information in every object; instead it is stored only once in the form of a single **Flyweight** object. As a result, the client application can realize considerable savings in terms of the memory-usage and the time.

Table 17.1 Flyweight Requirements

Serial Number	Description
1	There exists only one object of a given flyweight kind and is shared by all the other appropriate objects.
2	Client objects should not be allowed to create flyweight instances directly. At the same time, client objects should have a way of accessing a required `Flyweight` object when needed.

When the Flyweight pattern is applied, it is important to make sure that the requirements listed in Table 17.1 are satisfied.

HOW TO DESIGN A FLYWEIGHT IN JAVA

One of the ways to design a flyweight in Java is to design it as a singleton similar to the `Flyweight` class in Figure 17.1.

DESIGN HIGHLIGHTS

- The `Flyweight` class is designed with a private constructor. This is to prevent client objects from creating `Flyweight` instances by directly accessing its constructor.
- In general, a singleton is expected to maintain only one instance of itself. That is, the singleton nature is at the *class type level*. When a flyweight is designed as a singleton, it exhibits the singleton nature at the *flyweight type level*, not at the class type level. In other words, the singleton

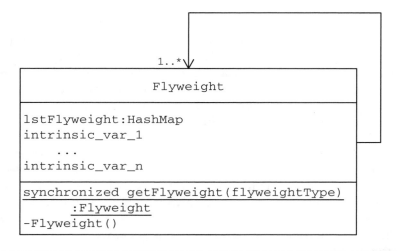

Figure 17.1 Flyweight as a Singleton

`Flyweight` maintains a single instance of itself for every possible flyweight type in the system. These flyweight objects are stored in the `lstFlyweight` static variable. This can be viewed as a variation of the Singleton pattern.

Whenever a client needs to create an instance of a given flyweight type, it invokes the static `getFlyweight` method, passing the required flyweight type as an argument. The `getFlyweight` method is designed as a synchronized class level method to make it thread safe.

As part of its implementation of the `getFlyweight` method, the `Flyweight` checks to see if an instance of itself corresponding to the requested flyweight type already exists in the `lstFlyweight  HashMap`.

- If it exists, the `Flyweight` returns the existing `Flyweight` object to the client.
- If it does not exist:
  - The `Flyweight` creates a new instance of itself corresponding to the requested flyweight type and adds it to the flyweights list maintained in the static `lstFlyweight HashMap` variable. Because the `getFlyweight` method is defined within the `Flyweight` class, it can access its private constructor to create an instance of itself.
  - It returns the newly created `Flyweight` object to the client.

The flyweight design discussed so far meets the requirements listed in Table 17.1. In general, a flyweight is designed solely to represent the intrinsic state of an object. Besides representing an object's intrinsic state, the flyweight contains the required data structures and the implementation to maintain different types of singleton `Flyweight` objects.

As an alternate design strategy, the responsibility of creating and maintaining different singleton `Flyweight` objects can be moved out of the `Flyweight` to a designated `FlyweightFactory`. The `Flyweight` can be designed as an inner class of the `FlyweightFactory` class. Since the `Flyweight` class is defined with a private constructor, external objects are prevented from creating its instances by directly invoking the constructor. But the `FlyweightFactory` can invoke the `Flyweight` class private constructor to create necessary `Flyweight` objects. This is because an outer class can access the private methods of its inner class.

In the new design (Figure 17.2), both the data structure (`lstFlyweight HashMap`) and the behavior (`getFlyweight` method) related to the creation and maintenance of singleton `Flyweight` objects are moved from the `Flyweight` class to the `FlyweightFactory` class. The `Flyweight` instances are used solely to represent an object's intrinsic state.

Whenever a client needs to create an instance of a given flyweight type, it invokes, the `getFlyweight` method on the singleton `FlyweightFactory` instance, passing the required flyweight type as an argument. The singleton `FlyweightFactory` object maintains the list of existing `Flyweight` objects in the `lstFlyweight` instance variable.

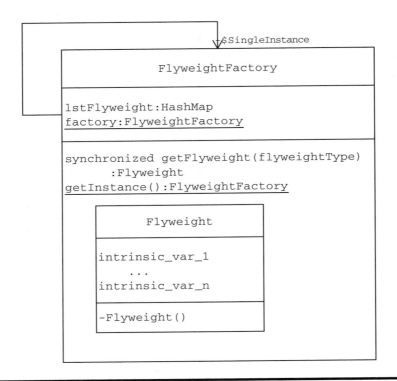

Figure 17.2   Flyweight as an Inner Class inside a Singleton Factory

As part of its implementation of the **getFlyweight** method, the **FlyweightFactory** checks to see if an instance of the **Flyweight** corresponding to the requested flyweight type already exists in the **lstFlyweight HashMap**.

- If it exists, the **FlyweightFactory** returns the existing **Flyweight** object to the client.
- If it does not exist:
  - The **FlyweightFactory** creates a new instance of the **Flyweight** corresponding to the requested flyweight type and adds it to the flyweights list maintained in the **lstFlyweight HashMap** variable.
  - It returns the newly created **Flyweight** object to the client.

The **FlyweighFactory** is designed as a singleton to prevent client objects from creating multiple instances of the **FlyweightFactory**, thereby creating multiple instances of a given flyweight kind.

Once the requested **Flyweight** object is received, the client can either:

- Create an object with the exclusive extrinsic data and associate the **Flyweight** object with it. This approach still results in the creation of a large number of objects but the design becomes more efficient as the intrinsic data is not duplicated in every object. Instead, it is kept inside a single shared **Flyweight** object (Design Approach I in the following example).

- Send the extrinsic data as part of a method call to the **Flyweight** object. This approach results in the creation of few objects with no duplication (Design Approach II in the following example).

EXAMPLE

To demonstrate the use of the Flyweight pattern, let us design an application that prints out the data for visiting cards of all the employees of a large organization with four major divisional offices. A typical visiting card can be assumed to have the following layout:

```
<<Name of the Employee>>
            <<Title>>
<<Company Name>>
<<Divisional_Office_Address_Lines>>
<<City>><<State>><<ZipCode>>
```

From the visiting card data layout, it can be observed that:

- The name and the title are unique for every employee and can be considered as the extrinsic data.
- The company name remains the same for all employees and every employee working under a divisional office is given the same divisional office address. Therefore the company name and division address part of a visiting card can be treated as the intrinsic data.

One of the simplest strategies for designing this example application is to create a **VCard** class representing a visiting card as in Figure 17.3. The **print()** method can be implemented to display the visiting card data.

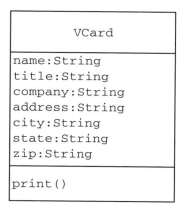

Figure 17.3   Visiting Card: Class Representation

Usually, there will be thousands of employees in a large organization and hence the application may need to create thousands of **VCard** objects. As discussed earlier, the address part of the **VCard** class remains constant for all employees working under a given divisional office. Hence, adapting the class representation depicted in Figure 17.3 could lead to duplicate data being created and maintained as part of every new **VCard** instance created. Using the Flyweight pattern, the need for storing the duplicate data can be eliminated.

DESIGN APPROACH I

In this approach, the extrinsic data is represented as an object and configured with a **Flyweight** object representing its intrinsic data.

Applying the Flyweight pattern, all the intrinsic data can be moved out of the **VCard** class into a separate **Flyweight** class. Let us define an interface **FlyweightIntr** to be implemented by the **Flyweight** class representing the visiting card intrinsic data.

```java
public interface FlyweightIntr {
  public String getCompany();
  public String getAddress();
  public String getCity();
  public String getState();
  public String getZip();
}
```

As we discussed under the "How to Design a Flyweight in Java" section earlier, let us define a singleton **FlyweightFactory** (Listing 17.1) with the responsibility of creating and maintaining single instances of different **Flyweight** objects corresponding to different divisions.

The actual **Flyweight** class can be defined within the **FlyweightFactory** as an inner class (Figure 17.4).

The design highlights of the concrete **Flyweight** and the **FlyweightFactory** classes are as follows:

■ The concrete **Flyweight** class is designed with a private constructor to prevent external objects from creating Flyweight instances directly by invoking its constructor.
■ The concrete **Flyweight** class is designed as an inner class within the **FlyweightFactory** to allow the **FlyweightFactory** to invoke its private constructor.
■ The **FlyweightFactory** is responsible for creating and managing different Flyweight instances. It maintains a list of different **Flyweight** objects inside the **lstFlyweight HashMap** instance variable. When a client requests a **Flyweight** object corresponding to a specific division, the **FlyweightFactory** checks the list of existing **Flyweight** objects to see if it is already created. If it is already created and available in the list, the **FlyweightFactory** returns the existing **Flyweight** object. If

Listing 17.1 Singleton `FlyweightFactory` Class with Inner `Flyweight` Class

```
//singleton Flyweight Factory
public class FlyweightFactory {
  private HashMap lstFlyweight;
  private static FlyweightFactory factory =
    new FlyweightFactory();
  private FlyweightFactory() {
    lstFlyweight = new HashMap();
  }
  public synchronized FlyweightIntr getFlyweight(
    String divisionName) {
    if (lstFlyweight.get(divisionName) == null) {
      FlyweightIntr fw = new Flyweight(divisionName);
      lstFlyweight.put(divisionName, fw);
      return fw;
    } else {
      return (FlyweightIntr) lstFlyweight.get(divisionName);
    }
  }
  public static FlyweightFactory getInstance() {
    return factory;
  }
  //Inner flyweight class
  private class Flyweight implements FlyweightIntr {
    private String company;
    private String address;
    private String city;
    private String state;
    private String zip;
    private void setValues(String cmp, String addr,
        String cty, String st, String zp) {
      company = cmp;
      address = addr;
      city = cty;
      state = st;
      zip = zp;
    }
```

(continued)

Listing 17.1 Singleton `FlyweightFactory` Class with Inner `Flyweight` Class (Continued)

```
  private Flyweight(String division) {
    //values are hard coded
    //for simplicity
    if (division.equals("North")) {
      setValues("CMP","addr1", "cty1","st1","10000");
    }
    if (division.equals("South")) {
      setValues("CMP","addr2", "cty2","st2","20000");
    }
    if (division.equals("East")) {
      setValues("CMP","addr3", "cty3","st3","30000");
    }
    if (division.equals("West")) {
      setValues("CMP","addr4", "cty4","st4","40000");
    }
  }
  public String getCompany() {
    return company;
  }
  public String getAddress() {
    return address;
  }
  public String getCity() {
    return city;
  }
  public String getState() {
    return state;
  }
  public String getZip() {
    return zip;
  }
 }//end of Flyweight
}//end of FlyweightFactory
```

not, the **FlyweightFactory** creates the requested **Flyweight** object, stores it inside the list and returns it to the client. Subsequently, when a client object requests a flyweight corresponding to the same division, the **Flyweight** object is not created. Instead, the corresponding **Flyweight**

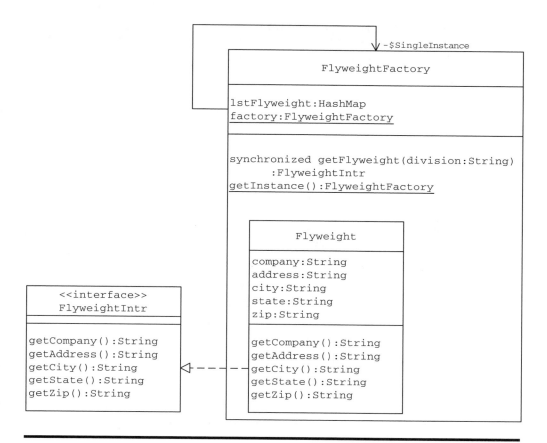

Figure 17.4 FlyweightFactory with an Inner Flyweight Class

object from the `lstFlyweight HashMap` instance variable is returned to the client.

■ The **FlyweightFactory** is designed as a singleton so that it guarantees the uniqueness of **Flyweight** objects.

After the intrinsic data is removed, the extrinsic data still remains within the **VCard** class (Listing 17.2). As part of its constructor, the **VCard** accepts a **Flyweight** instance representing its intrinsic data. The **print()** method displays extrinsic data from the **VCard** and intrinsic data from the associated **Flyweight** object.

With these objects in place, in order to print the visiting card data, a client object such as **FlyweightTest** (Listing 17.3):

1. Creates an instance of the singleton **FlyweightFactory**.
2. Requests an appropriate **Flyweight** object (for every employee) by invoking the **getFlyweight** method on the singleton **FlyweightFactory** instance, passing the division that the employee works for as an argument. In response, the **FlyweightFactory** returns a **Flyweight** instance corresponding to the specified division. Since the example organization is

Listing 17.2 VCard Class Using a Flyweight Object to Represent the Intrinsic Data

```java
public class VCard {
  String name;
  String title;
  FlyweightIntr objFW;
  public VCard(String n, String t, FlyweightIntr fw) {
    name = n;
    title = t;
    objFW = fw;
  }
  public void print() {
    System.out.println(name);
    System.out.println(title);
    System.out.println(objFW.getAddress() + "-" +
                        objFW.getCity() + "-" +
                        objFW.getState() + "-" +
                        objFW.getZip());
    System.out.println(" - - - - - - - - ");
  }
}
```

assumed to have only four divisions, there will be a maximum of four **Flyweight** objects created when the application is run.

3. Receives the requested **Flyweight** object and then associates the Flyweight with the **VCard** instance representing the extrinsic data by passing the **Flyweight** object as an argument to the **VCard** constructor.

Figure 17.5 shows the overall class association.

The following sequence diagram in Figure 17.6 depicts the message flow during the creation and display of the visiting card data of an employee working for a specific divisional office.

This approach requires the creation of a **VCard** object for every employee in addition to the four **Flyweight** objects. The fact that the intrinsic data is not duplicated in every **VCard** object results in savings in terms of the memory usage and the time it takes to create objects.

DESIGN APPROACH II

Extrinsic data passed to the flyweight as part of a method call and was not represented as an object (Listing 17.4).

This design approach requires the following two changes to the application design discussed in Design Approach I.

Listing 17.3   Client FlyweightTest Class

```
public class FlyweightTest {
  public static void main(String[] args) throws Exception {
  Vector empList = initialize();
    FlyweightFactory factory =
      FlyweightFactory.getInstance();
    for (int i = 0; i < empList.size(); i++) {
      String s = (String) empList.elementAt(i);
      StringTokenizer st = new StringTokenizer(s, ,"");
      String name = st.nextToken();
      String title = st.nextToken();
      String division = st.nextToken();
      FlyweightIntr flyweight =
        factory.getFlyweight(division);
      //associate the flyweight
      //with the extrinsic data object.
      VCard card = new VCard(name, title, flyweight);
      card.print();
    }
  }
  private static Vector initialize() {
        ...
        ...
  }
}
```

- The print method:
  - Needs to be moved from the **VCard** class to the **Flyweight** class.
  - Signature needs to be changed from

```
public void print()
```

   to

```
public void print(String name, String title)
```

   in order to accept the extrinsic data as arguments.
- Should be implemented to display the extrinsic data passed to it along with the intrinsic data it represents.

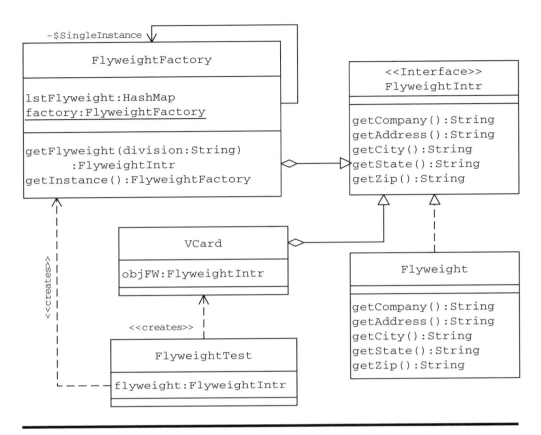

Figure 17.5   Design Approach I: Class Association

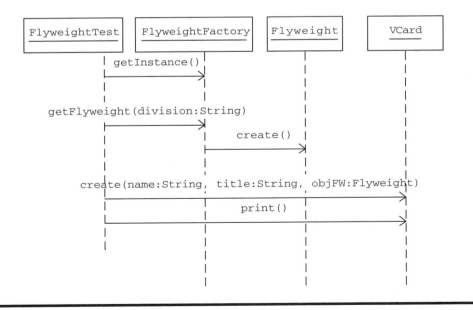

Figure 17.6   Message Flow: Design Approach I

Listing 17.4 Revised `FlyweightFactory` Class

```
public interface FlyweightIntr {
  public String getCompany();
  public String getAddress();
  public String getCity();
  public String getState();
  public String getZip();
  public void print(String name, String title);
}
//singleton Flyweight Factory
public class FlyweightFactory {

        ...

        ...

    //Inner flyweight class
    private class Flyweight implements FlyweightIntr {

        ...

        ...

      public void print(String name, String title) {
        System.out.println(name);
        System.out.println(title);
        System.out.println(getAddress() + "-" + getCity() +
                        "-" + getState() + "-" + getZip());
        System.out.println(" - - - - - - - - ");
      }
  }//end of Flyweight
}//end of FlyweightFactory
```

- **VCard** class:
  - Since the extrinsic data is to be passed to the **Flyweight** object and hence the **VCard** class is no longer needed, this class can be removed from the design.

In the new design, the client **FlyweightTest** (Listing 17.5):

- First creates an instance of the singleton **FlyweightFactory**. The design and implementation of the **FlyweightFactory** remains the same as in Design Approach I.
- For every employee, the application requests the **FlyweightFactory** for an appropriate **Flyweight** object by passing the division that the employee works for.

Listing 17.5 Client FlyweightTest Class

```
public class FlyweightTest {
  public static void main(String[] args) throws Exception {
    Vector empList = initialize();
    FlyweightFactory factory =
      FlyweightFactory.getInstance();
    for (int i = 0; i < empList.size(); i++) {
      String s = (String) empList.elementAt(i);
      StringTokenizer st = new StringTokenizer(s, ,"");
      String name = st.nextToken();
      String title = st.nextToken();
      String division = st.nextToken();
      FlyweightIntr flyweight =
        factory.getFlyweight(division);
      //pass the extrinsic data
      //as part of a method call.
      flyweight.print(name, title);
    }
  }
      ...
      ...
}
```

■ Once the requested **Flyweight** object is received, the client invokes the print method on the **Flyweight** object by passing the extrinsic data (employee name and title).

Figure 17.7 shows the class association in the revised design.

The sequence diagram in Figure 17.8 depicts the message flow in the new design during the creation and display of the visiting card data of an employee working for a specific divisional office.

Because the extrinsic data is not designed as an object, this approach requires the creation of only four **Flyweight** objects, each corresponding to a divisional office with no duplication. This substantially reduces the memory usage and the time required for the object creation.

PRACTICE QUESTIONS

1. Let us consider an online job site that receives XML data files from different employers with current openings in their organizations. When the number of vacancies is small, employers can enter details online. When the number

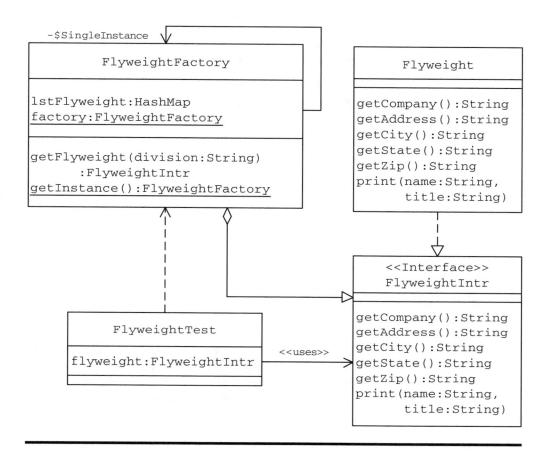

Figure 17.7   Design Approach II: Class Association

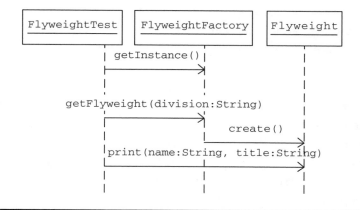

Figure 17.8   Message Flow: Design Approach II

of vacancies is large, employers upload details in the form of an XML file. Once the XML file is received, it needs to be parsed and processed. Let us assume the XML file to have the following details:

a. Job title
b. Minimum qualifications
c. Medical insurance
d. Dental insurance
e. Vision care
f. 401K
g. Minimum number of hours of work
h. Paid vacation
i. Employer name
j. Employer address

In general, details from (c) through (j) are all considered to be the same for all jobs posted by a given employer. Apply the Flyweight pattern to design the process of parsing the input XML file and creating different **Job** objects.

2. A computer user in a typical organization is associated with a user account. A user account can be part of one or more groups. Permissions on different resources (such as servers, printers, etc.) are defined at the group level. Users get all the permissions defined for all groups that their accounts are part of. Let us consider an organization with three different user groups — **Administrators**, **FieldOfficers** and **SalesReps**. Further assume that the organization is in the process of migrating user accounts from one server to a different server environment. As part of this process, all user accounts are first exported to an XML file as follows.

```
<Users>
  <User>
    <UserName>PKuchana</UserName>
    <Password>PKuchana</Password>
    <Group>FieldOfficers</Group>
    <Permissions>
      <Permission>Perm1</Permission>
      <Permission>Perm2</Permission>
    </Permissions>
  </User>
  <User>
    <UserName>VKuchana</UserName>
    <Password>VKuchana</Password>
    <Group>SalesReps</Group>
    <Permissions>
      <Permission>Perm1</Permission>
      <Permission>Perm4</Permission>
```

```
    </Permissions>
  </User>
    ...
    ...
</Users>
```

It is to be noted that permissions for all accounts in a given group are the same. This can be considered as the intrinsic data. The user name and the password details vary from user to user and should be treated as extrinsic data.

User accounts in the new server environment are created using the exported XML file. Make any necessary assumptions and design an application using the Flyweight pattern to parse the XML file to create different user account objects.

18

VISITOR

This pattern was previously described in GoF95.

DESCRIPTION

The Visitor pattern is useful in designing an operation across a heterogeneous collection of objects of a class hierarchy. The Visitor pattern allows the operation to be defined without changing the class of any of the objects in the collection.

To accomplish this, the Visitor pattern suggests defining the operation in a separate class referred to as a *visitor* class. This separates the operation from the object collection that it operates on. For every new operation to be defined, a new `visitor` class is created. Since the operation is to be performed across a set of objects, the visitor needs a way of accessing the public members of these objects. This requirement can be addressed by implementing the following two design ideas.

Design Idea 1

Every `visitor` class that operates on objects of the same set of classes can be designed to implement a corresponding `VisitorInterface` interface. A typical `VisitorInterface` declares a set of `visit(ObjectType)` methods, one for each object type from the object collection. Each of these methods is meant for processing instances of a specific class. For example, if the object collection consists of objects of `ClassA` and `ClassB`, then the `VisitorInterface` interface would declare the following two methods:

    visit(ClassA objClassA)

for processing `ClassA` objects.

    visit(ClassB objClassB)

for processing `ClassB` objects.

Every object from the object collection makes a call to the respective `visit(ObjectType)` method, passing itself as an argument. A typical implementer (visitor) of the `VisitorInterface` can access the information required for the operation it is designed for by accessing the public members (methods and attributes) of the object instance passed to it through the `visit` method call.

Design Idea 2

Classes of objects from the object collection need to define a method:

```
accept(visitor)
```

A client interested in executing the visitor operation needs to:

- Create an instance of the implementer (visitor) of the `VisitorInterface` interface that is designed to carry out the required operation.
- Create the object collection and invoke the `accept(visitor)` method on every member of the object collection by passing the visitor instance created above.

As part of the `accept(visitor)` method implementation, every object in the object collection invokes the `visit(ObjectType)` method on the visitor instance. Inside the `visit(ObjectType)` method, the visitor gathers the required data from the object collection to perform the operation it is designed for.

DEFINING NEW OPERATIONS ON THE OBJECT COLLECTION

Whenever a new operation is to be defined across the object collection, a new `visitor` class needs to be created with implementation for the new operation. The `visitor` class needs to implement all of the `visit(ObjectType)` methods declared in the `VisitorInterface` interface to process different types of objects.

With this design, defining a new operation does not require any changes to the classes of the object collection.

ADDING OBJECTS OF A NEW TYPE TO THE COLLECTION

Whenever a new type of object is to be added to the object collection and is to be referred within the scope of an already existing visitor operation:

- The class of the object must provide a method similar to `accept(visitor)` and as part of this method implementation it should invoke the `visit(ObjectType)` method on the `visitor` object passing itself as an argument to it.
- A corresponding `visit(ObjectType)` method needs to be added to the `VisitorInterface` interface and needs to be implemented by all the concrete `visitor` classes.

This means that for objects of an existing class to be added to the object collection and to be considered within the scope of an existing visitor operation, the class needs to be altered to implement a method similar to `accept(visitor)`, if one does not already exist. This implies that when the Visitor pattern is applied for the first time to a class, one should have access to its source code or the class needs to be subclassed to add the `accept(visitor)` method implementation.

EXAMPLE

Let us design an application to define operations over a collection of different `Order` objects. Orders can be of different types. Let us consider three different types of orders as follows:

- *Overseas order* — Order from countries other than the United States. Additional shipping and handling is charged for this type of order.
- *California order* — U.S. order with shipping address in California. Additional sales tax is charged on this type of order.
- *Non-California order* — U.S. order with shipping address not in California. Additional sales tax is not applicable.

DESIGN APPROACH I

Let us assume that we would like to define an operation `getMaxCAOrderAmount` to find the top dollar amount on a California order. We can define a generic `Order` class as in the following Figure 18.1.

The `Order` class maintains a static member variable `orderTotalCA` to keep track of the order amount. Whenever a new order is created, the `orderTotalCA` member variable is updated with the order amount if the new order amount is greater than the old order total already available in the `orderTotalCA` static member variable.

Let us say that we would like to add more methods, such as `getMinCAOrderAmount`, `getCAOrderTotal`, `getMinNonCAOrderAmount`, `getMaxOverseasOrderAmount`, etc., to find out different types of order amounts.

The `Order` class code needs to be altered for each such new operation. As a result, the class can quickly become cluttered (Figure 18.2).

```
┌─────────────────────────────────────┐
│              Order                   │
├─────────────────────────────────────┤
│ orderTotalCA:double                  │
├─────────────────────────────────────┤
│ getMaxCAOrderAmount():double         │
└─────────────────────────────────────┘
```

Figure 18.1   `Order` Class

```
┌─────────────────────────────────────────────┐
│                    Order                      │
├─────────────────────────────────────────────┤
│ orderTotalCA:double                           │
│ orderTotalNonCA:double                        │
├─────────────────────────────────────────────┤
│ getMaxCAOrderAmount():double                  │
│ getMinCAOrderAmount():double                  │
│ getMaxNonCAOrderAmount():double               │
│ getMinNonCAOrderAmount():double               │
└─────────────────────────────────────────────┘
```

Figure 18.2 Order Class with New Methods

DESIGN APPROACH II

Since orders are of three different types, we can design three subclasses of the Order class, each representing a specific order type (Figure 18.3).

With this new design, related operations can be kept within an appropriate Order subclass. Although this class structure is more manageable and less cluttered, it suffers from the following two limitations:

- There is no appropriate place to define operations involving different order types.
- Whenever a new operation is to be defined in any Order class, it requires a change to the class code.

DESIGN APPROACH III (COMPOSITE PATTERN)

During the discussion of the Composite pattern, we defined operations on an object collection containing objects from a class hierarchy. A Composite object is designed to maintain this object collection and operate on this collection.

Applying the Composite pattern, we can define a composite OrderComposite class as in Figure 18.4 to define operations on a collection of different order objects.

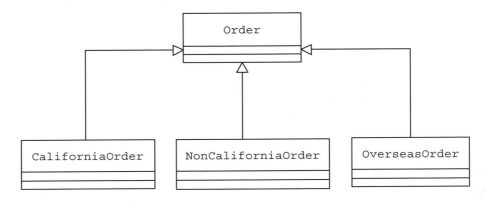

Figure 18.3 Order Class Hierarchy

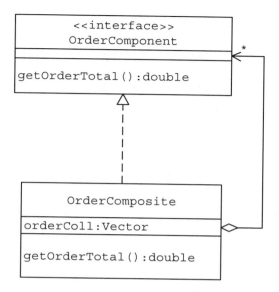

Figure 18.4 `OrderComposite`: **Class Structure**

The attribute `orderColl` can be used to store different types of `Order` objects and the `getOrderTotal` iterates over this collection to retrieve and sum up different order amounts.

This design does not fully address the limitations of the Design Approach II. It allows the definition of an operation over a heterogeneous collection of objects, but it requires changes to the `OrderComposite` hierarchy classes whenever a new operation is to be added.

DESIGN APPROACH IV (THE VISITOR PATTERN)

Let us define an order class hierarchy as in Figure 18.5 with an interface `Order` at the top of the hierarchy and three of its implementers — `CaliforniaOrder`, `NonCaliforniaOrder` and `OverseasOrder` — each representing a specific order type. The `Order` interface declares a method `accept(OrderVisitor)`. Each of the `Order` implementers provides implementation for the `accept(OrderVisitor)` method (Listings 18.1 through 18.4).

The `VisitorInterface` can be designed as a Java interface that declares a set of `visit(OrderType)` methods, one for each class in the order class hierarchy. In other words, these methods are meant to process different types of orders.

```
public interface VisitorInterface {
  public void visit(NonCaliforniaOrder nco);
  public void visit(CaliforniaOrder co);
  public void visit(OverseasOrder oo);
}
```

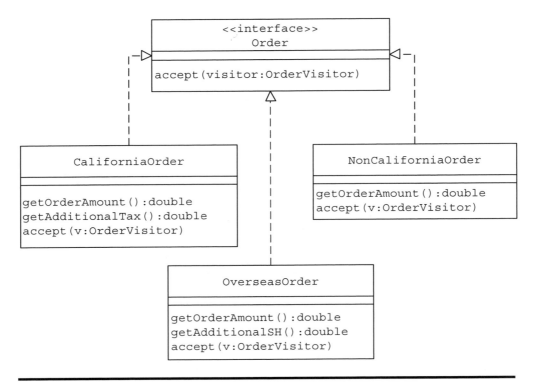

Figure 18.5 Order Class Hierarchy

Listing 18.1 Order Interface

```java
public interface Order {
  public void accept(OrderVisitor v);
}
```

Let us define a visitor OrderVisitor as an implementer of the VisitorInterface (Figure 18.6 and Listing 18.5), to calculate the sum of all order totals.

As part of its implementation of the VisitorInterface methods, the OrderVisitor retrieves the order amount, any additional tax or shipping and handling amounts from different Order objects and maintains a cumulative sum of these amounts in a private instance variable orderTotal.

Application Flow

When run, the client OrderManager creates an instance of the OrderVisitor and displays the necessary user interface to allow a user to create different types of orders (Figure 18.7).

Listing 18.2 `CaliforniaOrder` Class

```
public class CaliforniaOrder implements Order {
  private double orderAmount;
  private double additionalTax;
  public CaliforniaOrder() {
  }
  public CaliforniaOrder(double inp_orderAmount,
      double inp_additionalTax) {
    orderAmount = inp_orderAmount;
    additionalTax = inp_additionalTax;
  }
  public double getOrderAmount() {
    return orderAmount;
  }
  public double getAdditionalTax() {
    return additionalTax;
  }
  public void accept(OrderVisitor v) {
    v.visit(this);
  }
}
```

Listing 18.3 `NonCaliforniaOrder` Class

```
public class NonCaliforniaOrder implements Order {
  private double orderAmount;
  public NonCaliforniaOrder() {
  }
  public NonCaliforniaOrder(double inp_orderAmount) {
    orderAmount = inp_orderAmount;
  }
  public double getOrderAmount() {
    return orderAmount;
  }
  public void accept(OrderVisitor v) {
    v.visit(this);
  }
}
```

Listing 18.4 `OverseasOrder` Class

```java
public class OverseasOrder implements Order {
  private double orderAmount;
  private double additionalSH;
  public OverseasOrder() {
  }
  public OverseasOrder(double inp_orderAmount,
      double inp_additionalSH) {
    orderAmount = inp_orderAmount;
    additionalSH = inp_additionalSH;
  }
  public double getOrderAmount() {
    return orderAmount;
  }
  public double getAdditionalSH() {
    return additionalSH;
  }
  public void accept(OrderVisitor v) {
    v.visit(this);
  }
}
```

Every time a user enters the order data and clicks on the `CreateOrder` button, the client `OrderManager` (Listing 18.6):

■ Creates an `Order` object with the input data.
■ Invokes the `accept(OrderVisitor)` method on the `Order` object by passing the `OrderVisitor` object. The `Order` object internally calls the `OrderVisitor` visit method by passing itself as an argument. The `OrderVisitor` retrieves the required order amount, tax and shipping amounts using the public methods defined by different `Order` classes and adds these amounts, in a cumulative manner, to the order total kept inside the private instance variable `orderTotal`.

When the `GetTotal` button is clicked, the client `OrderManager` invokes the `getOrderTotal` method of the `OrderVisitor`. The `OrderVisitor` simply returns the value stored in the `orderTotal` instance variable, which is the total value of all orders created.

The sequence diagram in Figure 18.8 depicts the message flow, when the client `OrderManager` makes use of the visitor `OrderVisitor` to calculate the grand total of a set of different order amounts. In order to keep the diagram simple, only one type of order is included.

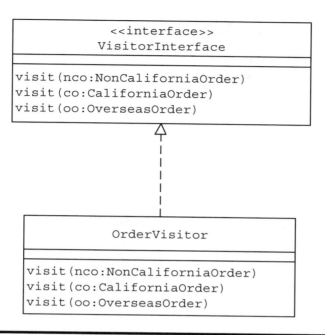

Figure 18.6 `OrderVisitor` Class Structure

DEFINING A NEW OPERATION ON THE ORDER OBJECT COLLECTION

Defining a new operation on the order object collection requires the creation of a new visitor. The new visitor needs to implement the `VisitorInterface` interface providing implementation for different `visit(OrderType)` methods to process different types of `Order` objects.

ADDING A NEW ORDER TYPE TO THE COLLECTION

If a new type of object (a new class) is to be added to the object structure such as a `DiscountOrder` that implements the `Order` interface, then a corresponding `visit(DiscountOrder)` method needs to be added to the `VisitorInter-face` and needs to be implemented by the `OrderVisitor` class.

PRACTICE QUESTIONS

1. As part of our discussion of the Composite pattern, we designed a composite `DirComponent` class. Redesign the `DirComponent` class operations applying the Visitor pattern.
2. The Practice Questions section of the Composite pattern discussion lists three applications involving operations on a heterogeneous object collection. Apply the Visitor pattern in designing these operations.

Listing 18.5 `OrderVisitor` Class

```
class OrderVisitor implements VisitorInterface {
  private Vector orderObjList;
  private double orderTotal;
  public OrderVisitor() {
    orderObjList = new Vector();
  }
  public void visit(NonCaliforniaOrder inp_order) {
    orderTotal = orderTotal + inp_order.getOrderAmount();
  }
  public void visit(CaliforniaOrder inp_order) {
    orderTotal = orderTotal + inp_order.getOrderAmount() +
                 inp_order.getAdditionalTax();
  }
  public void visit(OverseasOrder inp_order) {
    orderTotal = orderTotal + inp_order.getOrderAmount() +
                 inp_order.getAdditionalSH();
  }
  public double getOrderTotal() {
    return orderTotal;
  }
}
```

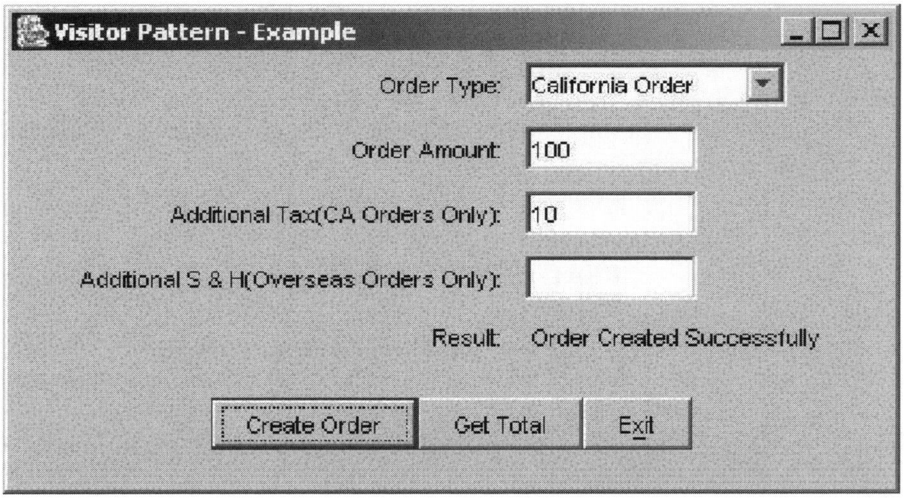

Figure 18.7   Order Manager: User Interface to Create Orders

Listing 18.6 OrderManager Class

```
        ...
        ...
public void actionPerformed(ActionEvent e) {
  String totalResult = null;
  if (e.getActionCommand().equals(OrderManager.EXIT)) {
    System.exit(1);
  }
  if (e.getActionCommand().equals(OrderManager.CREATE_ORDER)
      ) {
    //get input values
    String orderType = objOrderManager.getOrderType();
    String strOrderAmount =
      objOrderManager.getOrderAmount();
    String strTax = objOrderManager.getTax();
    String strSH = objOrderManager.getSH();
    double dblOrderAmount = 0.0;
    double dblTax = 0.0;
    double dblSH = 0.0;
    if (strOrderAmount.trim().length() == 0) {
      strOrderAmount = "0.0";
    }
    if (strTax.trim().length() == 0) {
      strTax = "0.0";
    }
    if (strSH.trim().length() == 0) {
      strSH = "0.0";
    }
    dblOrderAmount =
      new Double(strOrderAmount).doubleValue();
    dblTax = new Double(strTax).doubleValue();
    dblSH = new Double(strSH).doubleValue();
    //Create the order
    Order order = createOrder(orderType, dblOrderAmount,
                    dblTax, dblSH);
```

(continued)

Listing 18.6 `OrderManager` **Class (Continued)**

```
    //Get the Visitor
    OrderVisitor visitor =
      objOrderManager.getOrderVisitor();
    //accept the visitor instance
    order.accept(visitor);
    objOrderManager.setTotalValue(
      " Order Created Successfully");
  }
  if (e.getActionCommand().equals(OrderManager.GET_TOTAL)) {
    //Get the Visitor
    OrderVisitor visitor =
      objOrderManager.getOrderVisitor();
    totalResult = new Double(
                  visitor.getOrderTotal()).toString();
    totalResult = " Orders Total = " + totalResult;
    objOrderManager.setTotalValue(totalResult);
  }
}
public Order createOrder(String orderType,
    double orderAmount, double tax, double SH) {
  if (orderType.equalsIgnoreCase(OrderManager.CA_ORDER))
  {
    return new CaliforniaOrder(orderAmount, tax);
  }
  if (orderType.equalsIgnoreCase(
    OrderManager.NON_CA_ORDER)) {
    return new NonCaliforniaOrder(orderAmount);
  }
  if (orderType.equalsIgnoreCase(
      OrderManager.OVERSEAS_ORDER)) {
    return new OverseasOrder(orderAmount, SH);
  }
  return null;
}
        ...
        ...
```

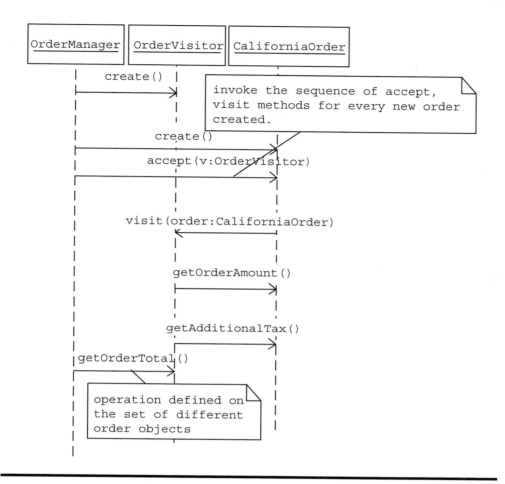

Figure 18.8 Application Message Flow

VI

STRUCTURAL PATTERNS

Structural patterns primarily:

- Deal with objects delegating responsibilities to other objects. This results in a layered architecture of components with low degree of coupling.
- Facilitate interobject communication when one object is not accessible to the other by normal means or when an object is not usable because of its incompatible interface.
- Provide ways to structure an aggregate object so that it is created in full and to reclaim system resources in a timely manner.

Chapter	Pattern Name	Description
19	Decorator	Extends the functionality of an object in a manner that is transparent to its clients without using inheritance.
20	Adapter	Allows the conversion of the interface of a class to another interface that clients expect. This allows classes with incompatible interfaces to work together.
21	Chain of Responsibility	Avoids coupling a (request) sender object to a receiver object. Allows a sender object to pass its request along a chain of objects without knowing which object will actually handle the request.
22	Façade	Provides a higher-level interface to a subsystem of classes, making the subsystem easier to use.
23	Proxy	Allows a separate object to be used as a substitute to provide controlled access to an object that is not accessible by normal means.
24	Bridge	Allows the separation of an abstract interface from its implementation. This eliminates the dependency between the two, allowing them to be modified independently.
25	Virtual Proxy	Facilitates the mechanism for delaying the creation of an object until it is actually needed in a manner that is transparent to its client objects.
26	Counting Proxy	When there is a need to perform supplemental operations such as logging and counting before or after a method call on an object, recommends encapsulating the supplemental functionality into a separate object.
27	Aggregate Enforcer	Recommends that when an aggregate object is instantiated, all of its member variables representing the set of constituting objects must also be initialized. In other words, whenever an aggregate object is instantiated it must be constructed in full.
28	Explicit Object Release	Recommends that when an object goes out of scope, all of the system resources tied up with that object must be released in a timely manner.
29	Object Cache	Stores the results of a method call on an object in a repository. When client objects invoke the same method, instead of accessing the actual object, results are returned to the client object from the repository. This is done mainly to achieve a faster response time.

19

DECORATOR

This pattern was previously described in GoF95.

DESCRIPTION

The Decorator Pattern is used to extend the functionality of an object *dynamically* without having to change the original class source or using inheritance. This is accomplished by creating an object wrapper referred to as a *Decorator* around the actual object.

CHARACTERISTICS OF A DECORATOR

- The Decorator object is designed to have the same interface as the underlying object. This allows a client object to interact with the Decorator object in exactly the same manner as it would with the underlying actual object.
- The Decorator object contains a reference to the actual object.
- The Decorator object receives all requests (calls) from a client. It in turn forwards these calls to the underlying object.
- The Decorator object adds some additional functionality before or after forwarding requests to the underlying object. This ensures that the additional functionality can be added to a given object externally at runtime without modifying its structure.

Typically, in object-oriented design, the functionality of a given class is extended using inheritance. Table 19.1 lists the differences between the Decorator pattern and inheritance.

EXAMPLE

Let us revisit the message logging utility we built while discussing the Factory Method and the Singleton patterns earlier. Our design mainly comprised a Logger interface and two of its implementers — FileLogger and ConsoleLogger — to log messages to a file and to the screen, respectively. In addition, we had the LoggerFactory class with a factory method in it.

Table 19.1   Decorator Pattern versus Inheritance

Decorator Pattern	Inheritance
Used to extend the functionality of a particular object.	Used to extend the functionality of a class of objects.
Does not require subclassing.	Requires subclassing.
Dynamic.	Static.
Runtime assignment of responsibilities.	Compile time assignment of responsibilities.
Prevents the proliferation of subclasses leading to less complexity and confusion.	Could lead to numerous subclasses, exploding class hierarchy on specific occasions.
More flexible.	Less flexible.
Possible to have different decorator objects for a given object simultaneously. A client can choose what capabilities it wants by sending messages to an appropriate decorator.	Having subclasses for all possible combinations of additional capabilities, which clients expect out of a given class, could lead to a proliferation of subclasses.
Easy to add any combination of capabilities. The same capability can even be added twice.	Difficult.

The `LoggerFactory` is not shown in Figure 19.1. This is because it is not directly related to the current example discussion.

Let us suppose that some of the clients are now in need of logging messages in new ways beyond what is offered by the message logging utility. Let us consider the following two small features that clients would like to have:

- Transform an incoming message to an HTML document.
- Apply a simple encryption by transposition logic on an incoming message.

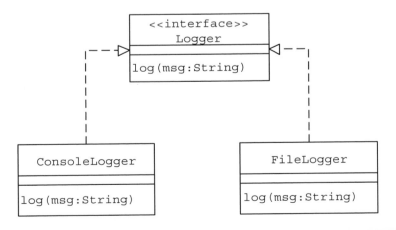

Figure 19.1   Logging Utility Class Hierarchy

Table 19.2 Subclasses of `FileLogger` and `ConsoleLogger`

Subclass	Parent Class	Functionality
HTMLFileLogger	FileLogger	Transform an incoming message to an HTML document and store it in a log file.
HTMLConsLogger	ConsoleLogger	Transform an incoming message to an HTML document and display it on the screen.
EncFileLogger	FileLogger	Apply encryption on an incoming message and store it in a log file.
EncConsLogger	ConsoleLogger	Apply encryption on an incoming message and display it on the screen.

Typically, in object-oriented design, without changing the code of an existing class, new functionality can be added by applying inheritance, i.e., by subclassing an existing class and overriding its methods to add the required new functionality.

Applying inheritance, we would subclass both the `FileLogger` and the `ConsoleLogger` classes to add the new functionality with the following set of new subclasses (Table 19.2).

As can be seen from the class diagram in Figure 19.2, a set of four new subclasses are added in order to add the new functionality. If we had additional `Logger` types (for example a `DBLogger` to log messages to a database), it would lead to more subclasses. With every new feature that needs to be added, there will be a multiplicative growth in the number of subclasses and soon we will have an exploding class hierarchy.

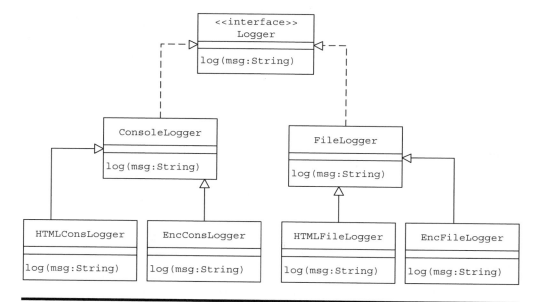

Figure 19.2 The Resulting Class Hierarchy after Applying Inheritance to Add the New Functionality

Listing 19.1 `LoggerDecorator` Class

```
public class LoggerDecorator implements Logger {
  Logger logger;
  public LoggerDecorator(Logger inp_logger) {
    logger = inp_logger;
  }
  public void log(String DataLine) {
    /*
      Default implementation
      to be overriden by subclasses.
    */
    logger.log(DataLine);
  }
}//end of class
```

The Decorator pattern comes to our rescue in situations like this. The Decorator pattern recommends having a wrapper around an object to extend its functionality by object composition rather than by inheritance.

Applying the Decorator pattern, let us define a default root decorator LoggerDecorator (Listing 19.1) for the message logging utility with the following characteristics:

- The LoggerDecorator contains a reference to a Logger instance. This reference points to a Logger object it wraps.
- The LoggerDecorator implements the Logger interface and provides the basic default implementation for the log method, where it simply forwards an incoming call to the Logger object it wraps. Every subclass of the LoggerDecorator is hence guaranteed to have the log method defined in it.

It is important for every logger decorator to have the log method because a decorator object *must* provide the same interface as the object it wraps. When clients create an instance of the decorator, they interact with the decorator in exactly the same manner as they would with the original object using the same interface.

Let us define two subclasses, HTMLLogger and EncryptLogger, of the default LoggerDecorator as shown in Figure 19.3.

CONCRETE LOGGER DECORATORS

HTMLLogger

The HTMLLogger (Listing 19.2) overrides the default implementation of the log method. Inside the log method, this decorator transforms an incoming message to an HTML document and then sends it to the Logger instance it contains for logging.

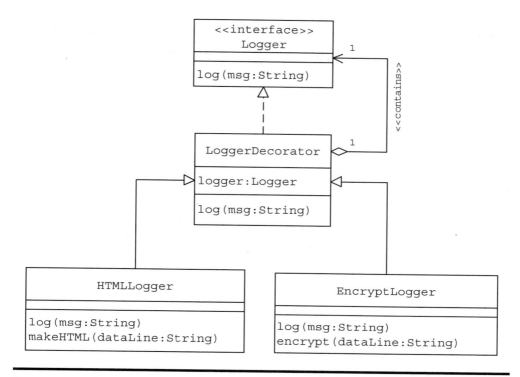

Figure 19.3 **The Decorator Class Structure for the Logging Utility to Add the New Functionality**

EncryptLogger

Similar to the HTMLLogger, the EncryptLogger (Listing 19.3) overrides the log method. Inside the log method, the EncryptLogger implements simple encryption logic by shifting characters to the right by one position and sends it to the Logger instance it contains for logging.

The class diagram in Figure 19.4 shows how different classes are arranged while applying the Decorator pattern.

In order to log messages using the newly designed decorators a client object (Listing 19.4) needs to:

- Create an appropriate Logger instance (FileLogger/ConsoleLogger) using the LoggerFactory factory method.
- Create an appropriate LoggerDecorator instance by passing the Logger instance created in Step 1 as an argument to its constructor.
- Invoke methods on the LoggerDecorator instance as it would on the Logger instance.

Figure 19.5 shows the message flow when a client object uses the HTMLLogger object to log messages.

Listing 19.2 `HTMLLogger` **Class**

```java
public class HTMLLogger extends LoggerDecorator {
  public HTMLLogger(Logger inp_logger) {
    super(inp_logger);
  }
  public void log(String DataLine) {
    /*
      Added functionality
    */
    DataLine = makeHTML(DataLine);
    /*
      Now forward the encrypted text to the FileLogger
      for storage
    */
    logger.log(DataLine);
  }
  public String makeHTML(String DataLine) {
    /*
      Make it into an HTML document.
    */
    DataLine = "<HTML><BODY>" + "<b>" + DataLine +
      "</b>" + "</BODY></HTML>";
    return DataLine;
  }
}//end of class
```

ADDING A NEW MESSAGE LOGGER

In case of the message logging utility, applying the Decorator pattern does *not* lead to a large number of subclasses with a fast growing class hierarchy as it would if we apply inheritance. Let us say that we have another Logger type, say a DBLogger, that logs messages to a database. In order to apply the HTML transformation or to apply the encryption before logging to the database, all that a client object needs to do is to follow the list of steps mentioned earlier. Because the DBLogger would be of the Logger type, it can be sent to any of the HTMLLogger or the EncryptLogger classes as an argument while invoking their constructors.

Listing 19.3 `EncryptLogger` **Class**

```
public class EncryptLogger extends LoggerDecorator {
  public EncryptLogger(Logger inp_logger) {
    super(inp_logger);
  }
  public void log(String DataLine) {
    /*
      Added functionality
    */
    DataLine = encrypt(DataLine);
    /*
      Now forward the encrypted text to the FileLogger
      for storage
    */
    logger.log(DataLine);
  }
  public String encrypt(String DataLine) {
    /*
      Apply simple encryption by Transposition...
      Shift all characters by one position.
    */
    DataLine = DataLine.substring(DataLine.length() - 1) +
               DataLine.substring(0, DataLine.length() - 1);
    return DataLine;
  }
}//end of class
```

ADDING A NEW DECORATOR

From the example it can be observed that a `LoggerDecorator` instance contains a reference to an object of type `Logger`. It forwards requests to this `Logger` object before or after adding the new functionality. Since the base `LoggerDecorator` class implements the `Logger` interface, an instance of `LoggerDecorator` or any of its subclasses can be treated as of the `Logger` type. Hence a `LoggerDecorator` can contain an instance of any of its subclasses and forward calls to it. In general, a decorator object can contain another decorator object and can forward calls to it. In this way, new decorators, and hence new functionality, can be built by wrapping an existing decorator object.

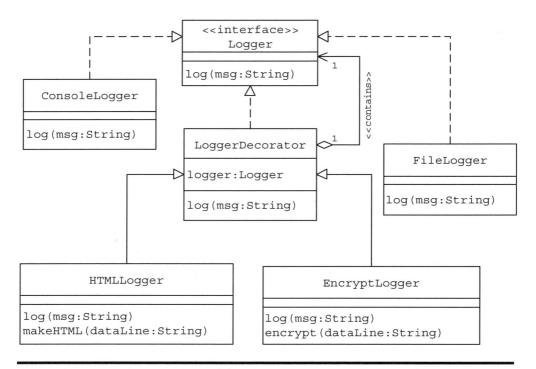

Figure 19.4   Association between Different Logger Classes and Logger Decorators

Listing 19.4   Client `DecoratorClient` Class

```java
class DecoratorClient {
  public static void main(String[] args) {
    LoggerFactory factory = new LoggerFactory();
    Logger logger = factory.getLogger();
    HTMLLogger hLogger = new HTMLLogger(logger);
    //the decorator object provides the same interface.
    hLogger.log("A Message to Log");
    EncryptLogger eLogger = new EncryptLogger(logger);
    eLogger.log("A Message to Log");
  }
}//End of class
```

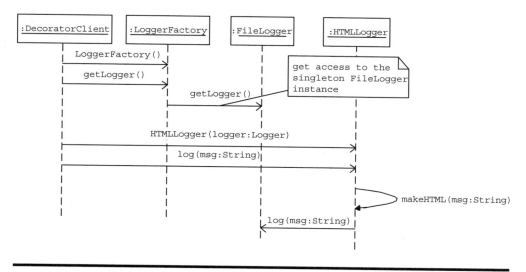

Figure 19.5   Message Flow When a Client Uses the HTMLLogger (Decorator) to Log a Message

PRACTICE QUESTIONS

1. Create a `FileReader` utility class with a method to read lines from a file.
2. The `EncryptLogger` in the example application encrypts a given text by shifting characters to the right by one position. Create a Decorator `DecryptFileReader` for the `FileReader` to add the decryption functionality, after reading data from a file.
3. Enhance `DecoratorClient` class to do the following:
   - Write a message to a file using the `EncryptLogger`.
   - Read using the `DecryptFileReader` decorator to display the message in an unencrypted form.

20

ADAPTER

This pattern was previously described in GoF95.

DESCRIPTION

In general, clients of a class access the services offered by the class through its interface. Sometimes, an existing class may provide the functionality required by a client, but its interface may not be what the client expects. This could happen due to various reasons such as the existing interface may be too detailed, or it may lack in detail, or the terminology used by the interface may be different from what the client is looking for.

In such cases, the existing interface needs to be converted into another interface, which the client expects, preserving the reusability of the existing class. Without such conversion, the client will not be able to use the functionality offered by the class. This can be accomplished by using the Adapter pattern. The Adapter pattern suggests defining a wrapper class around the object with the incompatible interface. This wrapper object is referred as an *adapter* and the object it wraps is referred to as an *adaptee*. The adapter provides the required interface expected by the client. The implementation of the adapter interface converts client requests into calls to the adaptee class interface. In other words, when a client calls an adapter method, internally the adapter class calls a method of the adaptee class, which the client has no knowledge of. This gives the client indirect access to the adaptee class. Thus, an adapter can be used to make classes work together that could not otherwise because of incompatible interfaces.

The term *interface* used in the discussion above:

- Does *not* refer to the concept of an interface in Java programming language, though a class's interface may be declared using a Java interface.
- Does *not* refer to the user interface of a typical GUI application consisting of windows and GUI controls.
- Does refer to the programming interface that a class exposes, which is meant to be used by other classes. As an example, when a class is designed as an abstract class or a Java interface, the set of methods declared in it makes up the class's interface.

CLASS ADAPTERS VERSUS OBJECT ADAPTERS

Adapters can be classified broadly into two categories — class adapters and object adapters — based on the way a given adapter is designed.

Class Adapter

A class adapter is designed by subclassing the adaptee class. In addition, a class adapter implements the interface expected by the client object. When a client object invokes a class adapter method, the adapter internally calls an adaptee method that it inherited.

Object Adapter

An object adapter contains a reference to an adaptee object. Similar to a class adapter, an object adapter also implements the interface, which the client expects. When a client object calls an object adapter method, the object adapter invokes an appropriate method on the adaptee instance whose reference it contains. Table 20.1 lists the differences between class and object adapters in detail.

EXAMPLE

Let us build an application to validate a given customer address. This application can be part of a larger customer data management application.

Let us define a Customer class as in Figure 20.1 (Listing 20.1).

Different client objects can create a Customer object and invoke the isValidAddress method to check the validity of the customer address. For the purpose of validating the address, the Customer class expects to make use of an address validator class that provides the interface declared in the AddressValidator interface (Listing 20.2).

Let us define one such validator USAddress to validate a given U.S. address as in Listing 20.3.

The USAddress class is designed to implement the AddressValidator interface so that Customer objects can use USAddress instances as part of the customer address validation process without any problems (Listing 20.4). Figure 20.2 shows the class association.

Let us say that the application needs to be enhanced to deal with customers from Canada as well. This requires a validator for verifying the addresses of Canadian customers. Let us assume that a utility class CAAddress, with the required functionality to validate a given Canadian address, already exists.

From the CAAddress class implementation in Listing 20.5, it can be observed that the CAAddress does offer the validation service required by the Customer class, but the interface it offers is different from what the Customer class expects.

The CAAddress class offers an isValidCanadianAddr method, but the Customer expects an isValidAddress method as declared in the AddressValidator interface.

This incompatibility in the interface makes it difficult for a Customer object to use the existing CAAddress class. One of the options is to change the interface

Table 20.1   Class Adapters versus Object Adapters

Class Adapters	Object Adapters
Based on the concept of inheritance.	Uses object composition.
Can be used to adapt the interface of the adaptee only. Cannot adapt the interfaces of its subclasses, as the adapter is statically linked with the adaptee when it is created.	Can be used to adapt the interface of the adaptee and all of its subclasses.
Because the adapter is designed as a subclass of the adaptee, it is possible to override some of the adaptee's behavior. **Note:** In Java, a subclass cannot override a method that is declared as final in its parent class.	Cannot override adaptee methods. **Note:** Literally, cannot "override" simply because there is no inheritance. But wrapper functions provided by the adapter can change the behavior as required.
The client will have some knowledge of the adatee's interface as the full public interface of the adaptee is visible to the client.	The client and the adaptee are completely decoupled. Only the adapter is aware of the adaptee's interface.
In Java applications: Suitable when the expected interface is available in the form of a Java interface and not as an abstract or concrete class. This is because the Java programming language allows only single inheritance. Since a class adapter is designed as a subclass of the adaptee class, it will not be able to subclass the interface class (representing the expected interface) also, if the expected interface is available in the form of an abstract or concrete class.	In Java applications: Suitable even when the interface that a client object expects is available in the form of an abstract class. Can also be used if the expected interface is available in the form of a Java interface. Or When there is a need to adapt the interface of the adaptee and also all of its subclasses.
In Java applications: Can adapt methods with protected access specifier.	In Java applications: Cannot adapt methods with protected access specifier, unless the adapter and the adaptee are designed to be part of the same package.

```
┌─────────────────────────────────┐
│           Customer              │
├─────────────────────────────────┤
│                                 │
├─────────────────────────────────┤
│ isValidAddress():boolean        │
└─────────────────────────────────┘
```

Figure 20.1   Customer Class

Listing 20.1 Customer Class

```
class Customer {
  public static final String US = "US";
  public static final String CANADA = "Canada";
  private String address;
  private String name;
  private String zip, state, type;
  public boolean isValidAddress() {

      ...

      ...

  }
  public Customer(String inp_name, String inp_address,
              String inp_zip, String inp_state,
              String inp_type) {
    name = inp_name;
    address = inp_address;
    zip = inp_zip;
    state = inp_state;
    type = inp_type;
  }
}//end of class
```

Listing 20.2 AddressValidator as an Interface

```
public interface AddressValidator {
  public boolean isValidAddress(String inp_address,
      String inp_zip, String inp_state);
}//end of class
```

of the CAAddress class, but it is not advisable as there could be other applications using the CAAddress class in its current form. Changing the CAAddress class interface can affect all of those current clients of the CAAddress class.

Applying the Adapter pattern, a class adapter CAAddressAdapter can be designed as a subclass of the CAAddress class implementing the AddressValidator interface (Figure 20.3 and Listing 20.6).

Because the adapter CAAddressAdapter implements the AddressValidator interface, client objects can access the adapter CAAddressAdapter objects without any problems. When a client object invokes the isValidAddress method

Listing 20.3   USAddress Class

```
class USAddress implements AddressValidator {
  public boolean isValidAddress(String inp_address,
      String inp_zip, String inp_state) {
    if (inp_address.trim().length() < 10)
      return false;
    if (inp_zip.trim().length() < 5)
      return false;
    if (inp_zip.trim().length() > 10)
      return false;
    if (inp_state.trim().length() != 2)
      return false;
    return true;
  }
}//end of class
```

Listing 20.4   Customer Class Using the USAddress Class

```
class Customer {
        ...

        ...

  public boolean isValidAddress() {
    //get an appropriate address validator
    AddressValidator validator = getValidator(type);
    //Polymorphic call to validate the address
    return validator.isValidAddress(address, zip, state);
  }
  private AddressValidator getValidator(String custType) {
    AddressValidator validator = null;
    if (custType.equals(Customer.US)) {
      validator = new USAddress();
    }
    return validator;
  }
}//end of class
```

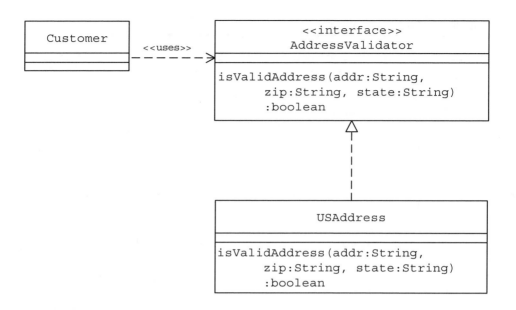

Figure 20.2 `Customer/USAddress Validator:` Class Association

Listing 20.5 `CAAdress` Class with Incompatible Interface

```
class CAAddress {
  public boolean isValidCanadianAddr(String inp_address,
     String inp_pcode, String inp_prvnc) {
   if (inp_address.trim().length() < 15)
     return false;
   if (inp_pcode.trim().length() != 6)
     return false;
   if (inp_prvnc.trim().length() < 6)
     return false;
   return true;
  }
}//end of class
```

on the adapter instance, the adapter internally translates it into a call to the inherited `isValidCanadianAddr` method.

Inside the `Customer` class, the `getValidator` private method needs to be enhanced so that it returns an instance of the `CAAddressAdapter` in the case of Canadian customers (Listing 20.7). The polymorphic call on the returned object (inside the `isValidAddress` method) does not need to be changed as both the `USAddress` and `CAAddressAdapter` implement the same `AddressValidator` interface.

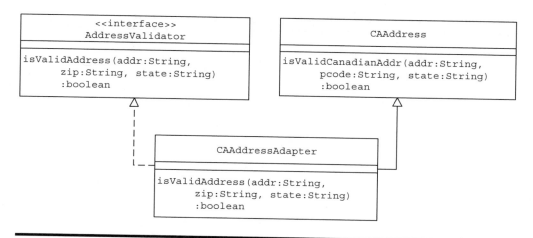

Figure 20.3   Class Adapter for the CAAddress Class

Listing 20.6   CAAddressAdapter as a Class Adapter

```
public class CAAddressAdapter extends CAAddress
  implements AddressValidator {
  public boolean isValidAddress(String inp_address,
      String inp_zip, String inp_state) {
    return isValidCanadianAddr(inp_address, inp_zip,
        inp_state);
  }
}//end of class
```

The combination of the CAAddressAdapter design and the polymorphic call on an object of the AddressValidator (that declares the expected interface) type object enables the Customer to make use of the services of the CAAddress class that has an incompatible interface.

The class diagram in Figure 20.4 shows the overall class association.

The sequence diagram in Figure 20.5 depicts the message flow when the CAAddressAdapter is designed as a class adapter.

ADDRESS ADAPTER AS AN OBJECT ADAPTER

While discussing the design of the address adapter as a class adapter, we saw that the AddressValidator interface expected by the client is defined in the form of a Java interface. Now let us assume that the client expects the Address-Validator interface to be available as an abstract class instead of a Java interface (Listing 20.8). Because the adapter CAAdapter has to provide the interface declared by the AddressValidator abstract class, the adapter needs to be

Listing 20.7 Customer Class Using the CAAddressAdapter Class

```
class Customer {

     ...

     ...

   public boolean isValidAddress() {
     //get an appropriate address validator
     AddressValidator validator = getValidator(type);
     //Polymorphic call to validate the address
     return validator.isValidAddress(address, zip, state);
   }
   private AddressValidator getValidator(String custType) {
     AddressValidator validator = null;
     if (custType.equals(Customer.US)) {
       validator = new USAddress();
     }
     if (type.equals(Customer.CANADA)) {
       validator = new CAAddressAdapter();
     }
     return validator;
   }
}//end of class
```

designed to subclass the AddressValidator abstract class and implement its abstract methods (Listing 20.9).

Because multiple inheritance is not supported in Java, now the adapter CAAddressAdapter cannot subclass the existing CAAddress class as it has already used its only chance to subclass from another class.

Applying the *object* Adapter pattern, the CAAddressAdapter can be designed to contain an instance of the adaptee CAAddress (Figure 20.6 and Listing 20.10). This adaptee instance is passed to the adapter by its clients, when the adapter is first created. In general, the adaptee instance contained by an object adapter may be provided in the following two ways:

- Clients of the object adapter may pass the adaptee instance to the adapter. This approach is more flexible in choosing the class to adapt from, but then the client may become aware of the adaptee or the fact of adaptation. It is more suitable when the adapter needs any specific state from the adaptee object besides its behavior.
- The adapter may create the adaptee instance on its own. This approach is relatively less flexible and suitable when the adapter does not need any specific state from the adaptee, but needs only its behavior.

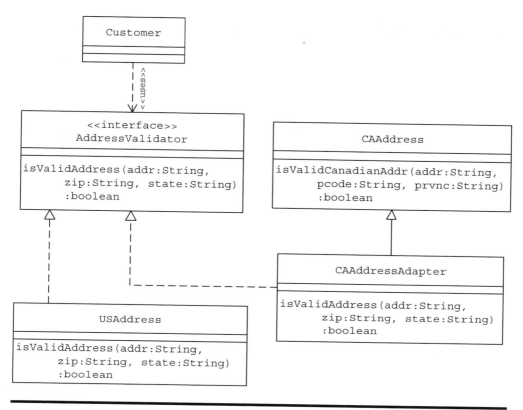

Figure 20.4   Address Validation Application: Using Class Adapter

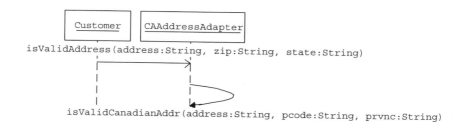

Figure 20.5   Address Validation Message Flow: Using Class Adapter

Listing 20.8   AddressValidator as an Abstract Class

```
public abstract class AddressValidator {
  public abstract boolean isValidAddress(String inp_address,
     String inp_zip, String inp_state);
}//end of class
```

Listing 20.9 CAAddressAdapter Class

```
class CAAddressAdapter extends AddressValidator {
    ...

    ...
  public CAAddressAdapter(CAAddress address) {
    objCAAddress = address;
  }
  public boolean isValidAddress(String inp_address,
      String inp_zip, String inp_state) {
      ...

      ...

  }
}//end of class
```

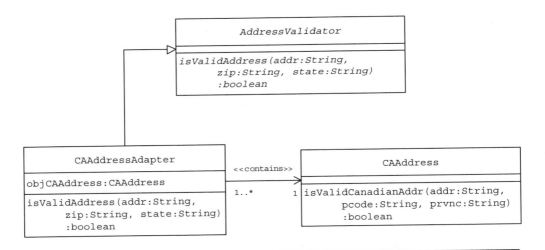

Figure 20.6 Object Adapter for the CAAddress Class

When a client object invokes the isValidAddress method on a CAAddressAdapter (adapter) instance, the adapter internally calls the isValidCanadianAddr method on the CAAddress (adaptee) instance it contains.

The class diagram in Figure 20.7 shows the overall class association when the address adapter is designed as an object adapter.

From the example application design it can be observed that an adapter enables the Customer (client) class to access the services offered by the CAAddress (adaptee) with an incompatible interface.

The sequence diagram in Figure 20.8 shows the message flow when the adapter CAAddressAdapter is designed as an object adapter.

Listing 20.10 `CAAddressAdapter` **as an Object Adapter**

```
class CAAddressAdapter extends AddressValidator {
  private CAAddress objCAAddress;
  public CAAddressAdapter(CAAddress address) {
    objCAAddress = address;
  }
  public boolean isValidAddress(String inp_address,
      String inp_zip, String inp_state) {
    return objCAAddress.isValidCanadianAddr(inp_address,
        inp_zip, inp_state);
  }
}//end of class
```

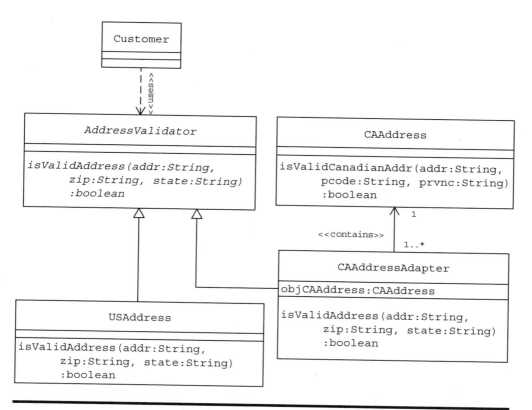

Figure 20.7   Address Validation Application: Using Object Adapter

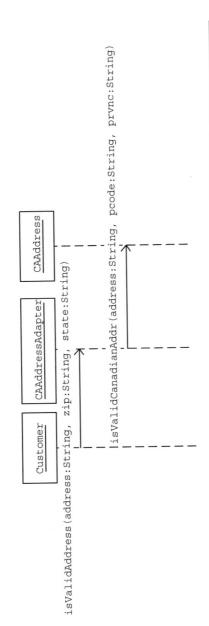

Figure 20.8 Address Validation Message Flow: Using Object Adapter

PRACTICE QUESTIONS

1. During the discussion of the Factory Method pattern, we designed a message logging class FileLogger with a method log(String) that can be used by client objects to log messages (Figure 20.9). Let us assume that a client LoggerClient expects a message logging class to provide an interface as follows:

```
public abstract class LoggerIntr{
  public abstract boolean logMessage(String msg);
}//end of class
```

   How would you design an adapter, say FileLoggerAdapter, to adapt the FileLogger class's existing interface?

2. In the above practice question, if the client LoggerClient expects a message logging class to provide an interface as follows:

```
public interface LoggerIntr{
  public boolean logMessage(String msg);
}//end of interface
```

   Can you design the adapter FileLoggerAdapter as a class adapter, an object adapter or both?

3. Design two subclasses — HTMLFileLogger and EncFileLogger — of the FileLogger as in Table 20.2. Each of these subclasses override the log(String) method of the parent FileLogger class to provide the required functionality. Assume that the client LoggerClient requires the functionality offered by the FileLogger and also its subclasses. If the client LoggerClient expects the message logging class to provide an interface as follows:

```
public interface LoggerIntr{
  public boolean logMessage(String msg);
}//end of interface
```

   Can you design the adapter FileLoggerAdapter as a class adapter, an object adapter or both? Why?

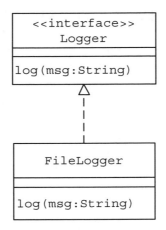

Figure 20.9   Messaging Logging Utility

Table 20.2   `FileLogger` Subclasses

Subclass	Functionality
HTMLFileLogger	Transform an incoming message into an HTML document and store it in a log file.
EncFileLogger	Apply encryption on an incoming message and store it in a log file.

21

CHAIN OF RESPONSIBILITY

This pattern was previously described in GoF95.

DESCRIPTION

The Chain of Responsibility pattern (CoR) recommends a low degree of coupling between an object that sends out a request and the set of potential request handler objects.

When there is more than one object that can handle or fulfill a client request, the CoR pattern recommends giving each of these objects a chance to process the request in some sequential order. Applying the CoR pattern in such a case, each of these potential handler objects can be arranged in the form of a chain, with each object having a pointer to the next object in the chain. The first object in the chain receives the request and decides either to handle the request or to pass it on to the next object in the chain. The request flows through all objects in the chain one after the other until the request is handled by one of the handlers in the chain or the request reaches the end of the chain without getting processed.

As an example, if A → B → C are objects capable of handling the request, in this order, then A should handle the request or pass on to B without determining whether B can fulfill the request. Upon receiving the request, B should either handle it or pass on to C. When C receives the request, it should either handle the request or the request falls off the chain without getting processed. In other words, a request submitted to the chain of handlers may not be fulfilled even after reaching the end of the chain.

The following are some of the important characteristics of the CoR pattern:

- The set of potential request handler objects and the order in which these objects form the chain can be decided dynamically at runtime by the client depending on the current state of the application.
- A client can have different sets of handler objects for different types of requests depending on its current state. Also, a given handler object may need to pass on an incoming request to different other handler objects depending on the request type and the state of the client application. For these communications to be simple, all potential handler objects should provide a consistent interface. In Java this can be accomplished by having

different handlers implement a common interface or be subclasses of a common abstract parent class.

■ The client object that initiates the request or any of the potential handler objects that forward the request do not have to know about the capabilities of the object receiving the request. This means that neither the client object nor any of the handler objects in the chain need to know which object will actually fulfill the request.

■ Request handling is not guaranteed. This means that the request may reach the end of the chain without being fulfilled. The following example presents a scenario where a purchase request submitted to a chain of handlers is not approved even after reaching the end of the chain.

EXAMPLE

Let us consider an application to simulate the purchase request (PR) authorization process in a typical organization. In general, a PR needs to be authorized by an appropriate management representative before an order to a vendor can be created. Let us consider an organization with four levels of management personnel listed in Table 21.1 who can authorize a PR with an amount less than their authorization limit.

We can define different classes (Listing 21.1) to represent each management level listed in Table 21.1.

Let us define a `PurchaseRequest` class (Figure 21.1 and Listing 21.2) that represents a purchase request.

A given PR could be authorized or handled by any of the management representatives listed in Table 21.1. In other words, each of the four classes representing different levels of management is a potential handler for a given PR and hence it is not advisable to tie a `PurchaseRequest` instance to any of the handlers. By using the CoR pattern, a low-coupling association between a `PurchaseRequest` object and the set of potential handler objects can be achieved.

Applying the CoR pattern, let us define an abstract `PRHandler` class (Listing 21.3) that declares the common interface to be offered by all of the potential PR handlers (Figure 21.2).

Each of the handlers can now be redesigned as a subclass of the abstract `PRHandler` class (Listing 21.4). As part of its implementation, each handler object compares the PR amount with the authorization limit of the management representative it represents. If the PR amount is less than the authorization limit, it

Table 21.1 Levels of PR Authorization

Management Level	Authorization Limit
Branch Manager	$25,000
Regional Director	$100,000
Vice President	$200,000
President and COO	$400,000

Listing 21.1   Classes Representing Different Management Levels

```
class BranchManager {
  static double LIMIT = 25000;
        …

        …
}//End of class
class RegionalDirector {
  static double LIMIT = 100000;
        …

        …
}//End of class
class VicePresident {
  static double LIMIT = 200000;
        …

        …
}//End of class
class PresidentCOO {
  static double LIMIT = 400000;
        …

        …
}//End of class
```

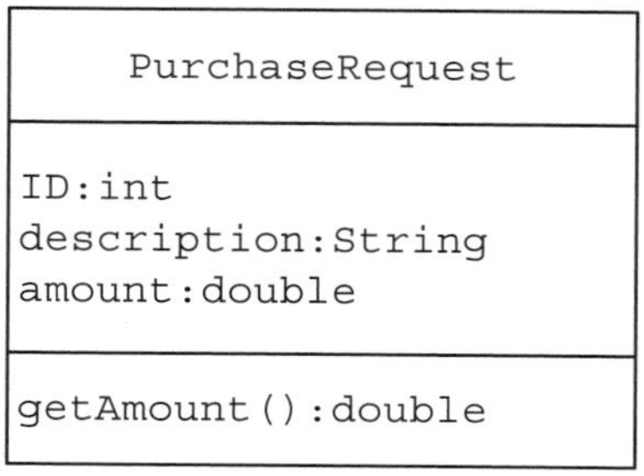

```
┌─────────────────────────────┐
│      PurchaseRequest         │
├─────────────────────────────┤
│ ID:int                       │
│ description:String           │
│ amount:double                │
├─────────────────────────────┤
│ getAmount():double           │
└─────────────────────────────┘
```

Figure 21.1   `PurchaseRequest` Class Representation

authorizes the PR. If not, it passes the PR authorization request to the next handler in the chain.

To authorize a PR, a client (Listing 21.5) would:

1. Create a set of potential PR authorization request handler objects and arrange them in an ascending order by authorization limit. Connect each handler to the next handler using the setNextHandler(PRHandler) method. This results in a chain of potential PR authorization request handlers (Figure 21.3).

Listing 21.2 `PurchaseRequest` Class

```java
class PurchaseRequest {
  private int ID;
  private String description;
  private double amount;
  public PurchaseRequest(int id, String desc, double amt) {
    ID = id;
    description = desc;
    amount = amt;
  }
  public double getAmount() {
    return amount;
  }
  public String toString() {
    return ID + ":" + description;
  }
}
```

Listing 21.3 Abstract `PRHandler` Class

```java
public abstract class PRHandler {
  private PRHandler nextHandler;
  private String handlerName;
  public PRHandler(String name) {
    handlerName = name;
  }
  public String getName() {
    return handlerName;
  }
  public abstract boolean authorize(PurchaseRequest request);
  public PRHandler getNextHandler() {
    return nextHandler;
  }
  public void setNextHandler(PRHandler handler) {
    nextHandler = handler;
  };
}
```

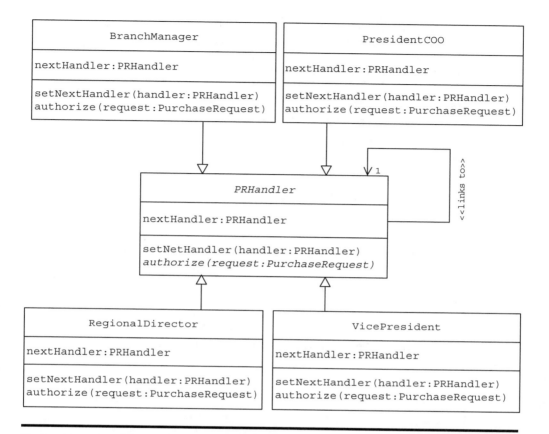

Figure 21.2 Purchase Request Approver Hierarchy

2. Send a PR authorization request to the first PRHandler object in the chain by invoking the authorize method on that object, passing the purchase request as an argument. As can be seen from the implementation of different PRHandler subclasses, a PR is authorized if the PR amount is less than the authorization limit of a specific handler. Otherwise, the authorization request is passed on to the next potential handler in the chain. If the PR is authorized by one of the handlers, it is not passed on to the next handler in the chain. The PR authorization is not guaranteed in this example. If the request reaches the last handler and the PR amount is higher than the authorization limit of the last handler, an appropriate message is displayed and the PR remains unauthorized.

When the client PRManager is run, output similar to the following is displayed:

```
Branch Manager Robin has authorized the PR - 1:Office Supplies
V.P. Kate has authorized the PR - 2:HardWare Procurement
PR - 3:AD Campaign couldn't be authorized.
Executive Board needs to be consulted for approval
reason: Amount too large
```

The sequence diagram in Figure 21.4 shows the message flow when a $150,000 PR authorization request is sent to the chain of potential handler objects.

Listing 21.4 PRHandler Concrete Subclasses

```java
class BranchManager extends PRHandler {
  static double LIMIT = 25000;
  public BranchManager(String name) {
    super(name);
  }
  public boolean authorize(PurchaseRequest request) {
    double amount = request.getAmount();
    if (amount <= LIMIT) {
      System.out.println(" Branch Manager " + getName() +
                        " has authorized the PR - " + request);
      return true;
    } else {
      //forward the request to the next handler
      return getNextHandler().authorize(request);
    }
  }
}//End of class
class RegionalDirector extends PRHandler {
  static double LIMIT = 100000;
  public RegionalDirector(String name) {
    super(name);
  }
  public boolean authorize(PurchaseRequest request) {
    double amount = request.getAmount();
    if (amount <= LIMIT) {
      System.out.println(" Regional Director " + getName() +
                        " has authorized the PR - " +
                        request);
      return true;
    } else {
      //forward the request to the next handler
      return getNextHandler().authorize(request);
    }
  }
}//End of class
```

(continued)

Listing 21.4 `PRHandler` Concrete Subclasses (Continued)

```java
class VicePresident extends PRHandler {
  static double LIMIT = 200000;
  public VicePresident(String name) {
    super(name);
  }
  public boolean authorize(PurchaseRequest request) {
    double amount = request.getAmount();
    if (amount <= LIMIT) {
      System.out.println(" V.P. " + getName() +
                         " has authorized the PR - " + request);
      return true;
    } else {
      //forward the request to the next handler
      return getNextHandler().authorize(request);
    }
  }
}//End of class
class PresidentCOO extends PRHandler {
  static double LIMIT = 400000;
  public PresidentCOO(String name) {
    super(name);
  }
  public boolean authorize(PurchaseRequest request) {
    double amount = request.getAmount();
    if (amount <= LIMIT) {
      System.out.println(" President & COO " + getName() +
                         " has authorized the PR - " + request);
      return true;
    } else {
      System.out.println("PR - " + request +
                         " couldn't be authorized.\n " +
                         "Executive Board needs to be " +
                         "consulted for approval \n" +
                         "reason: Amount too large");
      return false;
    }
  }
}//End of class
```

Listing 21.5   Client PRManager Class

```
public class PRManager {
  private BranchManager branchManager;
  private RegionalDirector regionalDirector;
  private VicePresident vicePresident;
  private PresidentCOO coo;
  public static void main(String[] args) {
    PRManager manager = new PRManager();
    manager.createAuthorizationFlow();
    PurchaseRequest request =
      new PurchaseRequest(1, "Office Supplies",10000);
    manager.branchManager.authorize(request);
    request = new PurchaseRequest(2, "HardWare Procurement",
            175000);
    manager.branchManager.authorize(request);
    request = new PurchaseRequest(3, "AD Campaign",800000);
    manager.branchManager.authorize(request);
  }
  public void createAuthorizationFlow() {
    branchManager = new BranchManager("Robin");
    regionalDirector = new RegionalDirector("Oscar");
    vicePresident = new VicePresident("Kate");
    coo = new PresidentCOO("Drew");
    branchManager.setNextHandler(regionalDirector);
    regionalDirector.setNextHandler(vicePresident);
    vicePresident.setNextHandler(coo);
  }
}//End of class
```

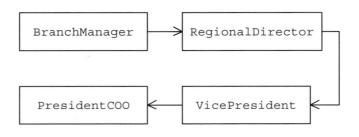

Figure 21.3   Chain of PR Authorization Request Handlers

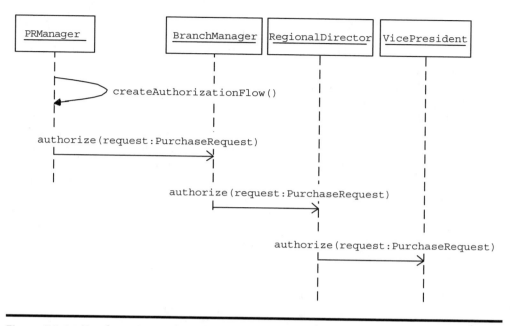

Figure 21.4   Purchase Request Authorization: Message Flow

PRACTICE QUESTIONS

1. In the example above, a given PR always needs to be approved by only one person in the chain with a higher approval limit than the PR amount. For example, a PR for $50,000 needs approval from a regional director (with approval limit $100,000). It does not need the approval of a branch manager (with approval limit $25,000). In general, if a PR is to be approved by one person in the approval chain, it does not need the approval of any other person in the chain. In some cases, it may be required that a given purchase request be approved by all individuals with the approval limit less than the purchase request amount until it is approved by an individual with a higher approval limit than the PR amount. Modify the example application to implement this purchase request approval process.

2. Let us consider an ISP (Internet service provider) with three levels of technical support as follows:

   a. *Service Level I (Basic)* — Aimed at resolving basic connectivity problems such as incorrect/forgotten passwords, incorrect dial-up number, etc.

   b. *Service Level II* — When the Basic Service Level I support team cannot resolve a problem, it will be sent to the Service Level II team. For problem resolution, the Service Level II team assumes the user to have a good understanding of computer concepts.

   c. *Service Level III* — When the Service Level I and II teams cannot resolve a problem, it will be sent to the Service Level III team. A technician schedules an appointment with the user for problem resolution at the user site.

Create an application using the CoR pattern to simulate the three-layer technical support structure explained above.

3. Let us consider an IT consulting firm with three levels of resource coordinators as follows:
   - Local resource manager
   - Regional resource coordinator
   - Corporate resource director

   Whenever a consultant becomes available, that consultant's profile is first sent to the local resource manager to see if there is any requirement locally that matches the skill set of the consultant. If there is no requirement that matches with the consultant's skill set, the consultant's details are sent to the regional resource coordinator.

   The regional resource coordinator, with access to a much broader area of current and prospective requirements within the region, will then look for a possible match for the consultant's skill set. If there is no match, the consultant's data is sent to the corporate resource director.

   The corporate resource director will be able to look for a matching assignment for the consultant's skill set across all regions of the company operation. Create an application using the CoR pattern to simulate this process.

22

FAÇADE

This pattern was previously described in GoF95.

DESCRIPTION

The Façade pattern deals with a subsystem of classes. A *subsystem* is a set of classes that work in conjunction with each other for the purpose of providing a set of related features (functionality). For example, an `Account` class, `Address` class and `CreditCard` class working together, as part of a subsystem, provide features of an online customer.

In real world applications, a subsystem could consist of a large number of classes. Clients of a subsystem may need to interact with a number of subsystem classes for their needs. This kind of direct interaction of clients with subsystem classes leads to a high degree of coupling between the client objects and the subsystem (Figure 22.1). Whenever a subsystem class undergoes a change, such as a change in its interface, all of its dependent client classes may get affected.

The Façade pattern is useful in such situations. The Façade pattern provides a higher level, simplified interface for a subsystem resulting in reduced complexity and dependency. This in turn makes the subsystem usage easier and more manageable.

A façade is a class that provides this simplified interface for a subsystem to be used by clients. With a Façade object in place, clients interact with the Façade object instead of interacting directly with subsystem classes. The Façade object takes up the responsibility of interacting with the subsystem classes. In effect, clients interface with the façade to deal with the subsystem. Thus the Façade pattern promotes a weak coupling between a subsystem and its clients (Figure 22.2).

From Figure 22.2, we can see that the Façade object decouples and shields clients from subsystem objects. When a subsystem class undergoes a change, clients do not get affected as before.

Even though clients use the simplified interface provided by the façade, when needed, a client will be able to access subsystem components directly through the lower level interfaces of the subsystem as if the Façade object does not exist. In this case, they will still have the same dependency/coupling issue as earlier.

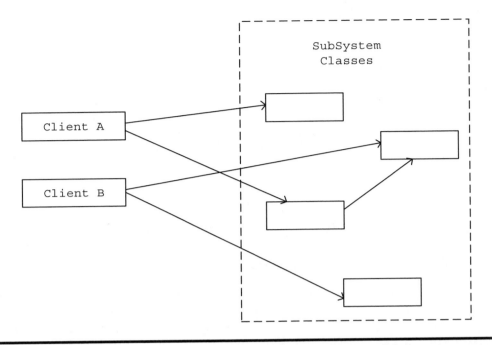

Figure 22.1   Client Interaction with Subsystem Classes before Applying the Façade Pattern

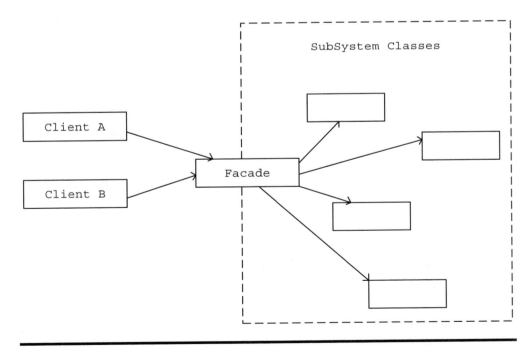

Figure 22.2   Client Interaction with Subsystem Classes after Applying the Façade Pattern

EXAMPLE

Let us build an application that:

- Accepts customer details (account, address and credit card details)
- Validates the input data
- Saves the input data to appropriate data files

Let us say that there are three classes — Account, Address and CreditCard — (Listing 22.1 through Listing 22.3) available in the system, each with its own methods for validating and saving the respective data (Figure 22.3).

Let us build a client AccountManager (Listing 22.4) that displays the user interface to a user to input the customer data.

When the client AccountManager is run, it displays the user interface shown in Figure 22.4.

In order to validate and save the input data, the client AccountManager would:

- Create Account, Address and CreditCard objects
- Validate the input data using these objects
- Save the input data using these objects

The sequence diagram in Figure 22.5 depicts the message flow between objects.

Applying the Façade pattern in this case can lead to a better design as it promotes low coupling between the client and the subsystem components (Address, Account and CreditCard classes in this case).

Applying the Façade pattern, let us define a Façade class CustomerFacade (Figure 22.6 and Listing 22.5) that offers a higher level, simplified interface to the subsystem consisting of customer data processing classes (Address, Account and CreditCard).

The CustomerFacade class offers a higher level business service in the form of the saveCustomerData method. Instead of interacting with each of the subsystem components directly, the client AccountManager can make use of the higher level, more simplified interface offered by the CustomerFacade object to validate and save the input customer data (Figure 22.7).

In the revised design, to validate and save the input customer data, the client needs to:

- Create or obtain an instance of the façade CustomerFacade class
- Send the data to be validated and saved to the CustomerFacade instance
- Invoke the saveCustomerData method on the CustomerFacade instance

The CustomerFacade handles the details of creating necessary subsystem objects and calling appropriate methods on those objects to validate and save the customer data. The client is no longer required to directly access any of the subsystem (Account/Address/CreditCard) objects.

Figure 22.8 shows the message flow in the revised design.

Listing 22.1 Account Class

```java
public class Account {
  String firstName;
  String lastName;
  final String ACCOUNT_DATA_FILE = "AccountData.txt";
  public Account(String fname, String lname) {
    firstName = fname;
    lastName = lname;
  }
  public boolean isValid() {
    /*
      Let's go with simpler validation
      here to keep the example simpler.
    */
        ...
        ...
  }
  public boolean save() {
    FileUtil futil = new FileUtil();
    String dataLine = getLastName() + "," + getFirstName();
    return futil.writeToFile(ACCOUNT_DATA_FILE, dataLine,
            true, true);
  }
  public String getFirstName() {
    return firstName;
  }
  public String getLastName() {
    return lastName;
  }
}
```

Listing 22.2 Address Class

```
public class Address {
  String address;
  String city;
  String state;
  final String ADDRESS_DATA_FILE = "Address.txt";
  public Address(String add, String cty, String st) {
    address = add;
    city = cty;
    state = st;
  }
  public boolean isValid() {
    /*
        The address validation algorithm
        could be complex in real-world
        applications.
        Let's go with simpler validation
        here to keep the example simpler.
      */
    if (getState().trim().length() < 2)
      return false;
    return true;
  }
  public boolean save() {
    FileUtil futil = new FileUtil();
    String dataLine = getAddress() + "," + getCity() + "," +
                      getState();
    return futil.writeToFile(ADDRESS_DATA_FILE, dataLine,
            true, true);
  }
  public String getAddress() {
    return address;
  }
  public String getCity() {
    return city;
  }
  public String getState() {
    return state;
  }
}
```

Listing 22.3 `CreditCard` **Class**

```java
public class CreditCard {
  String cardType;
  String cardNumber;
  String cardExpDate;
  final String CC_DATA_FILE = "CC.txt";
  public CreditCard(String ccType, String ccNumber,
                    String ccExpDate) {
    cardType = ccType;
    cardNumber = ccNumber;
    cardExpDate = ccExpDate;
  }
  public boolean isValid() {
    /*
      Let's go with simpler validation
      here to keep the example simpler.
    */
    if (getCardType().equals(AccountManager.VISA)) {
      return (getCardNumber().trim().length() == 16);
    }
    if (getCardType().equals(AccountManager.DISCOVER)) {
      return (getCardNumber().trim().length() == 15);
    }
    if (getCardType().equals(AccountManager.MASTER)) {
      return (getCardNumber().trim().length() == 16);
    }
    return false;
  }
  public boolean save() {
    FileUtil futil = new FileUtil();
    String dataLine =
      getCardType() + ,"" + getCardNumber() + "," +
      getCardExpDate();
    return futil.writeToFile(CC_DATA_FILE, dataLine, true,
            true);
  }
```

(continued)

Listing 22.3 CreditCard Class (Continued)

```
public String getCardType() {
  return cardType;
}
public String getCardNumber() {
  return cardNumber;
}
public String getCardExpDate() {
  return cardExpDate;
}
}
```

```
┌─────────────────────────────┐   ┌─────────────────────────────┐
│          Account            │   │          Address            │
├─────────────────────────────┤   ├─────────────────────────────┤
│firstName:String             │   │address:String               │
│lastName:String              │   │city:String                  │
│                             │   │state:String                 │
├─────────────────────────────┤   ├─────────────────────────────┤
│isValid():boolean            │   │isValid():boolean            │
│save():boolean               │   │save():boolean               │
│getFirstName():String        │   │getAddress():String          │
│getLastName():String         │   │getState():String            │
└─────────────────────────────┘   └─────────────────────────────┘

┌─────────────────────────────┐
│         CreditCard          │
├─────────────────────────────┤
│cardType:String              │
│cardNumber:String            │
│cardExpDate:String           │
├─────────────────────────────┤
│isValid():String             │
│save():String                │
│getCardType():String         │
│getCardNumber():String       │
│getCardExpDate():String      │
└─────────────────────────────┘
```

Figure 22.3 Subsystem Classes to Provide the Necessary Functionality to Validate and Save the Customer Data

Listing 22.4   Client `AccountManager` Class

```java
public class AccountManager extends JFrame {
  public static final String newline = "\n";
  public static final String VALIDATE_SAVE = "Validate & Save";
      ...

      ...
  public AccountManager() {
    super(" Facade Pattern - Example ");
    cmbCardType = new JComboBox();
    cmbCardType.addItem(AccountManager.VISA);
    cmbCardType.addItem(AccountManager.MASTER);
    cmbCardType.addItem(AccountManager.DISCOVER);
      ...

      ...
    //Create buttons
    JButton validateSaveButton =
      new JButton(AccountManager.VALIDATE_SAVE);
      ...

      ...
  }
  public String getFirstName() {
    return txtFirstName.getText();
  }
      ...

      ...
}//End of class AccountManager
```

IMPORTANT NOTES

Here are few notes to consider while applying the Façade pattern:

- A façade should not be designed to provide any additional functionality.
- Never return subsystem components from Façade methods to clients. As an example, having a method as follows:

```java
CreditCard getCreditCard()
```

would expose the subsystem to clients and the application may not be able to realize the full benefits of using the Façade pattern.

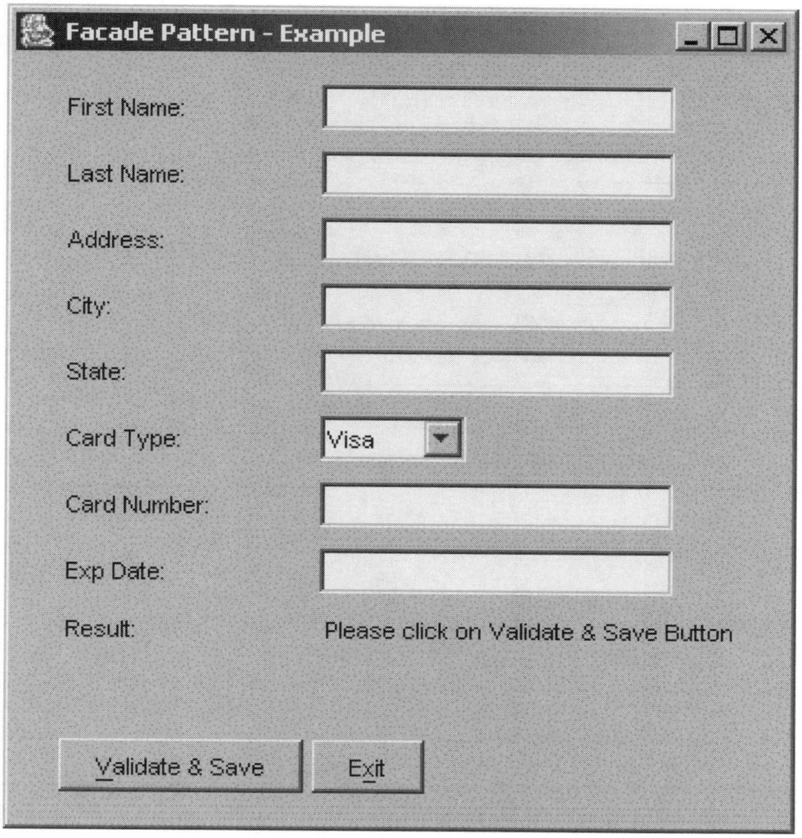

Figure 22.4   User Interface to Enter the Customer Data

■ The objective of a façade is to provide a higher level interface and hence most preferably a typical Façade method should offer a higher level business service rather than performing a lower level individual task.

PRACTICE QUESTIONS

1. Design and implement a façade that can be used by different client objects to create a purchase request consisting of different line items, header data and other information.
2. Enhance the same Façade class to offer business services methods to:
   ■ Retrieve a purchase request from a database
   ■ Create a new purchase request by copying an existing purchase request

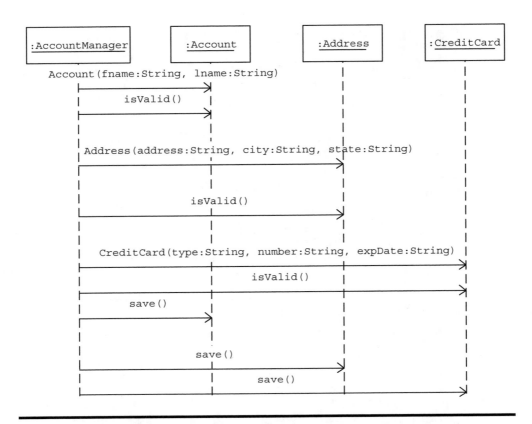

Figure 22.5   How a Client Would Normally Interact (Directly) with Subsystem Classes to Validate and Save the Customer Data

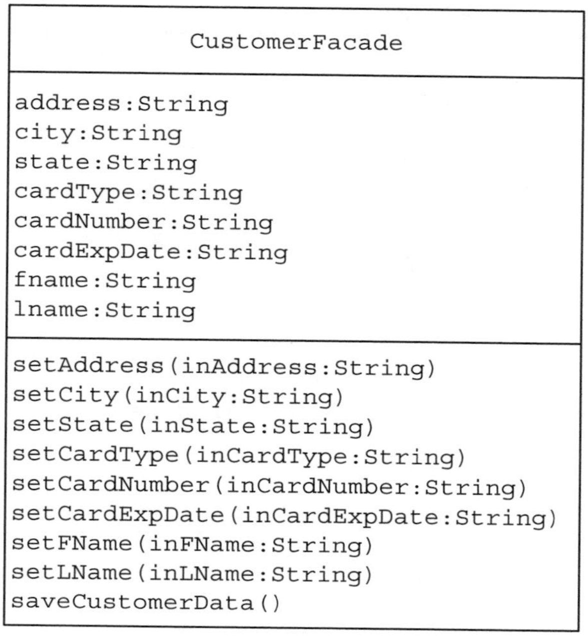

```
┌─────────────────────────────────────────────────────┐
│                   CustomerFacade                      │
├─────────────────────────────────────────────────────┤
│ address:String                                        │
│ city:String                                           │
│ state:String                                          │
│ cardType:String                                       │
│ cardNumber:String                                     │
│ cardExpDate:String                                    │
│ fname:String                                          │
│ lname:String                                          │
├─────────────────────────────────────────────────────┤
│ setAddress(inAddress:String)                          │
│ setCity(inCity:String)                                │
│ setState(inState:String)                              │
│ setCardType(inCardType:String)                        │
│ setCardNumber(inCardNumber:String)                    │
│ setCardExpDate(inCardExpDate:String)                  │
│ setFName(inFName:String)                              │
│ setLName(inLName:String)                              │
│ saveCustomerData()                                    │
└─────────────────────────────────────────────────────┘
```

Figure 22.6   Façade Class to Be Used by the Client in the Revised Design

Listing 22.5 CustomerFacade Class

```
public class CustomerFacade {
  private String address;
  private String city;
  private String state;
  private String cardType;
  private String cardNumber;
  private String cardExpDate;
  private String fname;
  private String lname;
  public void setAddress(String inAddress) {
    address = inAddress;
  }
  public void setCity(String inCity) {
    city = inCity;
  }
  public void setState(String inState) {
    state = inState;
  }
  public void setFName(String inFName) {
    fname = inFName;
  }
  public void setLName(String inLName) {
    lname = inLName;
  }
  public void setCardType(String inCardType) {
    cardType = inCardType;
  }
  public void setCardNumber(String inCardNumber) {
    cardNumber = inCardNumber;
  }
  public void setCardExpDate(String inCardExpDate) {
    cardExpDate = inCardExpDate;
  }
  public boolean saveCustomerData() {
    Address objAddress;
    Account objAccount;
    CreditCard objCreditCard;
    /*
```

(continued)

Listing 22.5 **CustomerFacade Class**

```
    client is transparent from the following
    set of subsystem related operations.
  */
  boolean validData = true;
  String errorMessage = "";
  objAccount = new Account(fname, lname);
  if (objAccount.isValid() == false) {
    validData = false;
    errorMessage = "Invalid FirstName/LastName";
  }
  objAddress = new Address(address, city, state);
  if (objAddress.isValid() == false) {
    validData = false;
    errorMessage = "Invalid Address/City/State";
  }
  objCreditCard = new CreditCard(cardType, cardNumber,
                  cardExpDate);
  if (objCreditCard.isValid() == false) {
    validData = false;
    errorMessage = "Invalid CreditCard Info";
  }
  if (!validData) {
    System.out.println(errorMessage);
    return false;
  }
  if (objAddress.save() && objAccount.save() &&
      objCreditCard.save()) {
    return true;
  } else {
    return false;
  }
 }
}
```

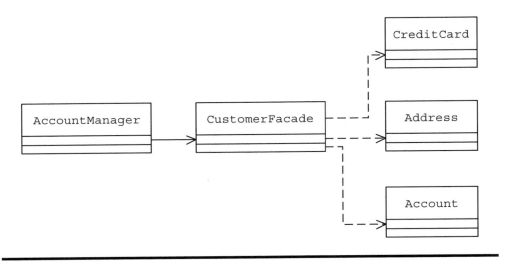

Figure 22.7   Class Association with the Façade Class in Place

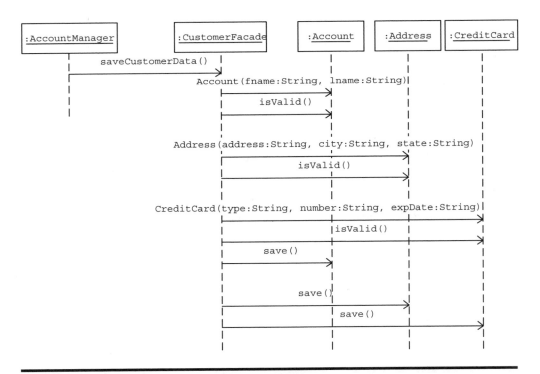

Figure 22.8   In the Revised Design, Clients Interact with the Façade Instance to Interface with the Subsystem

23

PROXY

This pattern was previously described in GoF95.

DESCRIPTION

Let us consider the following code sample:

```
//Client
class Customer{
  public void someMethod(){
    //Create the Service Provider Instance
    FileUtil futilObj=new FileUtil();
    //Access the Service
    futilObj.writeToFile("Some Data");
  }
}
```

As part of its implementation, the `Customer` class creates an instance of the `FileUtil` class and directly accesses its services. In other words, for a client object, the way of accessing a `FileUtil` object is fairly straightforward. From the implementation it seems to be the most commonly used way for a client object to access a service provider object. In contrast, sometimes a client object may not be able to access a service provider object (also referred to as a target object) by normal means. This could happen for a variety of reasons depending on:

- *The location of the target object* — The target object may be present in a different address space in the same or a different computer.
- *The state of existence of the target object* —The target object may not exist until it is actually needed to render a service or the object may be in a compressed form.
- *Special Behavior* —The target object may offer or deny services based on the access privileges of its client objects. Some service provider objects may need special consideration when used in a multithreaded environment.

In such cases, instead of having client objects to deal with the special require-ments for accessing the target object, the Proxy pattern suggests using a separate object referred to as a *proxy* to provide a means for different client objects to access the target object in a normal, straightforward manner.

The Proxy object offers the same interface as the target object. The Proxy object interacts with the target object on behalf of a client object and takes care of the specific details of communicating with the target object. As a result, client objects are no longer needed to deal with the special requirements for accessing the services of the target object. A client can call the Proxy object through its interface and the Proxy object in turn forwards those calls to the target object. Client objects need not even know that they are dealing with Proxy for the original object. The Proxy object hides the fact that a client object is dealing with an object that is either remote, unknown whether instantiated or not, or needs special authentication. In other words, a Proxy object serves as a trans-parent bridge between the client and an inaccessible remote object or an object whose instantiation may have been deferred.

Proxy objects are used in different scenarios leading to different types of proxies. Let us take a quick look at some of the proxies and their purpose.

Note: Table 23.1 lists different types of Proxy objects. In this chapter, only the remote proxy is discussed in detail. Some of the other proxy types are discussed as separate patterns later in this book.

PROXY VERSUS OTHER PATTERNS

From the discussion of different Proxy objects, it can be observed that there are two main characteristics of a Proxy object:

■ It is an intermediary between a client object and the target object.
■ It receives calls from a client object and forwards them to the target object.

In this context, it looks very similar to some of the other patterns discussed earlier in this book. Let us see in detail the similarities and differences between the Proxy pattern and some of the other similar patterns.

Proxy versus Decorator

■ Proxy
  – The client object cannot access the target object directly.
  – A proxy object provides access control to the target object (in the case of the protection proxy).
  – A proxy object does not add any additional functionality.
■ Decorator
  – The client object does have the ability to access the target object directly, if needed.
  – A Decorator object does not control access to the target object.
  – A Decorator adds additional functionality to an object.

Table 23.1   List of Different Proxy Types

Proxy Type	Purpose
Remote Proxy	To provide access to an object located in a different address space.
Virtual Proxy	To provide the required functionality to allow the on-demand creation of a memory intensive object (until required).
Cache Proxy/Server Proxy	To provide the functionality required to store the results of most frequently used target operations. The proxy object stores these results in some kind of a repository. When a client object requests the same operation, the proxy returns the operation results from the storage area without actually accessing the target object.
Firewall Proxy	The primary use of a firewall proxy is to protect target objects from bad clients. A firewall proxy can also be used to provide the functionality required to prevent clients from accessing harmful targets.
Protection Proxy	To provide the functionality required for allowing different clients to access the target object at different levels. A set of permissions is defined at the time of creation of the proxy. Subsequently, those permissions are used to restrict access to specific parts of the proxy (in turn of the target object). A client object is not allowed to access a particular method if it does not have a specific right to execute the method.
Synchronization Proxy	To provide the required functionality to allow safe concurrent accesses to a target object by different client objects.
Smart Reference Proxy	To provide the functionality to prevent the accidental disposal/deletion of the target object when there are clients currently with references to it. To accomplish this, the proxy keeps a count of the number of references to the target object. The proxy deletes the target object if and when there are no references to it.
Counting Proxy	To provide some kind of audit mechanism before executing a method on the target object.

Proxy versus Façade

- Proxy
  - A Proxy object represents a single object.
  - The client object cannot access the target object directly.
  - A Proxy object provides access control to the single target object.

■ Façade
  - A Façade object represents a subsystem of objects.
  - The client object does have the ability to access the subsystem objects directly, if needed.
  - A Façade object provides a simplified higher level interface to a subsystem of components.

Proxy versus Chain of Responsibility

■ Proxy
  - A Proxy object represents a single object.
  - Client requests are first received by the Proxy object, but are never processed directly by the Proxy object.
  - Client requests are always forwarded to the target object.
  - Response to the request is guaranteed, provided the communication between the client and the server locations is working.
■ Chain of Responsibility
  - Chain can contain many objects.
  - The object that receives the client request first could process the request.
  - Client requests are forwarded to the next object in the chain only if the current receiver cannot process the request.
  - Response to the request is not guaranteed. It means that the request may end up reaching the end of the chain and still might not be processed.

In Java, the concept of Remote Method Invocation (RMI) makes extensive use of the Remote Proxy pattern. Let us take a quick look at the concept of RMI and different components that facilitate the RMI communication process.

RMI: A QUICK OVERVIEW

RMI enables a client object to access remote objects and invoke methods on them as if they are local objects (Figure 23.1).

RMI Components

The following different components working together provide the stated RMI functionality:

■ *Remote Interface* — A remote object must implement a remote interface (one that extends `java.rmi.Remote`). A remote interface declares the

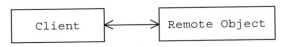

Figure 23.1   Client's View of Its Communication with a Remote Object Using RMI

methods in the remote object that can be accessed by its clients. In other words, the remote interface can be seen as the client's view of the remote object.

Requirements:

- Extend the `java.rmi.Remote` interface.
- All methods in the remote interface must be declared to throw `java.rmi.RemoteException` exception.

■ *Remote Object* — A remote object is responsible for implementing the methods declared in the associated remote interface.

Requirements:

- Must provide implementation for a remote interface.
- Must extend `java.rmi.server.UnicastRemoteObject`.
- Must have a constructor with no arguments.
- Must be associated with a server. The server creates an instance of the remote object by invoking its zero argument constructor.

■ *RMI Registry* — RMI registry provides the storage area for holding different remote objects.

- A remote object needs to be stored in the RMI registry along with a name reference to it for a client object to be able to access it.
- Only one object can be stored with a given name reference.

■ *Client* — Client is an application object attempting to use the remote object.
- Must be aware of the interface implemented by the remote object.
- Can search for a remote object using a name reference in the RMI Registry. Once the remote object reference is found, it can invoke methods on this object reference.

■ *RMIC: Java RMI Stub Compiler* — Once a remote object is compiled successfully, RMIC, the Java RMI stub compiler can be used to generate *stub and skeleton* class files for the remote object. Stub and skeleton classes are generated from the compiled remote object class. These stub and skeleton classes make it possible for a client object to access the remote object in a seamless manner.

The following section describes how the actual communication takes place between a client and a remote object.

RMI Communication Mechanism

In general, a client object cannot directly access a remote object by normal means. In order to make it possible for a client object to access the services of a remote object as if it is a local object, the RMIC-generated stub of the remote object class and the remote interface need to be copied to the client computer.

The *stub* acts as a *(Remote) proxy* for the remote object and is responsible for forwarding method invocations on the remote object to the server where the actual remote object implementation resides. Whenever a client references the remote object, the reference is, in fact, made to a local stub. That means, when a client makes a method call on the remote object, it is first received by the local stub instance. The stub forwards this call to the remote server. On the server the RMIC generated skeleton of the remote object receives this call.

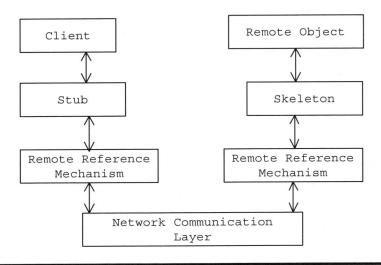

Figure 23.2   The Actual RMI Communication Process

The skeleton is a server side object and it *does not* need to be copied to the client computer. The *skeleton* is responsible for dispatching calls to the actual remote object implementation. Once the remote object executes the method, results are sent back to the client in the reverse direction.

Figure 23.2 shows the actual RMI communication process.

For more information on the Java RMI technology, I recommend reading the RMI tutorial at `java.sun.com`.

RMI AND PROXY PATTERN

It can be seen from the RMI communication discussion that the stub class, acting as a remote proxy for the remote object, makes it possible for a client to treat a remote object as if it is available locally. Thus, any application that uses RMI contains an implicit implementation of the Proxy pattern.

EXAMPLE

During the discussion of the Façade pattern, we built a simple customer data management application to validate and save the input customer data. Our design consisted of a set of three subsystem classes — `Account`, `Address` and `CreditCard` — representing different parts of the customer data.

Before applying the Façade pattern, the client `AccountManager` was designed to directly interact with the three subsystem classes to validate and save the customer data. Applying the Façade pattern, we defined a `CustomerFacade` Façade object to deal with the three subsystem classes on behalf of the client `AccountManager` (Figure 23.3).

In this application, both the subsystem components and the Façade object are local to the `AccountManager` client object.

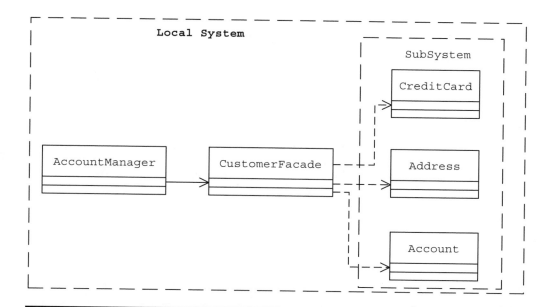

Figure 23.3 Customer Data Management Application for the Local Mode of Operation: Class Association

Let us build a different version of the same application that runs in the remote mode. In the remote mode, the application makes use of remote objects using the Java RMI technology.

In designing the application for the remote mode of operation, we would move all of the subsystem components (Account, Address and CreditCard) and the Façade (CustomerFacade) to a remote server (Figure 23.4) with the following advantages:

- Objects on the server can be shared by different client applications. Clients no longer have to maintain local copies of these classes and hence clients will be light-weighted.
- Leads to centralized control over processes involving changes, enhancements and monitoring.

Let us start designing our customer data management application for the remote mode of operation using the RMI technology.

As the first step, let us define a remote interface CustomerIntr that:

- Declares the methods to be implemented by the Façade
- Declares all such methods to throw the RemoteException exception
- Extends the built-in java.rmi.Remote interface

```
public interface CustomerIntr extends java.rmi.Remote {
    void setAddress(String inAddress) throws RemoteException;
    void setCity(String inCity) throws RemoteException;
```

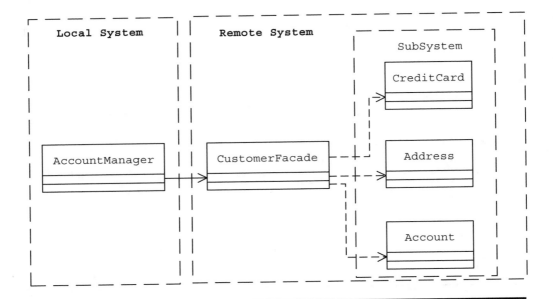

Figure 23.4 Customer Data Management Application for the Remote Mode of Operation: Class Association

```
void setState(String inState) throws RemoteException;
void setFName(String inFName) throws RemoteException;
void setLName(String inLName) throws RemoteException;
void setCardType(String inCardType) throws RemoteException;
void setCardNumber(String inCardNumber)
   throws RemoteException;
void setCardExpDate(String inCardExpDate)
   throws RemoteException;
boolean saveCustomerData() throws RemoteException;
}
```

Let us redesign the CustomerFacade Façade class (Listing 23.1) so that it now implements the CustomerIntr remote interface. Different client objects can interface with the subsystem objects by invoking the CustomerIntr methods on the concrete CustomerFacade. Figure 23.5 shows the structure and the association between the CustomerFacade and the remote interface CustomerIntr it implements.

Because the subsystem components are local to the CustomerFacade class, it continues to refer to them as local objects without any changes in the way it instantiates and invokes methods on them. When executed, the CustomerFacade creates an instance of itself and keeps it in the RMI registry with a reference name. Client objects will be able to obtain this copy of the remote object using the reference name.

Listing 23.1 CustomerFacade Class: Revised

```
public class CustomerFacade extends UnicastRemoteObject
  implements CustomerIntr {
  private String address;
  private String city;
  private String state;
  private String cardType;
  private String cardNumber;
  private String cardExpDate;
  private String fname;
  private String lname;
  public CustomerFacade() throws RemoteException {
    super();
    System.out.println("Server object created");
  }
  public static void main(String[] args) throws Exception {
    String port = "1099";
    String host = "localhost";
    //Check for hostname argument
    if (args.length == 1) {
      host = args[0];
    }
    if (args.length == 2) {
      port = args[1];
    }
    if (System.getSecurityManager() == null) {
      System.setSecurityManager(new RMISecurityManager());
    }
    //Create an instance of the server
    CustomerFacade facade = new CustomerFacade();
    //Bind it with the RMI Registry
    Naming.bind("//" + host + ":" + port + "/CustomerFacade",
                facade);
    System.out.println("Service Bound…");
  }
  public void setAddress(String inAddress)
    throws RemoteException {
    address = inAddress;
  }
```

(continued)

Listing 23.1   CustomerFacade Class: Revised (Continued)

```java
public void setCity(String inCity)
   throws RemoteException{ city = inCity;
}
public void setState(String inState)
   throws RemoteException{ state = inState;
}
public void setFName(String inFName)
   throws RemoteException{ fname = inFName;
}
public void setLName(String inLName)
   throws RemoteException{ lname = inLName;
}
public void setCardType(String inCardType)
   throws RemoteException {
   cardType = inCardType;
}
public void setCardNumber(String inCardNumber)
   throws RemoteException {
   cardNumber = inCardNumber;
}
public void setCardExpDate(String inCardExpDate)
   throws RemoteException {
   cardExpDate = inCardExpDate;
}
public boolean saveCustomerData() throws RemoteException{
   Address objAddress;
   Account objAccount;
   CreditCard objCreditCard;
   /*
    client is transparent from the following
    set of subsystem related operations.
   */
   boolean validData = true;
   String errorMessage = "";
   objAccount = new Account(fname, lname);
   if (objAccount.isValid() == false) {
    validData = false;
    errorMessage = "Invalid FirstName/LastName";
   }
```

(continued)

Listing 23.1 `CustomerFacade` **Class: Revised (Continued)**

```
objAddress = new Address(address, city, state);
if (objAddress.isValid() == false) {
  validData = false;
  errorMessage = "Invalid Address/City/State";
}
objCreditCard = new CreditCard(cardType, cardNumber,
                cardExpDate);
if (objCreditCard.isValid() == false) {
  validData = false;
  errorMessage = "Invalid CreditCard Info";
}
if (!validData) {
  System.out.println(errorMessage);
  return false;
}
if (objAddress.save() && objAccount.save() &&
    objCreditCard.save()) {
  return true;
} else {
  return false;
}
  }
}
```

Because a client does not need to access any of the subsystem components directly, none of the subsystem components undergoes any changes in the new design for the remote mode of operation of the application.

Let us redesign the client `AccountManager` class (Listing 23.2).

Similar to the local mode of operation, `AccountManager` displays the necessary user interface to accept the input customer data (Figure 23.6). When the user enters the data and clicks on the `Validate & Save` button, it retrieves the remote object reference from the RMI registry using the reference name.

Once the remote object reference is retrieved from the registry, the client can invoke operations on the remote object reference as if it is a local object. Figure 23.7 depicts this behavior.

Note that the stub class corresponding to the compiled `CustomerFacade` class must be copied onto the client `AccountManager` location before executing the application. After the `CustomerFacade` is compiled, the stub and skeleton classes can be generated using the RMIC compiler on the compiled `Customer-Facade` class. Detailed instructions on compiling and deploying different application components are provided under the following "Additional Notes" section.

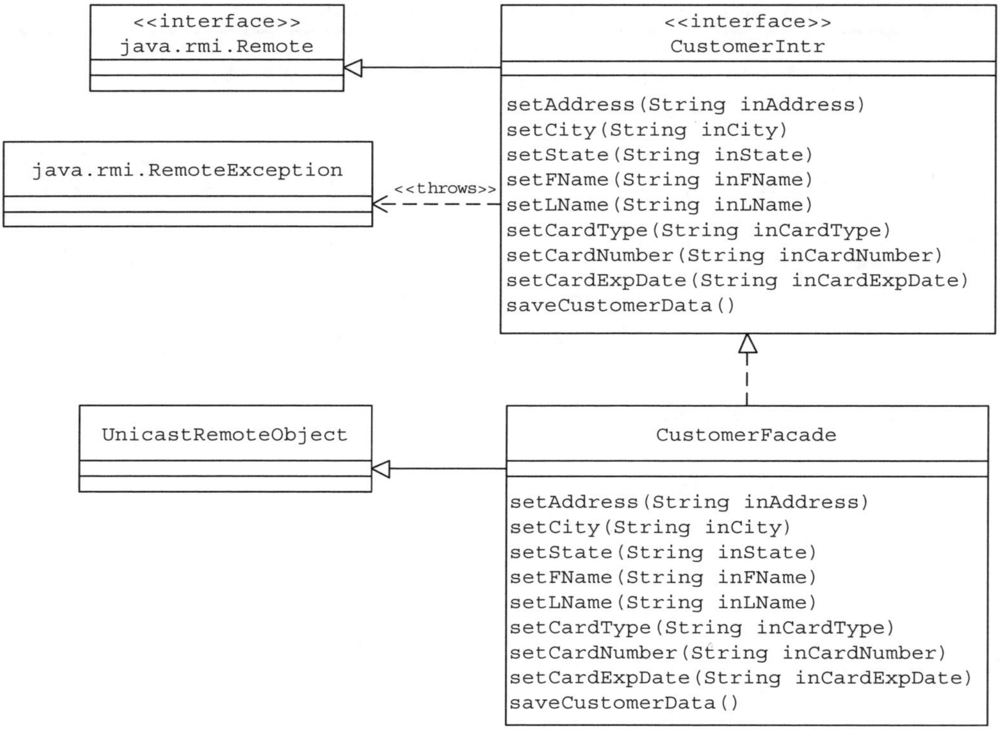

```
┌──────────────────────────┐              ┌──────────────────────────────────────────────┐
│      <<interface>>        │              │              <<interface>>                     │
│     java.rmi.Remote       │◁─────────────│              CustomerIntr                      │
├──────────────────────────┤              ├──────────────────────────────────────────────┤
│                           │              │  setAddress(String inAddress)                  │
└──────────────────────────┘              │  setCity(String inCity)                        │
                                          │  setState(String inState)                      │
┌──────────────────────────┐             │  setFName(String inFName)                      │
│  java.rmi.RemoteException │ <<throws>>  │  setLName(String inLName)                      │
├──────────────────────────┤◁─ ─ ─ ─ ─ ─ │  setCardType(String inCardType)                │
│                           │             │  setCardNumber(String inCardNumber)            │
└──────────────────────────┘             │  setCardExpDate(String inCardExpDate)          │
                                         │  saveCustomerData()                            │
                                         └──────────────────────────────────────────────┘
                                                              △
                                                              ┆
┌──────────────────────────┐             ┌──────────────────────────────────────────────┐
│   UnicastRemoteObject     │◁────────────│              CustomerFacade                    │
├──────────────────────────┤             ├──────────────────────────────────────────────┤
│                           │             │  setAddress(String inAddress)                  │
└──────────────────────────┘             │  setCity(String inCity)                        │
                                         │  setState(String inState)                      │
                                         │  setFName(String inFName)                      │
                                         │  setLName(String inLName)                      │
                                         │  setCardType(String inCardType)                │
                                         │  setCardNumber(String inCardNumber)            │
                                         │  setCardExpDate(String inCardExpDate)          │
                                         │  saveCustomerData()                            │
                                         └──────────────────────────────────────────────┘
```

Figure 23.5 Façade Design: Remote Mode of Operation

In reality, when the client invokes a method such as saveCustomerData on the CustomerFacade remote object, the CustomerFacade_stub object, which is local to the client, first receives it. The CustomerFacade_stub then transmits the method call to the server for processing.

On the server side the CustomerFacade_skel is responsible for receiving the method call through the lower levels of the communication network. It then dispatches it to the actual CustomerFacade object on the server. In case of the saveCustomerData method, the CustomerFacade object creates the necessary subsystem objects and invokes the required methods on these objects to validate and save the customer data. The result of the processing is carried back to the client in the reverse manner. Figure 23.8 depicts this actual communication mechanism.

As can be seen from above, the CustomerFacade_stub class enables the client object to invoke methods on the remote CustomerFacade object as if it is present locally, which, otherwise, is not accessible by normal means. Thus the stub functions as a remote proxy.

Listing 23.2 AccountManager Class: Revised

```
        …
          …

public void actionPerformed(ActionEvent e) {
          …
            …

   if (e.getActionCommand().equals(
          AccountManager.VALIDATE_SAVE)) {
     //get input values
     String firstName = objAccountManager.getFirstName();
     String lastName = objAccountManager.getLastName();
     String address = objAccountManager.getAddress();
            …
            …

     try {
       //Call registry for AddOperation
       facade = (CustomerIntr) Naming.lookup ("rmi://" +
                objAccountManager.getRMIHost() + ":" +
                objAccountManager.getRMIPort() +
                "/CustomerFacade");
       facade.setFName(firstName);
       facade.setLName(lastName);
       facade.setAddress(address);
            …
            …

     //Client is not required to access subsystem components.
     boolean result = facade.saveCustomerData();
     if (result) {
       validateCheckResult =
         " Valid Customer Data: Data Saved Successfully ";
     } else {
       validateCheckResult =
         " Invalid Customer Data: Data Could Not Be Saved ";
     }
```

(continued)

Listing 23.2 `AccountManager` Class: Revised (Continued)

```
      } catch (Exception ex) {
        System.out.println(
          "Error: Please check to ensure the " +
          "remote server is running" +
          ex.getMessage());
      }
      objAccountManager.setResultDisplay(
        validateCheckResult);
    }
  }
      ...
      ...
```

ADDITIONAL NOTES

Compilation and Deployment Notes

Download the source code from the following Web site: http://www.crcpress.com/ e_products/downloads/download.asp.

1. Compile all Java files in the *Proxy/Server* folder.
2. Execute the following command from the *Proxy/Server* folder:

```
Rmic CustomerFacade
```

This command invokes the RMI stub compiler and creates the stub and skeleton classes `CustomerFacade_Skel.class` and `CustomerFacade_ Stub.class`, respectively.

3. Copy the following files from the *Proxy/Server* folder to the *Proxy/Client* folder:

```
CustomerIntr.class

CustomerFacade_Stub.class
```

4. Compile all Java files in the *Proxy/Client* folder.
5. Start the `rmiregistry`:

```
start rmiregistry <objectRegistryPort> (Windows)
rmiregistry & (Solaris)
```

■ `<objectRegistryPort>` — This is where the RMI registry needs to listen. The default port value is 1099.
■ Example:

```
start rmiregistry
```

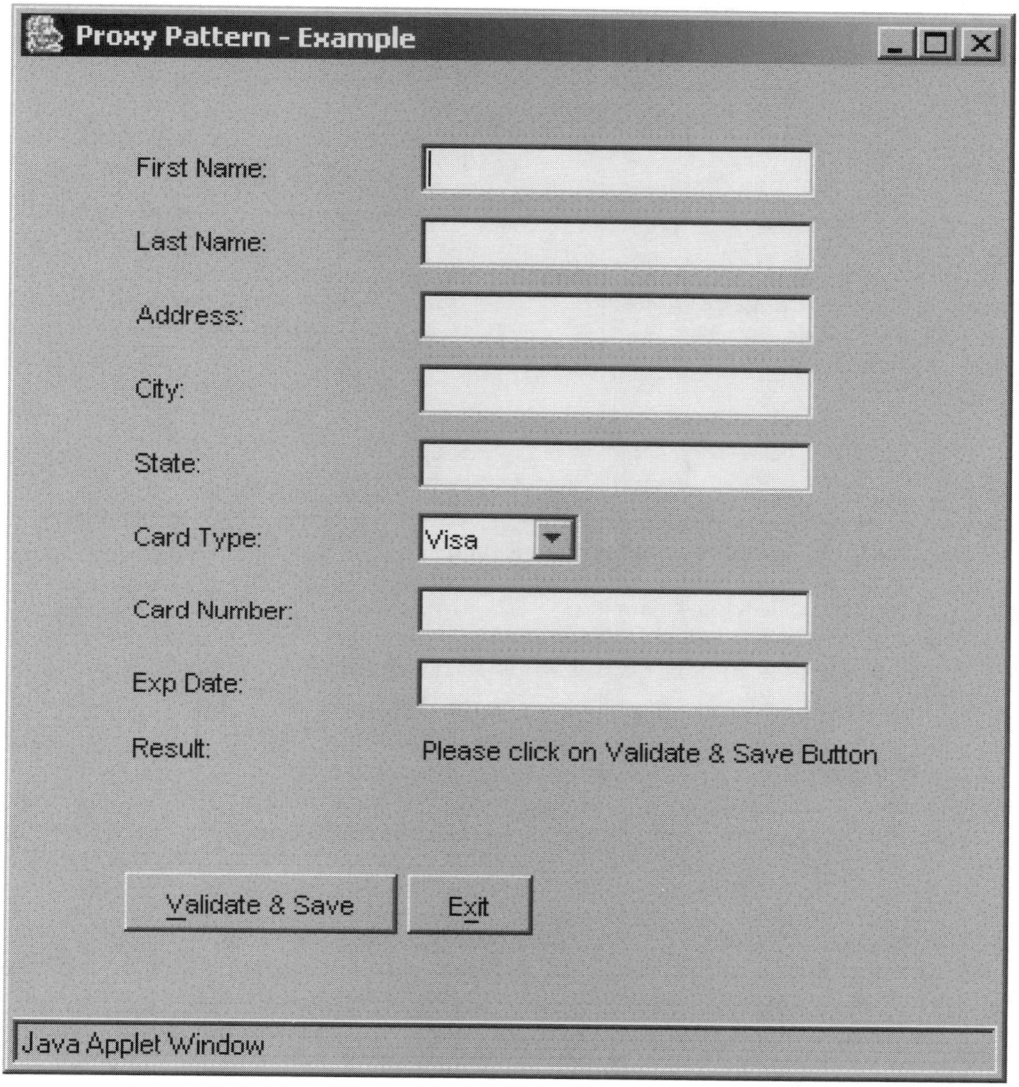

Proxy Pattern - Example

First Name:

Last Name:

Address:

City:

State:

Card Type: Visa ▼

Card Number:

Exp Date:

Result: Please click on Validate & Save Button

Validate & Save   Exit

Java Applet Window

Figure 23.6   The User Interface: Remote Mode of Operation

Figure 23.7   AccountManager View of Its Communication with the Remote Customer-Facade

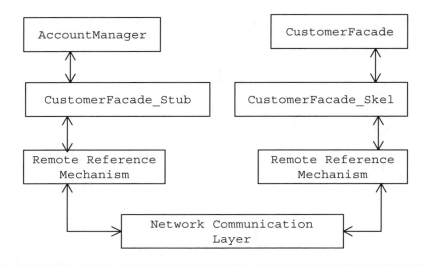

Figure 23.8   The Actual Flow of Communication

6. Run the following command:

```
java -Djava.security.policy=<PolicyFile> CustomerFacade
<RemoteRegistryHost>  <RemoteRegistryPort>
```

■ Example:

```
java -Djava.security.policy=java.policy CustomerFacade
localhost 1099
```

■ `<policyFile>` − This is the name of the security file with permissions set for the application. The location of the file in the file system of the underlying operating system needs to be specified.
   Note: The `java.policy` policy file is available in the server folder.
■ `<RemoteRegistryHost>` − This is the DNS (Domain Name System) name or the IP address of the host machine where the object registry is running. For the same computer, use "localhost."
■ `<RemoteRegistryPort>` − This is the port where the object registry is listening on the specified `RemoteRegistryHost`. The default is 1099.
7. The following output will be displayed:

```
Server object created
Service bound...
```

8. Go to the folder *Proxy/client* and execute the following command to run the client:

```
java -Djava.security.policy=<PolicyFile> AccountManager
<RemoteRegistryHost>  <RemoteRegistryPort>
```

■ Example:

```
java -Djava.security.policy=java.policy AccountManager
localhost 1099
```

■ <policyFile> — This is the name of the security file with permissions set for the application. The location of the file in the file system of the underlying operating system needs to be specified.
Note: The java.policy policy file is available in the client folder.
■ <RemoteRegistryHost> — This is the DNS name or the IP address of the host machine where the object registry is running. For the same computer, use "localhost."
■ <RemoteRegistryPort> — This is the port where the object registry is listening on the specified RemoteRegistryHost. The default is 1099.

This executes the client AccountManager and the user interface will be displayed.

PRACTICE QUESTIONS

1. In our example design, a client can access only the CustomerFacade remote object. The CustomerFacade internally interacts with the remote subsystem components directly. But a client cannot access any of the subsystem components (Account, Address or the CreditCard). Make necessary changes to the Account, Address and the CreditCard classes and to the deployment process, to enable a client to access these subsystem components directly without having to go through the CustomerFacade.
2. Design and implement the purchase request Façade as a remote object. (Refer to Practice Questions 1 and 2 of Chapter 22 — Façade.)

24

BRIDGE

This pattern was previously described in GoF95.

DESCRIPTION

The Bridge pattern promotes the separation of an abstraction's interface from its implementation. In general, the term *abstraction* refers to the process of identifying the set of attributes and behavior of an object that is specific to a particular usage. This specific view of an object can be designed as a separate object omitting irrelevant attributes and behavior. The resulting object itself can be referred to as an *abstraction*. Note that a given object can have more than one associated abstraction, each with a distinct usage.

A given abstraction may have one or more implementations for its methods (behavior). In terms of implementation, an abstraction can be designed as an interface with one or more concrete implementers (Figure 24.1).

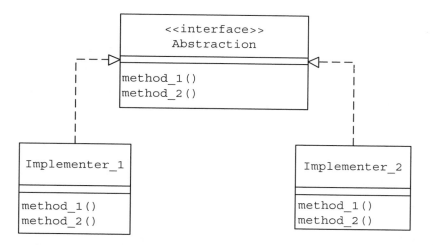

Figure 24.1   Abstraction as an Interface with a Set of Concrete Implementers

In the class hierarchy shown in Figure 24.1, the `Abstraction` interface declares a set of methods that represent the result of abstracting common features from different objects. Both `Implementer_1` and `Implementer_2` represent the set of `Abstraction` implementers. This approach suffers from the following two limitations:

1. When there is a need to subclass the hierarchy for some other reason, it could lead to an exponential number of subclasses and soon we will have an exploding class hierarchy.
2. Both the `abstraction` interface and its implementation are closely tied together and hence they cannot be independently varied without affecting each other.

Using the Bridge pattern, a more efficient and manageable design of an abstraction can be achieved. The design of an abstraction using the Bridge pattern separates its interfaces from implementations. Applying the Bridge pattern, both the interfaces and the implementations of an abstraction can be put into separate class hierarchies as in Figure 24.2.

From the class diagram in Figure 24.2, it can be seen that the Abstraction maintains an object reference of the `Implementer` type. A client application can

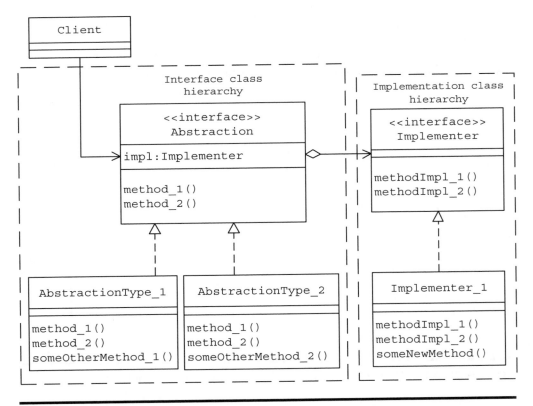

Figure 24.2 Interface and Implementations in Two Separate Class Hierarchies

choose a desired abstraction type from the `Abstraction` class hierarchy. The abstraction object can then be configured with an instance of an appropriate implementer from the `Implementer` class hierarchy. This ability to combine abstractions and implementations dynamically can be very useful in terms of extending the functionality without subclassing. When a client object invokes a method on the `Abstraction` object, it forwards the call to the `Implementer` object it contains. The `Abstraction` object may offer some amount of processing before forwarding the call to the `Implementer` object.

This type of class arrangement completely decouples the interface and the implementation of an abstraction and allows the classes in the interface and the implementation hierarchy to vary without affecting each other.

EXAMPLE

We designed the message logging functionality for an application during the discussion of the Factory Method pattern. Logging can be used for various purposes at different stages of an application and hence many different objects that are part of the application may need to have the ability to log messages. Because many different objects within an application may need the ability to log messages, the logging feature may be put into a separate class. The resulting class is an abstraction of the message logging functionality. From here on, we use the phrase *logger abstraction* to refer to the abstraction of the message logging functionality.

A message can be logged to different types of destinations such as a file, console and others. Depending on the destination type, a different implementation of the logger abstraction is needed. This requirement can be designed with a common `Logger` interface that declares the interface (methods) of the abstraction and different implementers corresponding to different destination types provide implementation for the logger abstraction. Let us define two such implementers — `FileLogger` and `ConsoleLogger` — to log messages to a file and console, respectively. Figure 24.3 depicts the resulting class hierarchy.

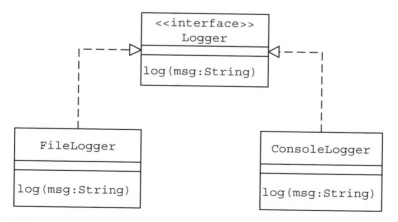

Figure 24.3   Logger Abstraction before Applying the Bridge Pattern

Different client objects can use one of the implementer (`FileLogger` or `ConsoleLogger`) objects to log messages to a desired destination in plain text format. After this design is implemented, let us suppose that an application object needs to log messages in a different format (e.g., in an encrypted form). The existing messaging logging functionality design is not sufficient without either:

■ Modifying different implementers
■ Extending the entire class hierarchy

Having to modify the existing code in order to extend the functionality is not advisable and violates the basic object-oriented open-closed principle.

The open-closed principle states that a software module should be:

■ *Open for extension* — It should be possible to alter the behavior of a module or add new features to the module functionality.
■ *Closed for modification* — Such a module should not allow its code to be modified.

In a nutshell, the open-closed principle helps in designing software modules whose functionality can be extended without having to modify the existing code.

This also means that whenever there is a change to be made to the `Logger` (Java)interface for a different type of (application)interface, each of its implementations needs to be modified, making the logger abstraction interface and its implementation dependent on each other.

Subclassing the class hierarchy for every different type of message format is also not recommended as it could result in an exponential number of subclasses and soon there will be an exploding class hierarchy. The Bridge pattern can be used in this case to provide the ability to add new message formats and new types of implementations to the logger abstraction. The Bridge pattern separates the interface and implementations into two separate class hierarchies so that they both can be modified without affecting each other.

Applying the Bridge pattern the interface and the implementation of the logger abstraction can be arranged into two separate class hierarchies.

Abstraction Implementation Design

Implementers of the logger abstraction need to provide the actual implementation required to log messages to different destination types. Let us define two such implementers — `FileLogger` and `ConsoleLogger` — to log messages to a file and console, respectively. These abstraction implementers can be designed as two concrete implementers of a common `MessageLogger` (Java)interface (Listing 24.1).

The common `MessageLogger` interface declares a method `logMsg(String msg)`, which can be used by objects that represent the interface of the logger abstraction. Figure 24.4 depicts the resulting abstraction implementation class hierarchy.

As part of its implementation of the `logMsg` method (Listing 24.2):

Listing 24.1 `MessageLogger` **Interface**

```
public interface MessageLogger {
  public void logMsg(String msg);
}
```

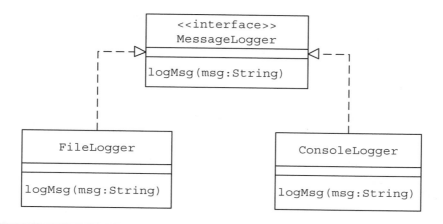

Figure 24.4 **Logger Abstraction: Implementer Hierarchy**

Listing 24.2 `MessageLogger` **Implementers:** `FileLogger` **and** `ConsoleLogger`

```
public class FileLogger implements MessageLogger {
  public void logMsg(String msg) {
    FileUtil futil = new FileUtil();
    futil.writeToFile("log.txt",msg, true, true);
  }
}
public class ConsoleLogger implements MessageLogger {
  public void logMsg(String msg) {
    System.out.println(msg);
  }
}
```

- The `FileLogger` writes a given message to a log file using a helper `FileUtil` class.
- The `ConsoleLogger` writes a given message on the screen.

Note that client objects should not directly access the message logging service offered by different logger abstraction implementers. To log a message, different

Listing 24.3   Message Interface

```
public interface Message {
  public void log(String msg);
}
```

client objects interact with instances of the classes representing the logger abstraction interface. These abstraction interface objects in turn use the services of the abstraction implementer classes.

Abstraction Interface Design

The interface for the logger abstraction can be designed in the form of a set of classes representing different types of messages that a client object would like to log. These classes can be designed as implementers of a common Message (Java)interface (Listing 24.3).

The Message interface declares a method log(String msg), which can be used by different client objects to log messages.

Let us define two logger abstraction interface classes — TextMessage and EncryptedMessage — (Listing 24.4) representing a plain text message and an encrypted message, respectively. These abstraction interface classes can be designed as concrete implementers of a common Message (Java)interface.

Figure 24.5 shows the resulting logger abstraction interface class hierarchy.

Design Highlights of the Abstraction Interface Classes

- Logger abstraction interface classes — TextMessage and Encrypted-Message — do not provide implementation for the actual message logging service. As seen earlier, classes such as the FileLogger and Console-Logger in the abstraction implementer class hierarchy provide the actual message logging implementation.
- Client objects do not directly use the interface exposed by the abstraction implementer classes.
- Each abstraction interface class maintains an object reference of the Mes-sageLogger (abstraction implementer) type. Whenever a client object creates an abstraction interface object, it configures the interface object with a MessageLogger object.
- Whenever a client object invokes the log method on an abstraction interface object, the interface object does any required preprocessing and uses the message logging service of the MessageLogger object it contains.
- The preprocessing functionality is meant to be used internally by abstraction interface objects only and it should not be available to client objects. To ensure this, the preProcess method in both the TextMessage and EncryptedMessage abstraction interface classes is designed as a private method. As part of its implementation of the preProcess method, the

Listing 24.4   Message Implementers: `TextMessage` and `EncryptedMessage`

```
public class TextMessage implements Message {
  private MessageLogger logger;
  public TextMessage(MessageLogger l) {
    logger = l;
  }
  public void log(String msg) {
    String str = preProcess(msg);
    logger.logMsg(str);
  }
  private String preProcess(String msg) {
    return msg;
  };
}
public class EncryptedMessage implements Message {
  private MessageLogger logger;
  public EncryptedMessage(MessageLogger l) {
    logger = l;
  }
  public void log(String msg) {
    String str = preProcess(msg);
    logger.logMsg(str);
  }
  private String preProcess(String msg) {
    msg = msg.substring(msg.length() - 1) +
          msg.substring(0, msg.length() - 1);
    return msg;
  };
}
```

EncryptedMessage encrypts an incoming message by shifting all characters to the right by one position.

As a result of keeping the interface and the implementation of the logger abstraction in two separate class hierarchies, the interfaces and the implementations of the logger abstraction are completely decoupled.

Whenever a client (Listing 24.5) needs to log a message:

1. It creates an instance of an appropriate `MessageLogger` implementer class such as `FileLogger` or `ConsoleLogger`.

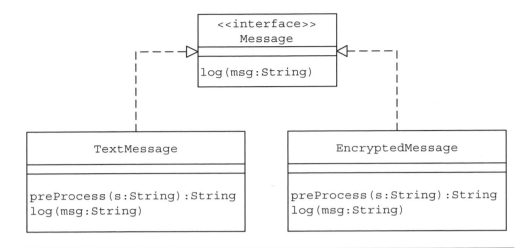

Figure 24.5   Logger Abstraction: Interface Hierarchy

Listing 24.5   Test Client Class

```
public class Client {
  public static void main(String[] args) {
    //Create an appropriate implementer object
    MessageLogger logger = new FileLogger();
    //Choose required interface object and
    //configure it with the implementer object
    Message msg = new EncryptedMessage(logger);
    msg.log("Test Message");
  }
}
```

2. It creates an instance of an appropriate `Message` implementer class such as `TextMessage` or `EncryptedMessage`.
3. It configures the `Message` implementer object with the `MessageLogger` implementer object created in Step 1. This object is maintained inside the `Message` implementer object.
4. It calls the `log(String)` method on the `Message` implementer object created in Step 2.
5. The `Message` implementer object carries out the required processing to transform the incoming message to the desired format (encrypt the input message in the case of the `EncryptedMessage`) and forwards the transformed message to the `MessageLogger` implementer object it contains by invoking its `logMessage(String)` method. This relationship between classes in the interface and the implementer class hierarchy can be viewed as a Bridge in this case.

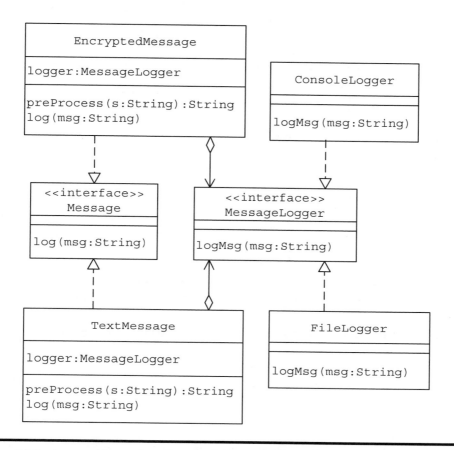

Figure 24.6 Logger Abstraction after Applying the Bridge Pattern

Figure 24.6 shows the overall class association.

The message flow when an application object uses the logger abstraction to log an encrypted message can be depicted as in Figure 24.7.

The separation of the logger abstraction interface from its implementation allows them to be modified independently without having to modify the other.

After the design is implemented, if a client object needs to log messages in a new format, say HTML, this requirement can be addressed easily by designing a new logger abstraction interface class HTMLMessage as an implementer of the existing Message interface. The HTMLMessage class can be designed to provide the required processing to transform an incoming message to HTML text and use an abstraction implementer class to actually log the transformed message. This addition of a new interface class does not affect any existing abstraction implementers. In addition, adding a new class for every new type of message format keeps the class growth linear.

Similarly, a new logger abstraction implementation such as a DBLogger to log messages to a database can be added without having to modify or subclass the class hierarchy.

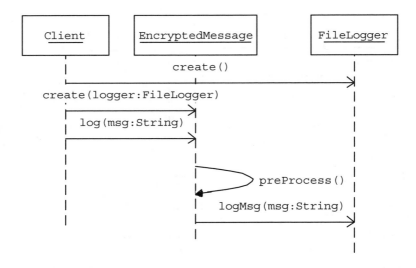

Figure 24.7   Message Flow When an Application Logs an Encrypted Message

BRIDGE PATTERN VERSUS ADAPTER PATTERN

Similarities:

■ Both the Adapter pattern and the Bridge pattern are similar in that they both work towards concealing the details of the underlying implementation from the client.

Differences:

■ The Adapter pattern aims at making classes work together that could not otherwise because of incompatible interfaces. An Adapter is meant to change the interface of an *existing object*. As we have seen during our discussion on the Adapter pattern, an Adapter requires an (existing) adaptee class, indicating that the Adapter pattern is more suitable for needs after the initial system design.

■ The Bridge pattern is more of a design time pattern. It is used when the designer has control over the classes in the system. It is applied before a system has been implemented to allow both abstraction interfaces and its implementations to be varied independently without affecting each other.

■ In the context of the Bridge pattern, the issue of incompatible interfaces does not exist. Client objects always use the interface exposed by the abstraction interface classes. Thus both the Bridge pattern and the Adapter pattern are used to solve different design issues.

PRACTICE QUESTIONS

1. Design an application that reads and writes different types of data (plain text, binary, etc.) to and from different destinations such as a file, a URL or a database. Apply the Bridge pattern in designing the data read/write abstraction.

2. Many applications with a database backend use ODBC/JDBC drivers from different vendors. Identify how the Bridge pattern is applied when an application uses an ODBC/JDBC driver.

3. Design a code formatting application using the Bridge pattern. In general, programs can be written in any computer language (e.g., Java, VB, etc.) and a given program can be formatted in different ways such as simple text formatting, HTML formatting, color formatting and others. In effect, the interface for code formatting can be implemented in many different ways. Apply the Bridge pattern to separate the interface from its implementations.

25

VIRTUAL PROXY

This pattern was previously described in GoF95.

DESCRIPTION

The Virtual Proxy pattern is a memory saving technique that recommends postponing an object creation until it is needed: when creating such an object is expensive in terms of the memory usage or the processing involved. In a typical application, different objects make up different parts of the functionality. When an application is started, it may not need all of its objects to be available immediately. In such cases, the Virtual Proxy pattern suggests deferring object creation until it is needed by the application. The object is created the first time it is referenced in the application and the same instance is reused from that point onwards. This approach has advantages and disadvantages.

Advantage

The advantage of this approach is a faster application start-up time, as it is not required to create and load all of the application objects.

Disadvantage

Because there is no guarantee that a given application object is created, *everywhere* the application object is accessed it needs to be checked to make sure that it is not null, i.e., the object is created. The time penalty associated with this check is the main disadvantage.

Applying the Virtual Proxy pattern, a separate object referred to as a *virtual proxy* can be designed with its interface the same as that of the actual object. Different client objects can create an instance of the corresponding virtual proxy and use it in place of the actual object. The Virtual Proxy object maintains a reference to the actual object as one of its instance variables. The proxy does not automatically create the actual object. When a client invokes a method on the Virtual Proxy object that requires the services of the actual object, it checks to see if the actual object is created.

- If the actual object is already created, the proxy forwards the method call to the actual object.
- If the actual object is not already created:
    - It creates the actual object.
    - It assigns the object to its object reference variable.
    - It forwards the call to the actual object.

With this arrangement, details such as the existence of the actual object and the method forwarding are hidden from client objects. Client objects interact only with the `Proxy` object as if it is the actual object. As a result, client objects are free from checking if the actual object is null. Also, because the time and the processing overhead is less to create a virtual proxy than the actual object it is associated with, the virtual proxy can be instantiated at the beginning of a client application in place of the actual object.

EXAMPLE

Suppose that you are creating an IDE (Integrated Development Environment) for editing Java programs with features to compile, execute and generate javadocs. Most often when a Java program is created or edited, it is compiled and run, but javadocs may not be generated for every Java program. Hence, instead of creating and loading all the application objects that provide the entire IDE functionality, it might be a good idea to create only those objects that are required for editing, compiling and executing programs, leaving the other objects that offer the service of generating javadocs. This type of object creation strategy results in an efficient memory usage model and the IDE application can be started quickly as there is no need to load all of the application objects.

Let us suppose that the compile, run and javadoc generation functionalities are offered by three utility classes — `Compiler`, `Runtime` and `JavaDoc` — respectively. The interface for different IDE operations to be accessed by client objects can be designed in the form of an abstract `IDEOperation` class.

```
public abstract class IDEOperation {
  private Compiler cmp;
  private Runtime rtime;
  public void compile(String javaFile) {
    cmp.compile(javaFile);
  }
  public void run(String classFile) {
    rtime.run (classFile);
  }
  //to be delayed until needed.
  public abstract void generateDocs(String javaFile);
  public IDEOperation() {
    cmp = new Compiler();
    rtime = new Runtime();
```

```
      }
    }
```

The IDEOperation class provides implementation for methods to compile and run Java programs. As part of its constructor, the IDEOperation creates and loads Compiler and Runtime objects required for the compile and execute operations. The javadoc generation method generateDocs is designed as an abstract method to be implemented by its subclasses.

Let us define a concrete subclass RealProcessor of the abstract IDEOperation class. The RealProcessor, as part of its constructor, creates a JavaDoc object that offers the javadoc generation service and implements the generateDocs method by using the JavaDoc object functionality.

```
public class RealProcessor extends IDEOperation {
  JavaDoc jdoc;
  public RealProcessor() {
    super();
    jdoc = new JavaDoc();
  }
  public void generateDocs(String javaFile) {
    jdoc.generateDocs(javaFile);
  }
}
```

With this implementation, the RealProcessor contains all the functionality to compile, run and generate javadocs for any Java program and can be readily used by client objects. As discussed earlier, however, the javadoc generation functionality may not be required for every Java program and the set of objects created when the RealProcessor is instantiated includes a JavaDoc object that is responsible for the javadoc generation. Creation of the JavaDoc objects can be deferred with the following advantages:

- Faster creation time of a RealProcessor object, as it needs to create fewer objects as part of its constructor.
- Efficient memory usage, as there is no need to hold an object in memory when there may be no need for its services.

Without altering the RealProcessor implementation, this can be accomplished by defining another subclass ProxyProcessor of the IDEOperation class. Because both the RealProcessor and the ProxyProcessor share the same interface, client objects can use the ProxyProcessor in place of the RealProcessor. Figure 25.1 shows the resulting class hierarchy.

```
public class ProxyProcessor extends IDEOperation {
  private RealProcessor realProcessor;
  public void generateDocs(String javaFile) {
```

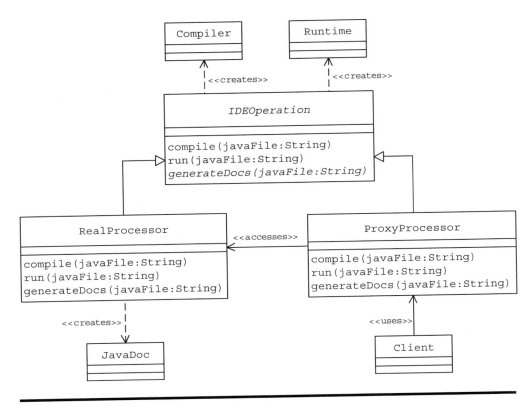

Figure 25.1 `IDEOperation` **Class Hierarchy**

```
/*
   In order to generate javadocs
   the proxy loads the actual object and
   invokes its methods.
   */
if (realProcessor == null) {
   realProcessor = new RealProcessor();
}
   realProcessor.generateDocs(javaFile);
   }
}
```

The `ProxyProcessor` maintains an object reference of the `RealProcessor` type as one of its instance variables. As part of the `generateDocs` method, the `ProxyProcessor` checks to see if this reference variable has been initialized with a `RealProcessor` object. If not, it creates a `RealProcessor` object and assigns it to the object reference instance variable. Once the `RealProcessor` object has been created, it invokes the `generateDocs` method on it.

In effect, it means that the `RealProcessor` is instantiated and loaded into the memory the first time when the javadoc generation functionality is requested by a client object. In turn, this means that the JavaDoc object is not created and loaded into the memory until a client needs to generate javadocs for a Java program.

Client objects do not need to know the existence of the RealProcessor and can invoke methods on the ProxyProcessor as if it is the real processor. Details such as the validations and checks involved and the communication between the ProxyProcessor and the RealProcessor are completely hidden from client objects.

```
public class Client {
  public static void main(String[] args) {
  /*
    At this point objects required for
    the compile and run operations are
    created, but not the objects that provide the
    generate Javadoc functionality.
  */
    IDEOperation IDE = new ProxyProcessor();
    IDE.compile("test.java");
    IDE.run("test.class");
  /*
    The Javadoc functionality is accessed
    For the first time and hence the
    Object offering the Javadoc generation
    Functionality is loaded at this point.
  */
    IDE.generateDocs("test.java");
  }
}
```

PRACTICE QUESTIONS

1. Consider an application that uses a DBManager class, which encapsulates all of the database access details. As soon as the application is run, the DBManager may not be needed. Because creating a database connection is considered as an expensive operation, it might be a good idea to defer the instantiation of the DBManager class until the application needs to access the database for the first time. Design a virtual proxy for the DBManager class, which allows the postponement of the DBManager object creation, at the same time hiding such details from client objects.

2. Identify how the virtual proxy is involved in the following examples:
   ■ When a word processor such as Microsoft® Word is installed, it does not automatically create the index for help topics. When the help is accessed

for the first time, it builds the help topics index (in the case of MS Word, it clearly displays a message to this effect).

■ Consider an application that uses JavaServer Pages™ technology. JSP scripts are not compiled automatically when they are placed in an application server specified directory. A JSP script is compiled the first time it is accessed.

26

COUNTING PROXY

This pattern was previously described in GoF95.

DESCRIPTION

The Counting Proxy pattern is useful in designing a set of additional operations such as logging and counting that need to be performed before and/or after a client object invokes a method on a service provider object. Instead of keeping these additional operations' implementation inside the service provider object, the Counting Proxy pattern suggests encapsulating the additional functionality in a separate object referred to as a *counting proxy*. One of the characteristics of a well-designed object is that it offers focused functionality. In other words, an object, ideally, should not do various unrelated things. Encapsulating the logging, counting and other similar functionality into a separate object leaves the service provider object with only the functionality that it is designed to offer. In other words, it allows the service provider object to perform a well-defined, definite task.

A counting proxy is designed to have the same interface as the service provider object that a client accesses. Instead of accessing the service provider object directly, client objects invoke methods on the counting proxy. The proxy performs the required logging and counting and forwards the method call to the service provider object (Figure 26.1).

The following example illustrates how a counting proxy can be used in an application scenario.

EXAMPLE

Let us design an `Order` class hierarchy as in Figure 26.2. The `OrderIF` interface declares a single method `getAllOrders` to read all orders from a database.

```
public interface OrderIF {
  public Vector getAllOrders();
}
```

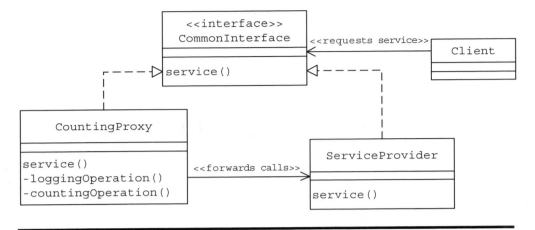

Figure 26.1   Generic Class Association When the Counting Proxy Pattern Is Applied

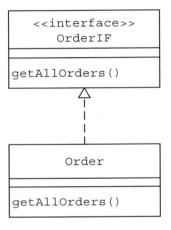

Figure 26.2   Order Class Hierarchy

As part of its implementation of the getAllOrders method, the Order class makes use of the FileUtil utility class to read order items from a data file orders.txt.

```
public class Order implements OrderIF {
  public Vector getAllOrders() {
    FileUtil fileUtil = new FileUtil();
    Vector v = fileUtil.fileToVector("orders.txt");
    return v;
  }
}
```

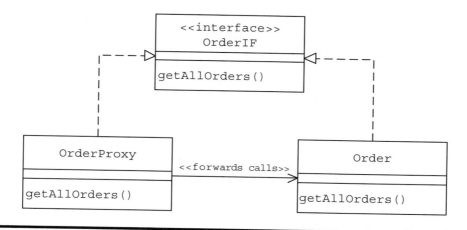

Figure 26.3   Order Class Hierarchy with the Counting Proxy

Let us suppose that the time it takes to read the data file and the number of times the getAllOrders operation is invoked need to be logged to a log file.

This additional functionality can be designed as a separate class OrderProxy that implements the same OrderIF interface as the actual Order object. This ensures that the OrderProxy offers the same interface to client objects as the actual Order object (Figure 26.3).

```
public class OrderProxy implements OrderIF {
  private int counter = 0;
  public Vector getAllOrders() {
    Order order = new Order();
    counter++;
    long t1 = System.currentTimeMillis ();
    Vector v = order.getAllOrders();
    long t2 = System.currentTimeMillis();
    long timeDiff = t2 - t1;
    String msg =
      "Iteration=" + counter + "::Time=" + timeDiff +
      "ms";
    //log the message
    FileUtil fileUtil = new FileUtil();
    fileUtil.writeToFile("log.txt",msg, true, true);
    return v;
  }
}
```

The client object MainApp can make use of the OrderProxy object as if it is the real Order object and invoke the OrderIF method getAllOrders on it. The `OrderProxy` forwards the call to the actual `Order` object, calculates the time it takes to read all orders and logs these details to a log file using the `FileUtil` helper class. In this process, the `OrderProxy` plays the role of a counting proxy.

```java
public class MainApp {
  public static void main(String[] args) {
    OrderIF order = new OrderProxy();
    Vector v = order.getAllOrders();
    v = order.getAllOrders();
    v = order.getAllOrders();
    v = order.getAllOrders();
  }
}
```

PRACTICE QUESTIONS

1. Design a counting proxy that keeps track of the number of orders created and provides the average order amount.
2. Consider items in a library. Library items can be divided into four categories — magazines, books, videos and DVDs. Design a proxy to keep track of the number of items of each category that are checked out every day.

27

AGGREGATE ENFORCER

DESCRIPTION

In general, classes are designed to carry related data and offer focused functionality. Sometimes an object may contain other objects as part of it. Such an object, which is a union of other objects, is called an *aggregate* object. For example, a computer is an Aggregate object that contains other objects such as a CPU unit and memory units. The Aggregate Enforcer pattern recommends that when an Aggregate object is constructed, it must be constructed in full. That means that when an Aggregate class is instantiated, all of its member variables representing the set of constituting objects must also be initialized. The idea is to make sure that an Aggregate object is created in full or is not created at all.

There are two types of aggregate relationships — aggregation and composition. In both of the relationships, an Aggregate object is composed of several constituting objects.

In the case of aggregation, the parts that make up the Aggregate object can exist meaningfully without the parent Aggregate object. Composition is a stronger form of aggregation. The set of constituting objects in a composition relationship with the parent Aggregate object cannot exist meaningfully on their own without the Aggregate object.

A member variable representing a constituting object can be initialized either at the time of creating the Aggregate object (early initialization) or on demand when there is a need to use the variable. Early initialization of constituting objects has the following advantages:

- An Aggregate object is always treated as a union of constituting objects. That means an Aggregate object cannot exist without its constituting objects. Hence, it follows the semantics of an Aggregate object to construct the Aggregate object in full by initializing all of its constituting objects.
- Early initialization reveals any problems with the construction of any of the constituting objects at the time of constructing the parent aggregate itself.
- All other client objects and different member functions within the Aggregate object can assume that the member variables representing constituting objects are always fully initialized. This eliminates the need for unwanted conditional statements to check if a member variable is initialized.

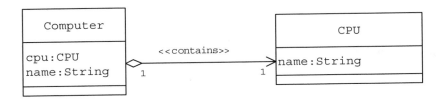

Figure 27.1   Computer Class Representation as an Aggregate

EXAMPLE

Let us design an `Aggregate` class representation for a typical computer with the CPU class as its constituting part (Figure 27.1). For simplicity, let us consider single processor computers only.

Design Approach I (On-Demand Initialization)

The object variable `cpu` can be initialized only when it is needed.

From the `Computer` class design in Listing 27.1 it can be observed that whenever the `cpu` object reference variable is accessed, a check is made to ensure that the object reference variable is properly initialized. Since there is no guarantee that the `cpu` variable is initialized, this check is crucial to prevent potential runtime errors.

Design Approach II (Early Initialization)

Initializing the `cpu` object reference variable with in the constructor (Listing 27.2) eliminates the need for a check to make sure that this object reference variable is properly initialized.

This does eliminate the need for the null value checking. But it does not always *force* the initialization of the `cpu` member variable when the `Aggregate` `Computer` object is created. In other words, even though it helps in eliminating the need for the null value checking, it is not an absolute requirement to initialize the `cpu` variable to be able to create an instance of the `Aggregate` `Computer` class. The `Computer` class must be designed in such a way that it becomes mandatory to initialize the `cpu` variable in its constructor. In general, what is needed is a way to make it *mandatory* to initialize the set of member variables that represent the objects constituting the `Aggregate` object.

Design Approach III (Final Variables)

A slight modification to the way the member variable `cpu` is declared, as in Listing 27.3, will do the trick. In Java, declaring a member variable as final ensures that the variable gets initialized fully as part of the object constructor (Figure 27.2). The compiler does not compile a class that does not fully initialize all of its final member variables.

Listing 27.1   Computer Class (On-Demand Initialization)

```java
public class Computer {
  //Constituting Object
  private CPU cpu;
  private String name;
  //Constructor
  public Computer(String n) {
    name = n;
  }
  public boolean start() {
    //…
    initCPU();
    System.out.println("CPU activated");
    return true;
  }
  public boolean executeTask() {
    //…
    initCPU();
    System.out.println("CPU is Executing the Task");
    return true;
  }
  public boolean stop() {
    //…
    initCPU();
    System.out.println("CPU is stopped");
    return true;
  }
  private void initCPU() {
    if (cpu == null) {
      cpu = new CPU("Intel");
    }
  }
}
class CPU {
  private String name;
  public CPU(String n) {
    name = n;
  }
}
```

Listing 27.2   Computer Class (Early Initialization)

```java
public class Computer {
  //Constituting Object
  private CPU cpu;
  private String name;
  //Constructor
  public Computer(String n) {
    name = n;
    cpu = new CPU("Intel");
  }
  public boolean start() {
    //...
    System.out.println("CPU activated");
    return true;
  }
      ...
      ...

}
```

Because the member variable initialization is guaranteed, different methods can safely eliminate the check for variable initialization.

The example deals with the construction of a single, small object as part of the Aggregate object creation. Sometimes, an Aggregate object may be composed of a number of large, complex objects. This could make it extremely expensive to construct all of the constituting objects when the Aggregate object is created. In such cases, the Virtual Proxy pattern can be used to design a proxy corresponding to each of the constituting objects. These Proxy objects can be constructed in place of actual constituting objects, as part of the Aggregate object creation.

PRACTICE QUESTIONS

1. Design a class representation for a country, which contains its capital. Ensure that the aggregate entity country is constructed in full at the time of its creation.

2. A general hospital consists of different departments. Design a representation for this relationship. Ensure that all constituting department objects are initialized when the aggregate hospital object is created.

Listing 27.3   Computer Class: Revised

```java
public class Computer {
  //Constituting Object
  private final CPU cpu;
  private String name;
  //Constructor
  public Computer(String n) {
    name = n;
    cpu = new CPU("Intel");
  }
  public boolean start() {
    //…
    System.out.println("CPU activated");
    return true;
  }
  public boolean executeTask() {
    //…
    System.out.println("CPU is Executing the Task");
    return true;
  }
  public boolean stop() {
    //…
    System.out.println("CPU is stopped");
    return true;
  }
}
class CPU {
  private String name;
  public CPU(String n) {
    name = n;
  }
}
```

Figure 27.2   Revised Computer Class Representation as an Aggregate

28

EXPLICIT OBJECT RELEASE

DESCRIPTION

In general, an object may need to deal with external resources such as files, databases and network connections as part of its implementation to provide the services it is designed for. The Explicit Object Release pattern suggests that when such an object is no longer needed, the external resources tied up with the object should be released *explicitly*, in a *timely* manner.

The Java programming language provides the following two ways to design the mechanism to release external resources explicitly:

- The finalize() method
- The finally statement

The finalize Method

Some object-oriented programming languages require a programmer to explicitly destroy objects when they are no longer needed. In the Java programming language, a programmer does not need to explicitly destroy objects. The Java Virtual Machine (JVM) is responsible for reclaiming the memory allocated to different objects when they go out of scope. This process is known as *garbage collection*. There are two main characteristics of the garbage collection process.

When an Object Goes Out of Scope, It Is Believed to Be Garbage Collected Immediately

This understanding is not entirely accurate. When an object goes out of scope, it is marked as eligible for garbage collection, but the process of garbage collection may not begin immediately. The garbage collection process runs periodically to reclaim the memory occupied by objects that are out of scope and no longer referenced. This happens in a recursive manner. But there is no exact specification as to when the JVM should run the garbage collection process.

When the garbage collection process runs, before an object is garbage collected, the Java runtime system invokes the object's finalize() method. Any required clean up operations to release any system resources such as open files or open sockets can be implemented as part of the `finalize()` method. The `finalize()` method must be declared as:

```
protected void finalize() throws Throwable
```

The Garbage Collection Process Runs as a Low-Level Background Daemon Thread

In general, it is not essential that a process running on a daemon thread be allowed to complete before an application terminates.

From these details of the garbage collection process, it can be seen that even though the `finalize()` method can be used to perform clean-up operations, it is not a reliable option to free system resources in a timely manner. This is mainly because the garbage collection process, which invokes the `finalize()` method on an object, runs at unpredictable times.

The `finally` Statement

Java provides another way of performing clean-up operations. This involves having a `finally` code block, where the implementation for explicitly releasing any external resources can be kept. Unlike the `finalize()` method, the `finally` statement code block is not dependent on the garbage collection process. Releasing resources inside the `finally` block is more advisable as the code inside the `finally` is *always guaranteed* to be executed even when there is an unexpected runtime exception.

The following example demonstrates how the `finally` statement can be used to release resources when an object goes out of scope.

EXAMPLE

Suppose that we are writing an application to write order data to a file.

One of the simplest ways of designing this functionality is to have an `Order-Log` utility class with a method such as `log` that takes the order data as input and writes it to a data file.

```java
public class OrderLog {
  public void log (Order order) {
    PrintWriter dataOut = null;
    try {
      dataOut =
        new PrintWriter (new FileWriter("order.txt"));
      String dataLine =
        order.getID() + "," + order.getItem() +
        "," + order.getQty();
      dataOut.println(dataLine);
      dataOut.close();
    } catch (IOException e) {
```

```
        System.err.println("IOException Occurred:  " +
                           e.getMessage());
      }
    }
  }
```

This implementation of the OrderLog class provides the mandatory exception handling as required by the compiler to compile successfully. Let us consider different possibilities when an application uses an OrderLog object to log different orders.

Best Case Scenario

In the best case scenario:

- The application invokes the log method on an OrderLog object by passing a fully initialized Order object.
- The OrderLog successfully retrieves different Order attribute values and writes them to the data file inside a try block using a PrintWriter object.
- The PrintWriter object is closed at the end of the try block.

Exception Scenario 1

Similar to the best case scenario:

- The application using an OrderLog object fully initializes an Order object and invokes the log method.
- An IOException occurs inside the try block when the OrderLog attempts to create a PrintWriter object.
- When the application is run, the application does not end abnormally as the IOException is caught inside the catch block.

Exception Scenario 2

Unlike both the above scenarios, if the Order object passed to the log method is not fully initialized, it could result in a NullPointerException. Because this is a runtime exception, the compiler cannot warn the user — even if it is not handled using a catch block. Because the log method implementation does not catch the NullPointerException, the application exits abnormally without closing the PrintWriter object. This can be avoided by declaring handlers for all possible runtime exceptions using individual catch statements and closing the PrintWriter object inside each of these handlers.

```
    public class OrderLog {
      public void log (Order order) {
        PrintWriter dataOut = null;
        try {
```

```
    dataOut =
      new PrintWriter (new FileWriter("order.txt"));
    String dataLine =
      order.getID() + "," + order.getItem() +
      "," + order.getQty();
    dataOut.println(dataLine);
    dataOut.close();//duplicate code
  }
  catch (IOException e) {
    System.err.println("IOException Occurred: " +
                         e.getMessage());
  }
  catch (NullPointerException ne) {
    dataOut.close();//duplicate code
  }
  catch (AnotherRuntimeException ne) {
    dataOut.close();//duplicate code
  }
 }
}
```

The implementation of the `log` method contains duplicate code segments for closing the `PrintWriter` object in each of the runtime exception handlers. Besides this disadvantage, it may not be possible for a typical programmer to anticipate all possible runtime exceptions, as the compiler does not require runtime exceptions to be handled to compile a Java class successfully.

Another solution is to define a generic exception handler to catch all possible exceptions — both checked and unchecked ones. Every Java exception is an instance of Throwable or a subclass of Throwable. The Exception class is high in the Throwable class hierarchy. Hence, declaring a handler to catch exceptions of the Exception class type can catch almost all of the checked and unchecked exceptions.

```
public class OrderLog {
  public void log (Order order) {
    PrintWriter dataOut = null;
    try {
      dataOut =
        new PrintWriter (new FileWriter("order.txt"));
      String dataLine =
        order.getID() + ,"" + order.getItem() +
        "," + order.getQty();
      dataOut.println(dataLine);
```

```
      dataOut.close();//duplicate code
    } catch (Exception e) {
      //Identify the type of runtime
      //exception occurred.
      if (e instanceof NullPointerException) {
        dataOut.close();//duplicate code
      }
      if (e instanceof IOException) {
        System.err.println("IOException Occurred: ");
      }
    }
  }
}
```

Ideally, an exception handler should be more specialized to handle a specific type of exception. In the case of a generalized exception handler, the handler needs to further identify the exact type of the exception that occurred to determine the recovery strategy. This results in a set of conditional statements in the `catch` block implementation corresponding to the set of all possible runtime exceptions. Having to check for all possible runtime exceptions defeats the purpose of having a generalized exception handler.

Another option is to provide the implementation for closing the `PrintWriter` object using the `finally` statement.

```
public class OrderLog {
  public void log (Order order) {
    PrintWriter dataOut = null;
    try {
      dataOut =
        new PrintWriter (new FileWriter("order.txt"));
      String dataLine =
        order.getID() + "," + order.getItem() +
        "," + order.getQty();
      dataOut.println(dataLine);
    } catch (IOException e) {
      System.err.println("IOException Occurred: ");
    }
    catch (NullPointerException ne) {
      System.err.println("NullPointerException Occurred: ");
    }
    finally{//Guaranteed to get executed
      if (dataOut != null) {
        dataOut.close();
```

```
            }
          }
        }
      }
```

The implementation looks similar to declaring multiple exception handlers, but using the `finally` statement to close the `PrintWriter` object does not require that the same code to close the `PrintWriter` instance be put in each of the exception handlers. This eliminates the code duplication. In addition, the code implementation to close the `PrintWriter` object inside the `finally` statement is *guaranteed to always get executed*. That means, even if an uncaught runtime exception occurs, the `PrintWriter` object will still be closed as a result of executing the `finally` statement code.

PRACTICE QUESTIONS

1. Design and implement an application to log messages to a database. Ensure that the database connection is released in a timely manner.
2. Design and implement an application to write messages to a remote server using a network socket. Ensure that the socket connection is released even for unhandled runtime exceptions.

29

OBJECT CACHE

This pattern was previously described in Grand98.

DESCRIPTION

During the discussion of the Counting Proxy we had developed an application to read all order records from a data file and log the time it takes to read these records. When the application is executed multiple times with a large number of orders in the data file, it can be observed that compared to the time taken to read orders from the data file during the first time execution, it takes less time to read the data file in subsequent application executions.

Every time the operation to read all orders is performed in the application, from the program code point of view, it should take exactly the same amount of time. This is because the code that gets executed and the data file remain the same every time orders are read from the data file. But the observation shows that it is not the case.

The reason for this behavior is that when the data file is read for the first time, the computer (the operating system) reads the file contents into the computer's memory. When the next immediate request is to read the same unchanged file, the operating system does not actually read the file again. Instead, it gives back the file contents that are already available in its memory. This results in a much faster response time to a client request.

The concept of keeping a copy of an object in the memory, in some form, with the goal of providing a faster response time to a client request is called *caching*. This is often done when the construction of a new object is expensive in terms of the processing involved. The object in the memory is not kept in the memory forever. Maintaining a large number of objects for a long time could have a negative effect on the application's performance. A strategy must be developed to decide on the optimal number of objects to be cached and how long these objects are to be kept in the memory. Such decisions constitute the cache management strategy. The following example shows how caching can be applied in an application scenario to improve the response time.

EXAMPLE

Let us design an application for product activation at a department store. Periodically, the store receives different product items from the distribution center. Before the items arrive, the department store receives the item data from the distribution center. These details include the item bar code, description and other related data. When the items arrive, the department store personnel need to scan each item bar code to activate it. Once an item is marked as active, it will be available for sale. The sequence of steps in this process can be summarized as follows:

■ Department store personnel use a bar code reader to read an item's bar code.
■ The bar code value is sent to an application object that updates the corresponding database entry with the current date as the date-of-activation.

One problem with this approach is that, every time the bar code of an item is scanned, the item gets updated in the database. This is true, even if the same item is scanned multiple times. Sometimes, department store personnel may doubt that an item is scanned properly and rescan the item to ensure that it gets activated. Scanning the same item more than once does not create any data integrity issues, but it results in waste of processing time due to redundant database updates. This can be avoided by applying the Object Cache pattern.

Let us begin our design with a representation for caching some of the most recently activated items. This can be designed in the form of a class `ItemCache` as in Listing 29.1.

The `ItemCache` offers two methods — `getItem` and `addItem` — which can be used by other objects to read item codes from and add item codes to the item cache. The `ItemCache` uses a `vector` to store different item bar codes. There is a limit on how many items can be maintained in the cache. For simplicity, the example defines a hard coded-value for the maximum limit. A more optimal number for the limit can be decided based on various application and infrastructure details. Details such as the duration for which these item bar codes should be maintained and what should be done when the maximum limit is reached constitute the application cache management strategy. In this example, when the maximum limit is reached, the least recently activated item is purged from the cache. Many different criteria can be taken into account to decide which one of the cached bar codes should be purged. For example, a cached item may be selected to be purged based upon the frequency of its access by other objects. That is, the least frequently referred cache entry needs to be purged.

Let us further define an `ItemManager` (Listing 29.2), which is responsible for the overall item management.

The `ItemManager` offers an `activate` method that can be used by other application objects to activate an item. The `ItemManager` maintains a cache of some of the most recently activated item bar codes in the form of an instance variable of the `ItemCache` type. Whenever a client needs to activate an item, it:

1. Creates an `ItemManager` instance.

Listing 29.1 `ItemCache` Class

```
public class ItemCache {
  private final static int Max_cache_size = 5;
  Vector cache;
  public ItemCache() {
    cache = new Vector();
  }
  public String getItem(String code) {
    String barCode = null;
    int pos = cache.indexOf(code);
    if (pos != -1)
      barCode = (String) cache.get(pos);
    return barCode;
  }
  public void addItem(String code) {
    //if the max limit is reached
    //remove the LRU item
    if (cache.size() == Max_cache_size) {
      cache.remove(0);
    }
    cache.add(code);
  }
}
```

2. Invokes the `activate` method on the `ItemManager` object passing the item bar code as an argument.

The `ItemManager` checks to see if the item already exists in the cache.

- If it exists then, it means that the item has been activated recently. The `ItemManager` simply returns with an appropriate message.
- If the item does not exist, then the `ItemManager` accesses the database using a helper class `DBManager` to check if the item is already in the active state.
  - If the item is already activated, the `ItemManager` returns with an appropriate message.
  - If not, the `ItemManager` updates the item as active with the current date as the date-of-activation and adds it to the item cache.

This approach eliminates the need for redundant database updates. Figure 29.1 shows the structure and the association of different classes in the application design.

Listing 29.2 `ItemManager` **Class**

```java
public class ItemManager {
  ItemCache cache;
  DBManager manager;
  public ItemManager() {
    cache = new ItemCache();
    manager = new DBManager();
  }
  public void activate(String code) {
    if (cache.getItem(code) != null) {
      System.out.println("Item Already Activated - cache");
    } else {
      if (manager.isActiveItem(code)) {
        System.out.println(
          "Item Already Activated - DB Access");
      } else {
        manager.activateItem(code);
        System.out.println(
          "Item Activated successfully");
        //add to the cache
        cache.addItem(code);
      }
    }
  }
}
```

The existence of the item cache remains transparent to the client object. The client can invoke methods on the `ItemManager` without having to know how the `ItemManager` uses the `ItemCache` internally.

```java
public class Client {
  public static void main(String[] args) {
    ItemManager manager = new ItemManager();
    manager.activate("1001001000");
    manager.activate("1001001001");
    manager.activate("1001001002");
    manager.activate("1001001000");
    manager.activate("1001001004");
    manager.activate("1001001005");
    manager.activate("1001001006");
```

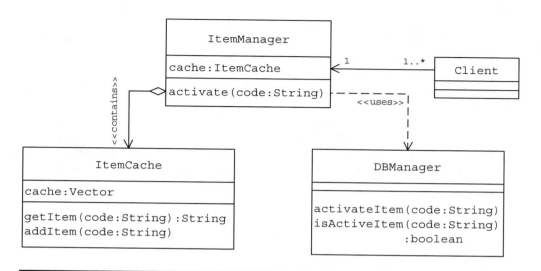

Figure 29.1   Class Association

```
    manager.activate("1001001002");
    manager.activate("1001001004");
    manager.activate("1001001002");
    manager.activate("1001001000");
  }
}
```

When the client application is run the following output will be displayed:

```
Item Activated successfully
Item Activated successfully
Item Activated successfully
Item Already Activated - cache
Item Activated successfully
Item Activated successfully
Item Activated successfully
Item Already Activated - cache
Item Already Activated - cache
Item Already Activated - cache
Item Activated successfully
```

PRACTICE QUESTIONS

1. Design an application to query the features of different items. Maintain the details of a set of recently read items in a cache. When a client object

requests the details of an item that are already available in the cache, they can be sent back to the client without retrieving details from the database.

2. Implement the purge criteria based on the frequency of access, i.e., each object in the cache is associated with a counter. When a cache object is returned to a client, its counter is incremented. When the maximum cache limit is reached and a new item needs to be added to the cache, one of the existing cached items needs to be purged. Using the access frequency as the criteria, the item in the cache with the least value for its frequency counter can be deleted. If there is more than one item with the same lower frequency counter value, then one of them can be chosen at random.

VII

BEHAVIORAL PATTERNS

Behavioral Patterns mainly:

- Deal with the details of assigning responsibilities between different objects
- Describe the communication mechanism between objects
- Define the mechanism for choosing different algorithms by different objects at runtime

Chapter	Pattern Name	Description
30	Command	Allows a request to be encapsulated into an object giving control over request queuing, sequencing and undoing.
31	Mediator	Encapsulates the direct object-to-object communication details among a set of objects in a separate (mediator) object. This eliminates the need for these objects to interact with each other directly.
32	Memento	Allows the state of an object to be captured and stored. The object can be put back to this (previous) state, when needed.
33	Observer	Promotes a publisher–subscriber communication model when there is a one-to-many dependency between objects so that when one object changes state, all of its dependents are notified so they can update their state.
34	Interpreter	Useful when the objective is to provide a client program or a user the ability to specify operations in a simple language. Helps in interpreting operations specified using a language, using its grammar. More suitable for languages with simple grammar.
35	State	Allows the state-specific behavior of an object to be encapsulated in the form of a set of state objects. With each state-specific behavior mapped onto a specific state object, the object can change its behavior by configuring itself with an appropriate state object.
36	Strategy	Allows each of a family of related algorithms to be encapsulated into a set of different subclasses (strategy objects) of a common superclass. For an object to use an algorithm, the object needs to be configured with the corresponding strategy object. With this arrangement, algorithm implementation can vary without affecting its clients.
37	Null Object	Provides a way of encapsulating the (usually do nothing) behavior of a given object type into a separate null object. This object can be used to provide the default behavior when no object of the specific type is available.

(continued)

Chapter	Pattern Name	Description
38	Template Method	When there is an algorithm that could be implemented in multiple ways, the template pattern enables keeping the outline of the algorithm in a separate method (Template Method) inside a class (Template Class), leaving out the specific implementations of this algorithm to different subclasses. In other words, the Template Method pattern is used to keep the invariant part of the functionality in one place and allow the subclasses to provide the implementation of the variant part.
39	Object Authenticator	Useful when access to an application object is restricted and requires a client object to furnish proper authentication credentials. Uses a separate object with the responsibility of verifying the access privileges of different client objects instead of keeping this responsibility on the application object.
40	Common Attribute Registry	Provides a way of designing a repository to store the common transient state of an application.

30

COMMAND

This pattern was previously described in GoF95.

DESCRIPTION

In general, an object-oriented application consists of a set of interacting objects each offering limited, focused functionality. In response to user interaction, the application carries out some kind of processing. For this purpose, the application makes use of the services of different objects for the processing requirement. In terms of implementation, the application may depend on a designated object that invokes methods on these objects by passing the required data as arguments (Figure 30.1). This designated object can be referred to as an *invoker* as it invokes operations on different objects. The invoker may be treated as part of the client application. The set of objects that actually contain the implementation to offer the services required for the request processing can be referred to as *Receiver* objects.

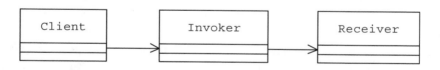

Figure 30.1   Object Interaction: Before Applying the Command Pattern

In this design, the application that forwards the request and the set of `Receiver` objects that offer the services required to process the request are closely tied to each other in that they interact with each other directly. This could result in a set of conditional *if* statements in the implementation of the invoker.

```
    ...
if (RequestType=TypeA){
  //do something
}
```

```
if (RequestType=TypeB){
  //do something
}
    ...
```

When a new type of feature is to be added to the application, the existing code needs to be modified and it violates the basic object-oriented open-closed principle.

```
    ...
if (RequestType=TypeA){
  //do something
}
    ...
if (RequestType=NewType){
  //do something
}
    ...
```

The open-closed principle states that a software module should be:

■ *Open for extension* — It should be possible to alter the behavior of a module or add new features to the module functionality.
■ *Closed for modification* — Such a module should not allow its code to be modified.

In a nutshell, the open-closed principle helps in designing software modules whose functionality can be extended without having to modify the existing code.

Using the Command pattern, the invoker that issues a request on behalf of the client and the set of service-rendering `Receiver` objects can be decoupled. The Command pattern suggests creating an abstraction for the processing to be carried out or the action to be taken in response to client requests.

This abstraction can be designed to declare a common interface to be implemented by different concrete implementers referred to as *Command objects*. Each `Command` object represents a different type of client request and the corresponding processing. In Figure 30.2, the `Command` interface represents the abstraction. It declares an `execute` method, which is implemented by two of its implementer (command) classes — `ConcreteCommand_1` and `ConcreteCommand_2`.

A given `Command` object is responsible for offering the functionality required to process the request it represents, but it does not contain the actual implementation of the functionality. `Command` objects make use of `Receiver` objects in offering this functionality (Figure 30.3).

When the client application needs to offer a service in response to user (or other application) interaction:

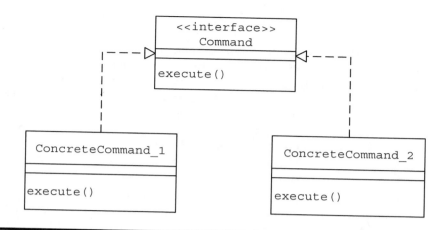

Figure 30.2 Command Object Hierarchy

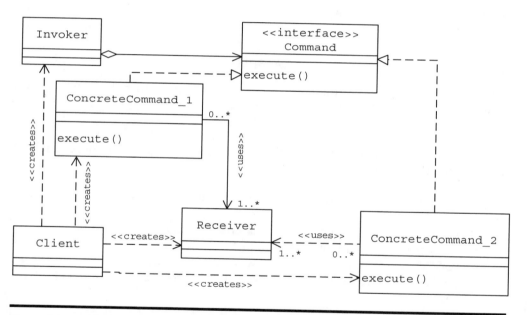

Figure 30.3 Class Association: After the Command Pattern Is Applied

1. It creates the necessary Receiver objects.
2. It creates an appropriate Command object and configures it with the Receiver objects created in Step 1.
3. It creates an instance of the invoker and configures it with the Command object created in Step 2.
4. The invoker invokes the execute() method on the Command object.
5. As part of its implementation of the execute method, a typical Command object invokes necessary methods on the Receiver objects it contains to provide the required service to its caller.

In the new design:

- The client/invoker does not directly interact with `Receiver` objects and therefore, they are completely decoupled from each other.
- When the application needs to offer a new feature, a new `Command` object can be added. This does not require any changes to the code of the invoker. Hence the new design conforms to the open-closed principle.
- Because the request is designed in the form of an object, it opens up a whole new set of possibilities such as:
  - Storing a `Command` object to persistent media:
    - To be executed later.
    - To apply reverse processing to support the undo feature.
  - Grouping together different `Command` objects to be executed as a single unit.

The following FTP (File Transfer Protocol) client example application provides a good understanding of how the `Command` pattern can be applied in real world applications.

EXAMPLE I

Let us build an application that simulates the working of an FTP client. In Java, a simple FTP client user interface can be designed using:

- Two `JList` objects for the local and remote file systems display
- Four `JButton` objects for initiating different types of requests such as upload, download, delete and exit

Once the user interface controls are arranged in a frame, the UI display looks as in Figure 30.4.

When each of the `JButton` objects is created, an instance of the `Button-Handler` class that implements the built-in `ActionListener` interface is set as its `ActionListener`. This means that whenever a `JButton` object in the UI display is clicked, the `actionPerformed` method of the `ButtonHandler` object gets executed.

```
public class FTPGUI extends JFrame {

    ...

    ...

//Create buttons
btnUpload = new JButton(FTPGUI.UPLOAD);
btnUpload.setMnemonic(KeyEvent.VK_U);

    ...

    ...

ButtonHandler vf = new ButtonHandler();
btnUpload.addActionListener(vf);
btnDownload.addActionListener(vf);
```

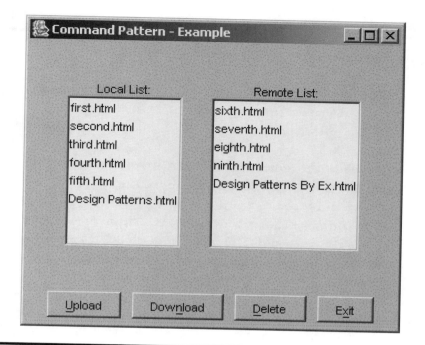

Figure 30.4 Simple FTP Client UI Display

```
    btnDelete.addActionListener(vf);
    btnExit.addActionListener(vf);

        ...

        ...
}//end of class
```

Because the same instance of the ButtonHandler is set as the Action-
Listener for all JButton objects in the UI display, the actionPerformed
method is called for all JButton objects. Hence the ButtonHandler object
must check which button is clicked and carry out the appropriate processing.

From Listing 30.1, it can be seen that code in the actionPerformed method
is a little inelegant with a set of conditional statements and as more button and
menu item objects are added to the FTP UI, the code could quickly become
cluttered. Also, when a new button object is to be added, the existing code in
the actionPerformed method needs to be modified. This violates the object-
oriented open-closed principle.

Let us redesign the application using the Command pattern. Applying the
Command pattern, let us define an abstraction in the form of a CommandInter-
face interface for the functionality associated with different button objects in the
FTP client UI.

```
interface CommandInterface {
  public void processEvent();
}
```

Listing 30.1 `ButtonHandler` Class

```java
class ButtonHandler implements ActionListener {
  public void actionPerformed(ActionEvent e) {
    //if statements - for different types of client requests
    if (e.getActionCommand().equals(FTPGUI.EXIT)) {
      System.exit(1);
    }
    if (e.getActionCommand().equals(FTPGUI.UPLOAD)) {
      int index = localList.getSelectedIndex();
      String selectedItem =
        localList.getSelectedValue().toString();
      ((DefaultListModel) localList.getModel()).remove(
        index);
      ((DefaultListModel) remoteList.getModel()).
      addElement(selectedItem);
    }
    if (e.getActionCommand().equals(FTPGUI.DOWNLOAD)) {
      int index = remoteList.getSelectedIndex();
      String selectedItem =
        remoteList.getSelectedValue().toString();
      ((DefaultListModel) remoteList.getModel()).remove(
        index);
      ((DefaultListModel) localList.getModel()).
      addElement(selectedItem);
    }
    if (e.getActionCommand().equals(FTPGUI.DELETE)) {
      int index = localList.getSelectedIndex();
      if (index >= 0) {
        ((DefaultListModel) localList.getModel()).
        remove(index);
      }
      index = remoteList.getSelectedIndex();
      if (index >= 0) {
        ((DefaultListModel) remoteList.getModel()).
        remove(index);
      }
    }
  }
}
```

Different button objects themselves can implement this interface and behave as individual command objects. But this is not recommended as:

- The JButton class is a highly reusable class and is used on many occasions where the Java Swing library is used to create an application user interface. Implementation specific to the CommandInterface may not be applicable in all such cases.
- If the JButton class is redesigned to implement the CommandInterface interface, it needs to implement the functionality required to process different types of requests such as upload, download and others corresponding to different JButton objects in the user interface. This results in adding unrelated functionality to the JButton class — low cohesion. In addition:
  - This could lead to inelegant conditional statements.
  - Every time a new button is added to the user interface, it would require changes to the existing implementation of the processEvent method, which is a violation of the object-oriented open-closed principle.

To overcome these problems, a set of new button classes, each corresponding to a different type of request, can be designed as subclasses of the JButton class (Listing 30.2). These subclasses can be designed to implement the CommandInterface. As part of its implementation of the processEvent method, each subclass of the JButton class offers the functionality required to process the request it represents (Figure 30.5).

The FTP UI can be built using objects of this new set of JButton subclasses. The rest of the application remains unchanged and the actionPerformed method gets highly simplified to a mere two lines of code.

```
class buttonHandler implements ActionListener {
  public void actionPerformed(ActionEvent e) {
    CommandInterface CommandObj =
      (CommandInterface) e.getSource();
    CommandObj.processEvent();
  }
}
```

In the new design whenever a new button or a menu item is to be added, a new Command object needs to be created as an implementer of the CommandInterface. The new Command object can be added to the application in a seamless manner without requiring changes to the existing actionPerformed method code. On the negative side, this results in a larger number of classes.

Listing 30.2 `JButton` Subclasses to Perform Different FTP Operations

```java
class UploadButton extends JButton
  implements CommandInterface {
  public void processEvent() {
    int index = localList.getSelectedIndex();
    String selectedItem =
      localList.getSelectedValue().toString();
    ((DefaultListModel) localList.getModel()).remove(
      index);
    ((DefaultListModel) remoteList.getModel()).addElement(
      selectedItem);
  }
  public UploadButton(String name) {
    super(name);
  }
}
class DownloadButton extends JButton
  implements CommandInterface {
  public void processEvent() {
    int index = remoteList.getSelectedIndex();
    String selectedItem =
      remoteList.getSelectedValue().toString();
    ((DefaultListModel) remoteList.getModel()).remove(
      index);
    ((DefaultListModel) localList.getModel()).addElement(
      selectedItem);
  }
  public DownloadButton(String name) {
    super(name);
  }
}
class DeleteButton extends JButton
  implements CommandInterface {
  public void processEvent() {
    int index = localList.getSelectedIndex();
    if (index >= 0) {
      ((DefaultListModel) localList.getModel()).remove(
        index);
    }
```

(continued)

Listing 30.2   JButton Subclasses to Perform Different FTP Operations (Continued)

```java
      index = remoteList.getSelectedIndex();
      if (index >= 0) {
        ((DefaultListModel) remoteList.getModel()).remove(
          index);
      }
    }
    public DeleteButton(String name) {
       super(name);
    }
  }
  class ExitButton extends JButton
    implements CommandInterface {
    public void processEvent() {
      System.exit(1);
    }
    public ExitButton(String name) {
      super(name);
    }
  }
```

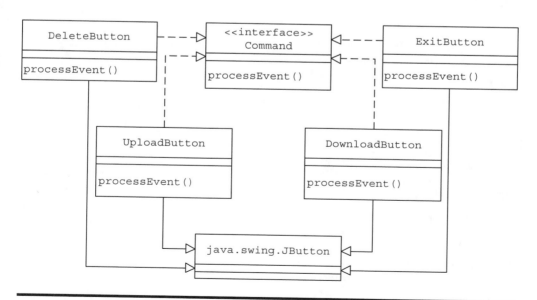

Figure 30.5   FTP UI: Command Object Hierarchy

EXAMPLE II

Let us build an application to manage items in a library item database. Typical library items include books, CDs, videos and DVDs. These items are grouped into categories and a given item can belong to one or more categories. For example, a new movie video may belong to both the Video category and the NewReleases category.

Let us define two classes — Item and Category — (Listing 30.3) representing a typical library item and a category of items, respectively (Figure 30.6).

From the design and the implementation of the Item and the Category classes, it can be seen that a Category object maintains a list of its current member items. Similarly, an Item object maintains the list of all categories which it is part of. For simplicity, let us suppose that the library item management application deals only with adding and deleting items. Applying the Command pattern, the action to be taken to process *add item* and *delete item* requests can be designed as implementers of a common CommandInterface interface. The CommandInterface provides an abstraction for the processing to be carried out in response to a typical library item management request such as add or delete item. The CommandInterface implementers — AddCommand and DeleteCommand — in Figure 30.7 represent the add and the delete item request, respectively.

Let us further define an invoker ItemManager class.

```
public class ItemManager {
  CommandInterface command;
  public void setCommand(CommandInterface c) {
    command = c;
  }
  public void process() {
    command.execute();
  }
}
```

The ItemManager:

■ Contains a Command object within
■ Invokes the Command object's execute method as part of its process method implementation
■ Provides a setCommand method to allow client objects to configure it with a Command object

The client CommandTest uses the invoker ItemManager to get its *add item* and *delete item* requests processed.

Application Flow

To add or delete an item, the client CommandTest (Listing 30.4):

1. Creates the necessary Item and Category objects. These objects act as receivers.
2. Creates an appropriate Command object that corresponds to its current request. The set of Receiver objects' created in Step 1 is passed to the Command object at the time of its creation.
3. Creates an instance of the ItemManager and configures it with the Command object created in Step 2.
4. Invokes the process() method of the ItemManager. The ItemManager invokes the execute method on the Command object. The Command object in turn invokes necessary Receiver object methods. Different Item and Category Receiver objects perform the actual request processing. To keep the example simple, no database access logic is implemented. Both Item and Category objects are implemented to simply display a message.

When the client program is run, the following output is displayed:

```
Item 'A Beautiful Mind' has been added to the 'CD' Category
Item 'Duet' has been added to the 'CD' Category
Item 'Duet' has been added to the 'New Releases' Category
Item 'Duet' has been deleted from the 'New Releases'
Category
```

The class diagram in Figure 30.8 depicts the overall class association.
The sequence diagram in Figure 30.9 shows the message flow when the client CommandTest uses a Command object to add an item.

PRACTICE QUESTIONS

1. In Example I above, different concrete Command classes are designed as inner classes. Redesign and implement the example application with different Command classes as external classes.
2. Add a new method undo() to the CommandInterface in Examples I and II. Enhance different command classes implementing this method to offer the functionality required to undo the effect of the execute() method.
3. Enhance the Example II application to include the ability to log the data and time when a specific add or delete operation is performed.
4. Enhance the Example II application to add the *move* functionality that allows an item to be moved from one category to another. Implement the *move* functionality as a combination of *delete* followed by an *add* operation. Both delete and add operations must be executed together as a unit to provide the move functionality.

Listing 30.3   Item and Category Classes

```java
public class Item {
  private HashMap categories;
  private String desc;
  public Item(String s) {
    desc = s;
    categories = new HashMap();
  }
  public String getDesc() {
    return desc;
  }
  public void add(Category cat) {
    categories.put(cat.getDesc(), cat);
  }
  public void delete(Category cat) {
    categories.remove(cat.getDesc());
  }
}
public class Category {
  private HashMap items;
  private String desc;
  public Category(String s) {
    desc = s;
    items = new HashMap();
  }
  public String getDesc() {
    return desc;
  }
  public void add(Item i) {
    items.put(i.getDesc(), i);
    System.out.println("Item '" + i.getDesc() +
                       "' has been added to the '" +
                       getDesc() + "' Category ");
  }
```

(continued)

Listing 30.3   Item and Category Classes (Continued)

```
public void delete(Item i) {
  items.remove(i.getDesc());
  System.out.println("Item '" + i.getDesc() +
                     "' has been deleted from the '" +
                     getDesc() + "' Category ");
}
}
```

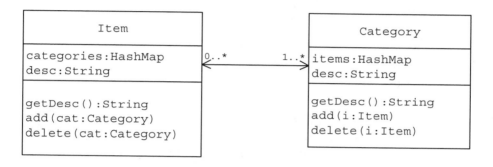

Figure 30.6   Item-Category Association

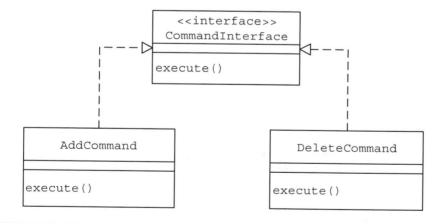

Figure 30.7   Command Object Hierarchy

Listing 30.4 Client CommandTest Class

```java
public class CommandTest {
  public static void main(String[] args) {
    //Add an item to the CD category
    //create Receiver objects
    Item CD = new Item("A Beautiful Mind");
    Category catCD = new Category("CD");
    //create the command object
    CommandInterface command = new AddCommand(CD, catCD);
    //create the invoker
    ItemManager manager = new ItemManager();
    //configure the invoker
    //with the command object
    manager.setCommand(command);
    manager.process();
    //Add an item to the CD category
    CD = new Item("Duet");
    catCD = new Category("CD");
    command = new AddCommand(CD, catCD);
    manager.setCommand(command);
    manager.process();
    //Add an item to the New Releases category
    CD = new Item("Duet");
    catCD = new Category("New Releases");
    command = new AddCommand(CD, catCD);
    manager.setCommand(command);
    manager.process();
    //Delete an item from the New Releases category
    command = new DeleteCommand(CD, catCD);
    manager.setCommand(command);
    manager.process();
  }
}
```

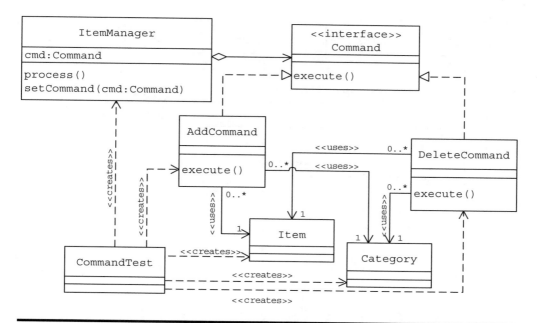

Figure 30.8   Class Association

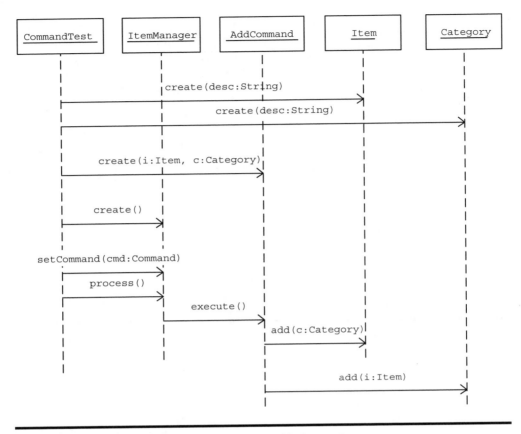

Figure 30.9   Message Flow When an Item Is Added to a Category

31

MEDIATOR

This pattern was previously described in GoF95.

DESCRIPTION

In general, object-oriented applications consist of a set of objects that interact with each other for the purpose of providing a service. This interaction can be direct (point-to-point) as long as the number of objects referring to each other directly is very low. Figure 31.1 depicts this type of direct interaction where ObjectA and ObjectB refer to each other directly.

As the number of objects increases, this type of direct interaction can lead to a complex maze of references among objects (Figure 31.2), which affects the maintainability of the application. Also, having an object directly referring to other objects greatly reduces the scope for reusing these objects because of higher coupling.

Figure 31.1 Point-to-Point Communication in the Case of Two Objects

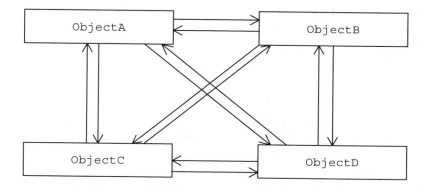

Figure 31.2 Point-to-Point Communication: Increased Number of Objects

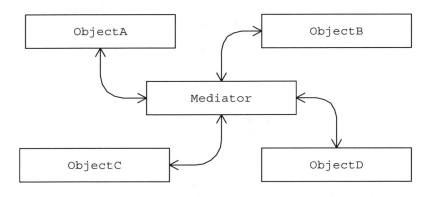

Figure 31.3   Object Interaction: `Mediator` as a Communication Hub

In such cases, the Mediator pattern can be used to design a controlled, coordinated communication model for a group of objects, eliminating the need for objects to refer to each other directly (Figure 31.3).

The Mediator pattern suggests abstracting all object interaction details into a separate class, referred to as a *Mediator*, with knowledge about the interacting group of objects. Every object in the group is still responsible for offering the service it is designed for, but objects do not interact with each other directly for this purpose. The interaction between any two different objects is routed through the `Mediator` class. All objects send their messages to the mediator. The mediator then sends messages to the appropriate objects as per the application's requirements. The resulting design has the following major advantages:

- With all the object interaction behavior moved into a separate (mediator) object, it becomes easier to alter the behavior of object interrelationships, by replacing the mediator with one of its subclasses with extended or altered functionality.
- Moving interobject dependencies out of individual objects results in enhanced object reusability.
- Because objects do not need to refer to each other directly, objects can be unit tested more easily.
- The resulting low degree of coupling allows individual classes to be modified without affecting other classes.

MEDIATOR VERSUS FAÇADE

In some aspects the Mediator pattern looks similar to the Façade pattern discussed earlier. Table 31.1 lists the similarities and differences between the two.

During the discussion of the Command pattern, we built two example applications. Let us revisit these applications and see how the direct object-to-object interaction can be avoided by applying the Mediator pattern.

Table 31.1 Mediator versus Façade

Mediator	Façade
A Mediator is used to abstract the necessary functionality of a group of objects with the aim of simplifying the object interaction.	A Façade is used to abstract the required functionality of a subsystem of components, with the aim of providing a simplified, higher level interface.
All objects interact with each other through the Mediator. The group of objects knows the existence of the Mediator.	Clients use the Façade to interact with subsystem components. The existence of the Façade is not known to the subsystem components.
Because the Mediator and all the objects that are registered with it can communicate with each other, the communication is bidirectional.	Clients can send messages (through the Façade) to the subsystem but not vice versa, making the communication unidirectional.
A Mediator can be assumed to stay in the middle of a group of interacting objects.	A Façade lies in between a client object and the subsystem.
Using a Mediator allows the implementation of any of the interacting objects to be changed without any impact on the other objects that interact with it only through the Mediator.	Using a Façade allows the implementation of the subsystem to be changed completely without any impact on its clients, provided the clients are not given direct access to the subsystem's classes.
By subclassing the Mediator, the behavior of the object interrelationships can be extended.	By subclassing the Façade, the implementation of the higher level interface can be changed.

EXAMPLE I

The FTP client simulation application built in the previous chapter has the following list of UI controls (Table 31.2) in the client display.

Figure 31.4 depicts the interaction between different UI objects.

Let us consider the following minor enhancements to the existing application to make it more user-friendly:

- When the UI is first displayed, all buttons except the Exit button should be disabled.
- When a file name is selected from the JList control displaying the local file system:
  - The Upload and Delete buttons should be enabled.
  - Any selected item in the remote file system display should be deselected.
  - The Download button should be disabled.
- When a file name is selected from the JList control displaying the remote file system:
  - The Download and Delete buttons should be enabled.
  - Any selected item in the local file system display should be deselected.
  - The Upload button should be disabled.

Table 31.2 List of User Interface Objects and the Associated Functionality

UI Control Object	Functionality
JList	Displays the local file system.
JList	Displays the remote file system.
JButton	Provides the upload functionality. When the Upload button is clicked, the selected file from the local file system is uploaded to the remote server and the file name is added to the remote file system JList control.
JButton	Provides the download functionality. When the Download button is clicked, the selected file from the remote file system is downloaded to the local system and the file name is added to the local file system display JList control.
JButton	Provides the delete functionality. When the Delete button is clicked, the selected file from the remote or local file system is deleted. The JList control is updated accordingly.

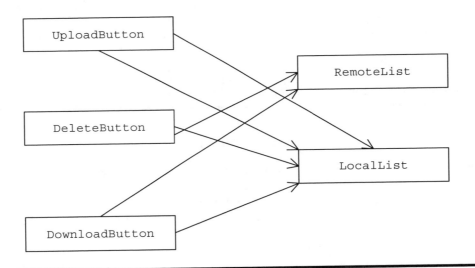

Figure 31.4 Object Interaction

– After executing the necessary upload/download operation, the Upload, Download and Delete buttons should be disabled. Similarly, after deleting the specified file, the Delete button should be disabled along with any Upload and Download buttons that are currently enabled. Both the local and remote file system displays should get refreshed after a delete, download or upload operation.

Figure 31.5 shows the resulting object interaction.

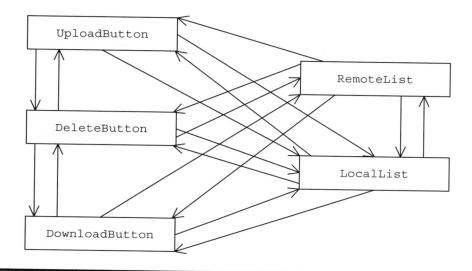

Figure 31.5 Object-to-Object Communication with Increased Direct Reference to Each Other

As more controls are added for additional functionality such as file rename, FTP server connect, disconnect and others, the direct communication between objects creates a complex maze of references among objects. This greatly reduces the maintainability of the application.

The Mediator pattern can be used in this case for a more efficient design of the object interaction. Applying the Mediator pattern, an abstraction for the object interaction details can be created. This abstraction can be designed as a separate Mediator class as in Figure 31.6 and Listing 31.1.

From the Mediator class implementation it can be seen that the Mediator offers methods for different UI objects to register themselves with the Mediator. The set of object interactions to be executed when each UI control is activated (or clicked) is designed as a separate method inside the Mediator.

Client Usage of the Mediator

The client (Listing 31.2) creates an instance of the Mediator. Whenever a UI object is created, the client passes the Mediator instance to it. The UI object registers itself with this instance of the Mediator.

User Interface Objects: Mediator Interaction

Because all the object interaction details are removed from individual UI objects to the Mediator object, the processEvent method of each of these UI objects gets reduced to a simple call to an appropriate Mediator method (Listing 31.3). Figure 31.7 shows the UI object interaction after the Mediator pattern is applied.

```
┌────────────────────────────────────────────────────────────┐
│                          Mediator                          │
├────────────────────────────────────────────────────────────┤
│ btnUpload:UploadButton                                     │
│ btnDownload:DownloadButton                                 │
│ btnDelete:DeleteButton                                     │
│ localList:LocalList                                        │
│ remoteList:RemoteList                                      │
├────────────────────────────────────────────────────────────┤
│ registerUploadButton(inp_ib:UploadButton)                 │
│ registerDownloadButton(inp_dnb:DownloadButton)            │
│ registerDeleteButton(inp_db:DeleteButton)                 │
│ registerLocalList(inp_arl:LocalList)                      │
│ registerRemoteList(inp_drl:RemoteList)                    │
│                                                            │
│ UploadItem()                                               │
│ DownloadItem()                                             │
│ DeleteItem()                                               │
│ LocalListSelect()                                          │
│ RemoteListSelect()                                         │
└────────────────────────────────────────────────────────────┘
```

Figure 31.6 Mediator

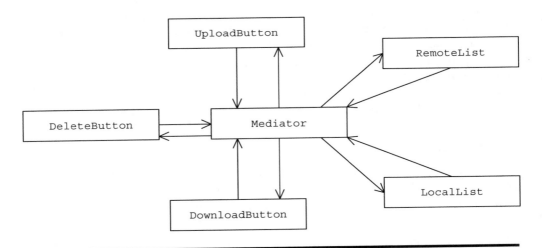

Figure 31.7 Object Interaction: Mediator as a Communication Hub

Listing 31.1 **Mediator Class**

```
class Mediator {
  private UploadButton btnUpload;
  private DownloadButton btnDownload;
  private DeleteButton btnDelete;
  private LocalList localList;
  private RemoteList remoteList;
  public void registerUploadButton(UploadButton inp_ib) {
    btnUpload = inp_ib;
  }
  public void registerDownloadButton(
    DownloadButton inp_dnb) {
    btnDownload = inp_dnb;
  }
  public void registerDeleteButton(DeleteButton inp_db) {
    btnDelete = inp_db;
  }
  public void registerLocalList(LocalList inp_arl) {
    localList = inp_arl;
  }
  public void registerRemoteList(RemoteList inp_drl) {
    remoteList = inp_drl;
  }
  public void UploadItem() {
    int index = localList.getSelectedIndex();
    String selectedItem =
      localList.getSelectedValue().toString();
    ((DefaultListModel) localList.getModel()).remove(
      index);
    ((DefaultListModel) remoteList.getModel()).addElement(
      selectedItem);
    btnUpload.setEnabled(false);
    btnDelete.setEnabled(false);
    btnDownload.setEnabled(false);
  }
```

(continued)

Listing 31.1 Mediator Class (Continued)

```java
    public void DownloadItem() {

        ...

        ...

    }
    public void DeleteItem() {

        ...

        ...

    }
    public void LocalListSelect() {

        ...

        ...

    }
    public void RemoteListSelect() {
      localList.setSelectedIndex(-1);
      btnUpload.setEnabled(false);
      btnDelete.setEnabled(true);
      btnDownload.setEnabled(true);
    }
  }
```

EXAMPLE II

During the discussion of the Command pattern, we built an application to add and delete items to a library item database. A given item can be part of one or more categories. Each Item object maintains a list of all categories which it is part of. Similarly, each Category object maintains a list of all items that currently are part of it. The class association diagram in Figure 31.8 depicts this relationship.

When an application has to deal with many items that belong to one or more categories, the object interactions can get complicated. The diagram in Figure 31.9 depicts a scenario where different Item and Category objects refer to each other directly.

The direct interaction between different Item objects and Category objects can be eliminated by moving the object interaction details out of the Item and Category classes to a separate Mediator class (Figure 31.10). The Mediator can be designed with the following two sets of methods:

- A set of methods to allow different Item and Category objects to register with the Mediator.
- A set of methods for adding and deleting items. The Mediator is responsible for implementing interactions between different objects as part of these methods.

Listing 31.2 Client FTPGUI Class

```
public class FTPGUI extends JFrame {
        …

        …

    private Mediator mdtr = new Mediator();
    public FTPGUI() throws Exception {
            …

            …

      //Create controls
      defLocalList = new DefaultListModel();
      defRemoteList = new DefaultListModel();
      localList = new LocalList(defLocalList, mdtr);
      remoteList = new RemoteList(defRemoteList, mdtr);
      pnlFTPUI = new JPanel();
          …

          …

      //Create buttons
      UploadButton btnUpload =
        new UploadButton(FTPGUI.UPLOAD, mdtr);
      btnUpload.setMnemonic(KeyEvent.VK_U);
      DownloadButton btnDownload =
        new DownloadButton(FTPGUI.DOWNLOAD, mdtr);
      btnDownload.setMnemonic(KeyEvent.VK_N);
      DeleteButton btnDelete =
        new DeleteButton(FTPGUI.DELETE, mdtr);
      btnDelete.setMnemonic(KeyEvent.VK_D);
          …

          …

    }
        …

        …
}//end of class
```

The Mediator can maintain the Item-Category association in the item-CatAssoc instance variable. Item objects do not need to refer to Category objects directly. Hence an Item object does not need to maintain the list of Categories it belongs to and vice versa. Similarly, both add and delete operations are not required to be implemented by the Item and the Category classes.

The execute method of the AddCommand and DeleteCommand Command objects gets reduced to a call to the addItem and deleteItem Mediator methods, respectively.

Listing 31.3   Simplified UI Object Classes

```
        ...

        ...
class UploadButton extends JButton
  implements CommandInterface {
  Mediator mdtr;
  public void processEvent() {
    mdtr.UploadItem();
  }
  public UploadButton(String name, Mediator inp_mdtr) {
    super(name);
    mdtr = inp_mdtr;
    mdtr.registerUploadButton(this);
  }
}
class DownloadButton extends JButton
  implements CommandInterface {
  Mediator mdtr;
  public void processEvent() {
    mdtr.DownloadItem();
  }
  public DownloadButton(String name, Mediator inp_mdtr) {
    super(name);
    mdtr = inp_mdtr;
    mdtr.registerDownloadButton(this);
  }
}
        ...

        ...
```

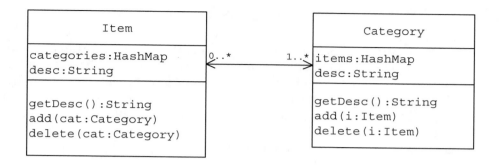

Figure 31.8 `Item-Category` Association

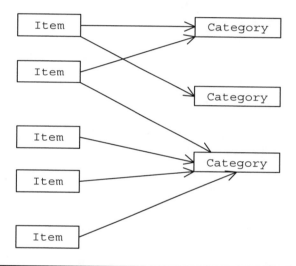

Figure 31.9 `Item-Category` Object Interaction

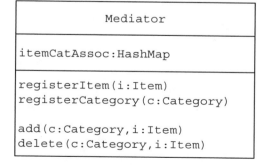

Figure 31.10 `Mediator`

PRACTICE QUESTIONS

1. Customer service representatives at some commercial banks handle queries from their existing and potential customers using an online chat application. At peak times, each representative may need to work with more than one customer simultaneously. Design this communication mechanism with a `Mediator` object between different `User` objects and `Representative` objects.
2. Implement the Example II application.

32

MEMENTO

This pattern was previously described in GoF95.

DESCRIPTION

The state of an object can be defined as the values of its properties or attributes at any given point of time. The Memento pattern is useful for designing a mechanism to capture and store the state of an object so that subsequently, when needed, the object can be put back to this (previous) state. This is more like an undo operation. The Memento pattern can be used to accomplish this without exposing the object's internal structure. The object whose state needs to be captured is referred to as the *originator*. When a client wants to save the state of the originator, it requests the current state from the originator. The originator stores all those attributes that are required for restoring its state in a separate object referred to as a *Memento* and returns it to the client. Thus a Memento can be viewed as an object that contains the internal state of another object, at a given point of time. A Memento object must hide the originator variable values from all objects except the originator. In other words, it should protect its internal state against access by objects other than the originator. Towards this end, a Memento should be designed to provide restricted access to other objects while the originator is allowed to access its internal state.

When the client wants to restore the originator back to its previous state, it simply passes the memento back to the originator. The originator uses the state information contained in the memento and puts itself back to the state stored in the Memento object.

EXAMPLE

Data conversion is almost always an integral part of any application that involves converting a legacy system to newer technologies. Let us consider one such application where customer data needs to be moved from a flat file to a relational database. The process validates every customer record before sending it to the database.

In reality, a customer record would contain many attributes, but for simplicity, let us consider only three attributes — first name, last name and the credit card number. The validations are also kept very simple. A customer record is considered as valid if the last name is not blank and the credit card number is composed of only digits (0 through 9). Whenever an invalid customer record is found, the process stops and prompts the user to correct the data and restart the process. At this point, the state of the data conversion process is saved inside a Memento object. When the user restarts the process, the conversion process state is restored from the Memento object and the process resumes from where it stopped, instead of starting from the beginning of the source data file. In general, a Memento object can be stored either in the memory or to persistent media. In this application, the state needs to be saved even after the application has been terminated and needs to be restored when the application is run subsequently. Hence, storing the Memento in the memory is not an option in this case. The Memento needs to be stored to persistent media instead.

Instead of storing valid customer records in a relational database, the application generates a text file consisting of SQL insert statements, which can be executed to insert data into any relational database.

Let us design different components required for this process to work.

DataConverter (Originator)

The DataConverter class (Figure 32.1 and Listing 32.1) is the implementer of the data conversion process.

ID

The instance variable ID constitutes the state of the DataConverter. It represents the customer ID of the last successfully processed customer record.

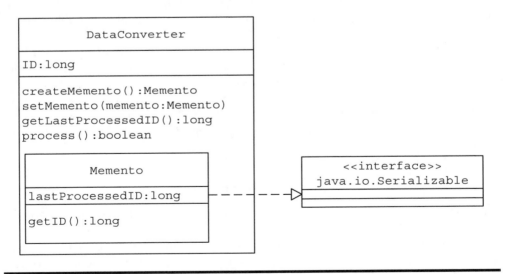

Figure 32.1 DataConverter Class: The Originator

Listing 32.1 DataConverter Class

```java
public class DataConverter {
  public static final String DATA_FILE = "Data.txt";
  public static final String OUTPUT_FILE = "SQL.txt";
  private long ID = 0;
  public Memento createMemento() {
    return (new Memento(ID));
  }
  public void setMemento(Memento memento) {
    if (memento != null)
      ID = memento.getID();
  }
  public long getLastProcessedID() {
    return ID;
  }
  public void setLastProcessedID(long lastID) {
    ID = lastID;
  }
  public boolean process() {
    boolean success = true;
    String inputLine = "";
    long currID = 0;
    try {
      File inFile = new File(DATA_FILE);
      BufferedReader br = new BufferedReader(
                      new InputStreamReader(
                        new FileInputStream(inFile)));
      long lastID = getLastProcessedID();
      while ((inputLine = br.readLine()) != null) {
        StringTokenizer st =
          new StringTokenizer(inputLine, ",");
        String strID = st.nextToken();
        currID = new Long(strID).longValue();
        if (lastID < currID) {
```

(continued)

Listing 32.1 `DataConverter` Class (Continued)

```java
        Customer c =
          new Customer(strID, st.nextToken(),
                      st.nextToken(), st.nextToken());
        if (!(c.isValid())) {
          success = false;
          break;
        }
        ID = new Long(strID).longValue();
        FileUtil util = new FileUtil();
        util.writeToFile(OUTPUT_FILE, c.getSQL(),
                        true, true);
      }
    }
    br.close();
  }//Try
  catch (Exception ex) {
    System.out.println(" An error has occurred " +
                      ex.getMessage());
    System.exit(1);
  }
  if (success == false) {
    System.out.println("An error has occurred at ID=" +
                      currID);
    System.out.println("Data Record=" + inputLine);
    return false;
  }
  return true;
}
class Memento implements java.io.Serializable {
  private long lastProcessedID;
  private Memento(long ID) {
    lastProcessedID = ID;
  }
  private long getID() {
    return lastProcessedID;
  }
}//end of class
}//end of class
```

Memento

The Memento class is defined as an inner class within the DataConverter. The Memento is defined with its constructor and other methods as private.

In Java, a class can access the private members of its inner classes.

The DataConverter will be able to access these methods while they remain inaccessible to other objects. Because the state of the DataConverter needs to be preserved even after the application ends, the Memento object needs to be serialized to a file. Hence the Memento is designed to implement the java.io.Serializable interface to identify itself as a Serializable class.

In Java, a Serializable class must:

- Explicitly specify nonserializable attributes using the *transient* keyword
- Implement the java.io.Serializable interface
- Have access to the first zero argument constructor of its first non-Serializable super class

---

process

The process method reads from the source data file, validates the customer data using a Customer helper class. For every valid customer record, a corresponding SQL insert statement is written to the output file. When a customer record with invalid data is encountered, the data conversion process stops.

createMemento

As the method name suggests, this method is responsible for the creation of the Memento object. It stores the DataConverter current state inside a Memento instance and returns it.

setMemento

Retrieves the state information from the input Memento object and resets the DataConverter back to this state.

DCClient (Client)

The client DCClient (Listing 32.2) first instantiates the DataConverter and starts the data conversion process by invoking the process method on this DataConverter instance. If the process method returns without processing the entire source data file due to invalid customer data, it invokes the create-Memento method on the DataConverter to capture its current state. The createMemento method returns a Memento object (See createMemento

Listing 32.2 `DCClient` **Class**

```
public class DCClient {
  public static void main(String[] args) {
    MementoHandler objMementoHandler = new MementoHandler();
    DataConverter objConverter = new DataConverter();
    objConverter.setMemento(objMementoHandler.getMemento());
    if (!(objConverter.process())) {
      System.out.println("Description: Invalid data - " +
                         "Process Stopped");
      System.out.println("Please correct the Data and " +
                         "Run the Application Again");
      objMementoHandler.setMemento(
        objConverter.createMemento());
    }
  }
}
```

method description above). The client `DCClient` uses a helper `MementoHandler` object to serialize this `Memento` instance to a file.

Once the data is corrected and the client `DCClient` is run again:

- The client `DCClient` invokes the `getMemento` method on the `MementoHandler` requesting it for the stored `Memento` object.
- The `MementoHandler` deserializes the previously serialized `Memento` object from the file and returns it to the client.
- The client passes it to the `DataConverter` as an argument to its `setMemento` method. The `DataConverter` puts itself back to the state stored in the memento and resumes with the data conversion process from where it stopped during the previous run.

MementoHandler

The `MementoHandler` (Listing 32.3) contains an object reference of `Memento` type. It is passed as a `Memento` instance by the client `DCClient`.

As discussed above, whenever the data conversion process returns without processing the entire source data file, the client captures the `DataConverter` state in a `Memento` and the application ends. For this `Memento` to be available during the next run of the application, it must be saved to persistent media. This involves object serialization. Also during the subsequent run if the `DataConverter` is to be put back to its previous state, this `Memento` needs to be reconstructed. This involves object deserialization. These details of `Memento` handling are maintained inside the `MementoHandler` class, freeing all clients

Listing 32.3 `MementoHandler` Class

```java
public class MementoHandler {
  public static final String ID_FILE = "ID.txt";
  private DataConverter.Memento objMemento = null;
  public DataConverter.Memento getMemento() {
    ObjectInputStream objStream = null;
    FileUtil util = new FileUtil();
    if (util.isFileExists(ID_FILE)) {
      //read the object from the file
      try {
        objStream = new ObjectInputStream(
                   new FileInputStream(new File(ID_FILE)));
        objMemento = (DataConverter.Memento)
                   objStream.readObject();
        objStream.close();
      } catch (Exception e) {
        System.out.println("Error Reading Memento");
        System.exit(1);
      }
      //delete the old memento
      util.deleteFile(ID_FILE);
    }
    return objMemento;
  }
  public void setMemento(DataConverter.Memento memento) {
    ObjectOutputStream objStream = null;
    //write the object to the file
    try {
      objStream = new ObjectOutputStream(
                 new FileOutputStream(new File(ID_FILE)));
      objStream.writeObject(memento);
      objStream.close();
    } catch (Exception e) {
      System.out.println("Error Writing Memento");
      System.exit(1);
    }
  }
}//end of class
```

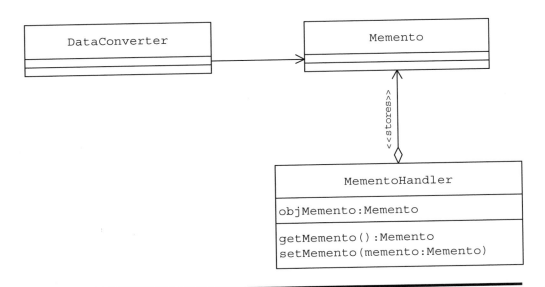

Figure 32.2   Data Conversion Application: Class Association

(that deal with the DataConverter and the associated Memento object) from having to deal with these details.

This also makes it easy to change the way the Memento is saved. For example, if the Memento needs to be saved to a database instead of a file, changes need to be made only to the MementoHandler, without having to alter the implementation of any client class that works with the Memento.

Figure 32.2 shows the association between different classes in the example data conversion application.

Figure 32.3 shows the application message flow.

PRACTICE QUESTIONS

1. Design and implement a Java applet that allows users to design a customized wedding gown. A preview of the dress should be displayed with default settings. Users should be able to select from a set of different neck and sleeve types. After every selection, the preview image should be updated. Users should be able to undo a selection to go back to their previous selection and the preview should get updated accordingly. Apply the Memento pattern in designing the undo operation.

2. Consider a simple shopping cart application that remembers shopping cart contents even after a user has logged out. Next time, when the user logs onto the Web site, the shopping cart should be shown with previously selected items and the user should be allowed to continue to shop in the new session. Identify how the Memento pattern can be used in preserving and restoring the state of an unfinished order.

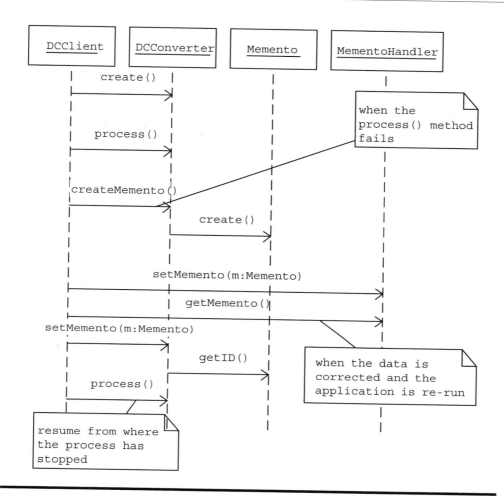

Figure 32.3 Application Message Flow

33

OBSERVER

This pattern was previously described in GoF95.

DESCRIPTION

The Observer pattern is useful for designing a consistent communication model between a set of dependent objects and an object that they are dependent on. This allows the dependent objects to have their state synchronized with the object that they are dependent on. The set of dependent objects are referred to as *observers* and the object that they are dependent on is referred to as the *subject*. In order to accomplish this, the Observer pattern suggests a *publisher-subscriber* model leading to a clear boundary between the set of Observer objects and the Subject object.

A typical observer is an object with interest or dependency in the state of the subject. A subject can have more than one such observer. Each of these observers needs to know when the subject undergoes a change in its state.

The subject cannot maintain a static list of such observers as the list of observers for a given subject could change dynamically. Hence any object with interest in the state of the subject needs to explicitly register itself as an observer with the subject. Whenever the subject undergoes a change in its state, it notifies all of its registered observers. Upon receiving notification from the subject, each of the observers queries the subject to synchronize its state with that of the subject's. Thus a subject behaves as a publisher by publishing messages to all of its subscribing observers.

In other words, the scenario contains a one-to-many relationship between a subject and the set of its observers. Whenever the subject instance undergoes a state change, all of its dependent observers are notified and they can update themselves. Each of the observer objects has to register itself with the subject to get notified when there is a change in the subject's state. An observer can register or subscribe with multiple subjects. Whenever an observer does not wish to be notified any further, it unregisters itself with the subject.

For this mechanism to work:

- The subject should provide an interface for registering and unregistering for change notifications.

- One of the following two must be true:
  - *In the pull model* — The subject should provide an interface that enables observers to query the subject for the required state information to update their state.
  - *In the push model* — The subject should send the state information that the observers may be interested in.
- Observers should provide an interface for receiving notifications from the subject.

The class diagram in Figure 33.1 describes the structure of different classes and their association, catering to the above list of requirements.

From this class diagram it can be seen that:

- All subjects are expected to provide implementation for an interface similar to the `Observable` interface.
- All observers are expected to have an interface similar to the `Observer` interface.

Several variations can be thought of while applying the Observer pattern, leading to different types of subject-observers such as observers that are interested only in specific types of changes in the subject.

ADDING NEW OBSERVERS

After applying the Observer pattern, different observers can be added dynamically without requiring any changes to the `Subject` class. Similarly, observers remain unaffected when the state change logic of the subject changes.

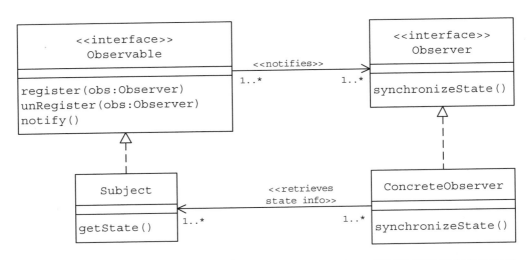

Figure 33.1   Generic Class Association When the Observer Pattern Is Applied

EXAMPLE

Let us build a sales reporting application for the management of a store with multiple departments. The features of the application include:

- Users should be able to select a specific department they are interested in.
- Upon selecting a department, two types of reports are to be displayed:
  - *Monthly report* — A list of all transactions for the current month for the selected department.
  - *YTD sales chart* — A chart showing the year-to-date sales for the selected department by month.
- Whenever a different department is selected, both of the reports should be refreshed with the data for the currently selected department.

From the proposed functionality described above, we can easily see that two of the reporting objects are dependent upon the object that carries the user-selected department. We can apply the Observer pattern in this case to design a consistent communication model between the object holding the user selection and both of the dependent report objects.

Let us define three classes with the stated functionality as in Table 33.1.

Applying the Observer pattern, let us define an `Observable` interface to be implemented by the `ReportManager` (Figure 33.2).

```
public interface Observable {
  public void notifyObservers();
  public void register(Observer obs);
  public void unRegister(Observer obs);
}
```

Table 33.1 Subject-Observer Classes

Class	Role	Functionality
ReportManager	Subject	Displays the necessary UI for the user to select a department. Maintains the user selected department in an instance variable.
MonthlyReport	Observer	Displays the monthly report for the selected department.
YTDChart	Observer	Displays the YTD sales chart for the selected department.

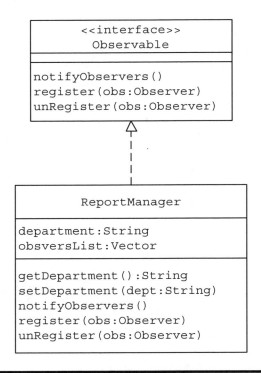

Figure 33.2   Observable Interface and Its Implementer

The ReportManager class (Listing 33.1) provides implementation for methods declared in the Observable interface. Both of the dependent report objects can use these methods to register themselves as observers. The ReportManager stores each of these registered observers in the observersList vector. The currently selected department constitutes the state of the ReportManager object and is maintained in the form of an instance variable named department. Whenever a new value is set for the department variable (this constitutes a change in the state), the notifyObservers method is invoked. As part of the notifyObservers method, the ReportManager invokes the refresh-Data(Observable) method on each of its currently registered observers.

Besides providing an implementation for the Observable interface methods, the ReportManager displays the necessary user interface as in Figure 33.3 to allow a user to select a specific department of interest.

Let us also define an interface Observer to be implemented by both the MonthlyReport and the YTDChart classes (Figure 33.4 and Listing 33.2):

```
public interface Observer {
  public void refreshData(Observable subject);
}
```

The ReportManager makes use of this interface to notify its observers.

Listing 33.1   ReportManager Class

```
public class ReportManager extends JFrame
  implements Observable {
          ...

          ...

  private Vector observersList;
  private String department;
  public ReportManager() throws Exception {
          ...

          ...

    observersList = new Vector();
          ...

          ...

  }
  public void register(Observer obs) {
    //Add to the list of Observers
    observersList.addElement(obs);
  }
  public void unRegister(Observer obs) {
    //remove from the list of Observers
  }
  public void notifyObservers() {
    //Send notify to all Observers
    for (int i = 0; i < observersList.size(); i++) {
      Observer observer =
        (Observer) observersList.elementAt(i);
      observer.refreshData(this);
    }
  }
  public String getDepartment() {
    return department;
  }
  public void setDepartment(String dept) {
    department = dept;
  }
```

(continued)

Listing 33.1 `ReportManager` **Class (Continued)**

```java
class ButtonHandler implements ActionListener {
  ReportManager subject;
  public void actionPerformed(ActionEvent e) {
    if (e.getActionCommand().equals(ReportManager.EXIT)) {
      System.exit(1);
    }
    if (e.getActionCommand().equals(ReportManager.SET_OK)) {
      String dept = (String)
                    cmbDepartmentList.getSelectedItem();
      //change in state
      subject.setDepartment(dept);
      subject.notifyObservers();
    }
  }
  public ButtonHandler() {
  }
  public ButtonHandler(ReportManager manager) {
    subject = manager;
  }
}
}//end of class
```

Figure 33.3 `ReportManager` **User Interface**

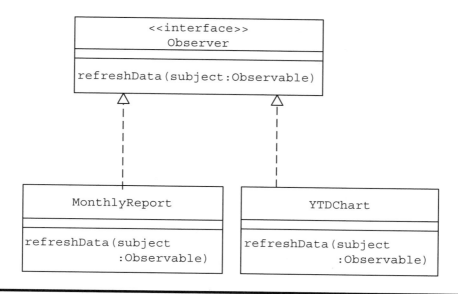

Figure 33.4   Observer Class Hierarchy

Subject–Observer Association

Typically, a client would first create an instance of the subject (ReportManager). Whenever an Observer (e.g., MonthlyReport, YTDChart) object is created, it passes the Subject instance reference to it as part of its Constructor method call. The Observer object registers itself with this Subject instance.

```
//Client Code
public class SupervisorView {

        ...

        ...

  public static void main(String[] args) throws Exception {
    //Create the Subject
    ReportManager objSubject = new ReportManager();
    //Create Observers
    new MonthlyReport(objSubject);
    new YTDChart(objSubject);
  }
}//end of class
```

The resulting class association can be depicted as in Figure 33.5.

Listing 33.2 MonthlyReport Class as an Observer

```java
public class MonthlyReport extends JFrame implements Observer {
      ...

      ...

  private ReportManager objReportManager;
  public MonthlyReport(ReportManager inp_objReportManager)
  throws Exception {
    super("Observer Pattern - Example");
    objReportManager = inp_objReportManager;
    //Create controls
        ...

        ...
    //Create Labels
        ...

        ...
    objReportManager.register(this);
  }
  public void refreshData(Observable subject) {
    if (subject == objReportManager) {
      //get subject's state
      String department = objReportManager.getDepartment();
      lblTransactions.setText(
        "Current Month Transactions - " +
        department);
      Vector trnList =
        getCurrentMonthTransactions(department);
      String content = "";
      for (int i = 0; i < trnList.size(); i++) {
        content = content +
                trnList.elementAt(i).toString() + "\n";
      }
      taTransactions.setText(content);
    }
  }
  private Vector getCurrentMonthTransactions(String department
                                            ) {
```

(continued)

Listing 33.2 **MonthlyReport Class as an Observer (Continued)**

```
      Vector v = new Vector();
      FileUtil futil = new FileUtil();
      Vector allRows = futil.fileToVector("Transactions.date");
      //current month
      Calendar cal = Calendar.getInstance();
      cal.setTime(new Date());
      int month = cal.get(Calendar.MONTH) + 1;
      String searchStr = department + "," + month + ",";
      int j = 1;
      for (int i = 0; i < allRows.size(); i++) {
        String str = (String) allRows.elementAt(i);
        if (str.indexOf(searchStr) > -1) {
          StringTokenizer st =
            new StringTokenizer(str, ",");
          st.nextToken();//bypass the department
          str = " " + j + ". " + st.nextToken() + "/" +
                  st.nextToken() + "~~~" +
                  st.nextToken() + "Items" + "~~~" +
                  st.nextToken() + " Dollars";
          j++;
          v.addElement(str);
        }
      }
      return v;
    }
  }//end of class
```

Logical Flow

1. Using the ReportManager user interface (Figure 33.3), whenever a user selects a particular department and clicks on the OK button, the Report-Manager undergoes a change in its internal state (i.e., the value of its instance variable department changes).
2. As soon as the new state is set, the ReportManager invokes the refreshData(Observable) method on both the currently registered MonthlyReport and the YTDChart objects.
3. As part of refreshData method, both the report objects:
   a. Check to make sure that the subject that invoked the refreshData method is in fact the same Subject instance they have registered with. This is to prevent the observers from responding to unintended calls.

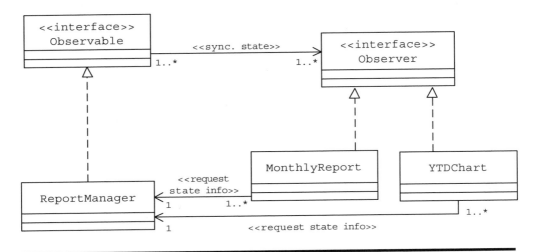

Figure 33.5 Example Application: Class Association

b. Query the `ReportManager` for its current state using the `getDepart-ment` method.

c. Retrieve appropriate data from the data file for display (Figures 33.6 and 33.7).

The sequence diagram in Figure 33.8 shows the communication between different objects when the application is run.

Whenever the state change logic implementation of the `ReportManager` changes, none of the observers will be affected. Similarly, when a new observer is added, the `ReportManager` class does not need to be changed.

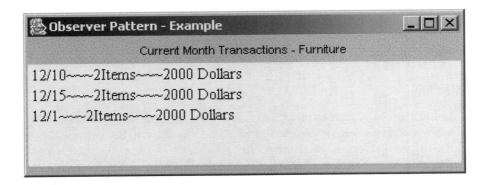

Figure 33.6 `MonthlyReport` View

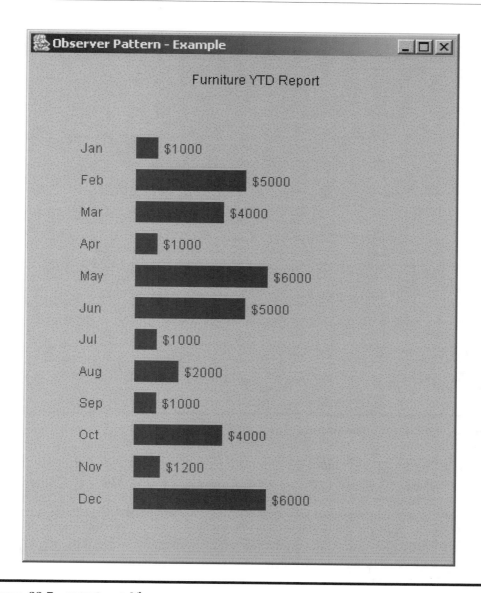

Figure 33.7 YTDChart View

PRACTICE QUESTIONS

1. Provide an implementation for the unRegister method of the Report-Manager class.
2. In general, it could lead to different problems if an observer changes the state of the subject (directly or indirectly) while attempting to update its state as part of its refreshData(Observable) method. Think of different ways of handling a scenario like this.

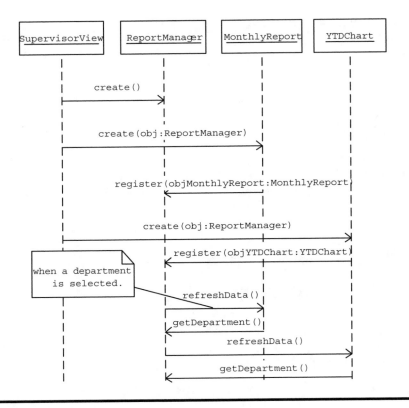

Figure 33.8 Application Message Flow

3. Design and implement an application for searching a jobs database that:
   - Allows a user to select a specific software skill and the number of years of experience.
   - Displays a list of all jobs that require the specific skill and the experience selected in one window with details.
   - Displays a list of all candidates with the specific skill and the experience selected in a third window.
4. Design and implement an application for monitoring and reporting different events with the following functionality:
   a. Whenever an event occurs, it is first sent to an EventManager object which functions as a publisher.
   b. Whenever the EventManager receives an event, it stores it to the database and sends notifications to the following three objects to take necessary action:
      i. An AlertSender object that sends notifications (e-mail or page) to different users depending on the event that occurred.
      ii. Two reporting objects that display the event data in different formats.

34

INTERPRETER

This pattern was previously described in GoF95.

DESCRIPTION

In general, languages are made up of a set of grammar rules. Different sentences can be constructed by following these grammar rules. Sometimes an application may need to process repeated occurrences of similar requests that are a combination of a set of grammar rules. These requests are distinct but are similar in the sense that they are all composed using the same set of rules. A simple example of this sort would be the set of different arithmetic expressions submitted to a calculator program. Though each such expression is different, they are all constructed using the basic rules that make up the grammar for the language of arithmetic expressions.

In such cases, instead of treating every distinct combination of rules as a separate case, it may be beneficial for the application to have the ability to interpret a generic combination of rules. The Interpreter pattern can be used to design this ability in an application so that other applications and users can specify operations using a simple language defined by a set of grammar rules.

Applying the Interpreter pattern:

- A class hierarchy can be designed to represent the set of grammar rules with every class in the hierarchy representing a separate grammar rule.
- An `Interpreter` module can be designed to interpret the sentences constructed using the class hierarchy designed above and carry out the necessary operations.

Because a different class represents every grammar rule, the number of classes increases with the number of grammar rules. A language with extensive, complex grammar rules requires a large number of classes. The Interpreter pattern works best when the grammar is simple. Having a simple grammar avoids the need to have many classes corresponding to the complex set of rules involved, which are hard to manage and maintain.

EXAMPLE

Let us build a calculator application that evaluates a given arithmetic expression. For simplicity, let us consider only add, multiply and subtract operations. Instead of designing a custom algorithm for evaluating each arithmetic expression, the application could benefit from interpreting a generic arithmetic expression. The Interpreter pattern can be used to design the ability to understand a generic arithmetic expression and evaluate it.

The Interpreter pattern can be applied in two stages:

1. Define a representation for the set of rules that make up the grammar for arithmetic expressions.
2. Design an interpreter that makes use of the classes that represent different arithmetic grammar rules to understand and evaluate a given arithmetic expression.

The set of rules in Table 34.1 constitutes the grammar for arithmetic expressions.

Table 34.1   Grammar Rules for Arithmetic Expressions

Arithmetic Expressions – Grammar
ArithmeticExpression::= ConstantExpression | AddExpression | MultiplyExpression | SubtractExpression
ConstantExpression::= Integer/Double Value
AddExpression::= ArithmeticExpression '+' ArithmeticExpression
MultiplyExpression::= ArithmeticExpression '*' ArithmeticExpression
SubtractExpression::= ArithmeticExpression '-' ArithmeticExpression

From Table 34.1, it can be observed that arithmetic expressions are of two types — individual (e.g., ConstantExpression) or composite (e.g., AddExpression). These expressions can be arranged in the form of a tree structure, with composite expressions as nonterminal nodes and individual expressions as terminal nodes of the tree.

Let us define a class hierarchy as Figure 34.1 to represent the set of arithmetic grammar rules.

Each of the classes representing different rules implements the common Expression interface and provides implementation for the evaluate method (Listing 34.1 through Listing 34.5).

The Context is a common information repository that stores the values of different variables (Listing 34.6). For simplicity, values are hard-coded for variables in this example.

While each of the NonTerminalExpression classes performs the arithmetic operation it represents, the TerminalExpression class simply looks up the value of the variable it represents from the Context.

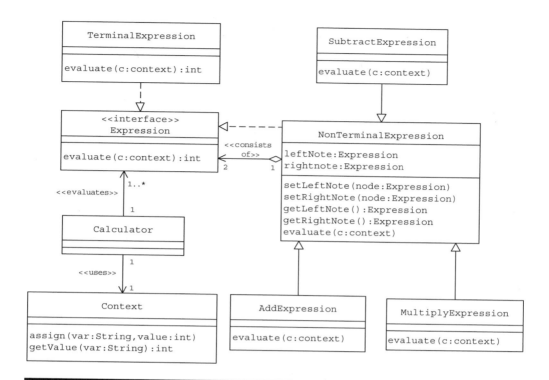

Figure 34.1 Class Hierarchy Representing Grammar Rules for Arithmetic Expressions

Listing 34.1 `Expression` Interface

```
public interface Expression {
  public int evaluate(Context c);
}
```

```
public class TerminalExpression implements Expression {
  private String var;
  public TerminalExpression(String v) {
    var = v;
  }
  public int evaluate(Context c) {
    return c.getValue(var);
  }
}
```

The application design can evaluate any expression. But for simplicity, the main `Calculator` (Listing 34.7) object uses a hard-coded arithmetic expression (a + b) * (c − d) as the expression to be interpreted and evaluated.

Listing 34.2 `NonTerminalExpression` Class

```java
public abstract class NonTerminalExpression
  implements Expression {
  private Expression leftNode;
  private Expression rightNode;
  public NonTerminalExpression(Expression l, Expression r) {
    setLeftNode(l);
    setRightNode(r);
  }
  public void setLeftNode(Expression node) {
    leftNode = node;
  }
  public void setRightNode(Expression node) {
    rightNode = node;
  }
  public Expression getLeftNode() {
    return leftNode;
  }
  public Expression getRightNode() {
    return rightNode;
  }
}//NonTerminalExpression
```

Listing 34.3 `AddExpression` Class

```java
class AddExpression extends NonTerminalExpression {
  public int evaluate(Context c) {
    return getLeftNode().evaluate(c) +
           getRightNode().evaluate(c);
  }
  public AddExpression(Expression l, Expression r) {
    super(l, r);
  }
}//AddExpression
```

The `Calculator` object carries out the interpretation and evaluation of the input expression in three stages:

Listing 34.4 SubtractExpression Class

```
class SubtractExpression extends NonTerminalExpression {
  public int evaluate(Context c) {
    return getLeftNode().evaluate(c) -
          getRightNode().evaluate(c);
  }
  public SubtractExpression(Expression l, Expression r) {
    super(l, r);
  }
}//SubtractExpression
```

Listing 34.5 MultiplyExpression Class

```
class MultiplyExpression extends NonTerminalExpression {
  public int evaluate(Context c) {
    return getLeftNode().evaluate(c) *
          getRightNode().evaluate(c);
  }
  public MultiplyExpression(Expression l, Expression r) {
    super(l, r);
  }
}//MultiplyExpression
```

1. *Infix-to-postfix conversion* — The input infix expression is first translated into an equivalent postfix expression.
2. *Construction of the tree structure* — The postfix expression is then scanned to build a tree structure.
3. *Postorder traversal of the tree* — The tree is then postorder traversed for evaluating the expression.

```
public class Calculator {
              ...
              ...
  public int evaluate() {
    //infix to Postfix
    String pfExpr = infixToPostFix(expression);
```

Listing 34.6 Context Class

```
class Context {
  private HashMap varList = new HashMap();
  public void assign(String var, int value) {
    varList.put(var, new Integer(value));
  }
  public int getValue(String var) {
    Integer objInt = (Integer) varList.get(var);
    return objInt.intValue();
  }
  public Context() {
    initialize();
  }
  //Values are hardcoded to keep the example simple
  private void initialize() {
    assign("a",20);
    assign("b",40);
    assign("c",30);
    assign("d",10);
  }
}
```

```
    //build the Binary Tree
    Expression rootNode = buildTree(pfExpr);
    //Evaluate the tree
    return rootNode.evaluate(ctx);
  }
      ...
      ...
}//End of class
```

Infix-to-Postfix Conversion (Listing 34.8)

An expression in the standard form is an infix expression.

Example: (a + b) * (c − d)

An infix expression is more easily understood by humans but is not suitable for evaluating expressions by computers. The usage of precedence rules and parentheses in the case of complex expressions makes it difficult for computer evaluation of

Listing 34.7 Calculator Class

```java
public class Calculator {
  private String expression;
  private HashMap operators;
  private Context ctx;
  public static void main(String[] args) {
    Calculator calc = new Calculator();
    //instantiate the context
    Context ctx = new Context();
    //set the expression to evaluate
    calc.setExpression("(a+b)*(c-d)");
    //configure the calculator with the
    //Context
    calc.setContext(ctx);
    //Display the result
    System.out.println(" Variable Values: " +
                     "a=" + ctx.getValue("a") +
                     ", b=" + ctx.getValue("b") +
                     ", c=" + ctx.getValue("c") +
                     ", d=" + ctx.getValue("d"));
    System.out.println(" Expression = (a+b)*(c-d)");
    System.out.println(" Result = " + calc.evaluate());
  }
  public Calculator() {
    operators = new HashMap();
    operators.put("+","1");
    operators.put("-","1");
    operators.put("/","2");
    operators.put("*","2");
    operators.put("(","0");
  }
        ...

        ...
}//End of class
```

these expressions. A postfix expression does not contain parentheses, does not involve precedence rules and is more suitable for evaluation by computers.

The postfix equivalent of the example expression above is ab+cd–*.

A detailed description of the process of converting an infix expression to its postfix form is provided in the Additional Notes section.

Listing 34.8 Calculator Class Performing the Infix-to-Postfix Conversion

```java
public class Calculator {
        ...

        ...

  private String infixToPostFix(String str) {
    Stack s = new Stack();
    String pfExpr = "";
    String tempStr = "";
    String expr = str.trim();
    for (int i = 0; i < str.length(); i++) {
      String currChar = str.substring(i, i + 1);
      if ((isOperator(currChar) == false) &&
          (!currChar.equals("(")) &&
          (!currChar.equals(")"))) {
        pfExpr = pfExpr + currChar;
      }
      if (currChar.equals("(")) {
        s.push(currChar);
      }
      //for ')' pop all stack contents until '('
      if (currChar.equals(")")) {
        tempStr = (String) s.pop();
        while (!tempStr.equals("(")) {
          pfExpr = pfExpr + tempStr;
          tempStr = (String) s.pop();
        }
        tempStr = "";
      }
      //if the current character is an
      //operator
      if (isOperator(currChar)) {
        if (s.isEmpty() == false) {
          tempStr = (String) s.pop();
          String strVal1 =
```

(continued)

Listing 34.8 Calculator Class Performing the Infix-to-Postfix Conversion (Continued)

```
              (String) operators.get(tempStr);
          int val1 = new Integer(strVal1).intValue();
          String strVal2 =
            (String) operators.get(currChar);
          int val2 = new Integer(strVal2).intValue();
          while ((val1 >= val2)) {
            pfExpr = pfExpr + tempStr;
            val1 = -100;
            if (s.isEmpty() == false) {
              tempStr = (String) s.pop();
              strVal1 = (String) operators.get(
                          tempStr);
              val1 = new Integer(strVal1).intValue();
            }
          }
          if ((val1 < val2) && (val1 != -100))
            s.push(tempStr);
        }
        s.push(currChar);
      }//if
    }//for
    while (s.isEmpty() == false) {
      tempStr = (String) s.pop();
      pfExpr = pfExpr + tempStr;
    }
    return pfExpr;
  }

          ...

          ...
}//End of class
```

Construction of the Tree Structure (Listing 34.9)

The postfix equivalent of the input infix expression is scanned from left to right and a tree structure is built using the following algorithm:

1. Initialize an empty stack.
2. Scan the postfix string from left to right.

Listing 34.9 `Calculator` Class Building a Tree with Operators as Nonterminal Nodes and Operands as Terminal Nodes

```java
public class Calculator {
    ...

    ...

  public void setContext(Context c) {
    ctx = c;
  }
  public void setExpression(String expr) {
    expression = expr;
  }

    ...

    ...

  private Expression buildTree(String expr) {
    Stack s = new Stack();
    for (int i = 0; i < expr.length(); i++) {
      String currChar = expr.substring(i, i + 1);
      if (isOperator(currChar) == false) {
        Expression e = new TerminalExpression(currChar);
        s.push(e);
      } else {
        Expression r = (Expression) s.pop();
        Expression l = (Expression) s.pop();
        Expression n =
          getNonTerminalExpression(currChar, l, r);
        s.push(n);
      }
    }//for
    return (Expression) s.pop();
  }

    ...

    ...

}//End of class
```

3. If the scanned character is an operand:
   a. Create an instance of the `TerminalExpression` class by passing the scanned character as an argument.
   b. Push the `TerminalExpression` object to the stack.

4. If the scanned character is an operator:
   a. Pop two top elements from the stack.
   b. Create an instance of an appropriate `NonTerminalExpression` sub-class by passing the two stack elements retrieved above as arguments.
5. Repeat Step 3 and Step 4 for all characters in the postfix string.
6. The only remaining element in the stack is the root of the tree structure.

The example postfix expression ab+cd–* results in the following tree structure as in Figure 34.2.

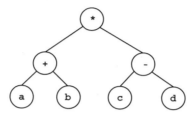

Figure 34.2   Example Expression: Tree Structure

Postorder Traversal of the Tree

The `Calculator` traverses the tree structure and evaluates different `Expression` objects in its postorder traversal path. There are four major tree traversal techniques. These techniques are discussed as part of the Additional Notes section. Because the binary tree in the current example is a representation of a postfix expression, the postorder traversal technique is followed for the expression evaluation. The `Calculator` object makes use of a helper `Context` object to share information with different `Expression` objects constituting the tree structure. In general, a `Context` object is used as a global repository of information. In the current example, the `Calculator` object stores the values of different variables in the `Context`, which are used by each of different `Expression` objects in evaluating the part of the expression it represents.

The postorder traversal of the tree structure in Figure 34.2 results in the evaluation of the leftmost subtree in a recursive manner, followed by the rightmost subtree, then the `NonTerminalExpression` node representing an operator.

ADDITIONAL NOTES

Infix-to-Postfix Conversion

Infix Expression

An expression in the standard form is an infix expression.

Example: a * b + c/d

Sometimes, an infix expression is also referred to as an in-order expression.

Postfix Expression

The postfix (postorder) form equivalent of the above example expression is ab*cd/+.

Conversion Algorithm

See Table 34.2 for the conversion algorithm.

Table 34.2   Conversion Algorithm

1. *Define operator precedence rules* — In general arithmetic, the descending order of precedence is as shown in the rules below:

Precedence Rules	
*, /	Same precedence
+, −	Same precedence
Expressions are evaluated from left to right.	

2. Initialize an empty stack.
3. Initialize an empty postfix expression.
4. Scan the infix string from left to right.
5. If the scanned character is an operand, add it to the postfix string.
6. If the scanned character is a left parenthesis, push it to the stack.
7. If the scanned character is a right parenthesis:
   a. Pop elements from the stack and add to the postfix string until the stack element is a left parenthesis.
   b. Discard both the left and the right parenthesis characters.
8. If the scanned character is an operator:
   a. If the stack is empty, push the character to the stack.
   b. If the stack is not empty:
      i. If the element on top of the stack is an operator:
         A. Compare the precedence of the character with the precedence of the element on top of the stack.
         B. If top element has higher or equal precedence over the scanned character, pop the stack element and add it to the Postfix string. Repeat this step as long as the stack is not empty and the element on top of the stack has equal or higher precedence over the scanned character.
         C. Push the scanned character to stack.
      ii. If the element on top of the stack is a left parenthesis, push the scanned character to the stack.
9. Repeat Steps 5 through 8 above until all the characters are scanned.
10. After all characters are scanned, continue to pop elements from the stack and add to the postfix string until the stack is empty.
11. Return the postfix string.

Example

As an example, consider the infix expression (A + B) * (C – D). Let us apply the algorithm described above to convert this expression into its postfix form.

Initially the stack is empty and the postfix string has no characters. Table 34.3 shows the contents of the stack and the resulting postfix expression as each character in the input infix expression is processed.

Table 34.3 Infix-to-Postfix Conversion Algorithm Tracing

Infix Expression Character	Observation and Action to Be Taken	Stack	Postfix String
(	Push to the stack.	(	
A	Operand. Add to the postfix string.	(	A
+	Operator. The element on top of the stack is a left parenthesis and hence push + to the stack.	(+	A
B	Operand. Add to the postfix string.	(+	AB
)	Right parenthesis. Pop elements from the stack until a left parenthesis is found. Add these stack elements to the postfix string. Discard both left and right parentheses.		AB+
*	Operator. The element on top of the stack is +. The precedence of + is less than the precedence of *. Push the operator to the stack.	*	AB+
(	Push to the stack.	*(	AB+
C	Operand. Add to the postfix string.	*(	AB + C
–	Operator. The element on top of the stack is a left parenthesis and hence push + to the stack.	*(–	AB + C
D	Operand. Add to the Postfix string.	*(–	AB + CD
)	Right parenthesis. Pop elements from the stack until a left parenthesis is found. Add these stack elements to the postfix string. Discard both left and right parentheses.	*	AB + CD–
All characters in the infix expression are scanned	Add all remaining stack elements to the postfix string.		AB + CD–*

Binary Tree Traversal Techniques

There are four different tree traversal techniques — Preorder, In-Order, Postorder and Level-Order. Let us discuss each of these techniques by using the following binary tree in Figure 34.3 as an example.

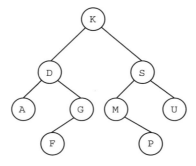

Figure 34.3 Example Sorted Tree Structure

Preorder (Node-Left-Right)

Start with the root node and follow the algorithm as follows:

- Visit the node first.
- Traverse the left subtree in preorder.
- Traverse the right subtree in preorder.

A preorder traversal of the above sorted tree structure to print the contents of the nodes constituting the tree results in the following display:

KDAGFSMPU

In-Order (Left-Node-Right)

Start with the root node and follow the algorithm as follows:

- Traverse the left subtree in in-order.
- Visit the node.
- Traverse the right subtree in in-order.

An in-order traversal of the above sorted tree structure to print the contents of the nodes constituting the tree results in the following display:

ADFGKMPSU

Postorder (Left-Right-Node)

Start with the root node and follow the algorithm as follows:

- Traverse the left subtree in in-order.
- Traverse the right subtree in in-order.
- Visit the node.

A postorder traversal of the above sorted tree structure to print the contents of the nodes constituting the tree results in the following display:

AFGDPMUSK

Level-Order

Start with the root node level and follow the algorithm as follows:

- Traverse different levels of the tree structure from top to bottom.
- Visit nodes from left to right with in each level.

A level-order traversal of the above sorted tree structure to print the contents of the nodes constituting the tree results in the following display:

KDSAGMUFP

PRACTICE QUESTIONS

1. Enhance the example application to include the division and the unary arithmetic negation operations.
2. Design an interpreter for the DOS copy command. The copy command can be used to create a new file with the contents of a single or multiple files:

- The Copy a.txt c.txt command copies the contents of the a.txt file to the new c.txt file.
- The Copy a.txt + b.txt c.txt command copies the contents of both the files a.txt and b.txt to the new c.txt file.

3. Design and develop an interpreter to display a given integer value in words.
4. Redesign the example application using the Visitor pattern.
   a. Design a Visitor with different visit(ExpressionObjectType) methods and a getResult() method.
   b. Convert the input infix expression to postfix expression.
   c. Scan the postfix expression from left to right.
      i. When an operand is found push to stack.
      ii. When an operator is found:
         A. Pop two operands from the stack.
         B. Create an appropriate Expression object.
         C. When the Expression object is created, it invokes an appropriate visit method on the Visitor instance by passing itself as an argument. The Visitor in turn calls the evaluate method on the Expression object. The integer result of the evaluate method call is then pushed to the stack.
         D. Once the postfix expression is scanned from left to right, the getResult() method can be invoked on the Visitor to get the final result. The Visitor can retrieve the only remaining stack element and return it.

35

STATE

This pattern was previously described in GoF95.

DESCRIPTION

The state of an object can be defined as its exact condition at any given point of time, depending on the values of its properties or attributes. The set of methods implemented by a class constitutes the behavior of its instances. Whenever there is a change in the values of its attributes, we say that the state of an object has changed.

A simple example of this would be the case of a user selecting a specific font style or color in an HTML editor. When a user selects a different font style or color, the properties of the editor object change. This can be considered as a change in its internal state.

The State pattern is useful in designing an efficient structure for a class, a typical instance of which can exist in many different states and exhibit different behavior depending on the state it is in. In other words, in the case of an object of such a class, some or all of its behavior is completely influenced by its current state. In the State design pattern terminology, such a class is referred to as a *Context* class. A `Context` object can alter its behavior when there is a change in its internal state and is also referred as a `Stateful` object.

STATEFUL OBJECT: AN EXAMPLE

Most of the HTML editors available today offer different views of an HTML page at the time of creation. Let us consider one such editor that offers three views of a given Web page as follows:

1. *Design view* — In this view, a user is allowed to visually create a Web page without having to know about the internal HTML commands.
2. *HTML view* — This view offers a user the basic structure of the Web page in terms of the HTML tags and lets a user customize the Web page with additional HTML code.
3. *Quick page view* — This view provides a preview of the Web page being created.

When a user selects one of these views (change in the state of the `Editor` object), the behavior of the `Editor` object changes in terms of the way the current Web page is displayed.

The State pattern suggests moving the state-specific behavior out of the `Context` class into a set of separate classes referred to as *State classes*. Each of the many different states that a `Context` object can exist in can be mapped into a separate `State` class. The implementation of a `State` class contains the context behavior that is specific to a given state, not the overall behavior of the context itself.

The context acts as a client to the set of `State` objects in the sense that it makes use of different `State` objects to offer the necessary state-specific behavior to an application object that uses the context in a seamless manner.

In the absence of such a design, each method of the context would contain complex, inelegant conditional statements to implement the overall context behavior in it. For example,

```
public Context{
      ...

      ...

   someMethod(){
     if (state_1){
       //do something
     }else if (state_2){
       //do something else
     }
         ...

         ...

   }
       ...

       ...

}
```

By encapsulating the state-specific behavior in separate classes, the context implementation becomes simpler to read: free of too many conditional statements such as if-else or switch-case constructs. When a `Context` object is first created, it initializes itself with its initial `State` object. This `State` object becomes the current `State` object for the context. By replacing the current `State` object with a new `State` object, the context transitions to a new state. The client application using the context is not responsible for specifying the current `State` object for the context, but instead, each of the `State` classes representing specific states are expected to provide the necessary implementation to transition the context into other states.

When an application object makes a call to a `Context` method (behavior), it forwards the method call to its current `State` object.

```
public Context{

        ...

        ...

    someMethod(){
      objCurrentState.someMethod();
    }

        ...

        ...

}
```

EXAMPLE

The following State pattern example takes advantage of polymorphism to implement such state-specific behavior. Polymorphism allows two objects with the same method signatures and completely different implementations to be treated in an identical manner.

To use polymorphism, classes that implement the same method differently are derived from a common parent class. Let us say that a client program is written to operate on objects of the superclass type. What the client program thinks of as a parent class object could in reality be an instance of any of its subclasses. The client remains oblivious to this fact. When the client program invokes a method defined in the superclass, the method that gets called is actually the subclass method that overrides the superclass version. In other words, polymorphism encapsulates (hides) the type of the object.

Let us consider a business account at a bank with the overdraft facility. Such an account can exist in any one of the following three states at any given point of time:

1. *No transaction fee state* — As long as the account balance remains greater than the minimum balance, no transaction fee will be charged for any deposit or withdrawal transaction. The example application has the minimum balance as $2,000.
2. *Transaction fee state* — An account is considered to be in the transaction fee state when the account balance is positive but below the minimum balance. A transaction fee will be charged for any deposit or withdrawal transaction in this state. The example application has the transaction fee in this state as $2.
3. *Overdrawn state* — This is the state of the account when an account balance is negative but within the overdraft limit. A transaction fee will be charged for any deposit or withdrawal transactions in this state. The example application has the transaction fee in this state as $5 and the overdraft limit is maintained as $1,000.

In all three states, a withdrawal transaction that exceeds the overdraft limit is not allowed. Figure 35.1 depicts possible state transitions for an account and Table 35.1 shows how these transitions can occur.

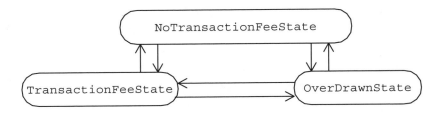

Figure 35.1 State Transitions among Different Account States

Table 35.1 State Transitions among Different Account States

From	To	What Causes the Transition
No transaction fee state	Transaction fee state	A withdrawal that can make the balance positive but less than the minimum balance.
	Overdrawn state	A withdrawal that can make the balance negative.
Transaction fee state	No transaction fee state	A deposit that can make the balance greater than the minimum balance.
	Overdrawn state	A withdrawal that can make the balance negative.
Overdrawn state	No transaction fee state	A deposit that can make the balance greater than the minimum balance.
	Transaction fee state	A deposit that can make the balance positive but less than the minimum balance.

Let us design a representation for the business account in the form of the BusinessAccount class as in Figure 35.2 and Listing 35.1.

The BusinessAccount class offers the basic functionality in the form of methods to enable a client object to perform deposit and withdrawal operations. In addition, the BusinessAccount class defines some of the transaction limits and offers accessor methods to read its state.

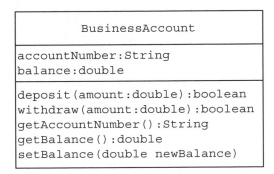

Figure 35.2 BusinessAccount Representation

Listing 35.1 BusinessAccount Class

```java
public class BusinessAccount {
  public static final double MIN_BALANCE = 2000.00;
  public static final double OVERDRAW_LIMIT = -1000.00;
  public static final double TRANS_FEE_NORMAL = 2.00;
  public static final double TRANS_FEE_OVERDRAW = 5.00;
  public static final String ERR_OVERDRAW_LIMIT_EXCEED =
    "Error: Transaction cannot be processed. " +
      "Overdraw limit exceeded.";
  private State objState;
  private String accountNumber;
  private double balance;
  public void setState(State newState) {
    objState = newState;
  }
  public State getState() {
    return objState;
  }
  public String getAccountNumber() {
    return accountNumber;
  }
  public boolean deposit(double amount) {
    //...
  }
  public boolean withdraw(double amount) {
    //...
  }
  public BusinessAccount(String accountNum) {
    accountNumber = accountNum;
    objState = State.InitialState(this);
  }
  public double getBalance() {
    return balance;
  }
  public void setBalance(double newBalance) {
    balance = newBalance;
  }
}
```

Let us define a common State class (Listing 35.2) that contains the business account behavior that is common across all states.

Instead of keeping the state-specific behavior inside the BusinessAccount class, by applying the State pattern, the behavior specific to each of the three states can be implemented in the form of three separate subclasses — NoTransactionFeeState, TransactionFeeState and OverDrawnState (Listing 35.3 through Listing 35.5) — of the State class. Figure 35.3 shows the resulting class hierarchy. The common parent State class declares the interface to be used by different client objects to access the services of the objects in the State class hierarchy. If a client object is designed to use the services of an object of the common parent State class type, it can access the services offered by its subclasses in a seamless manner.

Each of the State subclasses is designed to contain the behavior specific to a given state of the business account. In addition, these subclasses know the state it should transition to and when to make that transition. Each of these State subclasses implements this state transition functionality by overriding the parent class transitionState method as per the state transition rules detailed in Table 35.1.

While the state-specific behavior is separated out from the BusinessAccount, the state (i.e., the account balance) is still maintained within the BusinessAccount class. Because the behavior contained in each of the State objects is specific to a state of the business account represented by the BusinessAccount class, a State object should be able to read the BusinessAccount object state. To facilitate this, each of the State objects is designed to contain an object reference of the BusinessAccount type. When a State object is created, it is configured with a BusinessAccount instance. Using this BusinessAccount object, a state object can check or alter the state of the business account it represents.

Because the state-specific behavior of a business account is contained in the State class hierarchy, the BusinessAccount needs a way to access the behavior specific to its current state. This requirement can be addressed by enhancing the BusinessAccount class design so that a BusinessAccount object maintains an object reference instance variable of type State to store its current state object. When a BusinessAccount object is first created, it sets an instance of the NoTransactionFeeState class (the default state) as its current State object. Whenever a client object invokes a method such as deposit or withdraw on the BusinessAccount object, it forwards the method call to its current State object. Figure 35.4 and Listing 35.6 show the revised BusinessAccount class representation.

The BusinessAccount class represents the business account and acts as the context in this example. Figure 35.5 shows the overall class association.

Let us design a test client AccountManager to allow a user to perform different transactions on a business account. When executed, the AccountManager:

- Creates a BusinessAccount object that represents a business account.
- Displays the necessary user interface as in Figure 35.6 to allow a user to perform deposit and withdrawal transactions that can make the business account go through different states.

Listing 35.2 State Class

```java
public class State {
  private BusinessAccount context;
  public BusinessAccount getContext() {
    return context;
  }
  public void setContext(BusinessAccount newAccount) {
    context = newAccount;
  }
  public State transitionState() {
    return null;
  }
  public State(BusinessAccount account) {
    setContext(account);
  }
  public State(State source) {
    setContext(source.getContext());
  }
  public static State InitialState(BusinessAccount account) {
    return new NoTransactionFeeState(account);
  }
  public boolean deposit(double amount) {
    double balance = getContext().getBalance();
    getContext().setBalance(balance + amount);
    transitionState();
    System.out.println("An amount " + amount +
                       " is deposited ");
    return true;
  }
  public boolean withdraw(double amount) {
    double balance = getContext().getBalance();
    getContext().setBalance(balance - amount);
    transitionState();
    System.out.println("An amount " + amount +
                       " is withdrawn ");
    return true;
  }
}
```

Listing 35.3 NoTransactionFeeState Class

```java
public class NoTransactionFeeState extends State {
  public NoTransactionFeeState(BusinessAccount account) {
    super(account);
  }
  public NoTransactionFeeState(State source) {
    super(source);
  }
  public boolean deposit(double amount) {
    return super.deposit(amount);
  }
  public boolean withdraw(double amount) {
    double balance = getContext().getBalance();
    if ((balance - amount) >
        BusinessAccount.OVERDRAW_LIMIT) {
      super.withdraw(amount);
      return true;
    } else {
      System.out.println(
        BusinessAccount.ERR_OVERDRAW_LIMIT_EXCEED);
      return false;
    }
  }
  public State transitionState() {
    double balance = getContext().getBalance();
    if (balance < 0) {
      getContext().setState(new OverDrawnState(this));
    } else {
      if (balance < BusinessAccount.MIN_BALANCE) {
        getContext().setState(
          new TransactionFeeState(this));
      }
    }
    return getContext().getState();
  }
}
```

Listing 35.4 TransactionFeeState Class

```
public class TransactionFeeState extends State {
  public TransactionFeeState(BusinessAccount account) {
    super(account);
  }
  public TransactionFeeState(State source) {
    super(source);
  }
  public State transitionState() {
    double balance = getContext().getBalance();
    if (balance < 0) {
      getContext().setState(new OverDrawnState(this));
    } else {
      if (balance >= BusinessAccount.MIN_BALANCE) {
        getContext().setState(
          new NoTransactionFeeState(this));
      }
    }
    return getContext().getState();
  }
  public boolean deposit(double amount) {
    double balance = getContext().getBalance();
    getContext().setBalance(balance -
        BusinessAccount.TRANS_FEE_NORMAL);
    System.out.println(
      "Transaction Fee was charged due to " +
      "account status " +
      "(less than minimum balance)");
    return super.deposit(amount);
  }
  public boolean withdraw(double amount) {
    double balance = getContext().getBalance();
    if ((balance - BusinessAccount.TRANS_FEE_NORMAL -
        amount) > BusinessAccount.OVERDRAW_LIMIT) {
      getContext().setBalance(balance -
        BusinessAccount.TRANS_FEE_NORMAL);
```

(continued)

Listing 35.4 `TransactionFeeState` Class (Continued)

```
        System.out.println(
          "Transaction Fee was charged due to " +
          "account status " +
          "(less than minimum balance)");
        return super.withdraw(amount);
      } else {
        System.out.println(
          BusinessAccount.ERR_OVERDRAW_LIMIT_EXCEED);
        return false;
      }
    }
  }
}
```

Every deposit or withdrawal transaction initiated through the user interface translates to a `deposit(double)` or `withdraw(double)` method call on the `BusinessAccount` object that is created when the `AccountManager` is executed. The `BusinessAccount` object in turn forwards this call to its internal current `State` object. The current `State` object executes the behavior it contains and sets an appropriate `State` object as the `BusinessAccount` object's current `State` object. In this manner the `Context` class (`BusinessAccount`) and its state-specific behavior (`State` class hierarchy) are completely separated from each other. When a new state-specific behavior is added or the behavior specific to a state is altered, the actual `Context` class `BusinessAccount` remains unaffected.

Listing 35.5 `OverDrawnState` Class

```
  public class OverDrawnState extends State {
    public void sendMailToAccountHolder() {
      System.out.println (
        "Attention: Your Account is Overdrawn");
    }
    public OverDrawnState(BusinessAccount account) {
      super(account);
      sendMailToAccountHolder();
    }
    public OverDrawnState(State source) {
      super(source);
      sendMailToAccountHolder();
    }
```

(continued)

Listing 35.5 `OverDrawnState` **Class (Continued)**

```
    public State transitionState() {
   double balance = getContext().getBalance();
   if (balance >= BusinessAccount.MIN_BALANCE)
     getContext().setState(
       new NoTransactionFeeState(this));
   else if (balance >= 0)
     getContext().setState(new TransactionFeeState(this));
   return getContext().getState();
 }
 public boolean deposit(double amount) {
   double balance = getContext().getBalance();
   getContext().setBalance(balance -
       BusinessAccount.TRANS_FEE_OVERDRAW);
   System.out.println("Transaction Fee was charged " +
                     "due to account status(Overdrawn)");
   return super.deposit(amount);
 }
 public boolean withdraw(double amount) {
   double balance = getContext().getBalance();
   if ((balance - BusinessAccount.TRANS_FEE_OVERDRAW -
        amount) > BusinessAccount.OVERDRAW_LIMIT) {
     getContext().setBalance(balance -
       BusinessAccount.TRANS_FEE_OVERDRAW);
System.out.println(
       "Transaction Fee was charged due to " +
       "account status(Overdrawn)");
     return super.withdraw(amount);
   } else {
     System.out.println(
       BusinessAccount.ERR_OVERDRAW_LIMIT_EXCEED);
     return false;
   }
 }
}
```

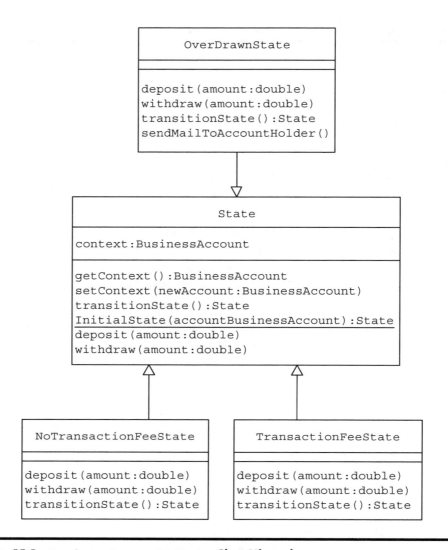

Figure 35.3 BusinessAccount State Class Hierarchy

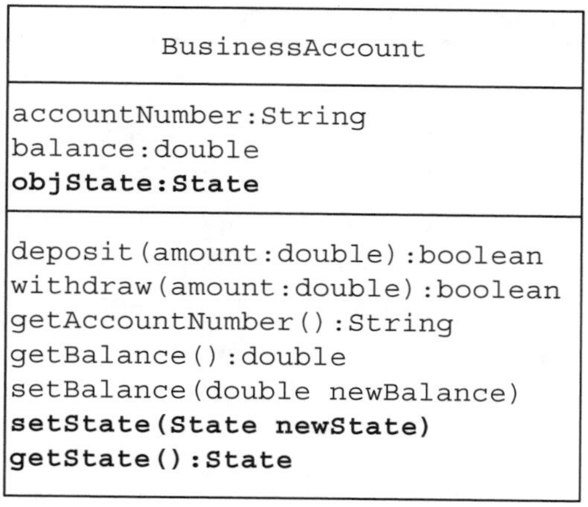

BusinessAccount
accountNumber:String
balance:double
objState:State
deposit(amount:double):boolean
withdraw(amount:double):boolean
getAccountNumber():String
getBalance():double
setBalance(double newBalance)
setState(State newState)
getState():State

Figure 35.4 **BusinessAccount Representation: Revised**

BusinessAccount
OverDrawnState
State
NoTransactionFeeState
TransactionFeeState

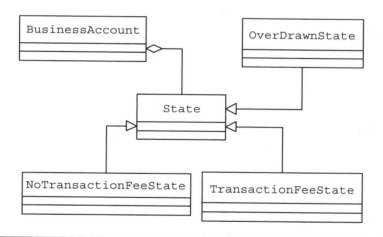

Figure 35.5 **Class Association**

Listing 35.6 BusinessAccount Class: Revised

```java
public class BusinessAccount {
  public static final double MIN_BALANCE = 2000.00;
  public static final double OVERDRAW_LIMIT = -1000.00;
  public static final double TRANS_FEE_NORMAL = 2.00;
  public static final double TRANS_FEE_OVERDRAW = 5.00;
  public static final String ERR_OVERDRAW_LIMIT_EXCEED =
    "Error: Transaction cannot be processed. " +
      "Overdraw limit exceeded.";
  private State objState;
  private String accountNumber;
  private double balance;
  public void setState(State newState) {
    objState = newState;
  }
  public State getState() {
    return objState;
  }
  public String getAccountNumber() {
    return accountNumber;
  }
  public boolean deposit(double amount) {
    return getState().deposit(amount);
  }
  public boolean withdraw(double amount) {
    return getState().withdraw(amount);
  }
  public BusinessAccount(String accountNum) {
    accountNumber = accountNum;
    objState = State.InitialState(this);
  }
  public double getBalance() {
    return balance;
  }
  public void setBalance(double newBalance) {
    balance = newBalance;
  }
}
```

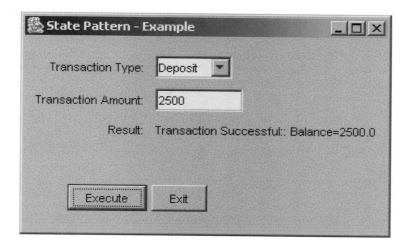

Figure 35.6 `AccountManager` **User Interface**

Table 35.2 Membership Account State Transitions

From	*To*	*What Causes the Transition*
Active	Due	From the 5th to the 10th of every month.
	Canceled	If a member wants to cancel the account explicitly.
Due	Active	If payment is made before the 10th of the month.
	Unpaid	If payment is not made before the 10th of the month.
	Canceled	If a member wants to cancel the account explicitly.
Unpaid	Active	If payment is made before the account is canceled.
	Canceled	If a member wants to cancel the account explicitly. If the account stays in the unpaid state for more than 15 days.
Canceled	Active	If all previous payment dues are cleared.

PRACTICE QUESTIONS

1. Assume that a membership account at a Web site can exist in one of four different states:
   - *Active* — This is the state of an account when it is in good standing.
   - *Due* — Every account is supposed to be paid for by the 5th of every month, but members are given up to the 10th to make the payment. An account remains in the due state until the 10th of every month, if not paid before the 10th.
   - *Unpaid* — If the payment is not made by the 10th of every month, the account enters into the unpaid state. In this state, members are not allowed to use premium services. But the membership still remains active and members can use basic services.

- *Canceled* — If an account remains in the unpaid state for more than 15 days then it is canceled. Table 35.2 lists different membership account state transitions.
  a. Design a `MemberAccount` class whose instances can be used to represent membership accounts.
  b. Apply the State pattern to design the state-specific behavior of a membership account in the form of a group of `State` classes that are part of a class hierarchy with a common parent.
2. An order at an online store can be in one of the following states:
   - Not Submitted
   - Submitted
   - Received
   - Processed
   - Shipped
   - Canceled
   a. Define a state transition table (similar to Table 35.1) for an order.
   b. Design an `Order` class whose instances can be used to represent orders. Design the state-specific behavior of an order in the form of a set of `State` classes with a common parent class.

36

STRATEGY

This pattern was previously described in GoF95.

DESCRIPTION

The Strategy pattern is useful when there is a set of related algorithms and a client object needs to be able to dynamically pick and choose an algorithm from this set that suits its current need.

The Strategy pattern suggests keeping the implementation of each of the algorithms in a separate class. Each such algorithm encapsulated in a separate class is referred to as a *strategy*. An object that uses a Strategy object is often referred to as a *context object*.

With different Strategy objects in place, changing the behavior of a Context object is simply a matter of changing its Strategy object to the one that implements the required algorithm.

To enable a Context object to access different Strategy objects in a seamless manner, all Strategy objects must be designed to offer the same interface. In the Java programming language, this can be accomplished by designing each Strategy object either as an implementer of a common interface or as a subclass of a common abstract class that declares the required common interface.

Once the group of related algorithms is encapsulated in a set of Strategy classes in a class hierarchy, a client can choose from among these algorithms by selecting and instantiating an appropriate Strategy class. To alter the behavior of the context, a client object needs to configure the context with the selected strategy instance. This type of arrangement completely separates the implementation of an algorithm from the context that uses it. As a result, when an existing algorithm implementation is changed or a new algorithm is added to the group, both the context and the client object (that uses the context) remain unaffected.

STRATEGIES VERSUS OTHER ALTERNATIVES

Implementing different algorithms in the form of a method using conditional statements violates the basic object-oriented, open-closed principle. Designing each algorithm as a different class is a more elegant approach than designing all different algorithms as part of a method in the form of a conditional statement. Because each algorithm is contained in a separate class, it becomes simpler and easier to add, change or remove an algorithm.

Another approach would be to subclass the context itself and implement different algorithms in different subclasses of the context. This type of design binds the behavior to a context subclass and the behavior executed by a context subclass becomes static. With this design, to change the behavior of the context, a client object needs to create an instance of a different subclass of the context and replace the current `Context` object with it.

Having different algorithms encapsulated in different `Strategy` classes decouples the context behavior from the `Context` object itself. With different `Strategy` objects available, a client object can use the same `Context` object and change its behavior by configuring it with different `Strategy` objects. This is a more flexible approach than subclassing.

Also, sometimes subclassing can lead to a bloated class hierarchy. We have seen an example of this during the discussion of the Decorator pattern. Designing algorithms as different `Strategy` classes keeps the class growth linear.

STRATEGY VERSUS STATE

From the discussion above, the Strategy pattern looks very similar to the State pattern discussed earlier. One of the differences between the two patterns is that the Strategy pattern deals with a set of related algorithms, which are more similar in what they do as opposed to different state-specific behavior encapsulated in different `State` objects in the State pattern.

Table 36.1 provides a detailed list of similarities and differences between the State and the Strategy patterns.

EXAMPLE

During the discussion of the Decorator pattern we designed a decorator class `EncryptLogger` that encrypts an incoming message before sending it to the `FileLogger` instance it contains for logging. For encrypting the message text, the `EncryptLogger` calls its `encrypt(String)` method. The encryption algorithm implemented inside the `encrypt(String)` method is very simple in that the characters of the message text are all shifted to the right by one position.

In general, there are many different ways of encrypting a message text using different encryption algorithms. Let us consider four different encryption algorithms including the simple encryption used by the `EncryptLogger` in the existing design.

SimpleEncryption

When this encryption is applied, characters in the plain text message are shifted to the right or left by one position.

Table 36.1   State versus Strategy

State Pattern	Strategy Pattern
Different types of possible behavior of an object are implemented in the form of a group of separate objects (`State` objects).	Similar to the State pattern, specific behaviors are modeled in the form of separate classes (`Strategy` objects).
The behavior contained in each `State` object is specific to a given state of the associated object.	The behavior contained in each `Strategy` object is a different algorithm (from a set of related algorithms) to provide a given functionality.
An object that uses a `State` object to change its behavior is referred to as a `Context` object. A `Context` object needs to change its current `State` object to change its behavior.	An object that uses a `Strategy` object to alter its behavior is referred to as a `Context` object. Similar to the State pattern, for a `Context` object to behave differently, it needs to be configured with a different `Strategy` object.
Often, when an instance of the context is first created, it is associated with one of the default `State` objects.	Similarly, a context is associated with a default `Strategy` object that implements the default algorithm.
A given `State` object itself can put the context into a new state. This makes a new `State` object as the current `State` object of the context, changing the behavior of the `Context` object.	A client application using the context needs to explicitly assign a strategy to the context. A `Strategy` object cannot cause the context to be configured with a different `Strategy` object.
The choice of a `State` object is dependent on the state of the `Context` object.	The choice of a `Strategy` object is based on the application need. Not on the state of the `Context` object.
A given `Context` object undergoes state changes. The order of transition among states is well defined. These are the characteristics of an application where the State pattern could be applied. **Example:** A bank account behaves differently depending on the state it is in when a transaction to withdraw money is attempted. When the minimum balance is maintained — no transaction fee is charged. When the minimum balance is not maintained — transaction fee is charged. When the account is overdrawn — the transaction is not allowed.	A given `Context` object does not undergo state changes. **Example:** An application that needs to encrypt and save the input data to a file. Different encryption algorithms can be used to encrypt the data. These algorithms can be designed as `Strategy` objects. The client application can choose a strategy that implements the required algorithm.

Example:
   Plain text:This is a message
   Cipher text:eThis is a messag

CaesarCypher

In its simplest form, the Caesar cipher is a rotation-substitution cipher where characters are shifted to the right by one position. It involves replacing the letter A with B, B with C, and so on, up to Z, which is replaced by A. This is called the rotate-1 Caesar cipher because it involves rotating the alphabet in the plain text by one position.

Example:
   Plain text:This is a message
   Cipher text:Uijt jt b nfttbhf

Similarly, a rotate-2 Caesar cipher replaces letter A with C, B with D, ... Z with B.

Julius Caesar is known to have used this simple rotate-n replacement cipher and hence the name *Caesar cipher*.

SubstitutionCypher

This encryption algorithm uses a letter substitution table to replace different letters in the plain text with corresponding entries from the substitution table.

Table 36.2 shows an example letter substitution table.

To encrypt a given plain text, look up letters from the plain text in the top row of the letter substitution table and replace it with the corresponding letter from the bottom row in the same column.

Example:
   Plain text: This is a Message
   Cipher text: mWNR NR T DXRRTnX

Table 36.2 Sample Letter Substitution Table

A	T	i	B	h	s	a	e	m	X	Y	M	P	C	g	F	Q	w	r	t
s	m	N	o	W	R	T	X	Y	A	B	D	F	I	n	d	i	a	U	S

CodeBookCypher

This algorithm involves replacing words from the plain text with corresponding word entries from a code-book table.

Table 36.3 shows an example code-book table.

Table 36.3 Sample Code-Book Table

This	Design
Is	Patterns
Book	CD
A	Are
Sun	Hello
True	Really
Moon	Country
Statement	Useful
Discovery	Old
Channel	Vaccum

To encrypt a given plain text message, look up every word from the plain text message in the first column of the code-book table and replace it with the corresponding word from the second column of the same row.

Example:
  Plain text:This Is A True Statement
  Cipher text:Design Patterns Are Really Useful

Let us suppose that clients of the EncryptLogger would like to be able to dynamically select and use any of the aforementioned encryption algorithms. This requirement can be designed in different ways, including:

■ Implementing all algorithms inside the existing encrypt(String) method of the EncryptLogger class using conditional statements
■ Applying inheritance, with each subclass of the EncryptLogger implementing a specific encryption algorithm

Though these options look straightforward, as discussed earlier under the "Strategies versus Other Alternatives" section, applying the Strategy pattern results in a more elegant and efficient design.

Applying the Strategy pattern, each of the encryption algorithms can be encapsulated in a separate (*strategy*) class (Listing 36.1 through Listing 36.4). Table 36.4 shows the list of these strategy classes and the algorithms they implement.

Let us define a common interface to be implemented by each of the strategy classes, in the form of a Java interface EncryptionStrategy, as follows:

```
public interface EncryptionStrategy {
  public String encrypt(String inputData);
}
```

Figure 36.1 shows the resulting class hierarchy.

Listing 36.1   SimpleEncryption Class

```
public class SimpleEncryption implements EncryptionStrategy {
  public String encrypt(String inputData) {
    inputData = inputData.substring(inputData.length() - 1) +
                inputData.substring(0, inputData.length() - 1);
    return inputData;
  }
}
```

Listing 36.2   CaesarCypher Class

```
public class CaesarCypher implements EncryptionStrategy {
  public String encrypt(String inputData) {
    char[] chars = inputData.toCharArray();
    for (int i = 0; i < chars.length; i++) {
      char c = chars[i];
      if (c == 'z') {
        c = 'a';
      }
      if ((c >= 'a') && (c < 'z')) {
        ++c;
      }
      chars[i] = c;
    }
    return new String(new String(chars));
  }
}
```

Each of the strategy classes listed in Table 36.4 provides the implementation of the algorithm it represents as part of the encrypt method declared by the EncryptionStrategy interface.

Because all of the strategy classes listed in Table 36.4 share the same interface, a client object that is designed to use an object of the EncryptionStrategy type will be able to access the encryption services offered by different strategy objects in a seamless manner.

Listing 36.3 SubstitutionCypher Class

```java
public class SubstitutionCypher implements EncryptionStrategy {
    char[] source = {'a','b','c','d','e','f','g','h','i','j','k',
                     'l','m','n','o','p','q','r','s','t','u','v',
                     'w','x','y','z'};
    char[] dest = {'m','n','o','p','q','r','a','b','c','d','e',
                   'f','g','h','i','j','k','l','y','z','s','t',
                   'u','v','w', 'x'};
    public String encrypt(String inputData) {
      char[] chars = inputData.toCharArray();
      for (int i = 0; i < chars.length; i++) {
        char c = chars[i];
        for (int j = 0; j < source.length; j++) {
          if (source[j] == chars[i]) {
            c = dest[j];
          }
        }
        chars[i] = c;
      }
      return new String(chars);
    }
}
```

With each encryption algorithm encapsulated in a separate strategy class, the EncryptLogger is no longer required to contain any implementation to encrypt an input message. The idea is that the EncryptLogger can make use of the services of any of the strategy objects as required to encrypt a message. To facilitate the usage of different strategy objects by the EncryptLogger in a seamless manner, the EncryptLogger needs to be redesigned (Figure 36.2 and Listing 36.5) so that:

- It contains an object reference variable currEncryptionStrategy of the EncryptionStrategy type. This variable is used to hold its current encryption strategy.
- It configures itself with the default encryption Strategy object when it is first created.
- It offers a method setEncryptionStrategy to enable a client object to configure it with a different Strategy object.
- As part of the encrypt method implementation, it accesses the encryption services offered by the EncryptionStrategy object that it is configured

Listing 36.4 CodeBookCypher Class

```java
public class CodeBookCypher implements EncryptionStrategy {
  HashMap codeContents = new HashMap();
  private void populateCodeEntries() {
    codeContents.put("This","Design");
    codeContents.put("is","Patterns");
    codeContents.put("a","are");
    codeContents.put("true","really");
    codeContents.put("statement","useful");
    //.........
    //.........
  }
  public String encrypt(String inputData) {
    populateCodeEntries();
    String outStr = "";
    StringTokenizer st = new StringTokenizer(inputData);
    while (st.hasMoreTokens()) {
      outStr = outStr + " " +
               codeContents.get(st.nextToken());
    }
    return new String(outStr);
  }
}
```

Table 36.4   Different Encryption Strategies

Strategy	Encryption Algorithm
CaesarCypher	Caesar
CodeBookCypher	Code-Book
SimpleEncryption	Basic
SubstitutionCypher	Substitution

with. In other words, the implementation of its encrypt method transforms to a simple method call to the encrypt method of its current encryption Strategy object stored in the currEncryptionStrategy instance variable.

Figure 36.3 shows the overall class association.

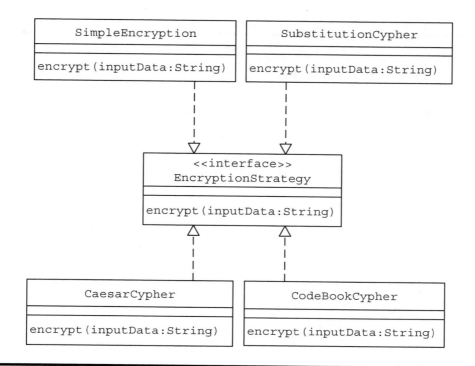

Figure 36.1 **EncryptionStrategy** Class Hierarchy

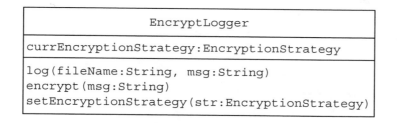

Figure 36.2 **EncryptLogger**

Note: The EncryptLogger contains an object reference of FileLogger type. This relationship is not included in the Figure 36.3 class diagram as it is not part of the pattern implementation.

The EncryptLogger uses different Strategy objects and hence acts as the context. A client object such as the LoggerClient that wants to log an encrypted message needs to create an instance of the EncryptLogger and invoke its log method. When the EncryptLogger is first instantiated, its current encryption strategy is set to SimpleEncryption inside its constructor. The EncryptLogger uses this strategy until the client explicitly changes the strategy to be used.

The client can create a different Strategy object and set it to be used as the current strategy by passing it to the EncryptLogger as part of the

Listing 36.5 `EncryptLogger` Class: Revised

```java
public class EncryptLogger {
  private EncryptionStrategy currEncryptionStrategy;
  private FileLogger logger;
  public EncryptLogger(FileLogger inp_logger) {
    logger = inp_logger;
    //set the default encryption strategy
    setEncryptionStrategy(new SimpleEncryption());
  }
  public void log(String fileName, String msg) {
    /*Added functionality*/
    msg = encrypt(msg);
    /*
      Now forward the encrypted text to the FileLogger
      for storage
    */
    logger.log(fileName, msg);
  }
  public String encrypt(String msg) {
    /*
      Apply encryption using the current encryption strategy
    */
    return currEncryptionStrategy.encrypt(msg);
  }
  public void setEncryptionStrategy(
    EncryptionStrategy strategy) {
    currEncryptionStrategy = strategy;
  }
}
```

`setEncryptionStrategy` method call. The `EncryptLogger` uses this new strategy until again changed by the client.

```java
class LoggerClient {
  public static void main(String[] args) {
    FileLogger logger = new FileLogger();
    EncryptLogger eLogger = new EncryptLogger(logger);
    eLogger.log("log1.txt",
              "this message is to be encrypted & logged");
    EncryptionStrategy strategy = new SubstitutionCypher();
```

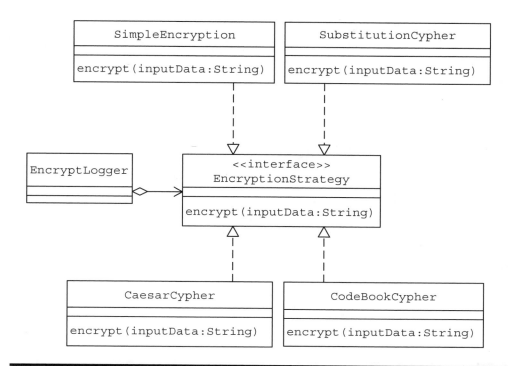

Figure 36.3   Class Association

```
        eLogger.setEncryptionStrategy(strategy);
        eLogger.log("log2.txt",
                    "this message is to be encrypted & logged");
        strategy = new CodeBookCypher();
        eLogger.setEncryptionStrategy(strategy);
        eLogger.log("log3.txt","This is a true statement");
    }
}//End of class
```

In the new design, the EncryptLogger (the context) is not affected when changes such as adding, changing or removing an algorithm are made. In addition, making such changes will be simpler as each algorithm is contained in a separate class.

The sequence diagram in Figure 36.4 depicts the message flow when a client uses the CodeBookCypher to encrypt a message.

PRACTICE QUESTIONS

1. Identify how the Strategy pattern is used when you build an applet setting its layout manager.
2. Design and implement an application to search for an item from a list of items. The application should decide the search algorithm to be used and

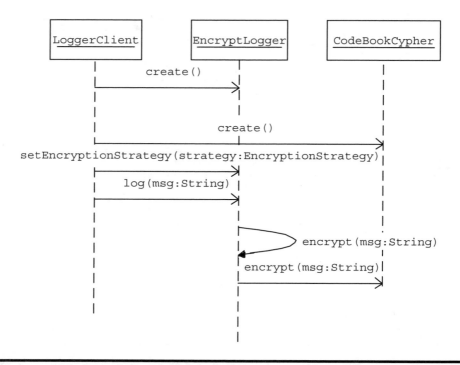

Figure 36.4 Client Object Using `CodeBookCypher` for Encryption

configure a search manager object (context) with this algorithm. For example, if the list is already sorted, the application should use the binary search algorithm as opposed to the linear search algorithm. Implement each algorithm as a different `Strategy` class.

3. The tax calculation varies from state to state in the United States. Design an application using the Strategy pattern to calculate taxes for different states in the United States.

4. Design an application that calculates simple and the compound interest. Identify the advantages and disadvantages of using the Strategy pattern in this case, compared to other alternatives.

37

NULL OBJECT

This pattern was previously described in Woolf96, Grand98.

DESCRIPTION

The term *null* is used in most computer programming languages to refer to a nonexisting object. The Null Object pattern is applicable when a client expects to use different subclasses of a class hierarchy to execute different behavior and refers these subclasses as objects of the parent class type. At times, it may be possible that a subclass instance may not be available when the client expects one. In such cases, what a client object receives is a nonexisting object or null. When a null is returned, the client cannot invoke methods as it would if a real object is returned. Hence the client needs to check to make sure that the object is not null before invoking any of its methods. In the case of a null, the client can either provide some default behavior or do nothing.

Applying the Null Object pattern in such cases eliminates the need for a client to check if an object is null every time the object is used.

The Null Object pattern recommends encapsulating the default (or usually the do nothing) behavior into a separate class referred to as a *Null Object*. This class can be designed as one of the subclasses in the class hierarchy. Thus the Null Object provides the same set of methods as other subclasses do, but with the default (or do nothing) implementation for its methods. With the Null Object in place, when no subclass with real implementation is available, the Null Object is made available to the client. This type of arrangement eliminates the possibility of a client receiving a nonexisting object and hence the client does not need to check if the object it received is null (or nonexisting). Because the Null Object offers the same interface as other subclass objects, the client can treat them all in a uniform manner.

The following example shows how the Null Object pattern can be used to address a special case requirement of the message logging utility we built as an example of the Factory Method pattern.

EXAMPLE

Our design of the message logging utility is mainly composed of a **Logger** interface and two of its implementers — **FileLogger** and **ConsoleLogger** — to log messages to a file and to the console, respectively. In addition, we had the **LoggerFactory** class (Listing 37.1) with a factory method in it. The factory method, when requested by the client, creates an instance of one of the **Logger** implementers based on the **FileLogging** property value specified in the **Logger.properties** file and returns it to the client.

Hence the message logging utility requires:

■ The **Logger.properties** property file to exist.
■ The **Logger.properties** property file to contain a value for the **FileLogging** property as per the values in Table 37.1.

Listing 37.1 LoggerFactory Class

```java
public class LoggerFactory {
  public boolean isFileLoggingEnabled() {
    Properties p = new Properties();
    try {
      p.load(ClassLoader.getSystemResourceAsStream(
        "Logger.properties"));
      String fileLoggingValue =
        p.getProperty("FileLogging");
      if (fileLoggingValue.equalsIgnoreCase("ON") == true)
        return true;
      else
        return false;
    } catch (IOException e) {
      return false;
    }
  }
  //Factory Method
  public Logger getLogger() {
    if (isFileLoggingEnabled()) {
      return new FileLogger();
    } else {
      return new ConsoleLogger();
    }
  }
}
```

Table 37.1 `Filelogging` Property Values

`FileLogging=ON`	Messages are logged to a file.
`FileLogging=OFF`	Messages are displayed on the console.

As can be seen from the implementation in Listing 37.1, the `LoggerFactory` makes an assumption that the properties file `Logger.properties` always exists with a value for the `FileLogging` property.

Let us enhance the message logging utility as in Listing 37.2 so that the utility works properly, even when the properties file does not exist.

The enhanced version of the `LoggerFactory` returns a null, when either the properties file is not available or when the parameter `FileLogging` is not given a value inside the property file.

With this new design, a client that uses the `LoggerFactory` has the possibility of receiving a null when it invokes the `getLogger` factory method. Because the client cannot invoke the `log` method when a null is returned, it needs to check if the returned object reference is null before invoking the `log` method. In other words, it needs to treat the returned `Logger` object reference differently depending on whether the reference is null or it refers to a real `Logger` object.

```
public class LoggerTest {
  public static void main(String[] args) {
    LoggerFactory factory = new LoggerFactory();
    Logger logger = factory.getLogger();
    if (logger != null) {
      logger.log("A Message to Log");
    }
  }
}
```

With the client having to check for null every time it tries to log a message, the code could quickly become very cluttered. The Null Object pattern can be applied in this case, eliminating the need for the client `LoggerTest` to check if the returned `Logger` instance is null.

Applying the Null Object pattern, let us define a new implementer `NullLogger` of the `Logger` interface as follows:

```
public class NullLogger implements Logger {
  public void log(String msg) {
  }
}
```

Figure 37.1 shows the `Logger` class hierarchy.

The `NullLogger` does not do anything as part of its implementation of the `log` method. Let us redesign the `LoggerFactory` class (Listing 37.3) so that

Listing 37.2 Enhanced `LoggerFactory` Class

```java
public class LoggerFactory {
  public boolean isFileLoggingEnabled() throws Exception {
    Properties p = new Properties();
    try {
      p.load(ClassLoader.getSystemResourceAsStream(
        "Logger.properties"));
      String fileLoggingValue =
        p.getProperty("FileLogging");
      if (fileLoggingValue.equalsIgnoreCase("ON") == true)
        return true;
      else
        return false;
    } catch (FileNotFoundException ex) {
      throw ex;
    }
    catch (IOException e) {
      throw e;
    }
  }
  //Factory Method
  public Logger getLogger() {
    Logger logger = null;
    try {
      if (isFileLoggingEnabled()) {
        logger = new FileLogger();
      } else {
        logger = new ConsoleLogger();
      }
    } catch (Exception e) {
      //
    }
    return logger;
  }
}
```

instead of returning a simple null, it now returns a **NullLogger** instance when either the property file is not available or when the parameter **FileLogging** is not given a value inside the property file.

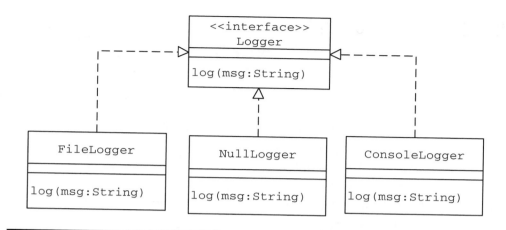

Figure 37.1   Message Logging Utility: Class Hierarchy

With this new design, the client is always assured of receiving an object of type **Logger**, which is *not null*. This in turn eliminates the need for a client to check for null. This reduces the clutter in the client code.

```
public class LoggerTest {
  public static void main(String[] args) {
    LoggerFactory factory = new LoggerFactory();
    Logger logger = factory.getLogger();
    logger.log("A Message to Log");
  }
}
```

Also, because the **NullLogger** implements the **Logger** interface, the client can treat all **NullLogger** objects in the same manner as the other **Logger** objects, without any special considerations.

PRACTICE QUESTIONS

During the discussion of the Strategy pattern, we built a message encryption application.

1. Design a new encryption strategy **NullCypher** that returns the input text as it is without applying any encryption.
2. Design a factory method **getCypherObject** that creates an appropriate encryption object and returns it as an object of **EncryptionStrategy** type. This factory method is to be used by the client **LoggerClient**.
3. Is it more advantageous to use a null encryption strategy such as **NullCypher** (as in practice question 1 above) or to have a check for null as part of the client implementation?

Listing 37.3   Revised LoggerFactory Class

```java
public class LoggerFactory {
  public boolean isFileLoggingEnabled() throws Exception {
    Properties p = new Properties();
    try {
      p.load(ClassLoader.getSystemResourceAsStream(
        "Logger.properties"));
      String fileLoggingValue =
        p.getProperty("FileLogging");
      if (fileLoggingValue.equalsIgnoreCase("ON") == true)
        return true;
      else
        return false;
    } catch (Exception e) {
      throw e;
    }
  }
  //Factory Method
  public Logger getLogger() {
    Logger logger = new NullLogger();
    try {
      if (isFileLoggingEnabled()) {
        logger = new FileLogger();
      } else {
        logger = new ConsoleLogger();
      }
    } catch (Exception e) {
      //
    }
    return logger;
  }
}
```

38

TEMPLATE METHOD

This pattern was previously described in GoF95.

DESCRIPTION

The Template Method pattern is one of the simplest and most frequently used design patterns in object-oriented applications.

The Template Method pattern can be used in situations when there is an algorithm, some steps of which could be implemented in multiple different ways. In such scenarios, the Template Method pattern suggests keeping the outline of the algorithm in a separate method referred to as a *template method* inside a class, which may be referred to as a *template class*, leaving out the specific implementations of the variant portions (steps that can be implemented in multiple different ways) of the algorithm to different subclasses of this class.

The Template class does not necessarily have to leave the implementation to subclasses in its entirety. Instead, as part of providing the outline of the algorithm, the Template class can also provide some amount of implementation that can be considered as invariant across different implementations. It can even provide default implementation for the variant parts, if appropriate. Only specific details will be implemented inside different subclasses. This type of implementation eliminates the need for duplicate code, which means a minimum amount of code to be written.

Using the Java programming language, the Template class can be designed in one of the following two ways.

Abstract Class

This design is more suitable when the Template class provides only the outline of the algorithm without any default implementation for its variant parts. Assuming that different steps of the algorithm can be made into individual methods:

- The Template method can be a concrete, nonabstract method with calls to other methods that represent different steps of the algorithm.
- The Template class can implement invariant parts of the algorithm as a set of nonabstract methods.

■ The set of variant steps can be designed as abstract methods. Specific implementations can be provided for these abstract methods inside a set of concrete subclasses of the abstract `Template` class.

In this design, the `Abstract` class declares methods and each of the subclasses implement these methods in a manner that is specific to it without altering the outline of the algorithm.

Concrete Class

This design is more suitable when the `Template` class provides, besides the outline of the algorithm, the default implementation for its variant parts. Assuming that different steps of the algorithm can be made into individual methods:

■ The `Template` method can be a concrete, nonabstract method with calls to other methods that represent different steps of the algorithm.
■ The `Template` class can implement invariant parts of the algorithm as a set of nonabstract methods.
■ The set of variant steps can be designed as nonabstract methods with the default implementation. Subclasses of the `Template` class can override these methods to provide specific implementations without altering the outline of the algorithm.

From both the design strategies, it can be seen that the Template pattern implementation relies heavily on inheritance and function overriding. Hence, whenever inheritance is used for implementing the specifics, it can be said that Template Method pattern is used in its simplest form.

EXAMPLE

Let us design an application to check the validity of a given credit card. For simplicity, let us consider only three types of credit cards — Visa, MasterCard and Diners Club. The application carries out a series of validations on the input credit card information. Table 38.1 lists different steps in the process of validating different credit cards.

As can be seen from Table 38.1, some steps of the validation algorithm are the same across all three of the credit cards while some are different. The Template Method pattern can be applied in designing this process.

Let us define an abstract `CreditCard` class (Figure 38.1 and Listing 38.1) with:

■ The `Template` method `isValid` that outlines the validation algorithm.
■ A set of concrete methods implementing Step 1, Step 4 and Step 5 from Table 38.1.
■ A set of abstract methods designated to implement Step 2, Step 3 and Step 6 from Table 38.1. It is to be noted that even after the `CheckSum` validation is successful, it cannot be guaranteed that a given credit card is valid. It is possible that the account may have been revoked or over the limit.

Table 38.1 Different Steps in the Validation Process

Step	Check	Visa	MasterCard	Diners Club
1	Expiration date	>Today	>Today	>Today
2	Length	13, 16	16	14
3	Prefix	4	51 through 55	30, 36, 38
4	Valid characters	0 through 9	0 through 9	0 through 9
5	Check digit algorithm	Mod 10	Mod 10	Mod 10
6	Account in good standing	Use custom Visa API	Use custom MasterCard API	Use custom Diners Club API

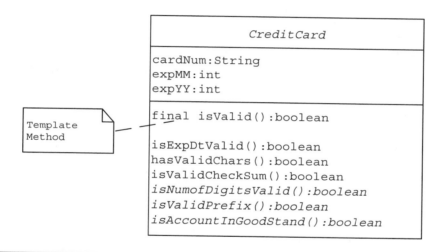

Figure 38.1 CreditCard Template Class

Hence, a check with the credit card company (Visa, MasterCard, Diners Club) is required to make sure that the account is in good standing. This step requires custom programming to interface with the credit card company database and is considered to be different for different credit card types. Hence the `isAccountInGoodStand` method is designed as an abstract method to be implemented by different subclasses.

The most significant method in the design is the `isValid` `Template` method. This method invokes different methods designed to implement different steps of the algorithm. It is to be noted that the `Template` method `isValid` is specified as a *final* method to prevent subclasses from overriding it. Subclasses are expected to override only abstract methods to provide specific implementation and are *not* supposed to alter the outline of the algorithm.

Listing 38.1   Abstract `CreditCard` Class

```java
public abstract class CreditCard {
  protected String cardNum;
  protected int expMM, expYY;
  public CreditCard(String num, int expMonth, int expYear) {
    cardNum = num;
    expMM = expMonth;
    expYY = expYear;
  }
  public boolean isExpDtValid() {
    Calendar cal = Calendar.getInstance();
    cal.setTime(new Date());
    int mm = cal.get(Calendar.MONTH) + 1;
    int yy = cal.get(Calendar.YEAR);
    boolean result =
      (yy > expYY) || ((yy == expYY) && (mm > expMM));
    return (!result);
  }
  private boolean hasValidChars() {
    String validChars = "0123456789";
    boolean result = true;
    for (int i = 0; i < cardNum.length(); i++) {
      if (validChars.indexOf(cardNum.substring(i, i + 1)) <
          0) {
        result = false;
        break;
      }
    }
    return result;
  }
  private boolean isValidCheckSum() {
    boolean result = true;
    int sum = 0;
    int multiplier = 1;
    int strLen = cardNum.length();
    for (int i = 0; i < strLen; i++) {
      String digit = cardNum.substring(strLen - i - 1,
                     strLen - i);
```

(continued)

Listing 38.1   Abstract `CreditCard` Class (Continued)

```
      int currProduct =
        new Integer(digit).intValue() * multiplier;
      if (currProduct >= 10)
        sum += (currProduct% 10) + 1;
      else
        sum += currProduct;
      if (multiplier == 1)
        multiplier++;
      else
        multiplier - ;
    }
    if ((sum% 10) != 0)
      result = false;
    return result;
  }
  /* methods to be overridden by sub-classes. */
  public abstract boolean isNumOfDigitsValid();
  public abstract boolean isValidPrefix();
  public abstract boolean isAccountInGoodStand();
  /* Final method - subclasses cannot override
      ***TEMPLATE METHOD***
  */
  public final boolean isValid() {
    if (!isExpDtValid()) {
      System.out.println(" Invalid Exp Dt. ");
      return false;
    }
    if (!isNumOfDigitsValid()) {
      System.out.println(" Invalid Number of Digits ");
      return false;
    }
    if (!isValidPrefix()) {
      System.out.println(" Invalid Prefix ");
      return false;
    }
```

(continued)

Listing 38.1   Abstract `CreditCard` Class (Continued)

```
      if (!hasValidChars()) {
        System.out.println(" Invalid Characters ");
        return false;
      }
      if (!isValidCheckSum()) {
        System.out.println(" Invalid Check Sum ");
        return false;
      }
      if (!isAccountInGoodStand()) {
        System.out.println(
          " Account is Inactive/Revoked/Over the Limit ");
        return false;
      }
      return true;
    }
  }
```

In Java programming language, a subclass cannot override the following two types of methods of its parent class:

- private methods
- final methods irrespective of the associated access specifier

Let us define three subclasses —VisaCard, MasterCard and DinersCard — of the CreditCard Template class, each providing implementation for all abstract methods declared in the parent class (Listing 38.2 through Listing 38.4).

The resulting class association can be depicted as in Figure 38.2.

With the above design in place, any client looking to validate credit card information would simply create an instance of an appropriate CreditCard subclass and invoke the isValid method.

```
  public class Client {
    public static void main(String[] args) {
      CreditCard cc =
        new VisaCard("1234123412341234,"11, 2004);
      if (cc.isValid())
        System.out.println("Valid Credit Card Information");
    }
  }
```

Listing 38.2 `VisaCard` Class

```java
public class VisaCard extends CreditCard {
  public VisaCard(String num, int expMonth, int expYear) {
    super(num, expMonth, expYear);
  }
  public boolean isNumOfDigitsValid() {
    if ((cardNum.length() == 13) ||
        (cardNum.length() == 16)) {
      return true;
    } else {
      return false;
    }
  }
  public boolean isValidPrefix() {
    String prefix = cardNum.substring(0, 1);
    if (prefix.equals("4")) {
      return true;
    } else {
      return false;
    }
  }
  public boolean isAccountInGoodStand() {
    /*
      Make necessary VISA API calls to
      perform other checks.
    */
    return true;
  }
}
```

ADDITIONAL NOTES

Mod 10 Check Digit Algorithm

In general, a check digit is a digit added to a number that helps in checking the authenticity of the number. The Mod 10 check digit algorithm can be used to validate such a number associated with a check digit.

Listing 38.3 MasterCard Class

```java
public class MasterCard extends CreditCard {
  public MasterCard(String num, int expMonth, int expYear) {
    super(num, expMonth, expYear);
  }
  public boolean isNumOfDigitsValid() {
    if (cardNum.length() == 16) {
      return true;
    } else {
      return false;
    }
  }
  public boolean isValidPrefix() {
    String prefix = cardNum.substring(0, 1);
    String nextChar = cardNum.substring(1, 2);
    String validChars = "12345";
    //51-55
    if ((prefix.equals("5")) &&
        (validChars.indexOf(nextChar) >= 0)) {
      return true;
    } else {
      return false;
    }
  }
  public boolean isAccountInGoodStand() {
    /*
      Make necessary MASTER CARD API calls to
      perform other checks.
    */
    return true;
  }
}
```

Listing 38.4 `DinersCard` Class

```java
public class DinersCard extends CreditCard {
  public DinersCard(String num, int expMonth, int expYear) {
    super(num, expMonth, expYear);
  }
  public boolean isNumOfDigitsValid() {
    if (cardNum.length() == 14) {
      return true;
    } else {
      return false;
    }
  }
  public boolean isValidPrefix() {
    String prefix = cardNum.substring(0, 1);
    String nextChar = cardNum.substring(1, 2);
    String validChars = "068";
    //51-55
    if ((prefix.equals("3")) &&
        (validChars.indexOf(nextChar) >= 0)) {
      return true;
    } else {
      return false;
    }
  }
  public boolean isAccountInGoodStand() {
    /*
      Make necessary DINERS CARD API calls to
      perform other checks.
    */
    return true;
  }
}
```

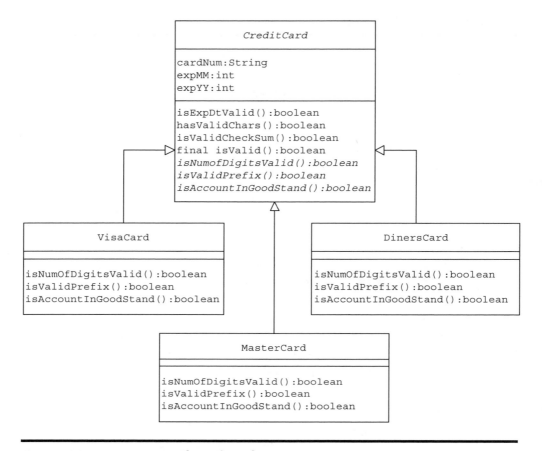

Figure 38.2 `CreditCard` **Class Hierarchy**

The following steps describe the validation process:

1. Use 194774915 (check digit 5 included) as an example.
   1 9 4 7 7 4 9 1 5
2. Starting from the second digit from right, multiply every alternate digit by 2.
   1 9x2 4 7x2 7 4x2 9 1x2 5
   Result:
   1 18 4 14 7 8 9 2 5
3. Add individual digits in the newly formed products.
   1 1+8 4 1+4 7 8 9 2 5
   Result:
   1 9 4 5 7 8 9 2 5
4. Now sum up all digits in the resultant number from the above step.
   1 +9 +4 +5 +7 +8 +9 +2 +5 = 50
5. Now divide the sum by 10.
   Result:
   50/10 leaves no remainder and a zero remainder proves that the number is valid.

PRACTICE QUESTIONS

1. Identify how the Template Method pattern is used when you design an applet with custom code in any of the applet life-cycle methods (init, start, paint, stop and destroy).
2. Some scenarios involving many different implementations for different steps of an algorithm could lead to a fast growing class hierarchy with a large number of subclasses. What alternatives would you consider in such cases?

39

OBJECT AUTHENTICATOR

The Object Authenticator pattern is also known as the Protection Proxy and was previously described in GoF95.

DESCRIPTION

In general, objects in an application interact with each other to offer the overall application functionality. Most application objects are generally accessible to all the other objects in the application. At times, it may be necessary to restrict the accessibility of an object only to a limited set of client objects based on their access rights. When a client object tries to access such an object, the client is given access to the services provided by the object only if the client can furnish proper authentication credentials. In such cases, a separate object can be designated with the responsibility of verifying the access privileges of different client objects when they access the actual object. In other words, every client must successfully authenticate with this designated object to get access to the actual object functionality. Such an object with which a client needs to authenticate to get access to the actual object can be referred as an *object authenticator*. The following example demonstrates how an object authenticator can be used in an application scenario.

EXAMPLE

Let us design the order creation functionality of an order management application. This functionality can be designed as part of an `Order` object.

Let us define an `OrderIF` interface that declares the functionality to be offered by `Order` objects.

```
public interface OrderIF {
  public void create(String item,
                     int qty) throws UnAuthorizedUserException;
}
```

The `OrderIF` interface declares a `create` method that can be used by client objects to create orders. The actual `Order` object can be designed as an implementer of the `OrderIF` interface.

```
public class Order implements OrderIF {
  public void create(String item, int qty) {
    System.out.println(qty + " Units of Item " + item +
                     " has been ordered. ");
  }
}
```

In this example, the `Order` object is kept simple, as the primary focus is to demonstrate the use of the authenticator object. As part of its implementation of the `create` method, an `Order` object simply writes the input order data to the console. In real world applications that order data is normally saved to a database.

By default, any other object in the order management application can freely access an `Order` object and invoke its `create` method without any problem.

Let us suppose that the access to the `Order` objects needs to be restricted only to authorized client objects. This can be easily accomplished by modifying the `Order` class's current implementation to include the responsibility of verifying the access privileges of different client objects.

One of the characteristics of a well-designed object is that it performs a well-defined, definite task. In other words, an object ideally should not do various unrelated things. Hence, instead of making an `Order` object responsible for client object access privilege verification and also to represent an order in the system, it might be a good idea to move the client object access privilege verification responsibility from the `Order` object to a separate designated object. This designated object serves as an object authenticator to the corresponding `Order` object. This leaves the `Order` object with only the order related functionality, rather than with the additional responsibility of authentication also.

The designated `Order` object authenticator, `OrderAuthenticator`, can be designed as an implementer of the same `OrderIF` interface, which the actual `Order` object also implements (Figure 39.1). As a result, both the `Order` and its authenticator offer the same interface and allow a client object to access both the `Order` and `OrderAuthenticator` in a seamless manner.

```
public class OrderAuthenticator implements OrderIF {
  private OrderManager client;
  private String accessCode;
  private String clientCode;
  public OrderAuthenticator(String aCode, String cCode) {
    accessCode = aCode;
    clientCode = cCode;
  }
  public void create(String item,
                   int qty) throws UnAuthorizedUserException {
```

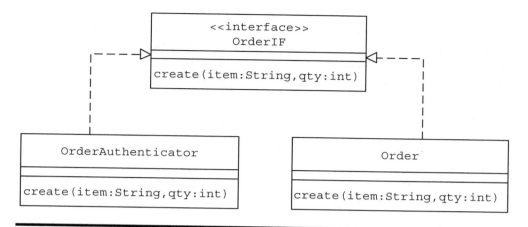

Figure 39.1 **Order** and **OrderAuthenticator** as Implementers of the **OrderIF** Interface

```
if (clientCode.equals(accessCode)) {
  Order ord = new Order();
  ord.create(item, qty);
} else {
  throw new UnAuthorizedUserException();
}
}
}
```

When an OrderAuthenticator object is created, it is configured with two types of access codes:

1. *Authentication code* — This is a valid code that a client object needs to provide to access the services offered by an Order object. Client objects that do not provide the right code are denied access to the Order object services.
2. *Client code* — This is the access code submitted by a client object that intends to use the Order object functionality. The client object is provided with the requested services only if this code matches with the authentication code.

As part of its implementation of the create method, the OrderAuthenticator checks to see if the client object has submitted the correct access code. If the client has submitted the correct access code, the authenticator creates an Order object and invokes the create method on the Order instance. The existence of the Order object is completely hidden from the client object. If the client has submitted an incorrect access code, the authenticator throws a custom UnAuthorizedUserException exception.

Further, let us define a factory object `AuthManager`, which is responsible for the creation of authenticator objects corresponding to different application objects. When the `AuthManager` creates an instance of an authenticator, it configures the authenticator with the correct authentication code. Every client object must authenticate by submitting the same access code with the authenticator to access the functionality offered by the actual object. In this example, the access code is hard-coded for simplicity. In real world applications, access codes are normally retrieved from a database.

```
public class AuthManager {
  public OrderIF getOrderAuthenticator(String clientCode) {
    return new OrderAuthenticator("xYzAbC", clientCode);
  }
}
```

When the client `OrderManager` needs to access an `Order` object to create an order (Figure 39.2):

1. It creates an instance of the `AuthManager` and requests an `OrderAuthenticator` object by invoking the `getOrderAuthenticator` method. As part of the `getOrderAuthenticator` method call the `OrderManager` object sends its access code as an argument.
2. The `AuthManager` creates an instance of the `OrderAuthenticator` and configures it with the correct authentication code and also the access code

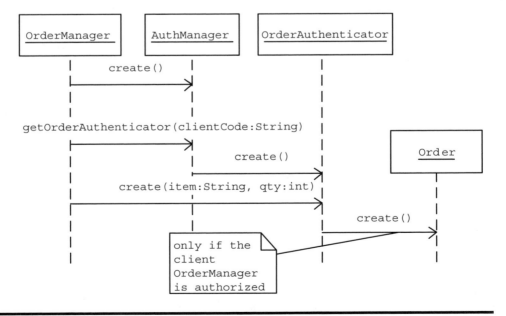

Figure 39.2   Message Flow

submitted by the client OrderManager in Step 1. The OrderAuthenticator does not offer any methods for external client objects to read the authentication code it is configured with.

3. The client OrderManager invokes the create method on the OrderAuthenticator with appropriate parameters.

4. The client OrderManager the OrderAuthenticator verifies the access code submitted by the client OrderManager.

- If the OrderManager has submitted the correct access code, the authenticator creates an actual Order object and forwards the method call to the corresponding Order object to create an order with the order data submitted by the OrderManager. The client OrderManager does not need to be aware of the existence of the Order object.

- If the OrderManager has submitted an incorrect access code, the OrderAuthenticator throws an exception indicating a denial of service.

```
public class OrderManager {
  public void createOrder(String item,
      int qty) throws UnAuthorizedUserException {
    AuthManager manager = new AuthManager();
    OrderIF authenticator =
      manager.getOrderAuthenticator("xYzAbC");
    authenticator.create(item, qty);
  }
}
public class MainApp {
  public static void main(String[] args) {
    OrderManager manager = new OrderManager();
    try {
      manager.createOrder("CDs", 10);
    } catch (Exception e) {
      System.out.println(e.getMessage());
    }
  }
}
```

Figure 39.3 depicts the structure and the associations between different classes.

PRACTICE QUESTIONS

1. Create an object authenticator for an Employee object.

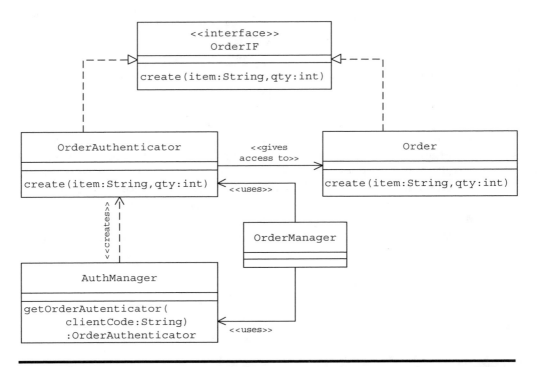

Figure 39.3 Order Management Application Using an Authenticator: Class Association

2. In the example application discussed above, the access code used during the creation of the authenticator object is hard-coded. Enhance the application to read access codes from a database.

40

COMMON ATTRIBUTE REGISTRY

DESCRIPTION

In general, objects in an application are designed to carry related data and perform well-defined tasks with clearly defined responsibilities. In an application, these objects interact with each other to provide the overall application functionality. During such interactions, instances of different classes may need to access the same set of data items or attributes. For example, different business objects in an application often use the same database connection string to connect to the application backend database. These common attributes are not always read-only. Consider the example of an application that operates in local and remote modes. While the application is operating in the remote mode, if an application object detects a problem in communicating with the remote server, it immediately informs all the other application objects so that they can take appropriate action such as changing to the local mode of operation. The remote server current status information is relevant and common for all objects in the application. Application objects both read and update this type of common information. The Common Attribute Registry (or CAR) is an object that is designated exclusively to handle the set of common data items or attributes in an application.

In a nutshell, CAR is an object that offers methods to allow different application objects to set and retrieve different attribute values and is not persistent. The data stored in CAR is available only during the lifetime of the application that is using CAR. As soon as the application execution is complete or in case of a system crash, the information stored in CAR is lost. In other words, CAR can be used to store only the common transient state of an application.

Because the purpose of CAR is to provide service to all the objects in an application, it requires that CAR be:

- Designed as a singleton, as there is a need for only one instance of CAR during the entire lifetime of an application. Applications can be built using more than one CAR instance as well. But in such cases, each client object needs to query every CAR instance in the application, which could become an overhead.
- Capable of handling concurrent updates to an attribute without problems. This ensures that CAR can safely be used in a multithreaded environment.

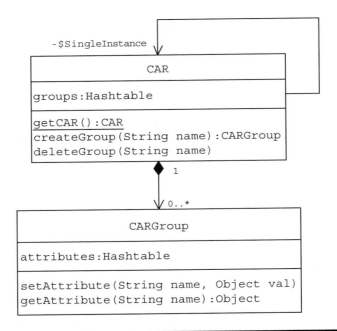

Figure 40.1   Generic CAR Design

- Capable of handling name collisions: When two objects try to store two different attributes with the same name, it should allow both operations to go through without any problems as long as the values are relevant and meaningful in two different parallel contexts.

With these specifications, a generic CAR can be designed as in Figure 40.1.

For the purpose of allowing the storage of more than one attribute with the same name, CAR can be thought of as consisting of a set of groups, which can be represented by instances of the CARGroup class in Figure 40.1. Each group in turn can hold a set of attributes along with their corresponding values. This allows two attributes with the same name to be stored in two groups. This is similar to storing two files with the same file name under two different directories in the file system and eliminates the possibility of name collisions.

The CARGroup (Listing 40.1) uses its instance variable named attributes of the Hashtable type to store different attributes and offers two methods — setAttribute and getAttribute — to set and retrieve the values of different attributes stored in the attributes instance variable. These methods internally use the built-in get and put Hashtable methods, which are designed as synchronized methods. This ensures that race conditions do not occur when the setAttribute and getAttribute methods are invoked in a multithreaded environment.

The CAR (Listing 40.2) class itself is designed as a singleton with a private constructor and a class-level method getCAR to return the singleton CAR instance. CAR stores CARGroup objects corresponding to different groups in its instance variable named groups of the Hashtable type. Similar to the CARGroup, CAR provides two methods — createGroup and deleteGroup — to allow

Listing 40.1 CARGroup **Class**

```
public class CAR {
  private static CAR car;
  private Hashtable groups;

        ...

        ...

  class CARGroup {
    private Hashtable attributes;
    private String name;
    private CARGroup(String grpName) {
      name = grpName;
      attributes = new Hashtable();
    }
    public void setAttribute(String name, Object val) {
      attributes.put(name, val);
    }
    public Object getAttribute(String name) {
      return attributes.get(name);
    }
  }
}
```

client objects to create and delete a group. Internally, these methods make use of the synchronized put and get Hashtable methods. This overall structure ensures that the singleton CAR object can safely be used in a multithreaded environment. Figure 40.2 provides the logical representation of CAR with internal CARGroup objects.

When a client object needs to store an attribute in a group inside CAR, it needs to:

1. Invoke the static getCAR method to get access to the singleton CAR object.
2. Invoke the createGroup method on the singleton CAR instance to obtain a reference to the required CARGroup object. This requires creating a CARGroup instance if a CARGroup instance corresponding to the required group does not already exist.
3. Create an attribute and set its value in CAR using the CARGroup object reference obtained in Step 2.

CAR is only useful to store simple data values and not suitable for storing large objects. Because the data stored within CAR is ephemeral, it is not recommended to store any data in CAR that is expected to be available after a system crash or after the application execution is complete.

Listing 40.2   CAR Class

```java
public class CAR {
  private static CAR car;
  private Hashtable groups;
  public static CAR getCAR() {
    if (car == null)
      car = new CAR();
    return car;
  }
  private CAR() {
    groups = new Hashtable();
  }
  public CARGroup createGroup(String name) {
    CARGroup group = (CARGroup) groups.get(name);
    if (group == null) {
      group = new CARGroup(name);
      groups.put(name, group);
    }
    return group;
  }
  public void deleteGroup(String name) {
  }
        ...
        ...
}
```

This design of CAR is generic and may be used directly in an application as a common data repository.

EXAMPLE

Let us build an application to query the details of different items in a library. Library items can be classified into five different categories — books, magazines, videos, DVDs and CDs. One of the simplest ways of designing the required functionality is to design a separate object, e.g., ItemManager (Listing 40.3), with the responsibility of retrieving the details of an item. Client objects can make use of the ItemManager to retrieve the details of an item. A client object may need to pass such information as the category and the item name to the Item-Manager to retrieve the details of an item. The ItemManager can be designed to make use of helper classes to access the database to retrieve the requested item details. Figure 40.3 provides a pictorial representation of this design.

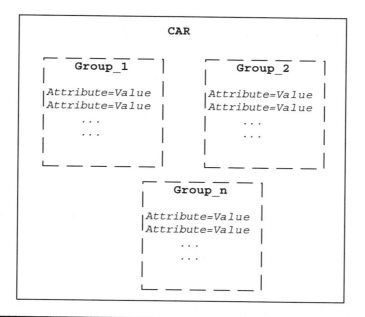

Figure 40.2 CAR: **Logical Representation**

Listing 40.3 `ItemManager` **Class**

```
public class ItemManager {
  public String getItemDetails(String item, String category) {
    DBManager objDBManager = new DBManager();
    String details =
      objDBManager.getItemDetails(item, category);
    return details;
  }
}
```

In this approach, every client request for item details results in a database operation. Because the item details do not change frequently, to improve the application performance some kind of a caching mechanism can be introduced so that every client request does not require the database to be accessed for details.

Because CAR offers a thread-safe mechanism to store data that is common across objects, details of some of the most recently queried items can be stored in CAR. The idea is to return the details of an item from CAR itself without having to access the database, if the requested item details are available in CAR. The requirement of storing the details of different items belonging to different categories maps well with the storage structure of CAR, where individual attributes or values are stored in groups. The generic CAR designed earlier in this section

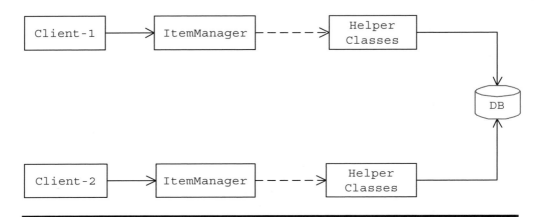

Figure 40.3 Item Details Query without Caching

can be used as-is in this case by the `ItemManager` (Listing 40.4). Because CAR
is designed as a singleton, all client objects can share the single instance of CAR.
Figure 40.4 shows the revised application design using CAR to improve the
application responsiveness.

In the new design (Figure 40.4, Listing 40.4), when a client object requests
the `ItemManager` for the details of an item in a category, the `ItemManager`
invokes the `createGroup` method on the singleton CAR object to obtain a
reference to the `CARGroup` object corresponding to the specified item category.
Inside the `createGroup` method, the CAR checks to see if a `CARGroup` object
corresponding to the requested item category already exists.

- If the `CARGroup` object exists, the `CARGroup` object reference is returned
  to the `ItemManager`.
- If the `CARGroup` object does not exist, CAR:
  - Creates a new `CARGroup` instance.
  - Associates it with the specified item category.
  - Returns it to the `ItemManager`.

Once the `CARGroup` instance is received, the `ItemManager` checks to see
if an attribute corresponding to the specified item exists in the group.

- If the attribute exists, item details are retrieved from CAR and returned to
  the client object.
- If the attribute does not exist:
  - The `ItemManager` retrieves item details from the database using helper
    objects.
  - The `ItemManager` creates an attribute with the item name by invoking
    the `setAttribute` method on the `CARGroup` corresponding to the
    item category. This essentially stores the item details in the `CARGroup`
    object.
  - Item details are returned to the client object.

Listing 40.4 ItemManager Class Using CAR

```java
public class ItemManager {
  private CAR car;
  public ItemManager() {
    car = CAR.getCAR();
  }
  public String getItemDetails(String item, String category) {
    String value =
      (String) car.createGroup(category).getAttribute(
        item);
    if (value == null) {
      DBManager objDBManager = new DBManager();
      String details =
        objDBManager.getItemDetails(item, category);
      CAR.CARGroup group = car.createGroup(category);
      group.setAttribute(item, details);
      value = details;
      System.out.println("From DB");
    } else {
      System.out.println("From Cache");
    }
    return value;
  }
}
```

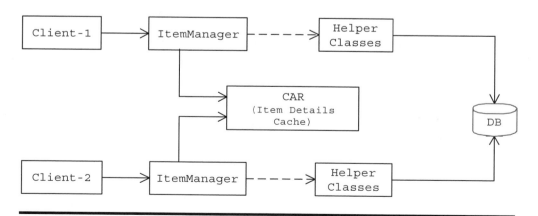

Figure 40.4 Item Details Query with Caching

Let us design the main application client `TestClient` (Listing 40.5) to make use of the `ItemManager` services to retrieve item details. For simplicity, different item and category details are hard-coded in the `TestClient` implementation. When executed, the `TestClient` interacts with the `ItemManager` to retrieve item details without having to know the presence of CAR and the role it plays in caching and retrieving item details.

The class diagram in Figure 40.5 shows the overall class association.

PRACTICE QUESTIONS

1. Redesign the example application to use a nonsingleton version of CAR. What changes are required to the application design to prevent unpredictable results when an application object attempts to read attribute values from CAR?
2. Enhance the example CAR design so that it can be used to share data across applications.
3. Design an application that uses a CAR instance to store the authentication credentials of different users.

Listing 40.5 `TestClient` Class

```java
public class TestClient {
  public static void main(String[] args) {
    ItemManager manager = new ItemManager();
    System.out.println(
      manager.getItemDetails("Commando","Video"));
    System.out.println(
      manager.getItemDetails("Commando","DVD"));
    System.out.println(
      manager.getItemDetails("Jaws","Video"));
    System.out.println(
      manager.getItemDetails("Jaws","Electronics"));
    System.out.println(
      manager.getItemDetails("Interview Tips","CD"));
    System.out.println(
      manager.getItemDetails("Jaws","Video"));
    System.out.println(
      manager.getItemDetails("Interview Tips","CD"));
  }
}
```

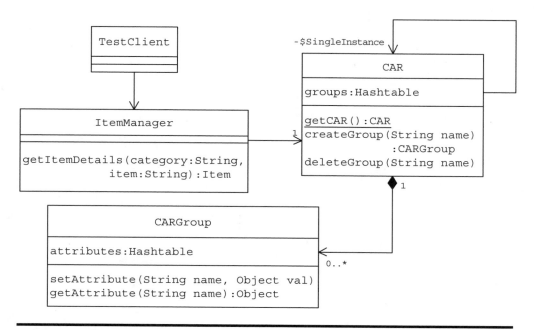

Figure 40.5   Class Association

VIII

CONCURRENCY PATTERNS

Concurrency patterns deal with:

- Ways to lock class code and an order of locking objects to prevent the occurrence of race conditions and deadlocks
- The details of streamlining access to an application resource to improve the overall application responsiveness
- The details of method execution while a required precondition is not met

Chapter	Pattern Name	Description
41	Critical Section	Stricter form of Monitor. Used to lock the code at the class level to keep multiple threads from executing the locked code even on two different instances of the same class.
42	Consistent Lock Order	Recommends identifying and documenting a well-defined order of locking objects to be followed consistently during the design and the development of an application to eliminate the possibility of the occurrence of a deadlock.
43	Guarded Suspension	Recommends a method to be designed to suspend its execution until the object is in a state that makes a required precondition true.
44	Read-Write Lock	Recommends allowing simultaneous read operations while preventing simultaneous updates to the values of an application resource in order to improve the overall application responsiveness.

41

CRITICAL SECTION

DESCRIPTION

A Critical Section is a segment of code that must be executed by only one thread at a time to produce the expected results. When more than one thread is allowed to execute this code segment, it could produce unpredictable results. By this definition, a critical section looks very similar to the concept of a Monitor discussed in Section III — Basic Patterns. The following is the list of similarities and differences between Monitors and Critical Sections:

- A Critical Section is a stricter form of a Monitor.
- A Monitor locks a single object whereas a Critical Section requires a lock on an entire class of objects.
- In Java:
  - The implementation of a Monitor on a method requires the method to be declared using the synchronized keyword.
  - A Critical Section can be implemented by using the combination of both the static and the synchronized keywords.
- In the case of a Monitor, no two threads are allowed to execute the synchronized code on the same object. Two threads can execute the same synchronized code on two different objects. In contrast, in the case of a critical section, no two threads are allowed to execute the code on two different objects. This is because the code is locked at the class level, not at the object level.

EXAMPLE

During the discussion of the Singleton pattern, we designed a message logging class FileLogger as a singleton. The FileLogger class maintains a class variable logger of the FileLogger type. This variable is used to hold the singleton FileLogger instance. The FileLogger class offers a class-level method get-FileLogger that can be used by different client objects to access the singleton FileLogger instance. As part of the getFileLogger method implementation, the FileLogger checks to see if the singleton instance has already been created. Checking to see if the class variable logger is null does this. If logger is found to be uninitialized, a `FileLogger` instance is created by invoking its private constructor and is assigned to the logger class variable. This implementation of the `getFileLogger` method works fine in a single-threaded environment. In a multithreaded environment, it is possible for two threads to simultaneously execute the `getFileLogger` method to see if the class variable logger is null and, as a result, initialize logger twice. This means that the `FileLogger` private constructor gets invoked twice.

```java
public class FileLogger implements Logger {
  private static FileLogger logger;
  private FileLogger() {
  }
  public static FileLogger getFileLogger() {
    if (logger == null) {
      logger = new FileLogger();
    }
    return logger;
  }
  public synchronized void log(String msg) {
    FileUtil futil = new FileUtil();
    futil.writeToFile("log.txt",msg, true, true);
  }
}
```

Initializing the logger variable twice in this example does not result in an error. This is because the `FileLogger` private constructor does not do any complex, critical initialization. In contrast, if the singleton constructor method executes such operations as opening a socket connection on a particular port, executing the constructor twice could result in an error.

Let us enhance the design of the `FileLogger` class to make it suitable for use in multithreaded environments. This can be accomplished in two ways.

Approach I (Critical Section)

This involves making the `getFileLogger` method a Critical Section so that only one thread can ever execute it at any given point in time. This can be accomplished by simply declaring the class-level method `getFileLogger` as synchronized.

```java
public class FileLogger implements Logger {
  private static FileLogger logger;
  private FileLogger() {
  }
```

```
   public static synchronized FileLogger getFileLogger() {
     if (logger == null) {
       logger = new FileLogger();
     }
     return logger;
   }
   public synchronized void log(String msg) {
     FileUtil futil = new FileUtil();
     futil.writeToFile("log.txt",msg, true, true);
   }
}
```

This simple change turns the getFileLogger method into a Critical Section and guarantees that no two threads ever execute the getFileLogger method at the same time. This completely eliminates the possibility of the FileLogger constructor getting invoked more than once inside the getFileLogger method.

Approach II (Static Early Initialization)

It is to be noted that synchronizing methods can have a significant effect on the overall application performance. In general, synchronized methods run much slower, as much as 100 times slower than their nonsynchronized counterparts. As an alternative to declaring the getFileLogger method as synchronized, the logger variable can be early initialized.

```
   public class FileLogger implements Logger {
     //Early Initialization
     private static FileLogger logger = new FileLogger();
     private FileLogger() {
     }
     public static FileLogger getFileLogger() {
       return logger;
     }
     public synchronized void log(String msg) {
       FileUtil futil = new FileUtil();
       futil.writeToFile("log.txt",msg, true, true);
     }
   }
```

This eliminates the need for any check or initialization inside the getFileLogger method. As a result, the getFileLogger becomes thread-safe automatically without having to declare it as synchronized.

PRACTICE QUESTIONS

1. Design a database connection class as a thread-safe singleton.
2. Design a printer spooler class as a thread-safe singleton.

42

CONSISTENT LOCK ORDER

DESCRIPTION

During the discussion of the Monitor and the Critical Section patterns earlier, we have seen that when the synchronized keyword is used to ensure single-threaded execution of a code block, a thread needs to wait while trying to acquire the lock associated with the specified object. Consider a scenario where two threads hold locks on two different objects and each one is waiting for a lock on the object that is locked by the other thread. Both threads will be waiting forever and are said to be in a state of deadlock. In terms of implementation, this type of situation most often occurs due to an inconsistent order of locking objects. Let us consider the code segment in Listing 42.1 to illustrate how inconsistent locking in a multithreaded environment can cause a deadlock.

Consider a scenario where:

- Two threads, A and B, simultaneously invoke methods — `Method_A` and `Method_B` — respectively on the same `SomeClass` object.
- Thread A acquires a lock on `objectA` and Thread B acquires a lock on `objectB` at the same time. At this point, each of the threads waits for a lock on the object locked by the other thread and this puts Thread A and Thread B in a deadlocked condition.

To address such deadlock issues, the Consistent Lock Order pattern recommends designing an object locking order to be followed consistently across an application. Simply following an object locking order consistently across the application (where objects of a particular class are to be locked before locking other class instances) can eliminate the deadlock problem associated with the example code block. In other words, by ensuring that objects are locked in a consistent order all across the application, the problem of deadlocks can be addressed.

The example code block in Listing 42.1 can be modified so that `ClassA` objects are locked prior to locking `ClassB` objects.

Listing 42.1   Class with Inconsistent Locking Order

```java
public class SomeClass {
  private ClassA objectA;
  private ClassB objectB;
  public SomeClass() {
    objectA = new ClassA();
    objectB = new ClassB();
  }
  public void Method_A() {
    synchronized (objectA) {
      synchronized (objectB) {
        process_A();
      }
    }
  }
  public void Method_B() {
    synchronized (objectB) {
      synchronized (objectA) {
        process_B();
      }
    }
  }
  private void process_A() {
    //
  }
  private void process_B() {
    //
  }
}
class ClassA {
}
class ClassB {
}
```

```
public void Method_A() {
  synchronized (objectA) {
    synchronized (objectB) {
      process_A();
    }
  }
}
public void Method_B() {
  synchronized (objectA) {
    synchronized (objectB) {
      process_B();
    }
  }
}
```

This type of object locking order based on the class type does not work when the objects to be locked are instances of the same class. A more sophisticated algorithm may be needed to decide the object locking order. The following example illustrates one such mechanism.

EXAMPLE

Let us build a utility class that offers the functionality to move the contents of a directory to a different directory in the file system.

Let us create a class Directory, instances of which can be used to represent directories in the file system.

```
public class Directory {
  private String name;
  public Directory(String n) {
    name = n;
  }
}
```

The utility class FileSysUtil in its simplest form can be designed with a method to move the contents between directories.

```
public class FileSysUtil {
  public void moveContents(Directory src, Directory dest) {
    synchronized (src) {
      synchronized (dest) {
        System.out.println("Contents Moved Successfully");
      }
    }
  }
}
```

To move the contents of a directory to another, a client object or thread needs to:

1. Create `Directory` objects corresponding to the source and destination directories.
2. Invoke the `moveContents` method by passing both the `Directory` objects created in Step 1.

As part of its implementation of the `moveContents` method, the `FileSysUtil` locks the `Directory` objects representing the source and destination directories in sequence before actually moving the directory contents. This is to prevent threads from changing or deleting the source or destination directories while the current thread is in the process of moving the source directory contents to the destination directory. For simplicity, the example application displays an appropriate message instead of actually moving the source directory contents.

Let us suppose that there exist two directories — `dir1` and `dir2` — in the file system. To move the contents of `dir1` to `dir2`, a thread (e.g., `Thread_A`) needs to create two `Directory` objects — `objDir_1` and `objDir_2` — corresponding to `dir1` and `dir2`, respectively and pass them as arguments to the `moveContents` method.

```
//For Thread_A objDir_1 is the source directory
   moveContents(objDir_1, objDir_2);
```

While executing the `moveContents` method, `Thread_A` attempts to acquire locks on `objDir_1` and `objDir_2` in sequence.

At the same time, a different thread (e.g., `Thread_B`) invokes the `moveContents` method on the same `FileSysUtil` object to move `dir2` contents to `dir1`. Using the same `Directory` objects used by `Thread_A`, `Thread_B` makes a call as follows:

```
//For Thread_B objDir_2 is the source directory
   moveContents(objDir_2, objDir_1);
```

Similar to `Thread_A`, while executing the `moveContents` method, `Thread_B` also attempts to acquire locks on `objDir_1` and `objDir_2` but in the reverse order.

If `Thread_A` and `Thread_B` acquire locks at the same time on `objDir_1` and `objDir_2`, respectively, then each thread continues to wait for a lock on the `Directory` object locked by the other thread and this causes a deadlock. Because both `objDir_1` and `objDir_2` are of the same `Directory` class type, defining an object locking order based on the class type does not work in this case. As an alternative, the built-in Java `hashCode` method can be used to define an order of locking `Directory` objects. The `hashCode` method is defined in the topmost `java.lang.Object` class and is inherited by all classes in Java.

The hashCode method returns the unique ID or hash code associated with an object. An object locking scheme can be defined based on some kind of order of the hash codes of the objects to be locked.

To eliminate the possibility of a deadlock situation, the moveContents method can be modified so that the objects representing the source and the destination directories are locked in the ascending order of their associated hash codes. This ensures that the Directory objects are always locked in the same order, even if they are passed to the moveContents method by two different threads in different order.

```
...

...

public void moveContents(Directory src, Directory dest) {
   if (src.hashCode() > dest.hashCode()) {
     synchronized (src) {
        synchronized (dest) {
           System.out.println("Contents Moved Successfully");
        }
     }
   } else {
      synchronized (dest) {
        synchronized (src) {
           System.out.println("Contents Moved Successfully");
        }
      }
   }
}

...

...
```

With this change in place, when two threads invoke the moveContents method at the same time to move the contents of two different directories in opposite directions, only one thread is granted lock on the first Directory object to be locked. The second thread simply waits for the lock on the first Directory object itself. The possibility of the second thread locking the second Directory object while the first thread locks the first Directory object does not arise.

The example application uses a simple mechanism to define the locking order for Directory objects. In the case of a real world application, a locking order that is suitable for the application needs to be identified and documented. This locking order can then be followed consistently during the design and the development of the application.

PRACTICE QUESTIONS

1. Design a class `AccountManager` with a method to transfer money from one bank account to another. For this class to be used in a multithreaded environment, it must lock both the account objects before performing the actual transfer. Implement a method to transfer money so that when two different threads attempt to transfer money between two different accounts at the same time in opposite directions, it does not result in a deadlock in a multithreaded environment.

2. Design a class `InventoryManager` with a method to move products from one distribution center to another. For this class to be used in a multi-threaded environment, it must lock the objects representing the two distribution centers that are participating in the transaction before performing actual updates to their inventory levels. The method to move products should be implemented in a manner that does not cause a deadlock when two different threads attempt to move items between two distribution centers at the same time in opposite directions.

43

GUARDED SUSPENSION

This pattern was previously described in Grand98 and is based on the material that appeared in Lea97.

DESCRIPTION

In general, each method in an object is designed to execute a specific task. Sometimes, when a method is invoked on an object, the object may need to be in a certain state, which is logically necessary for the method to carry out the action it is designed for. In such cases, the Guarded Suspension pattern suggests suspending the method execution until such a precondition becomes true. In other words, the requirement for the object to be in a particular state becomes a precondition for the method to execute its implementation of the intended task.

Every class in Java inherits the `wait,` `notify` and `notifyAll` methods from the base `java.lang.Object` class. When a thread invokes an object's `wait` method:

■ It makes the thread release the synchronization lock it holds on the object.
■ The thread remains in the waiting state until it is notified to return via the `notify` or `notifyAll` method.

Using these built-in `wait,` `notify` and `notifyAll` methods, the Guarded Suspension pattern can be implemented in Java.

The generic structure of a Java class when the Guarded Suspension pattern is applied using the built-in `wait,` `notify` and `notifyAll` methods is represented in Listing 43.1.

The class `SomeClass` consists of two synchronized methods — `guarded-Method` and `alterObjectStateMethod`. The `guardedMethod` represents a method that requires some kind of a precondition to become true before proceeding with its execution. Hence, it checks if the precondition is true and as long as the precondition is not true, it waits using the `wait` method.

The `alterObjectStateMethod` method enables different client objects (threads) to change the state of a `SomeClass` instance. This, in turn, could result in the required precondition becoming true. Once the state of the object is

Listing 43.1   Generic Class Structure

```java
public class SomeClass {
  synchronized void guardedMethod() {
    while (!preCondition()) {
      try {
        //Continue to wait
        wait();
        //...
      } catch (InterruptedException e) {
        //...
      }
    }
    //Actual task implementation
  }
  synchronized void alterObjectStateMethod() {
    //Change the object state
    //.....
    //Inform waiting threads
    notify();
  }
  private boolean preCondition() {
    //...
    return false;
  }
}
```

changed, this method notifies any waiting thread that is waiting inside the
guardedMethod using the notify method. If the change in the object state
makes the precondition true, the waiting thread resumes with the execution of
the guardedMethod. Otherwise, it continues to wait till the precondition
becomes true.

Both the guardedMethod and alterObjectStateMethod methods are
designed as synchronized methods to prevent race conditions in a multithreaded
environment.

EXAMPLE

Let us build an application to simulate the parking mechanism at a health club.
A member can park his car if there is an empty parking slot. If there is no empty
parking slot, a member needs to wait until one of the parking slots becomes
available.

Listing 43.2 ParkingLot Class

```java
class ParkingLot {
  //Assume 4 parking slots for simplicity
  public static final int MAX_CAPACITY = 4;
  private int totalParkedCars = 0;
  public synchronized void park(String member) {
    while (totalParkedCars >= MAX_CAPACITY) {
      try {
        System.out.println(" The parking lot is full " +
                           member + " has to wait ");
        wait();
      } catch (InterruptedException e) {
        //
      }
    }
    //precondition is true
    System.out.println(member + " has parked");
    totalParkedCars = totalParkedCars + 1;
  }
  public synchronized void leave(String member) {
    totalParkedCars = totalParkedCars - 1;
    System.out.println(member +
                       " has left, notify a waiting member");
    notify();
  }
}
```

A simple representation for the parking lot can be designed in the form of the ParkingLot class shown in Listing 43.2.

The ParkingLot maintains the total number of currently parked cars in its instance variable totalParkedCars. This constitutes the state of a ParkingLot object.

The existence of an empty slot is the precondition for a member to proceed with parking his car. It can be seen that the park method first checks to see if this precondition is satisfied. If the number of currently parked members is greater than or equal to the total number of available slots, it can be inferred that there is no empty parking slot available and the member needs to wait until this condition does not exist. When a member leaves the parking lot, the total number of currently parked members is decremented and the leave method notifies one of the waiting threads at random. Once the notification is received, the notified thread attempts to get a lock on the object. Once the lock is obtained, it checks to see if the precondition is satisfied by reentering the `while` loop. If the precondition is satisfied, it proceeds with the parking action. The example code simply displays a message and increments the total number of currently parked cars. Checking for the precondition by the notified thread may seem redundant but it is required in a multithreaded environment. This is because of the possibility of a different thread altering the object state between the time the waiting thread attempts to obtain a lock on the object and the time it obtains it, so that the precondition becomes false.

Use of `wait()` and `notify()` in the `ParkingLot` Class Design

- The `park` method uses the built-in `java.lang.Object` `wait()` method to keep a Member thread waiting while the precondition is not true. When the `wait()` method is called, the currently executed thread (in this case a Member) is placed in the wait queue and its lock on the `ParkingLot` object is released (it had a lock on the `ParkingLot` object because park is synchronized). The next Member thread is then free to enter the `park` method and checks if `totalParkedCars >= MAX_CAPACITY`, which if true, is also placed into the wait queue.
- The `leave` method uses the built-in `java.lang.Object` `notify` method to notify a single waiting thread at random. The choice of the thread is at the discretion of the specific JVM implementation. The notified thread regains a lock on the `ParkingLot` object and returns to executing in the `park` method where the `wait()` method was invoked. Using the built-in `notifyAll` method the `leave` method could also be implemented to notify all waiting threads at once. The waiting threads then contend for the `ParkingLot` object lock. Whatever thread obtains the lock continues execution in the `park` method where the `wait()` method was called.

The representation of a member can be designed as a Java Thread (Listing 43.3) to facilitate the simulation of more than one member looking to park their cars at the same time.

Let us design a test driver `GSTest` to make use of the `Member` class to simulate a real world scenario of multiple members trying to park their cars at the same time.

```
public class GSTest {
  public static void main(String[] args) {
    ParkingLot parking = new ParkingLot();
    new Member("Member1", parking);
    new Member("Member2", parking);
    new Member("Member3", parking);
    new Member("Member4", parking);
    new Member("Member5", parking);
    new Member("Member6", parking);
  }
}
```

Listing 43.3 Member Class

```
class Member extends Thread {
  private ParkingLot parking;
  private String name;
  Member(String n, ParkingLot p) {
    name = n;
    parking = p;
    start();
  }
  public void run() {
    System.out.println(name + " is ready to park");
    parking.park(name);
    try {
      sleep(500);
    } catch (InterruptedException e) {
      //
    }
    //leave after 500ms
    parking.leave(name);
  }
}
```

PRACTICE QUESTIONS

1. Design a queue data structure to be used by multiple threads in an application. A thread can retrieve an object from the queue only if the queue contains any elements. Apply the Guarded Suspension pattern in designing the queue class so that when a thread attempts to retrieve an object from the queue and the queue is empty, the thread is made to wait until an object is put into the queue by a different thread.

2. Apply the Guarded Suspension pattern to design the item check-out functionality at a library. Typically, a library maintains multiple copies of an item such as a movie or a book. Member A can check out an item only if the total number of its copies is greater than the number of members prior to Member A with interest in the same item.

44

READ-WRITE LOCK

This pattern was previously described in Grand98 and is based on the material that appeared in Lea97.

DESCRIPTION

During the discussion of the Monitor and the Critical Section patterns earlier, we saw that when multiple threads in an application simultaneously access a resource it could result in unpredictable behavior. Hence the resource must be protected so that only one thread at a time is allowed to access the resource. Though this may be required in most cases, it may lead to unwanted CPU overhead when some of the threads accessing the resource are interested only in reading the values or state of the resource but not in changing it. In such cases, it can be inefficient to prevent a thread from accessing the resource solely to read its values while a different thread is currently reading the same resource values. Because a read operation does not alter the values of the resource, multiple threads can safely be allowed to access the resource at the same time if all of these threads are interested only in reading the resource values. This kind of design improves the overall application responsiveness with reduced CPU overhead. That means, when a thread obtains a lock to simply read the values of a resource, it should not prevent other threads from accessing the resource to read its values. In other words, a read lock should be shared. If a thread is allowed to read a resource's data while a different thread is updating the same resource, the thread that is reading the data may receive an inconsistent view. Allowing more than one thread to update the values of a resource could also result in unpredictable results.

While some threads are interested only in reading the resource values, some other threads may access the resource to read and update its values. To eliminate concurrency problems, when such a thread needs to access the resource to update its values, it must get a write lock on the object representing the resource. A write lock is an exclusive lock on the object and prevents all other threads from accessing the resource at the same time. Further, if a read and a write lock are requested on an object at the same time, the write lock request should be granted first. The write lock is issued only if there are no threads currently holding a read lock on the same object.

Table 44.1 summarizes the criteria for issuing a read-write lock.

Table 44.1 Rules for Issuing Read-Write Locks

Lock	Rules
Read Lock	A read lock should be issued if there is no currently issued write lock and there are no threads waiting for the write lock.
Write Lock	A write lock should be issued if no thread is currently issued a (read or write) lock on the object.

In Java, there is no readily available feature for implementing read-write locks. But a custom class can be built (Listing 44.1) with the responsibility of issuing read-write locks on an object to different threads in an application.

Design Highlights of the `ReadWriteLock` Class

Lock Statistics

The `ReadWriteLock` maintains different lock statistics in a set of instance variables as follows:

- `totalReadLocksGiven` — To store the number of read locks already issued on the object.
- `writeLockIssued` — To indicate if a write lock has been issued or not.
- `threadsWaitingForWriteLocks` — To keep track of the number of threads currently waiting for a write lock.

These values are in turn used by the lock issuing methods — `getReadLock` and `getWriteLock`.

Lock Methods

The `ReadWriteLock` offers two methods — `getReadLock` and `getWrite-Lock` — which can be used by client objects to get read and write locks on an object, respectively. As part of its implementation of these two methods, the `ReadWriteLock` issues read-write locks as per the rules listed in Table 44.1.

Lock Release

A client object that currently holds a read-write lock can release the lock by invoking the `done` method. The `done` method updates appropriate lock statistics and allows the lock to be issued to any waiting thread as per the rules listed in Table 44.1.

The `ReadWriteLock` class is a generic implementation for issuing read-write locks and can be readily used in any application.

Listing 44.1   Generic `ReadWriteLock` Implementation

```java
public class ReadWriteLock {
  private Object lockObj;
  private int totalReadLocksGiven;
  private boolean writeLockIssued;
  private int threadsWaitingForWriteLock;
  public ReadWriteLock() {
    lockObj = new Object();
    writeLockIssued = false;
  }
  /*
    A read lock can be issued if
      there is no currently issued
      write lock and
      there is no thread(s) currently waiting for the
      write lock
  */
  public void getReadLock() {
    synchronized (lockObj) {
      while ((writeLockIssued) ||
        (threadsWaitingForWriteLock != 0)) {
      try {
        lockObj.wait();
      } catch (InterruptedException e) {
        //
      }
    }
    //System.out.println(" Read Lock Issued");
    totalReadLocksGiven++;
  }
}
}
/*
  A write lock can be issued if
    there is no currently issued
    read or write lock
*/
```

(continued)

Listing 44.1 Generic ReadWriteLock Implementation (Continued)

```java
public void getWriteLock() {
  synchronized (lockObj) {
    threadsWaitingForWriteLock++;
    while ((totalReadLocksGiven != 0) ||
      (writeLockIssued)) {
      try {
        lockObj.wait();
      } catch (InterruptedException e) {
        //
      }
    }
    //System.out.println(" Write Lock Issued");
    threadsWaitingForWriteLock -- ;
    writeLockIssued = true;
  }
}
//used for releasing locks
public void done() {
  synchronized (lockObj) {
    //check for errors
    if ((totalReadLocksGiven == 0) &&
      (!writeLockIssued)) {
      System.out.println(
        " Error: Invalid call to release the lock");
      return;
    }
    if (writeLockIssued)
      writeLockIssued = false;
    else
      totalReadLocksGiven -- ;
      lockObj.notifyAll();
  }
}
}
```

EXAMPLE

Applying the Read-Write Lock pattern, let us design an application to allow members of a library to:

- View details of different library items
- Check out an item if it is currently available

The application must ensure that multiple members are allowed to view an item status at the same time, but only one member is allowed to check out an item at a time. In other words, the application must support multiple simultaneous member transactions without producing unpredictable results.

The overall application design becomes much simpler using the ReadWrite-Lock class designed earlier. The representation of a library item can be designed in the form of an Item class (Listing 44.2) with methods to allow members to check the status of an item and to check in or check out an item.

Because the status check of an item does not involve changes to its status, the getStatus method acquires a read lock. This allows more than one thread to invoke the getStatus method to check the status of an item.

In contrast, both the checkIn and checkOut methods involve changes to the item status and hence acquire a write lock before changing the item status. This ensures that only one thread is allowed to alter the item status even though more than one thread invokes the checkIn/checkOut method at the same time. The Item class makes use of the services of a ReadWriteLock object to acquire an appropriate lock.

By using the exclusive write lock only when needed, the Item class allows multiple threads to access an item in a more controlled manner without the overhead of any unwanted waiting and eliminates the scope for unpredictable behavior at the same time.

The representation of a member transaction can be designed as a Java Thread (Listing 44.3) to facilitate the reflection of the real world scenario of different members accessing an item simultaneously.

The MemberTransaction class is designed in its simplest form and can be configured with an operation to check an item status or to check in or check out an item when it is instantiated.

To simulate a real world scenario, a test program RWTest can be designed to create multiple MemberTransaction objects to perform different operations to read the status of an item or check in or check out an item.

```
public class RWTest {
  public static void main(String[] args) {
    Item item = new Item("CompScience-I");
    new MemberTransaction("Member1", item, "StatusCheck");
    new MemberTransaction("Member2", item, "StatusCheck");
    new MemberTransaction("Member3", item, "CheckOut");
    new MemberTransaction("Member4", item, "CheckOut");
```

```
        new MemberTransaction("Member5", item, "CheckOut");
        new MemberTransaction("Member6", item, "StatusCheck");
    }
}
```

When the RWTest is executed, the order in which different read-write locks are issued will be displayed.

Listing 44.2   Item Class

```
public class Item {
  private String name;
  private ReadWriteLock rwLock;
  private String status;
  public Item(String n) {
    name = n;
    rwLock = new ReadWriteLock();
    status = "N";
  }
  public void checkOut(String member) {
    rwLock.getWriteLock();
    status = "Y";
    System.out.println(member +
                      " has been issued a write lock-ChkOut");
    rwLock.done();
  }
  public String getStatus(String member) {
    rwLock.getReadLock();
    System.out.println(member +
                      " has been issued a read lock");
    rwLock.done();
    return status;
  }
  public void checkIn(String member) {
    rwLock.getWriteLock();
    status = "N";
    System.out.println(member +
                      " has been issued a write lock-ChkIn");
    rwLock.done();
  }
}
```

Listing 44.3 MemberTransaction Class

```
public class MemberTransaction extends Thread {
  private String name;
  private Item item;
  private String operation;
  public MemberTransaction(String n, Item i, String p) {
    name = n;
    item = i;
    operation = p;
    start();
  }
  public void run() {
    //all members first read the status
    item.getStatus(name);
    if (operation.equals("CheckOut")) {
      System.out.println("\n" + name +
                          " is ready to checkout the item.");
      item.checkOut(name);
      try {
        sleep(1);
      } catch (InterruptedException e) {
        //
      }
      item.checkIn(name);
    }
  }
}
```

PRACTICE QUESTIONS

1. Design an application to allow different customers to buy airline tickets. Apply the Read-Write Lock pattern to ensure that multiple customers are allowed to check the seat availability on the same flight, but only one customer is allowed to buy the ticket at a time.
2. Design an application to allow different customers to bid on auctioned items. Apply the Read-Write Lock pattern to ensure that multiple customers are allowed to check the current bid but no two customers are allowed to alter the bid amount at the same time.

IX

CASE STUDY

45

CASE STUDY:
A WEB HOSTING COMPANY

OBJECTIVE

We have discussed 42 design patterns in earlier chapters in different sections of this book. Now it is time for us to see how some of these design patterns can be applied together in building a software solution. The objective of this case study is to identify and apply some of the design patterns discussed in this book in developing a software solution for the business requirements of a fictitious Web hosting company, KPS Hosting Solutions.

KPS HOSTING SOLUTIONS: A BRIEF OVERVIEW

- *About KPS Hosting Solutions* — KPS Hosting Solutions is a mid-sized Web hosting services provider based in the United States.
- *Customers* — KPS has customers from the United States and Canada. KPS expects to serve customers from Asia as well in the near future.
- *Hosting packages* — KPS currently hosts a few thousand Web sites and offers Web hosting on both Windows and UNIX platforms. KPS offers three different types of hosting packages — Basic, Premium and PremiumPlus — on both platforms.
- *Payment plans* — KPS allows its customers to pay for the hosting services on a monthly, quarterly, half-yearly or annual basis using credit cards. KPS intends to accept checking accounts and personal checks in the near future.
- *Employees* — KPS has both full-time and part-time employees. KPS guarantees an uptime of 99.99 percent to its customers. This requires some of the KPS employees to be available during night shifts.
- *Domain registration* — KPS does not serve as a domain registrar on its own. KPS works with different domain registrars to register new domains or transfer existing domains. KPS offers this complimentary service based on customer requests.
- *Resellers* — KPS attributes its fast growth to its committed, goal-oriented resellers. KPS classifies its resellers into two categories — Basic and

Premium. Resellers with more than 100 domains are considered Premium resellers and receive a higher rate of commission.

REQUIREMENTS

Functional

- *Customer management* — The system should have the ability to create a new customer profile, which includes the customer's personal information, Web site(s) information and the payment information. The system should allow modifications and deletions of the customer profile. Whenever the customer address or the credit card information is submitted, the system should validate it before saving it to the database. Because KPS expects to serve customers from Asia in the near future, the system should be able to accommodate any enhancements specific to customers from Asia with minimum or no changes to the existing design or implementation.
- *Search management* — The system should have the ability to search for customers, employees and resellers. Search results should be displayed with minimum details. The system should allow filtering from within the displayed search results based on user specified criteria. Upon selecting an item from the search results, a more detailed view of the selected item should be presented.
- *Billing* — The system should have the ability to charge the billing amount of a Web site to the associated credit card. KPS currently accepts Visa, MasterCard, Discover and Diners Club. KPS bills direct customers, including resellers. Resellers are responsible for billing their customers.
- *Reports* — The KPS management would like to see a set of predefined reports. In addition, the system should have an ad hoc report generation capability.
- *Employee management* — The system should have the ability to create, modify or delete an employee profile.
- *Data migration* — Currently, some of the tasks are accomplished using application software that is based on antiquated technology and is poorly architected. When the new system is built, data from the legacy system needs to be migrated to the new system. KPS intends to use the same data migration set up with minimum or no changes:
  - To migrate data from any other hosting firms it acquires.
  - To accept data from resellers (in case of bulk hosting requests) and move to the new system database.
- *Registrar interface* — KPS would like to submit domain registration requests in a batch to domain registrars. These requests are normally sent to different registrars in the form of an XML string. The system should have the ability to generate and submit the request.
- *Reseller management* — The system should have the ability to create, modify or delete a reseller profile. The system should provide the ability to calculate the commission to be paid to each reseller and generate checks to be mailed.

- *Trouble ticket management* — All Web site related issues are first received by the tech support team that creates a trouble ticket for each reported issue. Within the KPS tech support, there are different service levels that are responsible for different areas of tech support. Once a trouble ticket is issued, it gets routed through these service levels until it gets resolved.

Technical

- The overall system design should be component-based, manageable and reusable. System enhancements should be easy to apply.
- The system architecture and design must make use of best design practices to optimize the system performance and maintainability.
- Proper, consistent naming conventions must be followed.
- Reuse of any existing or available software is encouraged. For instance, KPS has access to a Java class that validates a given Canadian address. But the interface provided by the class is not compatible with the naming conventions of the development team.
- KPS Hosting Solutions currently uses only one database server with no secondary database server for fail-over. Sometimes the database server may be brought down for maintenance reasons. In the case of a new business request, if the database is down, the application should write the data to a flat file. The goal is not to turn down a customer request due to technical reasons. Because the customer information contains such sensitive data as the credit card information, the data must be encrypted before writing to the file.

BUSINESS OBJECTS AND THEIR ASSOCIATION

- Whenever a new customer is created, the personal information is collected.
- Whenever a customer requests hosting service for a Web site, the credit card information is collected from the customer and an account is created that allows the customer to access the Web site. Figure 45.1 shows the association of a `Customer` with other business objects such as `CreditCard`, `Website`, `Account` and `Address`.

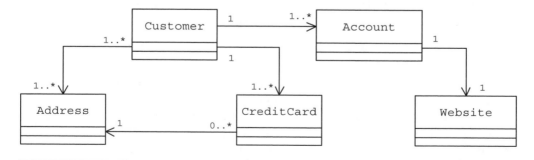

Figure 45.1   Customer Association with Other Business Objects

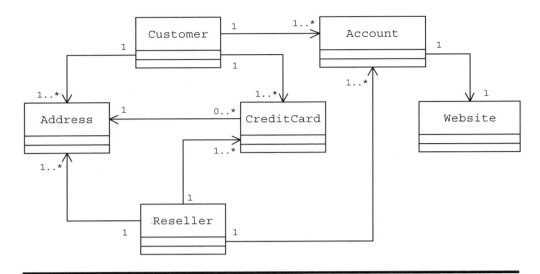

Figure 45.2 Reseller Association with Other Business Objects

- Whenever a customer contacts a reseller for hosting services, the reseller in turn contacts the KPS customer service for hosting the Web site. In this aspect, the system can treat resellers the same as a direct customer. Figure 45.2 depicts the association of a reseller with other business objects.
- KPS offers Basic, Premium and PremiumPlus Web hosting packages on both the Windows and UNIX platforms. Figure 45.3 shows the representation of hosting plans in the form of a class hierarchy.
- KPS provides tech support only for direct customers, not for those customers who have requested hosting services through a reseller. Resellers are responsible for providing billing and support services to their customers. Figure 45.4 depicts the relationship between a Web site and any associated trouble tickets.

FRAMEWORK FOR APPLICATION PROCESSING

As can be seen from the business requirements section, the application functionality consists of a set of services — customer management, search management, credit card services, address validation, employee management, etc. The overall application functionality may be modularized at two levels.

Enterprise Service Level

The first level of modularization can be accomplished at the service level. In other words, each of the services can be designed as an individual module. To provide client objects with a uniform interface to access these services, each service can be designed either as an implementer of an interface or as a subclass of an abstract or concrete class that declares the interface to be used by client objects. Figure 45.5 shows the design of different service modules as implementers of a common `EnterpriseService` interface.

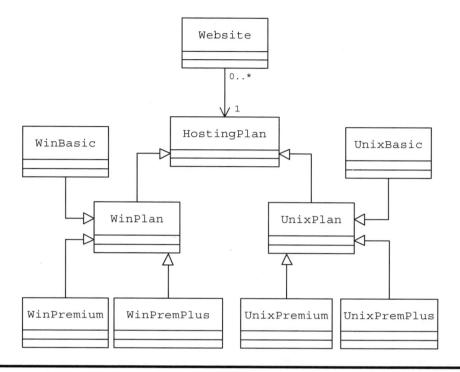

Figure 45.3   Hosting Plan Class Hierarchy

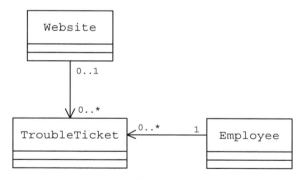

Figure 45.4   `Website–TroubleTicket-Employee` Association

An enterprise service offers a group of related lower-level services to its clients. In other words, an enterprise service allows the processing of a set of related tasks. The terms "lower-level service" and "task" are used synonymously in this discussion. Each of the `EnterpriseService` implementers expects to receive a client request in the form of an XML request. One of the advantages of sending the request as an XML string is that it does not bind the client to a particular method signature on the service module. Another advantage is that it provides language independence. That means, clients and service implementers can be implemented in different programming languages and thus allow

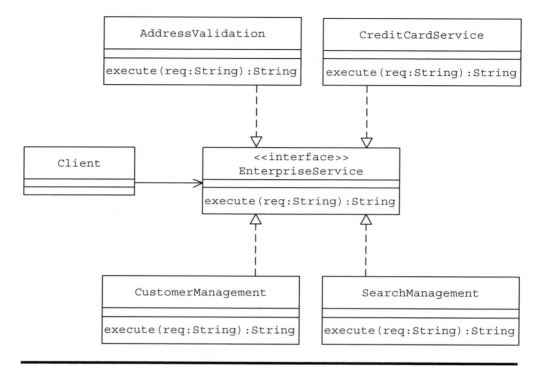

Figure 45.5 Service Module Class Hierarchy with Each Module as an Implementor of a Common Interface

for the integration of legacy applications written in Fortran, COBOL, C++ and other programming languages.

A service implementer is responsible for defining the required interface contract details to be used by different clients. This involves defining the request and the response structures for the service.

Generic Interface Contract

Request:

```
<ENT_SERVICE_NAME>
  <Task name='specificService'>
    <Input_1>abc</Input_1>
    <Input_2>xyz</Input_2>
      ...
      ...
    <Input_n>something else</Input_n>
  </Task>
</ENT_SERVICE_NAME>
```

Response:

```
<ENT_SERVICE_NAME ErrorMsg='N'>
  <RESPONSE>
    <Output_1>abc</Output _1>
    <Output _2>xyz</Output _2>
      ...
      ...
    <Output _n>something else</Output _n>
  </RESPONSE>
</ENT_SERVICE_NAME>
```

or

```
<ENT_SERVICE_NAME ErrorMsg='Y'>
  <ERRORS>
  <ERROR>
    <CODE>01</CODE>
    <MESSAGE> Error Message 1</MESSAGE>
  </ERROR>
    ...
    ...
    ...
  <ERROR>
    <CODE>0n</CODE>
    <MESSAGE> Error Message n</MESSAGE>
  </ERROR>
  </ERRORS>
</ENT_SERVICE_NAME>
```

Where:

<ENT_SERVICE_NAME> is the name of the enterprise service.
<Task> is the lower level service offered by the service.

Sample Interface Contract

Request:

```
<CREDIT_CARD_SERVICE>
  <Task name='validateCard'>
    <CardNumber>1234123412341234</CardNumber>
    <CardType>VISA</CardType>
```

```
      <ExpDate>01-12-2008</ExpDate>
      <CardHolderName>CardHolder</CardHolderName>
    </Task>
  </CREDIT_CARD_SERVICE>
```

Response:

```
  <CREDIT_CARD_SERVICE ErrorMsg='N'>
    <RESPONSE>
      <CardNumber>***********1234</CardNumber>
      <Status>Valid</Status>
    </RESPONSE>
  </CREDIT_CARD_SERVICE>
```

or

```
  <CREDIT_CARD_SERVICE ErrorMsg='Y'>
    <ERRORS>
      <ERROR>
        <CODE>05</CODE>
        <MESSAGE>Unable to Connect to the Provider For
  Verification</MESSAGE>
      </ERROR>
    </ERRORS>
  </CREDIT_CARD_SERVICE>
```

Whenever a client needs to access the services of an `EnterpriseService` implementer, it needs to:

- ■ Create an instance of the class representing the required enterprise service. The name of a service along with the corresponding implementation class can be specified using a Constant Data Manager.
- ■ Construct the service request as an XML string specifying the task name along with any data to be passed to the service as input as per the predefined contract.

Task Level

As mentioned earlier, an enterprise service component offers a set of related lower-level services (tasks). If the enterprise service module itself is made responsible for implementing these lower-level services, it could lead to a design that is very restrictive and hard to maintain. Whenever a new task needs to be added to the enterprise service or a task needs to be removed, it requires changes to the enterprise service module. To avoid these problems, an enterprise service module can be designed to make use of a set of predefined objects to handle the set of tasks that it is designed to process. The mapping between a lower-level task and its processor or handler can be specified in the form of an XML file.

Generic Task-Handler Mapping

```
<TaskMappings service='ENT_SERVICE_NAME'>
  <Task name='Task_Name'>
    <handler>package.class</handler>
  </Task>
</TaskMappings>
```

Sample Task-Handler Mapping

```
<TaskMappings service='CREDIT_CARD_SERVICE'>
  <Task name='validateCard'>
<handler>com.company.entservices.ccservice.CardValidator
</handler>
  </Task>
</TaskMappings>
```

Whenever an enterprise service component is initialized, it needs to read the corresponding *Task-Handler* mapping into memory. Maintaining a separate Task-Mapping XML file for each enterprise service works better in an environment where individual teams are responsible for developing specific enterprise services modules. When a client request is received, the service component can check the mapping list to find the handler. Once the handler is found, the service component instantiates the handler class and submits the request XML file to it. To make it possible for all enterprise service components to treat all handlers in the same manner, every handler must offer the same interface for an enterprise service module to forward a client request. Towards this end, every processor class can be designed as an implementer of a common Interface (Figure 45.6).

A handler can in turn make use of other helper classes in accomplishing the task it is designed for. The mapping between a task and a handler is one-to-many. In other words, a handler may process more than one task. For every task that a processor processes, there must be a method with the exact same name as the Task name specified in the mapping XML file.

Defining a Task-Handler mapping does not completely prevent the enterprise service module from offering any services on its own. For instance, in the case of a small but highly useful service such as the AddressValidation service, it may not be required to designate a separate object to receive the client request. In such cases, the service provider may intend to process the service on its own with the help of other utility or helper objects. Such a service provider needs to implement a method with same name as the Task name. In addition, the Task-Handler mapping must specify the processor as itself.

Because each of the enterprise service components needs to provide the same implementation to read the corresponding Task-Mapping XML file, it is likely to

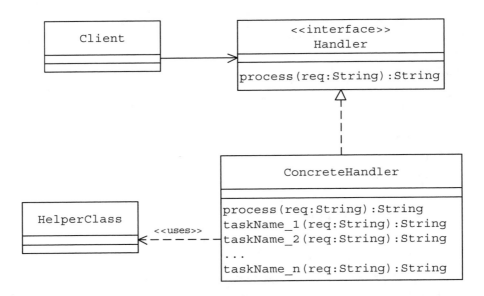

Figure 45.6 Client Accessing a Task-Handler Object

result in duplicate implementation across enterprise service modules. To avoid this problem, the `EnterpriseService` can be designed as an abstract class with the implementation to read the mapping XML file into memory. This requires each of the service modules to be redesigned as subclasses of the `Enterprise-Service` class (Figure 45.7).

Throughout the life of the application there will be a need for only one copy of the mapping data and it needs to be available to all service modules and it should not result in any concurrency problems. To accommodate these requirements, when the mapping XML file is read, mapping details can be stored inside a Common Attribute Registry where each service can be treated as a `CARGroup` with Task-Handler values as individual name-value pairs within the `CARGroup`. This allows the storing of the same Task-Handler combination across multiple service modules.

Error Processing

The method signatures of both the service module's `execute()` method and the handler's `process` method indicate that they return a string back to the caller. Any errors that occur during the processing can be communicated back to the caller in the form of an XML string. The caller can parse the returned XML string to check for specific errors and carry out any required error handling.

Enterprise Services Design

In accordance with the application framework discussed earlier, every service module needs to define an interface contract to be used by the clients that intend to access its services.

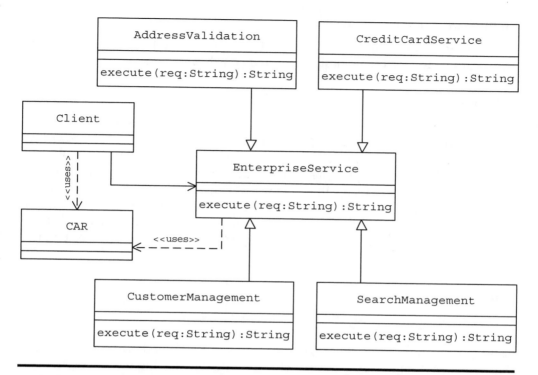

Figure 45.7 Service Module Class Hierarchy with Each Module as a Subclass of a Common Parent Class

Address Validation

Using the enterprise services architecture discussed above, the address validation can be designed as a service module subclass of the `EnterpriseServices` class. Using the interface contract, clients can send the address to be validated to the service module. The service returns the validation results by way of the response structure defined in the interface contract.

When the service module receives a validation request, it can be forwarded to a designated handler, `ValidationHandler` instance. From the technical requirements section, it can be seen that there exists a utility to validate Canadian addresses that has a method name which is not in conformance with KPS IT standards. While it is possible to create an address validator for U.S. addresses with the method name following the naming standards, it may not be possible to alter the existing utility to validate Canadian addresses to follow the naming standards. Without having to recreate the utility from scratch, using the Adapter pattern, an adapter can be designed to make it possible to leverage the existing utility functionality. This same procedure can be used for validation of Asian addresses if there exists a predefined validation module that may not have a compatible interface.

The `ValidationHandler` can be designed to make use of a designated method to accept a country code and return the appropriate address validator. Once the validator is received, the handler can access its service in a seamless manner irrespective of the concrete class of the validator that is returned.

Credit Card Service

The two services that the credit card service offers are credit card validation and credit card charging. Let us design the credit card validation functionality here.

Validation

From the business requirements section, it can be seen that the system should have the ability to validate Visa, MaterCard, Discover and Diners Club cards. All of these cards have a definite set of steps in checking their validity. Some of the steps in validating these cards are identical across all these cards while some are carried out differently. Using the Template Method pattern, the outline of the validation steps and the common invariant parts of the overall algorithm can be kept inside an abstract class leaving the implementation of variant parts of the algorithm to its subclasses (see the example discussion in Chapter 38 — Template Method).

Search Management

The search management should allow users to search for resellers, customers and Web sites. For performance reasons only a limited set of search results are to be displayed on the screen. Such parameters can be specified using the Constant Data Manager. The necessary UI panel can be designed using the Builder pattern (see the example in Chapter 14 — Builder Pattern) where each concrete Builder is responsible for creating the necessary UI for allowing a user to specify the search criteria. This allows the same series of steps to construct the UI panel specific to a search type. This gives the flexibility to use the same UI building logic when a new search, say an employee search, is to be added to the system. Without altering the existing implementation, a new concrete Builder specific to the employee search user-interface can be designed.

One of the requirements is to select an item from the result set on the screen and view more details on the selected item. Whenever an item is selected, a database query can be executed to retrieve its details. One of the ways of improving the performance is to introduce some amount of caching where some of the most recently accessed item details are kept in the memory. This can be designed as an Object Cache using a Common Attribute Registry (see the example discussion in Chapter 29 — Object Cache). Whenever a search results item is selected to view more details, item details are fetched from the cache, if it exists. Otherwise, details are fetched from the database for display and are also stored in the cache for later access.

Customer Management

Let us design one of the important tasks to be supported by the customer management service, the creation of a new customer profile. From the business requirements section above, it can be seen that the application must function even if the database is down. This means that the application must have the ability to write to files as well as to the database.

The functionality to save data to a file and the database can be encapsulated in two different classes — `FileManager` and `DBManager`, respectively. To allow client objects to deal with both the `FileManager` and `DBManager` in a seamless manner, they can be designed as implementers of a common interface `PersistenceManager` to provide the same interface to its clients. By virtue of polymorphism, client objects will be able to treat both the implementers as the `PersistenceManager` type.

Instead of having every client object to dealing with the choice of instantiating either `FileManager` or `DBManager`, the implementation of this decision logic can be kept inside a separate Factory Method. If there is a change in the way one of the `PersistenceManager` objects is to be selected, the Factory Method can be overridden in a subclass of the class that contains the Factory Method.

One of the important steps in creating a new customer profile is the selection of a hosting plan for the customer Web site. From the "Business Objects" section, it can be seen that there exist two families of hosting plans — Windows and UNIX. Instead of requiring client objects to be aware of the existence of the families of concrete classes (such as `WinBasic`, `WinPremium`,..., `UnixPremium` and `UnixPremPlus`) and have the knowledge of the concrete `HostingPlan` class to be instantiated, the Abstract Factory pattern can be used to encapsulate these details into a set of concrete factories that share a common interface. Clients can get access to an appropriate `HostingPlan` instance using the common interface without having to know the class type of the object returned.

In addition to the hosting plan selection, the customer profile creation involves address validation, credit card validation, account creation and saving customer data to the database or file. For address and credit card validation, the handler makes use of the `AddressValidation` and the `CreditCardService` enterprise services, respectively. While performing these lower-level tasks, the handler presents a very high level interface to its clients. In other words, client objects do not need to directly deal with the details of creating an account, validating addresses, credit card information and saving the data using an appropriate `PersistenceManager`. A client only needs to formulate its request to create a new customer profile in accordance with the interface contract defined by the `CustomerManagement` service and forward the request to the `CustomerManagement` enterprise service. In this aspect the handler functions as a Façade object.

The `FileManager` can be designed to make use of a utility to write data to the file. While designing the utility to write data to the file may seem like a trivial task, it requires special care to ensure that the utility functions as desired in a multithreaded environment. Applying the concept of the Critical Section ensures this by allowing only a single thread to access the utility method to write to the file. Such a utility can be used in other parts of the application for other purposes such as logging messages. From the requirements section, it can be seen that when the data is written to the file, it must be encrypted to avoid easy exposure. It may not be a good idea to alter the utility to implement the necessary encryption to the data being written. This is because encrypting the data before writing to a file may not be required everywhere the utility is used. As a work around, a Decorator object may be designed to provide the necessary encryption implementation before sending data to the utility to write to the file.

CONCLUSION

As part of the preceding discussion, we have designed:

- The address validation service
- The credit card service
- The new customer profile creation part of the customer management service
- The search management services

Interested readers may enhance the business requirements and design the rest of the system.

X

APPENDICES

Appendix A

LIST OF DESIGN PATTERNS

Basic:

- Interface
- Abstract Parent Class
- Private Methods
- Accessor Methods
- Constant Data Manager
- Immutable Object
- Monitor

Creational:

- Factory Method
- Abstract Factory
- Singleton
- Prototype
- Builder

Collectional:

- Composite
- Iterator
- Flyweight
- Visitor

Concurrency:

- Critical Section
- Consistent Lock Order
- Guarded Suspension
- Read-Write Lock

Structural:

- Decorator
- Adapter
- Chain of Responsibility
- Façade
- Proxy
- Bridge
- Virtual Proxy
- Counting Proxy
- Aggregate Enforcer
- Explicit Object Release
- Object Cache

Behavioral:

- Command
- Mediator
- Memento
- Observer
- Interpreter
- State
- Strategy
- Null Object
- Template Method
- Object Authenticator
- Common Attribute Registry

Appendix B

REFERENCES

Alexander, Christopher. *A Timeless Way of Building*. Oxford, England: Oxford University Press, 1979.

Alexander, Christopher, S. Ishikawa and Murray Silverstein. *A Pattern Language: Towns, Buildings, Construction*. Oxford, England: Oxford University Press, 1977.

Alpert, Sherman, Kyle Brown and Bobby Woolf. *The Design Patterns Smalltalk Companion*. Reading, MA: Addison-Wesley, 1988.

Arnold, Ken and James Gosling. *The Java™ Programming Language*. Reading, MA: Addison-Wesley, 1988.

Bertrand, Meyer. *Object Oriented Software Construction*. New York: Prentice Hall, 1988.

Booch, Grady, James Rumbaugh and Ivar Jacobson. *The Unified Modeling Language User Guide*. Reading, MA: Addison-Wesley, 1999.

Buschman, Frank, Regine Meunier, Hans Rohnert, Peter Sommerlad and Michael Stal. *Pattern-Oriented Software Architecture: A System of Patterns*. New York: John Wiley and Sons, 1996.

Cooper, James W. *Java™ Design Patterns*. Boston, MA: Addison-Wesley, 2000.

Coplien, James O. *Advanced C++ Programming Styles and Idioms*. Reading, MA: Addison-Wesley, 1992.

Coplien, James O. and Douglas Schmidt. *Pattern Languages of Program Design*. Reading, MA: Addison-Wesley, 1995.

Fowler, Martin and Kendall Scott. *UML Distilled: A Brief Guide to the Standard Object Modeling Language*. Reading, MA: Addison-Wesley, 1997.

Gamma, Erich, R. Helm, R. Johnson and J. Vlissides. *Design Patterns: Elements of Reusable Object-Oriented Software*. Reading, MA: Addison-Wesley, 1995. [GoF95].

Grand, Mark. *Patterns in Java™ Vol.1*. New York: John Wiley and Sons, 1998. [Grand98].

Kuchana, Partha. Create Your Own Web Server. http://members.itjobslist.com/partha/Web-Server.pdf

Lea, Doug. *Concurrent Programming in Java™*. Reading, MA: Addison-Wesley, 1997. [Lea97].

Metsker, Steven J. *Design Patterns: Java™ Workbook*. Boston, MA: Addison-Wesley, 2002.

Pree, Wolfgang. *Design Patterns for Object-Oriented Software Development*. Reading, MA: Addison-Wesley, 1994.

Riel, Arthur J. *Object-Oriented Design Heuristics*. Reading, MA: Addison-Wesley, 1996.

Vlissides, John. *Pattern Hatching: Design Patterns Applied*. Reading, MA: Addison-Wesley, 1998.

Woolf, Bobby. *The Null Object Pattern*. PLoP'96 Final Papers. [Woolf96].

WEB REFERENCES

http://www.sqlsecurity.com/faq-inj.asp
http://www.objectmentor.com/mentoring/OOPrinciples
http://www.object-arts.com/EducationCentre/Patterns/AccessorMethods.htm

http://www.object-arts.com/OldStuff/Patterns/PrivateMethods.htm
http://java.sun.com
http://www.javaworld.com/javaworld/jw-10-2001/jw-1012-deadlock.html
Discussions with www.ITJobsList.com web administrator
http://www.research.ibm.com/designpatterns/pubs/7habits.html
http://www.w3.org/TR/REC-html40/present/frames.html

INDEX